Ultimate Azure Data Scientist Associate (DP-100) Certification Guide

Simplified Concepts and Effective ML Solutions to Crack the Azure Data Scientist DP-100 Exam

Rajib Kumar De

www.orangeava.com

First published: June 2024

Published by: Orange Education Pvt Ltd, AVA™

Address: 9, Daryaganj, Delhi, 110002, India

275 New North Road Islington Suite 1314 London,

N1 7AA, United Kingdom

ISBN: 978-81-97256-22-6

www.orangeava.com

Dedicated To

My Beloved Sons:

Rishabh and Rishan

Who Fills My Days With Laughter and Inspires Me to Dream Big, My Strength and Constant Source of Support. This Book is for You

About the Author

Rajib Kumar De is a seasoned Data Scientist with a Master's in Statistics and over a decade of industry experience. He excels in Analytics, Predictive Modeling, Machine Learning, Cloud Computing (Microsoft Azure), AI, Deep Learning, and NLP. With a strong research mindset, he tackles complex problems using supervised and unsupervised learning methods.

Proven Qualifications and Certifications:

- **Master's Degree in Statistics**: Equips him with advanced data analysis skills.
- **Microsoft Certifications**:
  - Azure Data Scientist Associate, Azure AI Fundamentals, and Microsoft Professional Program for Data Science
- **Additional Certifications**:
  - Data Science Core, Data Science Fundamentals, and Trifacta Data Wrangler and Knight Certification

Delivering Value and Efficiency: Rajib is committed to timely, budget-conscious project delivery, emphasizing client satisfaction and long-term partnerships.

Commitment to Quality and Communication: He ensures clear communication, providing timely updates and meticulously planning tasks to meet deadlines and budgets.

Technical Expertise and Team Collaboration:

- **Programming Languages**: R, Python
- **Cloud Platforms**: Microsoft Azure, Azure Databricks, Microsoft Fabric
- **Data Science Tools**: Azure ML, MLFlow, Fabric Data Science

Rajib collaborates with a team of experts to tackle complex projects and ensure client satisfaction. Outside of work, he enjoys stock market analysis and travel. His blend of technical skills, certifications, and client-focused approach makes him an ideal partner for data science and machine learning projects.

About the Technical Reviewer

Nehaa Bansal is a trailblazing thought leader and data scientist, driven by a relentless passion for early innovation. With a wealth of experience spanning multiple industries including banking, finance, telecom, and insurance, Nehaa has mastered the art of developing predictive models that drive impactful outcomes. Her ability to excel both as an independent contributor and a collaborative team player sets her apart in the field.

Nehaa's academic journey showcases a string of remarkable achievements. Earning top honors in her graduating class, Nehaa obtained a bachelor's degree in computer science, laying a strong foundation for her future endeavors. Building upon her academic success, she further honed her skills by earning a master's in data science from the esteemed BITS Pilani.

At the core of Nehaa's professional ethos lie values that shape her every action. She thrives on taking ownership, putting people first, and asking the fundamental question of "why" before embarking on any endeavor. Her agile mindset propels her to act swiftly, embrace failure as a learning opportunity, iterate continuously, and always strive to play fair.

Driven by her deep-rooted passion for solving user problems, Nehaa leverages her expertise in analytics capabilities, product strategy, and leadership to craft innovative solutions. She approaches every challenge with unwavering dedication, consistently pushing the boundaries of what is possible.

Beyond her professional pursuits, Nehaa finds fulfillment in various personal interests. She relishes the power of continuous learning and remains at the forefront of emerging trends in her field. Furthermore, she is an avid advocate for creating a more inclusive and diverse work environment, fostering collaboration and empathy among team members.

With an indomitable spirit and a commitment to excellence, she continues to inspire and pave the way for others in the realm of technology and data science. Her unwavering dedication to her craft, coupled with her deep empathy for others, has solidified her as a thought leader and a catalyst for positive change.

Acknowledgements

Embarking on the journey of writing *Ultimate Azure Data Scientist Associate (DP-100) Certification Guide* has been an incredible experience, and I am deeply grateful to the individuals who have played a crucial role in bringing this book to fruition. This endeavor wouldn't have been possible without the unwavering support, guidance, and expertise generously shared by many.

Firstly, my heartfelt thanks go to the Microsoft Azure community and the development team behind Azure, whose dedication to the platform has shaped this book. The Azure documentation, an invaluable resource at www.docs.microsoft.com, served as a guiding light, enriching the content and ensuring accuracy. Special thanks to Sanjay Soni, Director, Global Analytics and AI Sales Enablement Leader at Microsoft, for providing me with the opportunity to work within the Microsoft AI world. His support and leadership have been instrumental in my professional growth and the development of this book.

To my family, your unwavering support has been invaluable. I am deeply grateful for my parents' blessings, which have been a constant source of strength throughout this writing journey. To my wife, your steadfast support and encouragement have been instrumental in making this book possible. To my sons, your inspiration and energy have fueled my dedication and passion. Thank you all for being my pillars of strength.

To all those at the publication house who have contributed in various capacities, your collective efforts have enriched this endeavor. I appreciate the collaborative spirit that has fueled the creation of *Ultimate Azure Data Scientist Associate (DP-100) Certification Guide*.

Finally, a heartfelt thank you to the readers, the **Certification Aspirants, Aspiring Data Scientists, IT Professionals and Developers, Data Analysts, Students and Researchers, and Business Professionals**, who have chosen this book as their guide to mastering data science within the Microsoft Azure environment. Whether your goal is to achieve the DP-100 certification or simply to expand your data science skill set in Azure, this book is designed to empower your journey.

Get ready to elevate your data science game and emerge as a certified Azure Data Scientist Associate!

Preface

In the fast-evolving landscape of Azure data science, embracing a framework that seamlessly blends power with elegance is paramount. Welcome to the modern cloud-based data science world – a journey that transcends the ordinary and propels you into the extraordinary.

This book comprises 12 chapters, each a complete module in itself, serving as your comprehensive guide to mastering data science on Azure. It covers a wide array of topics, from the fundamentals to advanced techniques. Whether you are a seasoned developer looking to expand your skills or a newcomer eager to dive into data science, this book has something for everyone.

Chapter 1. Introduction to Data Science and Azure: In this chapter, you will be introduced to the world of data science and Microsoft Azure. You will understand the significance of data science in today's business landscape and explore the capabilities that Azure offers for data science projects. Topics include an overview of data science concepts, Azure's role in data science, and setting the stage for your journey in designing and implementing data science solutions on the Azure platform.

Chapter 2. Setting Up Your Azure Environment: This chapter focuses on the practical aspects of getting started with Azure. You will learn how to create an Azure account and subscription and gain insights into relevant Azure services for data science. The core part of this chapter is setting up your Azure Machine Learning workspace, which serves as a hub for managing and running data science experiments.

Chapter 3. Data Ingestion and Storage in Azure: Understanding data ingestion is pivotal. You will delve into Azure Data Lake Storage and Azure SQL Database, exploring how these services facilitate data storage and management. The chapter covers various techniques for data ingestion, including batch and real-time methods, ensuring a holistic understanding of data movement in Azure.

Chapter 4. Data Transformation and Cleaning: Effective data transformation and cleaning are essential for accurate analysis. You will grasp the significance of preprocessing and learn how to use Azure Data Factory for data transformation.

The chapter also delves into data cleaning techniques using both Python and Azure services, ensuring your data is ready for analysis.

Chapter 5. Introduction to Machine Learning: This chapter provides a foundational understanding of machine learning. It covers the basics of supervised and unsupervised learning algorithms, giving you a clear grasp of the fundamental concepts that underpin machine learning techniques.

Chapter 6. Azure Machine Learning Studio: Explore Azure Machine Learning Studio in-depth. This includes creating and training machine learning models within the studio, understanding hyperparameter tuning, and evaluating model performance. The chapter empowers you to harness the power of Azure's machine learning capabilities effectively.

Chapter 7. Model Deployment and Monitoring: Deploying and monitoring machine learning models is critical for successful integration. This chapter guides you through deploying models using Azure services, ensuring you understand the steps involved. You will also learn about monitoring and managing deployed models, as well as integrating CI/CD practices for machine learning projects.

Chapter 8. Embracing AI Revolution Azure: This enlightening chapter delves comprehensively into the Generative AI and Large Language Models, focusing on their implementation and application using Microsoft Azure's robust tools and services. Beginning with an exploration of Azure's advanced capabilities like OpenAI, Semantic Kernel, and the Model Catalog, we further examine the utilization of Generative AI in various applications. The chapter also dives deep into the nuances of creating engaging conversational experiences with Azure's PromptFlow and wraps up by addressing critical aspects such as Responsible AI. Moreover, it encompasses a detailed walkthrough on how to leverage Azure's multi-modal AI services, including Azure Speech and Azure Vision, to build more inclusive AI models.

Chapter 9. Responsible AI and Ethics: The ethical considerations of AI and data science are explored in this chapter. Learn about responsible AI practices, including fairness, transparency, and bias mitigation, ensuring that your data science solutions adhere to ethical standards.

Chapter 10. Big Data Analytics with Azure: This chapter introduces you to big data analytics using Azure. Gain an understanding of Apache Spark and how Azure Databricks facilitates big data processing and analytics. Topics covered include big data concepts, Databricks architecture, and real-world applications.

Chapter 11. Real-World Applications and Case Studies: Dive into real-world applications of data science on Azure. This chapter showcases case studies that highlight successful implementations of data science solutions, providing valuable insights into how these concepts are put into practice.

Chapter 12. Conclusion and Next Steps: The concluding chapter recaps the key takeaways from the book and encourages you to continue your journey in data science on Azure. It offers guidance on further enhancing your skills and exploring advanced topics.

This book is a hands-on guide filled with practical examples, real-world scenarios, and best practices. We hope this journey through Azure empowers you to build cutting-edge machine learning applications and enhances your skills in the dynamic field of data science. Happy learning!

Get a Free eBook

We hope you are enjoying your recently purchased book! Your feedback is incredibly valuable to us, and to all other readers looking for great books.

If you found this book helpful or enjoyable, we would truly appreciate it, if you could take a moment to leave a short review with a 5 star rating on Amazon. It helps us grow, and lets other readers discover our books.

As a thank you, we would love to send you a free digital copy of this book, and a **30%** discount code on your next cart value on our official websites:

www.orangeava.com

www.orangeava.in (For Indian Subcontinent)

☑ **Here's how:**

Leave a review for the book on Amazon.

Take a screenshot of your review, and send an email to **info@orangeava.com** (it can be just the confirmation screen).

Once, we receive your screenshot, we will send you the digital file, within 24 hours.

Thank you so much for your support – it means a lot to us!

Colored Images

Please follow the links or scan the QR codes to download the ***Images*** of the book:

You can find code bundles of our books on our official Github Repository. Go to the following link to and QR code to explore the further:

https://github.com/orgs/ava-orange-education/repositories

Please follow the link to download the Colored Images of the book:
https://rebrand.ly/65e9b7

In case there's an update to the code, it will be updated on the existing GitHub repository.

Errata

We take immense pride in our work at **Orange Education Pvt Ltd,** and follow best practices to ensure the accuracy of our content to provide an indulging reading experience to our subscribers. Our readers are our mirrors, and we use their inputs to reflect and improve upon human errors, if any, that may have occurred during the publishing processes involved. To let us maintain the quality and help us reach out to any readers who might be having difficulties due to any unforeseen errors, please write to us at :

errata@orangeava.com

Your support, suggestions, and feedback are highly appreciated.

DID YOU KNOW

Did you know that Orange Education Pvt Ltd offers eBook versions of every book published, with PDF and ePub files available? You can upgrade to the eBook version at **www.orangeava.com** and as a print book customer, you are entitled to a discount on the eBook copy. Get in touch with us at: **info@orangeava.com** for more details.

At **www.orangeava.com**, you can also read a collection of free technical articles, sign up for a range of free newsletters, and receive exclusive discounts and offers on AVA™ Books and eBooks.

PIRACY

If you come across any illegal copies of our works in any form on the internet, we would be grateful if you would provide us with the location address or website name. Please contact us at **info@orangeava.com** with a link to the material.

ARE YOU INTERESTED IN AUTHORING WITH US?

If there is a topic that you have expertise in, and you are interested in either writing or contributing to a book, please write to us at **business@orangeava.com**. We are on a journey to help developers and tech professionals to gain insights on the present technological advancements and innovations happening across the globe and build a community that believes Knowledge is best acquired by sharing and learning with others. Please reach out to us to learn what our audience demands and how you can be part of this educational reform. We also welcome ideas from tech experts and help them build learning and development content for their domains.

REVIEWS

Please leave a review. Once you have read and used this book, why not leave a review on the site that you purchased it from? Potential readers can then see and use your unbiased opinion to make purchase decisions. We at Orange Education would love to know what you think about our products, and our authors can learn from your feedback. Thank you!

For more information about Orange Education, please visit **www.orangeava.com**.

Table of Contents

1. Introduction to Data Science and Azure **1**
Introduction 1
Structure 1
Introduction to Data Science 2
Definition of Data Science 2
Importance of Data Science in Modern Businesses 2
Overview of Data Science 2
Understanding Data Science Concepts 3
Process of Data Science 3
Data Science Tools and Techniques 4
Role of Data Science in Decision Making 5
Introduction to Microsoft Azure 5
Overview of Microsoft Azure 6
Azure Architecture 6
Benefits of Using Azure in Businesses 6
Azure for Data Science 7
Overview of Azure Services for Data Science 8
Azure Machine Learning 8
Azure Databricks 9
Azure Data Lake Storage 9
Azure Synapse Analytics 10
Azure AI Capabilities 10
Azure Subscription Models and Pricing 11
Overview of Azure Subscription Models 12
Understanding Azure Pricing 12
Setting Up Azure for Data Science 12
Creating an Azure Account 13
Buying an Azure Subscription 13
Managing Azure Services and Permissions 13

Azure Resource Manager 14
Azure Role-Based Access Control 14
Azure Advisor 14
Azure Policy 15
Azure Portal and Azure Resource Manager 16
Navigating the Azure Portal 16
Introduction to Azure Resource Manager 17
Exploring Resource Groups in Azure 17
Conclusion 18
Exercises 20
2. Setting Up Your Azure Environment 21
Introduction 21
Structure 21
Introduction to Azure Environment Setup 22
Creating an Azure Account and Subscription 22
Establishing Your Azure Account 22
Selecting An Azure Subscription 23
Overview of Azure Services for Data Science 23
Azure Services for Data Science 24
Azure Machine Learning (Azure ML) 24
Azure Databricks 24
Azure Synapse Analytics 25
Azure Cognitive Services 25
Utilizing Azure Services for Data Science Optimally 25
For Start-ups or Small Projects 25
For Big Data Operations 25
Setting Up Azure Machine Learning Workspace 26
Exploring Features and Benefits of Azure Machine Learning Workspace 27
Understanding Azure Machine Learning Studio Interface 27
Exploring Azure Machine Learning Studio Interface 28
Authoring 28

Assets 28
Manage 29
Familiarizing with Tools and Functionalities 30
Authoring 30
Assets 32
Manage 34
Managing and Configuring Compute Resources 35
Importance of Compute Resources 35
Guideline to Effectively Manage and Configure Compute Resources in Azure 36
Using Azure Notebooks 37
Introducing Azure Notebooks 37
Executing Data Science Experiments Using Azure Notebooks 38
Collaboration Between Azure Notebooks and AutoML 38
Version Control and Collaboration with Git Integration 39
Importance of Version Control and Collaboration in Data Science Projects 40
Steps to Integrate Git for Version Control in Azure 40
Collaboration Features in Azure 42
Azure DevOps 43
Azure Notebooks 43
Azure Boards 43
Azure Pipelines 43
Conclusion 44
Questions 44
Multiple Choice Questions 45
Answers 48
3. Data Ingestion and Storage in Azure 49
Introduction 49
Structure 49
Introduction to Data Ingestion in Azure 50
Explaining Data Ingestion and Its Significance 50

Overview of Azure Data Storage and Management Services 51

Azure Data Storage Options 51

Azure Data Lake Storage (ADLS) Gen2 51

Azure SQL Database 54

Azure Blob Storage 56

Choosing the Right Azure Storage for Your Needs 58

Data Ingestion Techniques in Azure 59

Azure Data Factory 59

Azure Stream Analytics 61

Building Azure's Data Ingestion Pipeline 62

Introduction to Azure Data Lake Storage Gen2 62

Elucidation of the Azure Data Lake Gen2 Services 62

Highlighting the Distinguished Features and Advantages 62

Real-World Applications of Azure Data Lake Storage Gen2 63

Data Access and Security in Azure 63

Understanding Azure's Data Security Measures 64

Encryption Types and Data Protection Tactics 64

User Authentication and Access Control in Azure 65

Importance of Data Security in Cloud Storage 66

Data Governance and Compliance in Azure 67

Understanding the Role and Principles of Data Governance in Azure 67

Compliance Policies as per Different Jurisdictions 67

Azure's Support Tools for Governance and Compliance 68

Role of Governance and Compliance in Data Trustworthiness 71

Conclusion 71

Questions 72

Multiple Choice Questions 72

Answers 75

4. Data Transformation and Cleaning 76

Introduction 76

Structure 76

Overview of Data Transformation and Cleaning....77
Understanding Data Preprocessing and Cleaning....77
Definition and Importance....77
Basic Techniques of Data Cleaning....78
Azure Data Factory for Data Transformation....79
Introduction to Azure Data Factory....79
Benefits of Using Azure Data Factory in Data Transformation....80
Step-by-Step Guide to Using Azure Data Factory....80
Data Wrangling Using Azure Databricks....81
Introduction to Data Wrangling....82
Introduction to Azure Databricks....83
Step-by-Step Guide on Implementation of Data Wrangling with Azure Databricks....83
Dealing with Structured and Unstructured Data....86
Differences Between Structured and Unstructured Data....86
Understanding the Challenges....87
Techniques to Deal with Structured and Unstructured Data....88
Structured Data....89
Unstructured Data....89
Focus on Data Transformation Pipelines and Orchestration....90
Understanding Data Transformation Pipelines....91
The Role of Orchestration in Data Transformation Pipelines....91
Use of Azure Features in Pipeline Orchestration....92
Conclusion....92
Questions....93
Multiple Choice Questions....93
Answers....96
5. Introduction to Machine Learning....97
Introduction....97
Structure....98
Fundamentals of Machine Learning....98
Supervised Learning....98

Unsupervised Learning ... 98

Reinforcement Learning ... 100

Overview of Machine Learning Algorithms ... 101

Classification ... 101

Types of Classification Algorithms ... 102

Regression ... 103

Types of Regression Algorithms ... 103

Clustering ... 105

Feature Engineering and Selection ... 106

Steps in Feature Engineering ... 107

Variable Transformation ... 107

Variable Creation ... 107

Strategies for Attribute Selection ... 108

Methods for Feature Selection ... 108

Evaluation Metrics for Machine Learning Models ... 109

Classification Metrics ... 110

Accuracy ... 111

Precision ... 111

Recall (Sensitivity) ... 111

F1 Score ... 111

Specificity (True Negative Rate) ... 111

Receiver Operating Characteristic (ROC) Curve ... 111

Regression Metrics ... 112

Mean Absolute Error (MAE) ... 112

Mean Squared Error (MSE) ... 112

Root Mean Squared Error (RMSE) ... 113

R-squared (Coefficient of Determination) ... 113

Bias, Fairness, and Ethics Considerations in Machine Learning ... 113

Understanding Bias in Machine Learning ... 113

Types of Bias ... 114

Sample Bias ... 114

Prejudice Bias ... 115

xix

Measurement Bias 115

Exclusion Bias 115

Selection Bias 116

Outlier Bias 116

Algorithmic Bias 116

Importance of Fairness in Machine Learning 116

Techniques to Ensure Fairness 117

Data Preprocessing 118

Stratified Sampling 118

Feature Selection 118

Algorithm Modification 118

Post-processing 118

Evaluation Metrics 118

Bias-Awareness Training 118

Ethics in Machine Learning 119

Ethical Considerations 120

Informed Consent 120

Transparency 120

Privacy Protection 121

Conclusion 121

Questions 122

Multiple Choice Questions 122

Answers 125

6. Azure Machine Learning Studio 126

Introduction 126

Structure 127

Overview of Azure Machine Learning Studio 127

Introduction to Azure Machine Learning Studio and Its Capabilities 127

Navigating the Azure Machine Learning Studio Interface 128

Role of Azure Machine Learning Studio in Model Development and Deployment 131

Practical Application 132
Introducing Our Project: Predicting House Prices 132
Setting Up the Project on Azure Machine Learning Studio 132
Creating and Managing Experiments in Azure Machine Learning Studio 137
Setting Up a Workspace and Creating New Experiments 137
Organizing Resources Within the Azure Machine Learning Studio Environment 138
Monitoring Experiments and Logging Runs 139
Monitoring Experiments 139
Logging Runs 139
Output Files 140
Preparing Data for Training and Evaluation 140
Accessing and Importing Data into Azure Machine Learning Studio 140
Data Pre-processing Techniques Supported by Azure Machine Learning 143
Loading the Data 143
Inspecting the Data 145
Handling Missing Values 145
Handling Duplicates 146
Handling Outliers 147
Converting Data Types 148
Data Transformation 148
Encoding Data 149
Splitting Data into Training and Test Sets 150
Data Scaling 150
Reasons to Scale Data After Splitting 151
Building and Training Machine Learning Models Using Azure Machine Learning SDK 152
Overview of the Azure Machine Learning SDK for Python 152
Workspace 152
Experiment 153

xxi

Run 153
Model 154
Selecting and Constructing Machine Learning Models Using SDK 154
Training Models on Cloud Resources 158
Hyperparameter Tuning and Model Selection 159
Introduction to Hyperparameter Tuning 160
Azure Machine Learning SDK Hyperparameter Tuning 161
Strategies for Selecting the Best Model 162
Model Evaluation Techniques and Metrics 164
Different Evaluation Metrics for Various Machine Learning Tasks 164
Regression Task Metrics 164
Classification Task Metrics 164
Clustering Task Metrics 165
Ranking Task Metrics 165
Visualizing and Interpreting Evaluation Results 165
Model Validation and Cross-Validation in Azure Machine Learning Studio 166
Deploying Models and Real-time Prediction 166
Preparing a Model for Deployment 167
Setting Up a Deployment Environment 168
Creating and Consuming Real-Time Prediction Endpoints 169
Managing and Monitoring Deployed Models 170
Techniques for Managing Deployed Models 170
Monitoring Model Performance and Data Drift 171
Strategies for Model Retraining and Updating 172
Automated Retraining 172
Validation Process 172
Champion-Challenger Framework 172
Seamless Model Updates 173
Model Version Control 173

Best Practices and Considerations....173

Ensuring Model Reproducibility and Version Control....173

Security and Compliance Considerations in Azure Machine Learning....174

Access Control and Identity Management....174

Encryption and Isolation....175

Compliance....175

Protections Against Threats....175

Cost Management and Optimization for Machine Learning Projects in Azure....175

Conclusion....176

Questions....177

Multiple Choice Questions....178

Answers....179

Practical Exercise....179

7. Model Deployment and Monitoring....181

Introduction....181

Structure....181

Introduction to Model Deployment and Monitoring....182

Overview of Model Deployment and Monitoring....182

Importance of Model Deployment and Monitoring....182

Deploying Models with Azure Machine Learning Service....183

Gaining Insight into Azure Machine Learning Service....183

Navigating Through the Deployment Process....184

Setting Up Deployment Environments....185

Preparing Azure Kubernetes Service....185

Establishing Azure Container Instances....186

Monitoring Deployed Models....187

Leveraging Azure Monitor for Model Monitoring....187

Implementing Azure Application Insights for Model Monitoring....188

Continuous Integration and Deployment (CI/CD) in Machine Learning 189
Understanding and Highlighting the Importance of CI/CD in ML 189
Implementing CI/CD in ML: A Step-by-Step Guide 190
Model Version Control and Rollback 191
Overview of Model Version Control and Rollback 192
Process and Guidelines for Model Version Control and Rollback 192
Conclusion 193
Questions 194
Multiple Choice Questions 195
Answers 198
8. Embracing AI Revolution Azure 199
Introduction 199
Structure 199
Introduction to Generative AI and Large Language Models 199
Definition and Overview 200
Importance and Benefits 201
Applications 202
Azure's Role in Advancing Generative AI 204
Azure OpenAI 204
Steps to Create an Azure OpenAI Resource 206
Model Catalog 208
Function and Usage 209
Relationship with Generative AI 209
Steps for Using Model Catalog 209
Exploring Azure's PromptFlow for Developing Applications Powered by LLMs 214
Understanding Azure's PromptFlow 214
Advantages of PromptFlow in LLM Application 215
Prompt Engineering Agility 215
Enterprise Readiness 215

Unveiling the LLM-based Application Development Lifecycle............215
Creating an Azure's PromptFlow: A Step-By-Step Guide....................216
Going in Depth...221
Working with Multimodal AI Services: Azure Speech and Vision 225
Azure's Speech Services: The Voice of AI..225
Azure Vision Services: AI's Optical Powerhouse..226
Azure Speech..226
Utilization in AI Models..227
Practical Implementation...227
Azure Vision..227
Role in AI Models...228
Walkthrough of Implementation..228
Responsible AI in Azure: Creating Ethical and Unbiased
AI Models 228
Importance of Ethical and Unbiased AI Models..228
Azure's Approach to Responsible AI..229
Azure AI Content Safety..229
Steps to Create Content Safety Resource...230
Purpose..232
Application in Current Technological Landscape.......................................233
Conclusion...233
Exercise..234
Multiple Choice Questions...235
Answers..236
9. Responsible AI and Ethics.. **237**
Introduction..237
Structure..237
The Crucial Role of AI Ethics...238
Understanding the Importance of Ethics in Artificial
Intelligence...238
Consequences of Unethical AI..238
Understanding Responsible AI...239

Definition and Overview of Responsible AI....239
Importance of Responsible AI....239
Responsible AI Principles and Practices....240
Introduction to Responsible AI Principles....240
Implementation of Responsible AI Practices....241
Ethical Considerations in Data Science Projects....242
Importance of Ethics in Data Science....242
Ethical Considerations and Their Practical Applications....242
Fairness, Transparency, and Interpretability of Machine Learning Models....243
Defining Fairness, Transparency, and Interpretability....243
Importance of These Principles in Machine Learning....244
Practices to Enhance These Principles in ML Models....244
Mitigating Bias and Discrimination in AI Models....245
Understanding Bias and Discrimination in AI....245
Techniques for Mitigating Bias and Discrimination....245
Case Studies: Impact of Mitigation Strategies....245
Privacy and Security Concerns in AI Solutions....246
Importance of Privacy and Security in AI....246
Impact of Security Breaches on AI Solutions....246
Strategies to Ensure Privacy and Security in AI Solutions....247
Implementing Responsible AI with Azure....247
Overview of Azure's Role in Responsible AI....247
Using Azure Machine Learning for Ethical AI Practices....248
Conclusion....249
Questions....250
Multiple Choice Questions....250
Answers....253
10. Big Data Analytics with Azure....254
Introduction....254
Structure....254
Introduction to Big Data Analytics and Processing....255

Defining Big Data: Understanding its Scope and Importance 255
Overview of Big Data Analytics: Techniques and Tools 256
Big Data Processing: Steps and Challenges 259
Using Azure Databricks for Scalable Data Processing 260
Introduction to Azure Databricks: Benefits and Features 260
Setting Up Azure Databricks: A Step-by-Step Guide 262
Using Azure Databricks for Data Processing: Best Practices 263
Implementing Apache Spark Jobs on Azure 264
Understanding Apache Spark: Its Role in Big Data Processing 264
Role of Apache Spark in Big Data Processing 265
Apache Spark and Azure: A Powerful Duo 265
Running Apache Spark Jobs on Azure: A Comprehensive Guide 267
Leveraging Azure HDInsight for Big Data Solutions 267
Introduction to Azure HDInsight: Capabilities and Functions 268
Integrating Azure HDInsight with Big Data Analytics: Mastering the Process 269
Best Practices for Using Azure HDInsight in Big Data Solutions 270
Real-Time Data Processing with Azure Stream Analytics 271
Understanding Azure Stream Analytics: Features and Benefits 271
Setting Up Azure Stream Analytics: Practical Steps 272
Implementing Real-Time Data Processing with Azure Stream Analytics 273
Conclusion 274
Questions 275
Multiple Choice Questions 276
Answers 279

11. Real-World Applications and Case Studies 280
Introduction 280
Structure 280
Overview of Real-World Data Science Applications on Azure 281

Explanation of Data Science Projects: Success Stories........................282
Real-World Examples of Successful Data Science Projects on Azure........................282
Project A: Predictive Maintenance for the Manufacturing Industry........................283
Project B: Customer Segmentation in E-commerce........................285
Project C: Fraud Detection in Financial Services........................286
Case Studies: Data Science Applications in Various Industries........................288
Finance........................288
Healthcare........................289
E-Commerce........................289
Identifying Business Problems and Formulating Data Science Solutions........................290
Understanding Business Problems: Tips and Techniques........................290
Creating Suitable Data Science Solutions: A Step-by-Step Guide........................291
Lessons Learned from Implementing Data Science Projects........................291
Challenges and How to Overcome Them........................292
Key Takeaways from Past Projects........................292
Best Practices for Delivering Value through Data Science on Azure........................293
Conclusion........................293
Q&A: Frequently Raised Concerns and Expert Responses........................294
12. Conclusion and Next Steps........................296
Introduction........................296
Structure........................297
Recap of Key Concepts........................297
Review of Data Science and Azure........................297
Reflection on Setting Up Your Azure Environment........................297
Recap on Data Ingestion and Storage in Azure........................297
Summary of Data Transformation and Cleaning........................297
Review of Machine Learning........................298

Reflection on Azure Machine Learning Studio......298
Summary of Model Deployment and Monitoring......298
Recap on Embracing AI Revolution with Azure......298
Reflection on Responsible AI and Ethics......298
Summary of Big Data Analytics with Azure......298
Review of Real-World Applications and Case Studies......299
Reflection on the Journey from Designing to Implementing Data Science Solutions......299
Importance of Designing to Implementing Data Science Solutions......299
Reflection on Learned Skills and Techniques......299
Progressing Further: Diving Deeper into Azure and Data Science......300
Emphasizing Continuous Learning in Data Science......300
A Glimpse into Advanced Azure Topics......300
Inspiring More Engagement with Real-World Applications......300
Future Directions: Amplifying Your Data Science Expertise in Azure......301
Strategies for Skill Augmentation in Data Science......301
Resources for Continued Learning......301
Future Trends and Technologies to Look Out......301
Certifications to Validate Your Skills......301
Conclusion: Reflecting, Engaging, and Envisioning the Future in Data Science with Azure......302
Reflection on the Learning Journey......303
Encouraging Engagement in Data Science Endeavors......303
Envisioning the Future – Data Science and Azure......303
Index......304

CHAPTER 1
Introduction to Data Science and Azure

Introduction

This chapter provides an extensive overview and introduction to the rapidly growing field of data science, with a particular focus on the application and utility of Microsoft Azure in the context of data science. Starting with a basic concept of data science, we delve deeper into the concept, methodologies, and the vast potential the domain offers.

We further enhance the perspective by introducing Microsoft Azure, emphasizing how it provides a robust platform for numerous data science activities. This chapter provides a detailed explanation of Azure, focusing on its specific functions for data science. It will feature essential capabilities of Microsoft Azure from storage and networking to compute resources that help in managing and analyzing big data. The chapter also explores Azure's subscription models and pricing strategies, enabling the readers to make an informed decision based on their needs and budget. It offers a comprehensive guide for setting up Azure for data science, which would be especially beneficial for first-time users. In addition, we take a closer look at the crucial components of Azure such as the Azure Portal and Azure Resource Manager, offering a granular view of their functionalities.

Structure

In this chapter, the following topics will be covered:

- Introduction to Data Science
- Overview of Data Science
- Introduction to Microsoft Azure
- Azure for Data Science
- Azure Subscription Models and Pricing

- Setting Up Azure for Data Science
- The Azure Portal and Azure Resource Manager

Introduction to Data Science

Data Science is an emerging interdisciplinary field that uses scientific methods, algorithms, and systems to draw actionable insights from both structured and unstructured data. It is the lifeblood of our current digitally inclined era, shaping diverse sectors from business to health, education, and beyond.

Definition of Data Science

"Science is what we understand well enough to explain to a computer. Data Science is when the computer understands it well enough to explain it to you."

- Geoffrey Hinton (renowned as the "*Godfather of Deep Learning*")

Essentially, data science can be characterized as a systematic approach aimed at interpreting large volumes of data. By deploying various tools, algorithms, and principles of machine learning, data science strives to identify latent patterns within raw data. It is a transformative process where data is turned into valuable insights, influencing decision-making and forecasting trends.

Importance of Data Science in Modern Businesses

In the current business context, enterprises are inundated with data. This data can originate from a myriad of sources such as transaction records, customer feedback, or social media platforms. Data science is pivotal in leveraging this immense volume of data into actionable outcomes. It enables businesses to comprehend customer behaviors, optimize operations, improve decision-making processes, and ultimately, bolster their competitive stance in the market.

As we move forward in this chapter, we will delve deeper into the core concepts of data science, its working process, as well as the array of tools and techniques employed within this field. Following that, we will pivot towards unveiling Microsoft Azure, a robust cloud platform that offers impressive capabilities for orchestrating data science projects. Keep reading; there's much more to unfold.

Overview of Data Science

Stepping into the realm of data science, we encounter a dynamic world encapsulated by concepts, processes, tools, and the consequential impact on decision-making capabilities. Let's dive deeper to better understand these facets.

Understanding Data Science Concepts

Data science is a multidisciplinary field that uses scientific methods, algorithms, systems, and processes to derive insights from structured or unstructured data. It brings together three significant concepts: data, programming, and statistics.

Data is an assembly of information that is quantitative or qualitative, structured or unstructured. They hold deep knowledge but are typically unsorted and in the raw form, which needs to be refined to be useful. The quantity of data collected in modern digital systems is vast and can't be processed manually. This is where programming becomes a vital component.

Programming is the method by which we instruct computers to perform specific tasks. For a data scientist, programming languages such as Python, R, SQL, and others are used to work with large quantities of data. They write algorithms and create computer models to clean, organize, and interpret the data. Programming skills help manipulate the data and produce analyses that are meaningful and digestible.

Statistics is the third key component. It brings in quantitative reasoning to consider the variability, uncertainty, sampling, and inference in the data. The implementation of statistical depth allows a data scientist to draw reliable conclusions from the data analyses. It helps differentiate between correlation and causation, thus allowing for meaningful insights to be drawn.

Data science thereby is not just about the individual capabilities in handling data, programming, and statistics, but the specific prowess in coalescing these into a single effective tool. It takes data, breaks it down, refines it, analyzes it, and ultimately changes it into actionable knowledge. This knowledge, in turn, helps businesses in decision-making processes, predictive assessments, and more. It empowers organizations to drive strategic planning, foster innovation, and gain a competitive edge.

Process of Data Science

Data science process can be viewed as a journey that starts with an initial query or issue and gradually reveals deeper insights and information.

It begins with a question or problem. This could be a business query, a technical issue, or any general query that needs to be analyzed. It forms the basis and direction of the analysis to follow. For example, a business could be interested in finding out why a particular product is not performing well in certain regions.

The next stage involves collecting relevant data that can help answer the query or solve the problem. This could involve gathering data from various sources such as databases, web scraping, surveys, and many others.

Once data is collected, the next step is data cleaning or preprocessing. This is an essential step as the collected data can have many inconsistencies such as missing values, duplicate values, errors, and more. Data cleaning helps in rectifying these and transforming the data into a format that can be easily analyzed.

Following data cleaning is the exploratory data analysis. This involves analyzing and investigating datasets and summarizing their main characteristics, often using visual methods like graphs and charts. It helps data scientists to gain insights and identify any patterns or relations in the data that may be underlying the problem or query.

The refined data is then used for statistical modeling and machine learning. In statistical modeling, mathematical equations are used to represent the relationships between different variables. Machine learning, on the other hand, involves using algorithms to parse data, learn from it, and then make a determination or prediction about something.

These models and algorithms help in making predictions or conclusions about the query. They are tested and validated using various metrics for accuracy, precision, and other parameters.

The final step involves interpreting and communicating the insights derived from the analysis. Effective communication of these insights is vital as it impacts decision making. These insights can influence changes or improvements in business strategies, technical solutions, and other areas.

This is a cyclic and iterative process. Once an insight is derived and communicated, it can lead to other questions, and the process begins again. The more the cycle is repeated, the more insights are gained, making it an ongoing journey.

Data Science Tools and Techniques

Data science is a comprehensive field that focuses on extracting meaningful insights from large quantities of structured or unstructured data. This process involves using different programming languages, machine learning techniques, predictive analytics, and visualization tools.

One of the important programming languages used in data science is Python, known for its simplicity and versatility. It offers numerous libraries and frameworks, such as Pandas for data manipulation, Matplotlib for data visualization, and Scikit-learn for machine learning, making it widely used amongst data scientists.

R, another key programming language, is largely used for statistical analysis and graphical models. Its vast collection of packages makes it possible to conduct complex statistical operations.

SQL or Structured Query Language is essential in dealing with databases. It allows data scientists to retrieve, manipulate, and analyze data stored in relational databases.

When it comes to AI techniques, machine learning forms the crux of many data science operations, helping in creating predictive models based on patterns and inferences from the data.

Predictive analytics is another critical aspect of data science, using data, statistical algorithms, and machine learning techniques to identify the likelihood of future outcomes based on historical data.

Visualization tools, such as Tableau or Power BI, allow data to be represented graphically, making it easier to understand trends, patterns, and outliers. These tools are user-friendly and can turn complex data into digestible visualizations.

As data science is largely conducted in cloud environments due to the significant volumes of data, knowledge of cloud platforms like Microsoft Azure is crucial. Azure offers a range of services, including Azure Databricks, an Apache Spark-based analytics platform, and Azure Machine Learning service for building, deploying, and managing machine learning models. Azure also integrates seamlessly with many of the aforementioned tools and has powerful computing capabilities to handle the heavy workloads associated with data science.

Essentially, data science blends various tools and techniques to help organizations make data-driven decisions. The cloud, particularly Azure, offers a flexible and scalable environment for carrying out these extensive operations.

Role of Data Science in Decision Making

"Without big data, you are blind and deaf and in the middle of a freeway."

- Geoffrey Moore (acclaimed consultant and author)

Applying data science in decision-making adds precision, speeds up the process, and mitigates the risks associated with erroneous judgments. Leveraging past data and predicting future tendencies, it empowers businesses to make data-backed, insightful decisions.

All in all, while it may seem overwhelming initially, data science, in essence, revolves around transforming data into a strategic asset for decision-making.

Introduction to Microsoft Azure

Welcome to the world of Microsoft Azure, a comprehensive, ever-evolving cloud platform that's bringing a paradigm shift in how businesses operate today. Azure's versatility extends to an array of functionalities, including but not limited to, computing, networking, storage, and data analytics.

Overview of Microsoft Azure

Think of Microsoft Azure as a global supermarket for all your digital, cloud-based needs. The entire digital landscape is at your fingertips' reach! It's a cloud computing service created by Microsoft, providing an extensive suite of cloud services that users can pick and choose from to develop and scale new applications or run existing ones in the public cloud.

Azure stacks up well in the cloud game by not only offering considerable storage and speed but also an extensive array of integrated cloud services that include analytics, computing, database, mobile, networking, storage, and web.

Azure Architecture

Azure's architecture is flexible and dynamic, empowering developers and IT professionals with a scalable, secure, and responsive framework apt for aligning with the businesses' unique needs. This architecture consists of three key components:

- **Azure Management:**

  This includes the administrative services, tools, and features that help in managing, configuring, and setting up the Azure environment.

- **Azure Compute:**

  These are the services that allow developers to host apps. They include virtual machines, container services, and Azure Functions, which handle event-driven computing tasks.

- **Data and Storage:**

  These services store, retrieve, and analyze data, including Azure Database, Azure Cosmos DB, Azure Data Lake Storage, Azure Blob Storage, and more.

Benefits of Using Azure in Businesses

Embracing Azure means signing up for a multitude of benefits it offers. It renders scalability, helping business applications to meet a change in demand. With high-speed and high-performance computing, Azure processes tasks effectively, saving time. By offering robust disaster recovery capabilities, it significantly reduces the financial impact of critical IT outages.

Additionally, Azure ensures flexible expenditure, meaning businesses only pay for what they use, driving cost optimization. Not to forget, Azure not only provides secure cloud data storage but also ensures strict compliance with regulatory standards and data privacy laws.

Finally, Azure seamlessly blends with other Microsoft products, ensuring effortless integrations and smooth transitions.

As we tread further in this chapter, we will focus on how all these elements morph to create a powerful infrastructure for supporting data science activities in Azure's environment.

Azure for Data Science

Microsoft Azure is not merely a provider of cloud services, rather it serves as an all-inclusive platform that offers a vast toolkit specifically designed to accommodate applications related to data science. In essence, Azure is much more akin to a fully equipped workshop where data scientists can execute their projects with high efficiency and precision.

Cloud refers to servers that are accessed over the Internet, and the software and databases that run on those servers. Cloud servers are located in data centers all over the world. Unlike traditional on-premise servers, by using cloud services, companies can access software, storage, compute, and other IT infrastructure elements without the burden of maintaining and upgrading them.

Azure's cloud services are at the bedrock of its capabilities. Through its cloud service offerings, Azure provides a high degree of scalability, flexibility, and cost-efficiency. This allows businesses to only pay for what they use and scale up or down as their needs change.

Focusing more closely on Azure's role in data science, it is important to emphasize that Azure provides several tools and services that aid data scientists in their work. It provides services for big data, machine learning, analytics, and much more, enabling data scientists to create efficient and powerful data models.

Azure's Machine Learning Studio is a prime example of Microsoft's commitment to streamlining data science processes. It's a visual interface for building, testing, and deploying machine learning models, which significantly reduces the need for coding, thereby making the process more approachable and efficient.

The platform's versatility is another strength, accommodating various programming languages used in data science such as Python, R, and SQL. Azure Databricks, an Apache Spark-based analytics platform, is designed to consolidate the process of building big data and AI solutions. This accelerates the work, allowing scientists to swiftly go from data ingestion to insight.

Additionally, Azure's high level of security and compliance standards helps ensure that data is stored and processed under strict standards, making it a reliable choice for businesses across various industries.

Overall, Microsoft Azure is a complete, robust, and reliable cloud platform with a strong focus on enabling efficient data science processes. This makes it much more than just a cloud service provider.

Overview of Azure Services for Data Science

Azure Cloud Platform, created by Microsoft, is a platform for public cloud computing. It provides features that are customized explicitly for data science projects. This means it is built with services and tools that data scientists can utilize for their theoretical or experimental protocols. It integrates the diverse components of data science such as Machine Learning, Artificial Intelligence (AI), Internet of Things (IoT), analytics, and data storage, enabling a smooth transition and management throughout the whole data science project.

In the realm of machine learning, Azure takes pride in its Azure Machine Learning service, a cloud-based predictive analytics service. It allows scientists to build, deploy, and share predictive models, using simplified machine-learning tools. Coupled with AI, Azure permits the creation and training of models that are capable of improving their performance over time.

Regarding IoT, Azure IoT suite provides solutions designed to analyze untapped data, integrate business systems, and transform a business digitally. Azure recognizes the power of IoT in transforming ordinary data into useful insights that can provide businesses with strategies for optimization.

Moreover, Azure specializes in multiple analytics services such as Azure Stream Analytics for real-time analytics and Azure Data Lake Analytics for big data analytics. These can be used to analyze huge volumes of complex data speedily and thoroughly. Undeniably, the ability to manage large amounts of data and turn them into meaningful analytical results is vital in providing a solid foundation for business decisions.

Close to that is data storage. Azure provides scalable and secure data storage services through Azure Blob Storage, Azure Table Storage, Azure Queue Storage, and Azure File Storage. This provides users with reliable, cost-effective options to store, retrieve, and manipulate huge amounts of data.

In modern times, where digital landscapes continuously evolve, time is a valuable resource, and data is the new currency. Azure Cloud Platform acknowledges this fact. Its fast and versatile way of accessing, processing, and analyzing data with its extensive suite of services makes it a highly preferential cloud platform for many businesses. By empowering data scientists with this platform, it helps them drive successful data science projects.

Azure Machine Learning

Azure Machine Learning (AML) is an indispensable tool for data scientists, providing a comprehensive and streamlined environment for developing, training, and deploying machine learning models. AML's automated machine learning capabilities minimize manual efforts and reduce the chances of error, enabling even those with limited expertise to build models more efficiently.

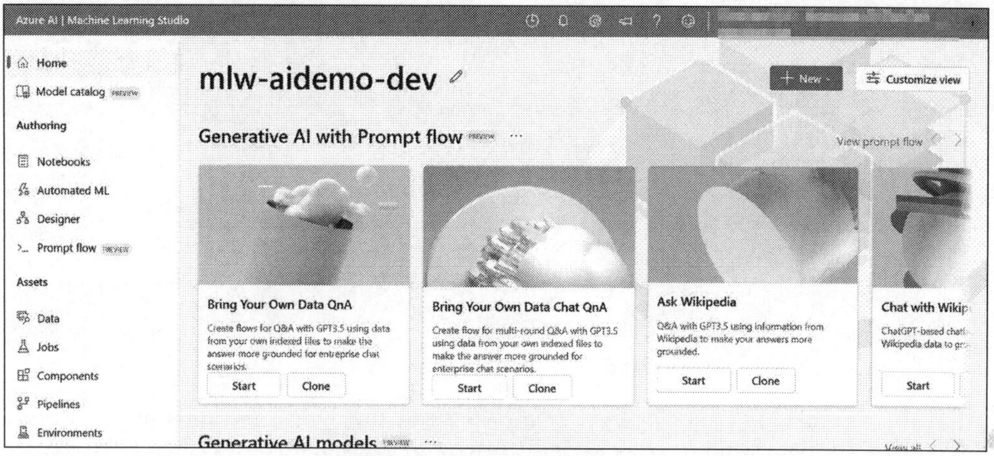

***Figure 1.1:** Machine Learning portal*

Azure Databricks

Azure Databricks is an Apache Spark-based analytics platform that has been optimized for the Microsoft Azure cloud services platform. Designed with the founders of Apache Spark, it combines the best of Databricks and Azure to provide the high-performance analytics that businesses require to boost their big data strategies. Azure Databricks allows organizations to simplify big data and artificial intelligence workflows and collaborate in real time. This platform fully automates the setup and provides collaborative notebooks, integrated workflows, and robust security controls, making it a powerful tool for data scientists and engineers. Its scalability and native integration with the Azure ecosystem make it a top choice for many businesses deploying big data solutions.

Azure Data Lake Storage

Azure Data Lake Storage is a highly scalable and secure data lake functionality launched by Microsoft as part of its Azure Cloud platform. This service allows businesses to perform big data analytics, machine learning, and other advanced analytics on data of any size or type. It can handle structured and unstructured data, stream data, and bulk uploads efficiently and quickly. Azure Data Lake offers a premium level of performance, security, and analytics capabilities, enabling users to seamlessly integrate it with existing IT infrastructure. It supports the most recent big data open-source frameworks, providing developers with the flexibility to write code in multiple languages. Azure Data Lake Storage is encrypted and protected by Azure Active Directory, ensuring comprehensive data protection.

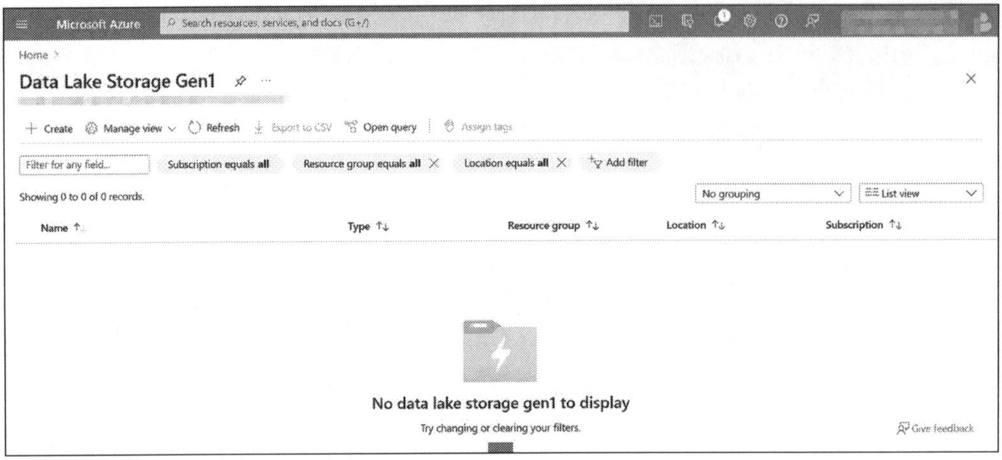

Figure 1.2: *The Data Lake portal*

Hence, it is revolutionizing the way businesses approach vast amounts of raw data, as it possesses the potential to turn data into transformative insights.

Azure Synapse Analytics

Azure Synapse Analytics, formerly known as SQL Data Warehouse, is a cloud-based integrated analytics service provided by Microsoft. It blends big data and data warehousing, providing users with real-time analytics capabilities. Azure Synapse Analytics uses both on-demand and provisioned resources to deliver a powerful and comprehensive analytics solution.

This cutting-edge service enables businesses to visualize, ingest, prepare, manage, and serve data for immediate business intelligence and machine learning needs. It also includes built-in security at different levels, offering extensive protection to the vital business data. Azure Synapse Analytics is fast, flexible, and easy to use, making big data analysis more accessible and manageable for businesses of all sizes.

Azure AI Capabilities

Azure AI is an advanced toolkit offering state-of-the-art artificial intelligence capabilities that aid data scientists in effectively utilizing their machine learning models. By incorporating Azure AI into workflows, it allows the development of intelligent applications in an intuitive and uncomplicated manner. This is possible without necessitating an extensive immersion into AI programming.

The pre-configured services available on Azure make aspects like image recognition, text analysis, and predictive modeling straightforward. A particularly noteworthy feature is Azure Machine Learning Studio, which hosts a variety of pre-trained models.

This enables developers to deploy a range of different models, thus encouraging flexible and dynamic machine-learning practices.

In addition to this, Azure has developed a tool called Prompt Flow, designed to streamline the creation of applications using Little Language Models (LLMs). This user-friendly tool simplifies the overall process, enabling users to develop their applications with ease.

Microsoft Azure provides a secure, highly scalable infrastructure that is particularly beneficial for data-driven processes. Its extensive suite of services makes managing the entire data science lifecycle - from data collection and processing to building, training, and deployment of models - an efficient and smooth exercise.

Azure's dedication to security is evident in their practices, ensuring a secure data pipeline throughout the process. This security-focused approach, combined with its comprehensive suite of tools and services, makes Azure an ideal platform for businesses seeking to leverage the benefits of data science. It provides businesses with both the capability and confidence needed to push their data-driven strategies forward, by knowing their data is not only used to its maximum potential but also secure.

Azure Subscription Models and Pricing

Microsoft Azure provides a variety of services such as analytics, storage, and networking. Users can select and configure these services based on their needs.

Azure offers flexible subscription models as part of its strategy to cater to the different needs of businesses, developers, and users. This means, depending on your needs, you can choose different plans with different levels of service, capacity, and price.

For instance, if you are a small business with minimal data storage needs, you might want to go for a basic plan. On the other hand, if you are a large corporation with extensive data storage, processing, and analytics needs, you might opt for a more advanced plan.

This flexibility extends to the pricing as well. The cost for Azure services is not set in stone but is determined based on the specific services and capacity that a user opts for. Therefore, customers are not obligated to pay for resources or services that they do not need, thus making Azure a cost-effective solution.

At the same time, despite the competitive pricing, Azure does not compromise on operational efficiency. Regardless of the pricing model chosen, users can expect high-quality, efficient, and reliable services. This ensures that businesses can run smoothly and efficiently while keeping their costs at a manageable level.

Overview of Azure Subscription Models

Azure offers two primary subscription models: Pay-As-You-Go and Enterprise Agreement.

Pay-As-You-Go

As the name implies, this model charges customers for resources as they use them. It's an excellent option for businesses or individuals who want to try out Azure services or have short-term requirements.

Enterprise Agreement

The Enterprise Agreement is for larger organizations and requires a commitment to Azure for a specific duration, such as one or three years. This model offers cost benefits for significant usage and brings additional support and management features.

Understanding Azure Pricing

Understanding Azure pricing is crucial to efficiently manage resources and costs. Azure's pricing is consumption-based, meaning you only pay for what you use.

Azure's Total Cost of Ownership (TCO) Calculator is a handy tool to estimate the cost savings you can realize by migrating your workloads to Azure. Azure Pricing Calculator can provide detailed price estimates based on factors like required services, scale, and location.

Moreover, Azure offers an array of cost management tools such as Azure Cost Management and Azure Advisor, which provide actionable recommendations to optimize costs while maximizing resource efficiency.

Lastly, Azure offers a unique Azure Hybrid Benefit, which lets users bring their on-premises Windows Server and SQL Server license with software assurance to Azure. This feature can result in significant cost savings.

As we deep dive into Azure's world, knowing about its subscription models and pricing strategy will empower you to make informed decisions and adopt a financially savvy strategy, thereby maximizing your return on investment. Azure's adaptability ensures that its services align with your financial comfort, making it an apt choice for businesses and developers prepared to harness the power of the Cloud.

Certainly, let's dive deeper into the process of setting up Azure for data science.

Setting Up Azure for Data Science

Beginning to use Azure entails some critical steps, all of which play a pivotal role towards unlocking the full potential of Microsoft's robust cloud service. The first step necessitates the creation of an Azure account. This process requires you to provide specific details like your Microsoft account information and is often followed by a verification procedure.

Once you have established your Azure account, the next crucial step is to buy an Azure subscription. Azure subscriptions enable users to gain access to the vast range of cloud services Azure offers. By purchasing a subscription, one essentially enters into a service agreement with Microsoft that details the amount and nature of Azure services one can make use of – a process that can easily be customized to individual or corporate needs.

Lastly, while having an Azure subscription allows you to use Azure services, managing these services efficiently necessitates an understanding of Azure's service management and permissions. From configuring services to monitoring their performance and granting permissions to different users, this step is a continual learning process that equips Azure users with tools for optimal service utilization. Each of these steps is indispensable in the successful navigation of Azure's cloud infrastructure and facilities.

Creating an Azure Account

Setting foot on Azure's platform requires an Azure account. To create one, visit the Azure website and click '`Start Free`.' You will be required to sign in with your Microsoft account or create a new one. As part of the account setup, you would be asked for your credit card details for identification and to prevent misuse, but no charges will be initiated without your explicit approval.

Buying an Azure Subscription

Once the account is set up, the next move is the acquisition of an Azure subscription. Subscriptions allow you to group and manage resources and provide a way to consolidate billing. This is where you would choose between a pay-as-you-go or enterprise agreement, depending on your needs and scale of usage.

Azure also offers "*Azure Free Account*", providing users with free access to selected Azure products for 12 months, and a limited quantity of free services for the next 30 days.

Managing Azure Services and Permissions

Managing Azure services and permissions involves the efficient handling of resources and their associated roles, which ensures secure and efficient functioning. Azure offers several tools to help you manage resources.

Azure Resource Manager

Azure Resource Manager (ARM) is a management interface provided by Microsoft Azure, designed to create and manage various resources in Azure. ARM is essentially a solution that helps you manage and organize resources in your application, instead of handling them individually. It provides a layered approach where you can manage related resources together in a Resource Group. With Azure Resource Manager, you can handle your application as a single entity, which enhances efficiency, security, and auditability.

Moreover, ARM provides a wholesome deployment model, tagging of resources, robust access control, and effective consistency checks in Azure. It allows the development of complex, sophisticated applications by supporting reusable and reliable templates. Azure Resource Manager also provides organizations with a unified approach to handle infrastructure scaling. Templates can be used to define dependencies between resources, enabling users to specify deployment orders effectively. All these features of Azure Resource Manager make it an indispensable tool in managing Azure solutions.

Azure Role-Based Access Control

Azure Role-Based Access Control (RBAC) is a system within Azure that provides fine-grained access management to Azure resources. This system allows administrators to segment users into groups based on their roles and responsibilities, and grant or deny permissions to these groups based on their roles. In RBAC, roles are used to define what actions are allowed on specific resources, including the ability to read, write, and delete resources. These roles can also define what types of tasks are permissible, such as restarting a virtual machine or reading from a database.

Azure RBAC is a crucial security feature that helps organizations manage who has access to Azure resources. The use of RBAC can reduce the risk of errant or malicious changes affecting these resources. It also ensures that only authorized individuals can perform specific tasks in Azure. RBAC is deeply integrated into Azure and is automatically applied when you create resources and perform operations. It handles any request to perform an operation by determining if the user or application making the request is allowed to perform the operation based on RBAC roles and permissions.

Azure Advisor

Azure Advisor is a personalized cloud consultant provided by Microsoft's Azure cloud computing service that helps users follow best practices to optimize their Azure deployments. It analyses your resource configuration and usage and then provides you with recommendations that can help you to improve the cost-effectiveness, performance, high availability, and security of your Azure resources. Azure Advisor's capabilities enable organizations to understand their current state and to make necessary amendments for enhanced resource management.

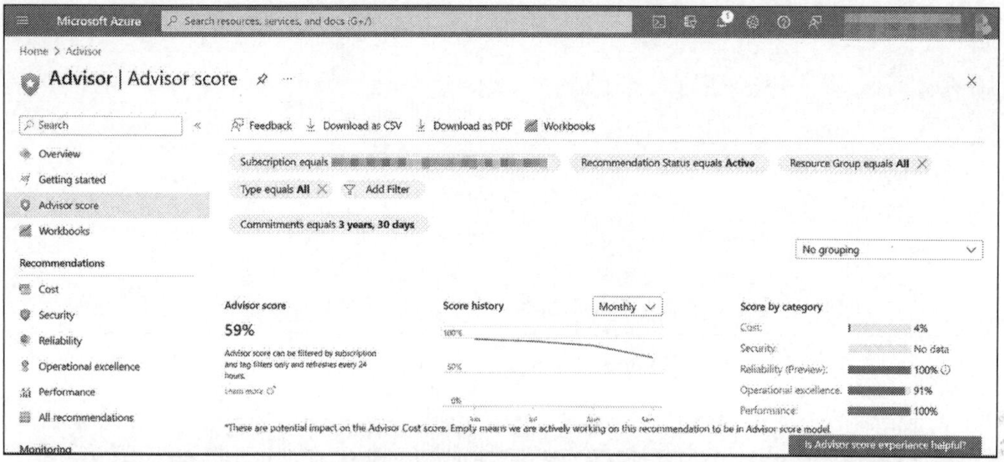

Figure 1.3: *Azure Advisor portal*

Azure Advisor works via machine learning algorithms and offers suggestions keeping in mind the five pivotal aspects of a robust Azure environment: Reliability, Security, Performance, Operational Excellence, and Cost. Those using Azure Advisor can expect recommendations such as right-sizing or eliminating underutilized resources, buying reserved instances to save money over pay-as-you-go costs, and more. All these recommendations are aimed to simplify, optimize, and amplify the resource handling capabilities of an organization.

Azure Policy

Azure Advisor is a personalized cloud consultancy service provided by Microsoft Azure. This service operates by analyzing your Azure resource configurations as well as usage data to provide recommendations for optimum business processes. These recommended best practices are designed to help streamline your Azure deployments, improve performance, enhance security, and increase cost efficiency.

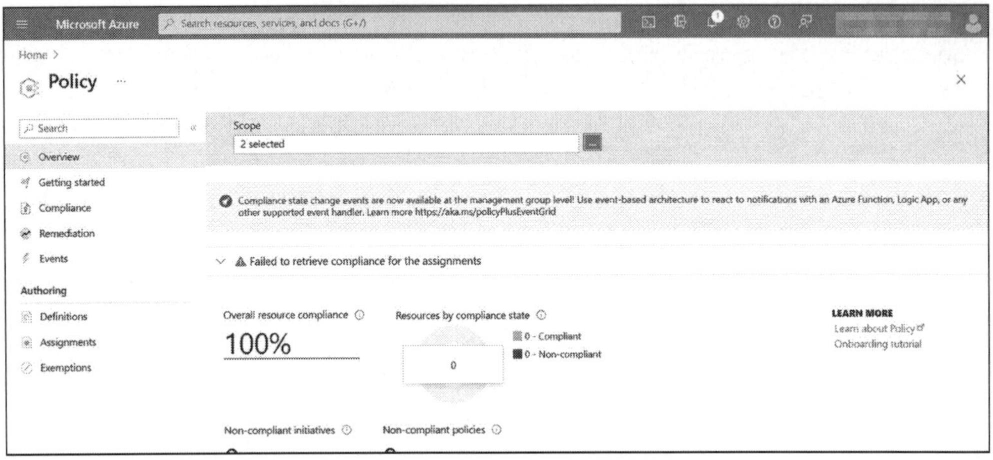

Figure 1.4: *Azure Policy portal*

The primary focus of Azure Advisor is to provide high-quality recommendations across four main pillars: cost, security, performance, and reliability. It offers advice in these areas by using a set of advanced algorithms and machine learning. For example, by suggesting resizing or shutting down underutilized resources to save costs, offering suggestions to improve your system security using Azure Security Center, recommending solutions to enhance the performance of your service, or offering insight on fault-tolerant architecture solutions. Through such detailed and useful advice, Azure Advisor helps organizations to make the best use of their Azure resources.

Navigating these setup processes holistically prepares data scientists to hit the ground running with Azure. The flexibility of the Azure subscription, coupled with its free offerings, enables users to explore and make the most out of this platform regardless of their data science needs and scale. Moreover, the account management capacities ensure you have robust and secure control over your Azure services, aligning it proficiently with your data science workflows.

Azure Portal and Azure Resource Manager

Regardless of the services and functionalities chosen within Azure, two key components tie everything together: the Azure portal and Azure Resource Manager. These essential parts of Azure's infrastructure offer a user-friendly interface and a robust management system to streamline operations and resources.

Navigating the Azure Portal

The Azure portal is the primary point of interaction between the user and the vast array of Azure's services. It provides a web-based, unified console to manage all of your applications in one place. Through intuitive dashboards, one can build, manage, and monitor everything from simple web apps to complex cloud deployments.

The Azure portal provides customizable dashboards where one can pin frequently accessed resources, choose favorite services for easier access, and monitor key metrics. It also offers features like Azure Cloud Shell, giving you direct command-line access from your browser.

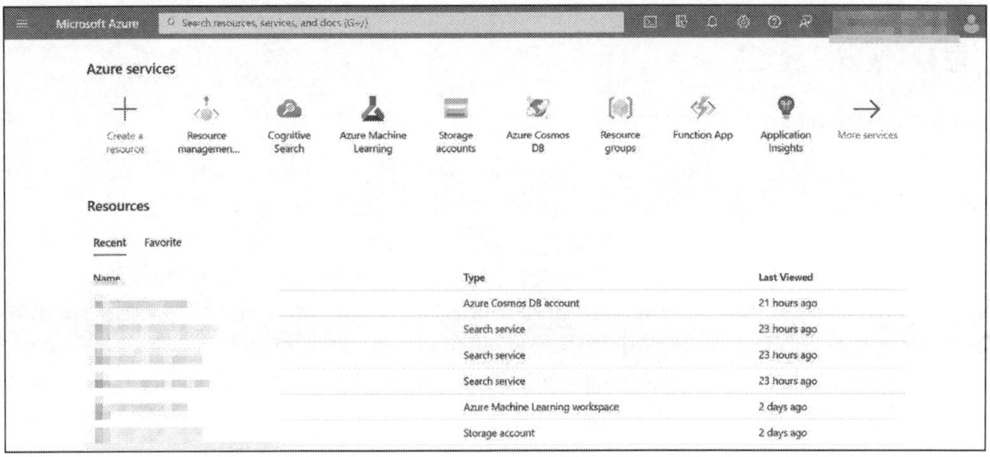

Figure 1.5: *Azure Home (we can see all the resource shortcuts and recently visited resources)*

Introduction to Azure Resource Manager

Azure Resource Manager (ARM) is the deployment and management service provided by Azure. It offers a consistent management layer to create, update, and delete resources in your Azure account.

ARM organizes resources in groups, allowing you to manage and visualize resources related to your application in a unified manner. It enables templated deployments, where you define your infrastructure through declarative templates rather than scripts. Thus, it fosters repeatable deployments and helps maintain consistency across development, testing, and production environments.

Exploring Resource Groups in Azure

At the heart of ARM are resource groups, logical containers where Azure resources like web apps, databases, and storage accounts are deployed and managed. They play a crucial role in applying consistent policies, access control, and managing billing in an organized manner.

Resource groups make it effortless to manage and monitor resources that serve a common purpose or are related to each other in terms of lifecycle and functionality.

They encourage resource organization based on lifecycle, application type, or even department-wise in an organization.

In conclusion, Azure portal and Azure Resource Manager encapsulate the necessary toolset to manage your Azure services effectively and efficiently. As we advance through our Azure journey, understanding these tools will undoubtedly provide a smoother and more streamlined experience.

Conclusion

Recap of Data Science and Azure

We have journeyed through the dynamic domain of data science, exploring its significance in the modern business world, and the impressive capabilities of Microsoft Azure as a comprehensive platform for data science projects. From understanding crucial data science concepts, processes, tools, and techniques to navigating the vast landscape of Azure, we've laid a strong foundation. We have seen Azure's seamless service integration, flexible subscription models, user-friendly portal, and resource management capabilities, and how everything comes together to form an invincible platform for data science activities.

Future Prospects of Data Science with Azure

Azure, being a Microsoft product, comes with its robustness, security, and scale, making it a favored platform for building and deploying machine learning models and conducting in-depth analytics. Considering these factors, here's a potential future outlook for data science with Azure, across a few key domains:

- **Healthcare:** Considering the increasing need for telehealth solutions and personalized medicine, data science with Azure may see a surge in the healthcare sector. Data Scientists can use Azure ML to build predictive models helping doctors in diagnosing diseases sooner or identify patients at high risk. For example, Microsoft Teams is integrated with Azure AI to improve virtual health care with transcription services and other AI-based capabilities.
- **Retail:** Retailers will continue leveraging data science in Azure to optimize their supply chains, enhance customer experiences, and predict market trends. For instance, Azure's data analytics capabilities can help businesses analyze customer shopping patterns and customize their product offerings, thus fostering customer loyalty.
- **Finance:** The sheer amount of financial data, coupled with the need for fraud detection and risk management, will drive further growth for data science with Azure in the financial domain. For example, Azure's AI/ML services can be used to detect anomalous patterns and potential fraud activities.

- **Education:** With an increasing emphasis on personalized learning and online education, the educational sector will need data science to develop student-specific learning plans and enhance virtual learning. Azure's AI services like Azure Bot Services can be used to build interactive chatbots for student onboarding or query resolution.
- **Manufacturing:** With Industry 4.0 and IoT, manufacturing needs advanced data analytics and predictive modeling. Azure's IoT capabilities, coupled with AI, can help optimize assembly lines, improve quality control procedures, and predict maintenance requirements, thereby reducing cost and improving efficiency.
- **Energy:** As the energy sector shifts towards renewable resources and decentralization, predictive models and IoT are becoming increasingly important. Azure can help here with real-time data handling and predictive analytics to optimize energy efficiency and maintenance for power generation equipment.

Moreover, Azure's edge computing capabilities will also open new avenues in real-time data processing and decision-making in various sectors, including autonomous vehicles, smart cities, and more. Azure is also improving its AutoML capabilities, which will make AI/ML accessible to non-technical users.

Therefore, the future prospects of data science with Azure look quite promising as it will continue to be instrumental in allowing businesses to tap into their data and extract meaningful insights, improving decision-making and operational efficiency.

Looking Ahead: Setting Up Your Azure Environment

In the upcoming chapter, "*Setting Up Your Azure Environment*," we will kick-off by guiding you through the process of creating an Azure account and subscription. This is your key to accessing the powerful data science capabilities of Azure. We will then present an overview of the various Azure services, specifically catered towards data science, which will streamline and enhance your data handling processes. The chapter will deepen your understanding of the Azure Machine Learning Workspace - the space you'll use to craft and manage machine learning models. It will also equip you with practical knowledge of managing and configuring compute resources. You'll become skilled in working with Azure Notebooks, a tool paramount to any data scientist for efficient code development and documentation.

Lastly, we will highlight the importance of collaboration and version control in data science, introducing you to Git Integration for Azure. This concise but robust chapter aims to equip you with the practical know-how of setting up and optimizing your Azure environment for best performance in data science tasks.

Exercises

- Brainstorm an organizational challenge that could potentially be addressed through data science. Write a brief paragraph outlining the issue and how data science could provide a solution.
- Navigate to Microsoft Azure's official website. Familiarize yourself with the various services offered under Azure's AI + Machine Learning and Data + Analytics sections.
- Sign up for an Azure free account (if possible) and navigate the Azure portal. Explore the various sections and services available.
- Based on what you've learned about Azure's pricing and subscription, try to estimate the monthly costs for a hypothetical data science project using the Azure Pricing Calculator.
- Explore a recent real-world case study where a company has used Azure for data science or AI purposes. Write a brief summary of the case study.

CHAPTER 2
Setting Up Your Azure Environment

Introduction

In this chapter, we will delve into the practicalities of commencing your journey with Azure, a comprehensive suite of cloud services that empowers businesses to innovate and grow. Azure provides an extensive range of services tailored towards data science, enabling you to handle complex data processing tasks and generate valuable insights. Understanding how to set up your Azure environment effectively is a crucial stepping stone on the path to leveraging these cutting-edge services to their fullest potential.

The heart of this chapter is focused on setting up your Azure Machine Learning workspace, which acts as a central hub for managing and running your data science experiments. Alongside this, you will be guided through the processes of creating an Azure account and subscription, exploring the Azure Machine Learning Studio interface, managing and configuring resources, and leveraging Azure Notebooks. Lastly, we will touch on the vital topic of version control and collaboration with Git integration in an Azure environment. With an aim to craft a solid foundation for your data science endeavors, this chapter promises to equip you with valuable insights and applicable skills.

Structure

In this chapter, the following topics will be covered:

- Introduction to Azure Environment Setup
- Creating an Azure Account and Subscription
- Overview of Azure Services for Data Science
- Setting Up Azure Machine Learning Workspace
- Understanding Azure Machine Learning Studio Interface
- Managing and Configuring Compute Resources

- Using Azure Notebooks
- Version Control and Collaboration with Git Integration

Introduction to Azure Environment Setup

This chapter is designed to shed light on the practicalities of initiating your journey with Azure in the field of data science. An appropriate setup of your Azure environment acts as a cornerstone for the construction, management, and execution of successful data science projects.

Appreciating the importance of setting up Azure correctly is the first stepping stone to effectively unlocking its potent capabilities for data science. A well-structured Azure environment is directly proportional to the performance, efficiency, and ease of operations in your data science projects. With the goal of empowering you to smoothly navigate this process with clarity and confidence, this chapter provides guidance on creating an Azure account and subscription, setting up an Azure Machine Learning workspace, understanding the Azure Machine Learning Studio interface, managing compute resources, and effectively utilizing Azure Notebooks. Lastly, it discusses how to enhance collaboration and version control via Git integration. So, let us put theory into practice and get started on setting up your Azure environment!

Creating an Azure Account and Subscription

This section provides a step-by-step walkthrough of setting up an account and aims to guide users in selecting the most fitting subscription according to their specific needs and preferences.

Establishing Your Azure Account

Starting your exploration of Azure's diverse offerings begins with creating an Azure account. This is a necessary and straightforward process that involves a few simple steps.

1. **Step 1**: Visit the Azure [https://portal.azure.com] home page. Here, you will find the Start free option which you need to click on to commence the registration process.
2. **Step 2**: If you already own a Microsoft account, you can conveniently use those credentials to log in. If not, do not worry. You can create a new Microsoft account. This can be done by providing the necessary information such as a valid email address and creating a strong password.

3. **Step 3**: For enhanced security, Microsoft requires you to verify your account. You can do this through either a linked email address or a phone number. By adding this extra layer of security, Microsoft ensures your account is protected.
4. **Step 4**: At this point, you will be asked to fill out some personal details. Once completed, make sure to take a moment to review Microsoft's terms of usage carefully. Upon agreeing to these terms, your registration will be completed, and you will officially own an Azure account.

Selecting An Azure Subscription

Upon successful creation of your account, the next step is to activate a subscription. In Azure, a subscription serves as a logical container for the Azure services that are linked to an account. Microsoft provides an array of subscription options to cater to the varying needs and financial plans of different users.

1. **Step 1**: To activate a subscription, you need to navigate to the 'Subscriptions' page on your account dashboard. Here, you will find a catalog of all the subscription plans that Azure has on offer.
2. **Step 2**: Take your time to explore each subscription plan. Pay attention not only to the cost of each plan but also to the features and limits accompanying it. Also, keep your eyes peeled for any special offers that Azure might have at the moment.
3. **Step 3**: Once you have settled on the subscription that aligns best with your needs, select it. This choice should ideally take into consideration both your present requirements and plans for future expansion.
4. **Step 4**: With the selection made, proceed to the next level of confirming your choice. Fill out the payment details and confirm your selection. Your account will now be linked to your chosen subscription.

Choosing the right subscription is of paramount importance as it directly impacts your cost efficiency and the extent of services available to you. It is wise to take into account your project's needs, the budgetary limitations, potential future growth, and specific Azure services required when deciding on a subscription plan. With the Azure account and subscription now up and running, you are equipped to start exploring and capitalizing on the boundless potential that Azure offers.

Overview of Azure Services for Data Science

In this segment, we offer a succinct overview of the diverse Azure Services that are crucial in Data Science. Furthermore, we provide insights into their optimal utilization and the most opportune times to utilize these services.

Azure Services for Data Science

Data Science is this dynamic crossroads where valuable insights are extracted from raw, often complex, data. The ability to understand and interpret data is more crucial than ever in the digital age, given the sheer volume and speed at which data is created. With data production growing exponentially, leveraging data science effectively has emerged as a strategic differentiator for organizations across industries and sectors.

This massive data surge, often referred to as the '*Big Data*' phenomenon, has transformed data science from a niche specialization into a pivotal player in business, technology, and decision-making models. In that light, data science aids organizations in various ways. It helps understand market trends, customer behaviors, operational inefficiencies, and strategic opportunities. By unearthing hidden patterns, correlations, and trends, data science formulations turn the abstract concept of data into actionable business insights. Decoding this data-dense world with data science enhances decision making, drives efficiencies, and creates new products and services, fostering a data-driven culture that fuels both innovation and growth.

Microsoft Azure, with a keen sense of the data revolution, offers a comprehensive suite of services tailor-made for data science applications. Azure empowers users to build analytical models that understand and tackle real-world situations seamlessly. From building, deploying, and managing applications with Microsoft's Azure Machine Learning, analyzing big data with Azure HDInsight, to predicting and optimizing with Cognitive Services, Azure allots an array of tools built for advanced analytics. With these in-depth services, Azure provides an excellent testing ground for data science innovations, thereby changing the way businesses deal with complex data. It helps predict future trends, and make significant decisions for strategic benefit to businesses.

Azure Machine Learning (Azure ML)

Azure ML is a fundamental service that allows you to build, deploy, and share predictive analytics solutions. It is a cloud-based environment, which means you can access it from anywhere. Azure ML is extremely versatile – it supports Python, allows automated hyper-parameter tuning, and provides MLOps capabilities (DevOps for machine learning) to manage the lifecycle of your models.

Azure Databricks

It is an Apache Spark-based analytics platform optimized for Azure. It combines the best of Databricks and Azure to provide a one-stop solution for data exploration, machine learning model training, and production pipelines creation.

Azure Synapse Analytics

Previously known as SQL Data Warehouse, it integrates big data, data warehousing, and data analytics into a single service. It gives you complete analytics solutions for ingestion, data preparation, data management, and serving.

Azure Cognitive Services

It offers AI services with pre-trained models that can be used for vision, speech, language, decision-making, and personalized recommendations.

Azure HDInsight

It is a fully managed cloud service that simplifies processing large amounts of data using popular open-source frameworks such as Hadoop and Spark.

Utilizing Azure Services for Data Science Optimally

The choice of the Azure Data Science service to utilize largely depends on the business problem at hand, the nature of the data, the required processing speed, and the desired outcomes.

For Start-ups or Small Projects

Azure Machine Learning is an excellent place to get started. Its user-friendly nature enables beginners or small teams to quickly create, test, and deploy ML models.

For Big Data Operations

Services such as Azure Databricks and HDInsight are significantly useful when dealing with large datasets. Databricks provides a collaboration-focused platform that moderate to large teams can use for big data analytics and AI solutions. Meanwhile, HDInsight suits scenarios in which open-source frameworks are in use.

If your project calls for a full-fledged analytics solution that covers the steps from data ingestion to visualization, Azure Synapse Analytics or Power BI come into play.

When the project requires minimal code, AI plug and play solutions like Azure Cognitive Services can be a savior.

Remember, many of the Azure services for data science are interchangeable depending on the requirement or the stage of the data science project. It is all about choosing the right tool at the right time. Having both an overarching understanding and a situational approach to Azure services will help you make optimal use of the platform, and advance your data science tasks in the most efficient, reliable, and innovative way.

Setting Up Azure Machine Learning Workspace

Creating an Azure Machine Learning workspace can be seen as the first practical step into the crux of Azure's capabilities for machine learning and data science operations. The workspace in Azure is a high-level, centralized repository for all the artifacts created as part of your machine learning work. It conveniently groups together the resources required for various operations such as data exploration, model training, and service deployment. With Azure ML Workspace, Azure decidedly enhances efficiency, management, and collaboration in your project.

Commence by logging into your Azure portal. In the left-hand-side panel, select `'Create a resource,'` then input `'Machine Learning'` into the search bar and select the `'Machine Learning'` result. Here, you will be required to provide pertinent information such as the Workspace name, Subscription, Resource group, and Location. After taking note of the cost details, click on `'Review + Create,'` validate your information, and finally click **`Create`**. Within a few moments, your workspace will be ready. Once the workspace creation is complete, you can access the new workspace by navigating to the Dashboard and selecting the workspace name.

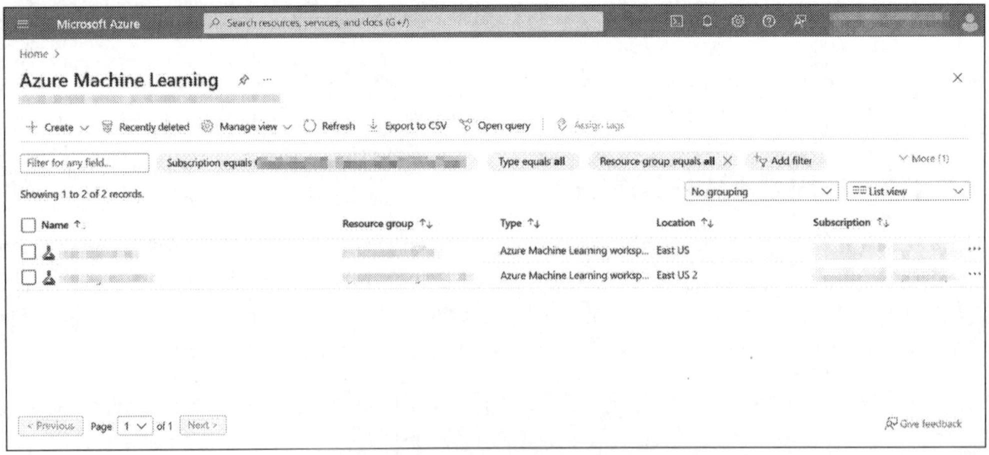

Figure 2.1: *Machine Learning workspaces*

Exploring Features and Benefits of Azure Machine Learning Workspace

Azure Machine Learning Workspace offers a myriad of features tailored towards streamlined and intuitive machine learning operations. The workspace's unique features such as pre-configured computing resources (Compute Instances and Compute Clusters), datastores, and datasets essentially give you a readily available machine learning studio. It also hosts exploratory data analysis tools and aids in creating machine learning models through designer and trained algorithms.

The Azure ML workspace acts as a collaborative platform where data scientists and developers can work together synchronously. One crucial benefit of it is the ease of management as all resources are centrally located, making organization and navigation of resources seamless. It allows secure sharing, offers version control, preserves and reproduces work, all of which are essential attributes in a collaborative environment.

In conclusion, setting up the Azure ML Workspace is a crucial stepping stone in initiating your machine learning journey with Azure. The workspace, with its plethora of features and advantages, lays a firm foundation, making data exploration, model creation, training, deployment, and management a streamlined, efficient, and collaborative process.

Understanding Azure Machine Learning Studio Interface

Azure Machine Learning Studio is the next-generation web-based integrated development environment (IDE) for machine learning. A powerful hub built with both beginners and experienced data scientists in mind, Machine Learning Studio aims to offer a unified, consolidated workspace where users can build, train, deploy, and manage their machine learning models. Its interface strikes the right balance between powerful capabilities and user friendliness; it eliminates the need for extensive coding knowledge, thus making machine learning accessible for anyone with a basic understanding.

Machine Learning Studio is designed to foster collaborative work, serving as an interactive space where developers and data scientists can seamlessly share and publish their work, fostering team collaboration in any machine learning project. Its user-friendly nature does not diminish the power it packs for tackling advanced projects. From skilled coders preferring the versatility of Python or R to developers leveraging the drag-and-drop interface, Azure Machine Learning Studio spans a wide range of capabilities to cater to diverse user requirements. Whether you are a novice just beginning to navigate the landscape or a seasoned professional seeking a robust platform for complex workloads, the Azure Machine Learning Studio is equipped to serve you effectively.

Exploring Azure Machine Learning Studio Interface

Upon signing in, you are greeted with the home page that provides a high-level snapshot of your workspace. From here, you can navigate through the various sections of the studio using the tabs on the left sidebar, which include the following.

Authoring

The **Authoring** tab in Azure Machine Learning is the main workspace for data scientists and machine learning practitioners. Here is where you can create, build, and work on cutting-edge machine learning models. Whether you are opting to code your own machine learning algorithms or take advantage of Azure's AutoML, the Authoring tab provides a comprehensive and intuitive interface for building machine learning pipelines. You can experiment with different features, parameters, and algorithms and instantly visualize the results. Notably, it also supports many popular notebook platforms, such as Jupyter and JupyterLab, which offer an interactive environment for writing, running, and sharing code across a variety of programming languages prevalent in the data science community.

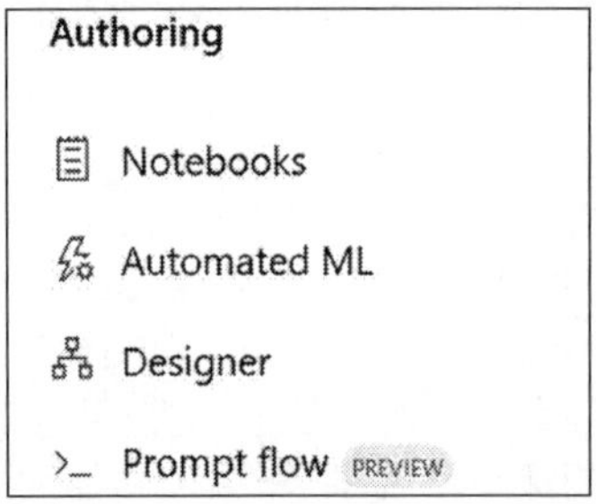

***Figure 2.2:** Options under the Authoring section*

Assets

Assets in Azure Machine Learning is a one-stop-shop for all your machine learning resources. All the datasets, experiments, models, and computing resources that you have interfaced with throughout the machine learning pipeline are neatly and conveniently organized here. This section is incredibly useful as it provides a quick overview of all the elements of your project. It allows you to manage your datasets, ensuring that they are kept up-to-date and version-controlled. You can track experiments, compare model performances and keep a log of different computations used throughout your machine learning pipeline. Essentially, the **Assets** section serves as an organizational backbone behind your machine learning operations, helping streamline your projects, maintain orderliness, and vastly improve productivity and efficiency.

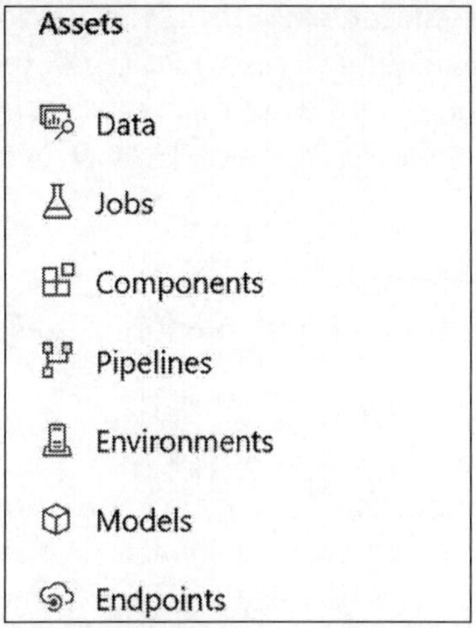

Figure 2.3: *Options under the Assets section*

Manage

The **Manage** section in Azure Machine Learning is critical for managing the operational and administrative aspects of machine learning projects. Here, you can assign roles and provide access levels to team members, keeping in mind the principle of least privilege to reduce potential security risks. You can also monitor and manage quotas to ensure fair resource allocation and prevent over-usage. More so, this section gives a detailed insight into cost management, allowing you to keep track of your spending, set budgets, and optimize costs in real-time. This is vital for enterprises to understand the operational and financial implications of running machine learning workloads on Azure, allowing them to align these workflows with their budget and business objectives. Thus, the **Manage** section acts as the control panel, managing operations, security, and costs effectively.

Figure 2.4: *Options under the Manage section*

Familiarizing with Tools and Functionalities

This section delves into acquainting users with various tools and functionalities such as authoring, assets, and managing. It provides a comprehensive guide on how to effectively utilize these features for a smoother, more efficient workflow.

Authoring

This section dives into the process of creating and editing documents or datasets in Azure, elaborating on the tools and functionalities employed for robust data manipulation.

- **Notebooks**

Jupyter and JupyterLab notebooks in the Authoring section are an interactive platform where you can write and execute code, visualize data, and see results and outputs dynamically. It provides data scientists with a user-friendly environment that boosts prototype development and enriches the process of data analysis. All the packages, libraries, and dependencies are handled by Azure, allowing you to focus entirely on developing and executing your computational workflows. These notebooks are excellent tools for creating machine learning models, preprocessing data, and even developing advanced analytics models.

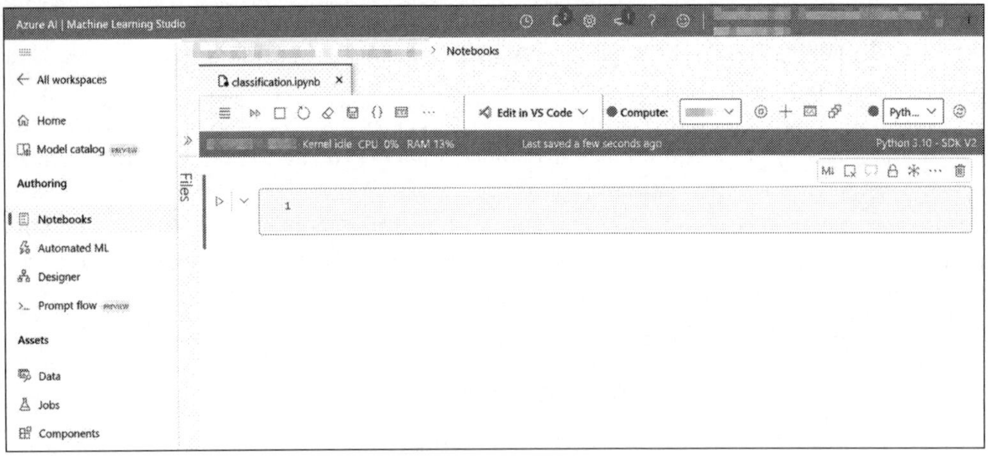

***Figure* 2.5:** *Azure Notebook*

- **Designer**

Using the Designer component in Azure Machine Learning allows you to build machine learning models with a minimum amount of code. With a drag and drop interface, you can create data processing and model pipelines visually, which makes it accessible for individuals without a solid coding background. The designer provides various modules for data transformation, model creation, training, and evaluation, and these can be interlinked to create a complete pipeline. This highly interactive tool not only accelerates ML model development but also makes the complete pipeline visible, hence making it easier for collaboration and understanding.

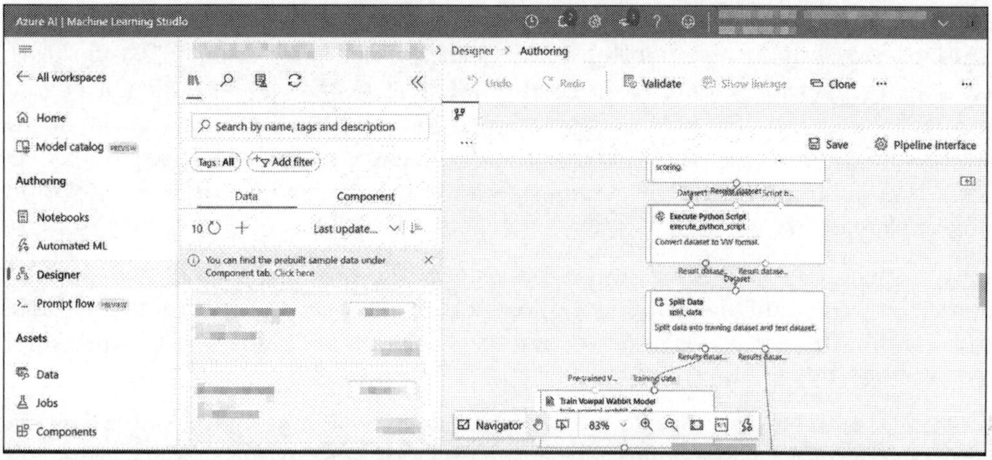

Figure 2.6: *A sample project in Azure Designer*

- **AutoML**

Azure's AutoML interface in the Authoring section is aimed at simplifying the process of model creation by automatically choosing the best model based on problem type and data fed. It accelerates the creation of machine learning models by managing sophisticated tasks such as feature selection, hyperparameter tuning, and iteration over multiple models. Additionally, it provides an explainability feature, which gives transparency into how the model makes predictions. AutoML is not just a boon for beginners in the field of machine learning, but it also helps seasoned professionals to save time and effort.

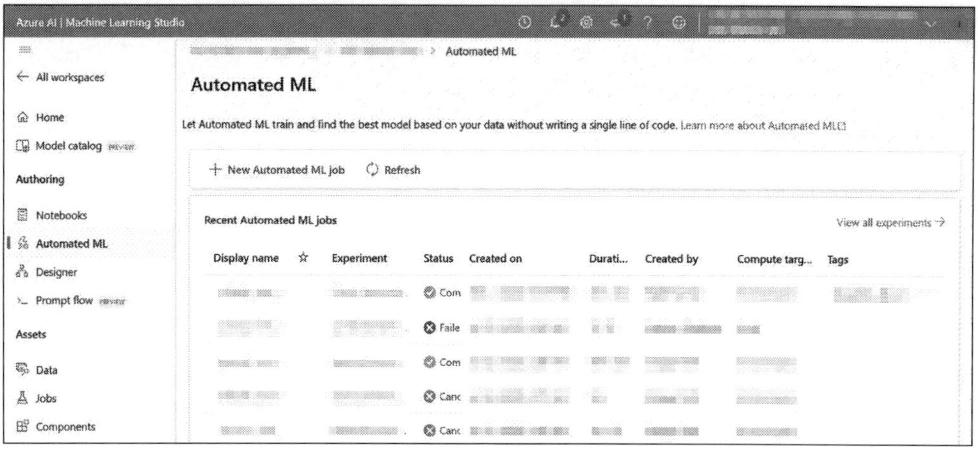

Figure 2.7: Azure AutoML Portal

- **Prompt flow**

`Prompt flow`, a cutting-edge feature currently in preview mode on Azure, heralds an exciting era of innovation and accessibility in creating applications with Large Language Models (LLMs). As we are witnessing the rapid evolution and adoption of LLMs in various industries, Prompt Flow stands as an important milestone in this technological advancement. This user-friendly feature is a game-changer, enabling seamless manipulation of LLMs, and fostering a more intuitive approach to application development. With its capabilities extending to include AI orchestration, **`Prompt flow`** offers broad compatibility with numerous LLM models, including high-performers such as Llama and ChatGPT.

However, where **`Prompt flow`** truly revolutionizes the process, is in its real-time LLM monitoring. This added component allows developers to evaluate their LLM-based applications on various crucial parameters, including coherence, groundedness, similarity, relevance, and fluency.

In essence, with **`Prompt flow`**, Azure is dramatically recalibrating the way we interact with, develop, and assess applications based on LLMs. It is not just a new feature, but a significant marker in the evolutionary timeline of machine learning, aligning well with the accelerated growth and potential of LLMs in the technology landscape.

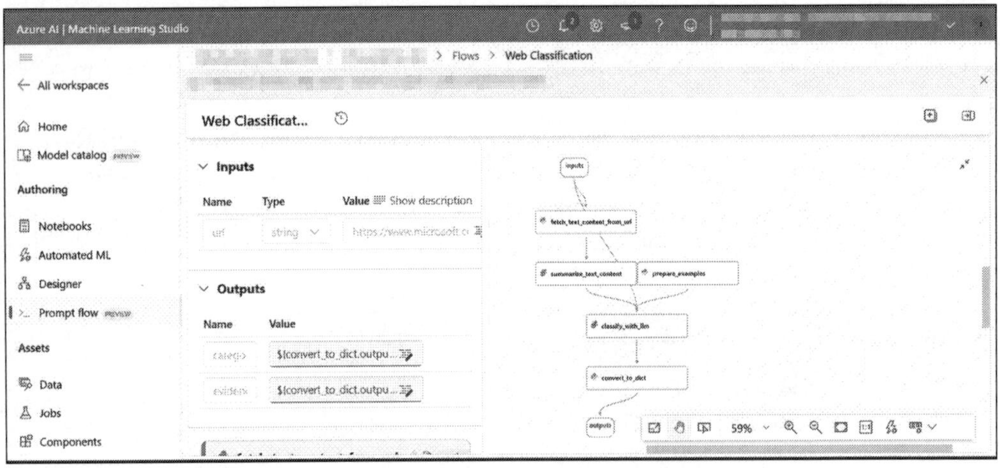

***Figure 2.8:** A sample flow in Azure Prompt Flow*

Assets

Here, we dissect how Azure handles resources like data, models, and applications, providing a clear understanding of managing, sharing, and leveraging these assets effectively within the platform.

- **Data**

Data, in the context of Azure Machine Learning, refers to the various datasets that users can import, curate, transform, and manage for their machine learning projects.

The '*Data*' functionality supports a wide array of formats including structured data like CSVs, unstructured data like images or text, and even real-time data streams. It provides tools for preparing and cleaning data, feature engineering, and even visualizing the data, making it a vital component in the process of creating high-performance models.

- **Jobs**

Jobs in Azure Machine Learning represent the execution of a specific task, such as a data preprocessing job or a machine learning training job. Users can monitor the progress of these jobs, stop or pause them, and even view the logs and output of completed jobs. This feature enhances productivity, transparency, and effective resource management, given its ability to queue jobs and execute them based on resource availability.

- **Components**

Components in Azure Machine Learning form the basic building blocks of machine learning pipelines. These are self-contained, reusable units of a pipeline that perform a single task like data transformation or model training. Users can create and share these components, making it easier to reproduce and modularize their work. This functionality aids efficient, scalable, and faster development of machine learning solutions.

- **Pipelines**

Pipelines in Azure Machine Learning enforce a structured format to machine learning workflows. A pipeline visualizes the series of steps or stages in a machine learning process, right from data preparation to model deployment. Each stage in the pipeline is a 'component' that performs a specific task. Pipelines make it easier to re-run experiments, ensure consistency, and manage complex processes in a more modular way.

- **Environment**

In Azure Machine Learning, the '*Environment*' pertains to the runtime context where your experiments run. It can encompass various dependencies, including Python packages, R packages, software settings, and even hardware configurations. Azure takes care of compatibility issues and makes it easier to replicate experiments consistently across different compute targets. It is essentially a reusable specification to run your machine learning experiments.

- **Model**

Models in Azure Machine Learning represent the output of a machine learning training process. The '*Model*' functionality allows you to register, version, and manage these trained models, making them ready for deployment in production or for further experimentation. It also provides model interpretability features, ensuring transparency in how the model makes predictions.

- **Endpoints**

Endpoints in Azure Machine Learning provide a platform for deploying your machine learning models. They are the URL and associated resources where your models are published for real-time scoring or batch inferencing. This feature simplifies the process of integrating your machine learning models into production applications, manages traffic splitting for A/B testing, and monitors performance and data drift, thereby making machine learning operations more manageable and scalable.

Manage

In this section, we illustrate the art of efficiently controlling and coordinating Azure's resources and services, ensuring optimal performance and maximum benefits from your Azure setup.

- **Compute**

The Compute tool in Azure's Management suite controls all the computational resources utilized in your machine learning processes. It includes various compute targets like Azure Machine Learning Compute, Azure Databricks, and Azure Kubernetes Service (AKS), and more. These resources can be allocated to different tasks matching the computational requirements of each task, making resource utilization flexible and cost-effective. Having a centralized view of all compute resources ensures efficient handling, straightforward scalability, and better monitoring.

- **Monitoring**

Monitoring is a crucial tool within Azure Management that oversees the performance of your machine learning models once they are deployed in production environments. It provides real-time insights into how your models are behaving and performing, enabling you to detect anomalies, predict issues before they escalate, and make informed decisions about maintenance or improvements. This tool also allows you to track data drift, model fairness, and other model performance indicators, providing deep visibility into the model's lifecycle.

- **Data Labeling**

Data Labeling, in Azure, is a user-friendly tool that facilitates the process of annotating your image datasets. Creating accurate labels for your data is a vital step in developing supervised machine learning models and the tool offers a diverse set of labeling tasks including image classification, object identification, object tracking and semantic segmentation. You can manage projects, control quality metrics, and even use Azure's automated data labeling feature, accelerating the typically labor-intensive process of data annotation and making your datasets ready for training more efficiently.

- **Linked Service**

Linked Services in Azure is a pivotal feature that creates connections between your workspace and external resources. It encapsulates connection details to these external services, letting you securely access different data resources or services without exposing sensitive details. Be it a data store, compute resource, or an AI service, linked services ensure seamless integration with your workspace. This feature strengthens the inter-operability of your Azure workspace and promotes a more unified and secure machine learning workflow.

The Azure Machine Learning Studio also supports the integration of open-source tools and libraries, providing a comprehensive platform capable of catering to varied user needs. It allows for version control to track changes and maintain a record of the entire modeling process, fostering effective collaboration and development practices.

In conclusion, Azure Machine Learning Studio provides an all-in-one platform for creating, training, and deploying machine learning models. The interface's well-organized structure makes for an intuitive and effective experience, enabling you to focus more on building accurate models rather than managing the environment. Getting familiar with the portal and understanding its functions allows for maximum use of all its features, making your data science projects more efficient and effective.

Managing and Configuring Compute Resources

The role of compute resources within a cloud-based environment like Microsoft Azure is of immense significance and cannot be emphasized enough. Compute resources act as the powerhouse, the engine that drives data processing and the execution of applications within the cloud. Residing at the heart of all the key operations within the Azure environment, compute resources essentially care for the performance of data-intensive tasks, thereby contributing to the backbone of a robust, responsive, and efficient cloud computing ecosystem.

For data scientists, the variety and capability of compute resources take on increased importance. In fact, these resources are extensively leveraged by data scientists while configuring machine learning models, conducting intricate data manipulations, or executing analytics on large voluminous datasets. Whether it is running a resource-hungry deep learning model or churning vast amounts of data in real-time for actionable insights, compute resources make it possible for data scientists to execute their data-oriented tasks with utmost efficiency. Thus, a comprehensive understanding of how to efficiently manage and configure these computational resources within Azure becomes a fundamental skill, a prerequisite for data scientists aspiring to optimize productivity while working in the Azure environment.

Importance of Compute Resources

Compute resources form the crux of all data processing and management tasks in an

Azure environment. As they deal with how data is stored, processed, and accessed, their role is of paramount importance to a data scientist.

Compute resources include anything that features a compute component. Some classic examples are Virtual Machines (VMs), Azure Kubernetes Service (AKS), Azure Functions, Azure Logic Apps, and Azure Batch. Specifically, in the case of data science endeavors, compute resources typically entail Machine Learning Compute Instances and Clusters. These components undertake hefty computational tasks of complex algorithms on large datasets.

Importantly, the utilization of compute resources affects the performance, cost, and complete project time frame. Thus, understanding the right type and amount of compute resources for any task is critical. It will optimize processing time while minimizing costs – a crucial aspect in the contemporary development world where optimized task execution and budgeting are vital.

Guideline to Effectively Manage and Configure Compute Resources in Azure

Properly managing compute resources is as important as comprehending their importance. An improperly managed and configured compute resource will defeat its purpose, theoretically driving up costs, extending execution time, and potentially causing the mismanagement of data.

Understand Your Needs

Before you venture into managing and configuring your resources, having a comprehensive grasp of your requirements is a must. The type of compute resources you should configure relies heavily on what you seek to accomplish.

Type and Size of Compute Resource

Azure offers a variety of compute resources. Select the resource that aligns with your needs – for instance, VMs for large jobs, or AKS for managing cluster applications. Understand that each type and each size will have its own capabilities, costs, and pros and cons.

Configure According to Your Preference

Azure's adjustable configurations further add to its versatility. For instance, you can choose the OS type, disk type, and VM type, among other things.

Autoscaling

Use Azure's Autoscale feature for managing your resource output. It automatically scales up or down to match your needs, benefitting cost and resource management.

Monitor Your Resources

Azure Monitor and Log Analytics can provide you the insights you need to optimize the utilization of your resources. They can assist in detecting any anomalies, tracking performance, and identifying areas for improvement.

By adequately managing and configuring your compute resources, you can greatly increase efficiency and productivity, ultimately meeting the project's needs in the Azure environment more adequately. Remember that this management is an ongoing process, which requires regular monitoring, adjusting, and strategizing.

Using Azure Notebooks

Azure Notebooks, a Microsoft product, are designed to facilitate web-based data analytics and scientific programming in Python, R, and F#. They feature best-in-class support for Jupyter, a popular open-source platform around which a bustling community has developed, with full integration with the Azure suite.

Azure Notebooks offer a simple, robust platform for data scientists to pursue large-scale, collaborative projects with ease and efficiency. Whether you are analyzing data, developing models or sharing results with colleagues, Azure notebooks are an essential tool in the data scientist's kit.

Introducing Azure Notebooks

Azure Notebooks, part of the Azure Machine Learning service, are a cloud-based version of Jupyter Notebooks. This setting offers an excellent environment for developing, testing, and executing algorithms, and working with data in a flexible, integrated platform.

As an online application, Azure Notebooks permits collaborative real-time editing, akin to Google Docs, but with advanced functionalities specific to computational sciences. Render graphical visualizations, write in LaTeX, or write and execute code in over 40 programming languages, all within an Azure notebook. Furthermore, Azure Notebooks come with a variety of pre-installed packages, sparing users the hassle of managing their software dependencies.

Understanding how to set up and manage Azure Notebooks is the first step toward exploiting this advanced environment to execute your data science tasks. With this tool, anyone can create a project space, invite collaborators, share data and code, and publish results, making it not only a platform for data analysis but also a database of collective wisdom that can be shared with the world.

Executing Data Science Experiments Using Azure Notebooks

Executing data science projects on Azure Notebooks combines the dynamism of Jupyter with the robustness of Azure. From data cleaning and exploration to model development and deployment, the entire scientific pipeline can be undertaken within a given notebook.

Import your data directly to your notebook from your local files, cloud storage, or real-time database, and conduct preliminary analyses using pre-installed Python, R or F# packages. Once your dataset is cleaned and prepared, Azure Notebooks present a variety of machine learning and statistical modeling techniques to extract patterns and insights from your data.

Beyond these analytical capabilities, Azure Notebooks allow users to build and deploy predictive models, like logistical and linear regression models, decision trees, and artificial neural networks. Trace your metrics easily using the automatic logging feature, which keeps iterations organized and readily available.

Interactive widgets allow for the dynamic presentation of results, with charts, images, videos, and LaTeX equations all supported. After fine-tuning their analyses and models, users can share their Jupyter notebooks as fully interactive documents, rendering the output cells as live code that can be edited and executed. Better yet, Azure users can publish their final products as articles or dashboards, thereby communicating their insights actively to a broader audience.

Collaboration Between Azure Notebooks and AutoML

Using Azure Notebooks alongside AutoML presents a powerful, streamlined approach to your data science workflows. Together, they enhance efficiency, foster collaboration, and promote robust and reproducible outcomes.

Azure Notebooks initially provide a comprehensive environment for your data pre-processing and cleaning tasks. With Azure Notebooks, you can visualize your data, perform exploratory analysis, and carry out preliminary statistical checks, all to ensure your data is ready for the modeling stage. Once your data is adequately prepared, it is ready to be utilized in an AutoML experiment.

Azure Notebooks and AutoML work together seamlessly in this phase. AutoML takes your cleaned data and applies advanced feature engineering techniques automatically. Using your Azure Notebook, you can monitor each step of the process undertaken by AutoML, retaining full control and transparency throughout the modeling process.

Upon completion of the chosen model, AutoML allows for predictions using your new data. You can then interpret these model results within your Azure Notebook environment, translating predictive outcomes into actionable insights quickly and efficiently.

The sharing features of Azure Notebooks make it easy to present your findings to your team and encourage wider collaboration. An Azure Notebook, complete with live code blocks and explanatory commentary, can be shared at the click of a button. This reproducible document can assist other team members in understanding your analysis or inspire new directions for future data projects.

By leveraging the robust combination of Azure Notebooks and AutoML, you significantly streamline the machine learning process and foster efficient problem-solving in your data science projects. This synergy not only enhances productivity but also promotes a culture of collaboration and transparency in your data science team.

In conclusion, Azure Notebooks are a powerful, scalable, and highly interactive platform for data scientists. They provide a complete environment for executing data science tasks, facilitating everything from data preparation and exploration to predictive modeling and results communication.

Version Control and Collaboration with Git Integration

The Azure cloud platform is a crucial toolkit for the modern data scientist. It provides comprehensive cloud services that empower scientists to build, deploy, and manage applications through Microsoft-managed data centers. These services range from data storage and security to machine learning and analytics capabilities. The platform is not merely a host for these services, but a conducive environment that caters to the needs of data scientists at each stage of the data lifecycle. It, therefore, becomes imperative to have a well-configured Azure Environment to allow for the seamless execution of data science tasks and projects.

As you set up your Azure environment, one integral feature to focus on is Git integration. Git, which is a distributed version control system, is fundamental in managing and tracking changes to codes, be it a small tweak or a complete modification. The integration of Git with Azure presents an opportunity to enhance the functionality of your data science projects. It establishes a platform where data scientists can collaborate and work on projects simultaneously without the fear of overwriting each other's work. In addition, it provides the flexibility to work on multiple versions of code and seamlessly merge them without losing any changes. We will delve deeper into this, discussing the importance of version control, steps to integrate Git into Azure, and collaboration features in Azure.

Importance of Version Control and Collaboration in Data Science Projects

Version control systems are essential in data science as they allow teams to manage changes to projects over time. Complex data science projects often require the collective efforts of a team, and version control ensures seamless team collaboration by allowing team members to work on different parts of the project simultaneously without causing conflicts. Even in individual projects, version control allows scientists to keep track of changes, revert to previous versions if necessary and compare different versions of code or data analysis.

Collaboration in data science projects goes beyond mere teamwork. It encourages idea sharing and peer reviews that contribute to better project outcomes. Collaboration tools like Git make it easier for teams to work synchronously or asynchronously on several parts of a project across different locations and time zones.

Steps to Integrate Git for Version Control in Azure

Integrating Git for version control in Azure is a simple process that involves:

1. **Creating a Git repository:**

   This is where all project files and their history will be stored. You can create a repository in several ways, including on GitHub, Azure Repos, or other platforms.

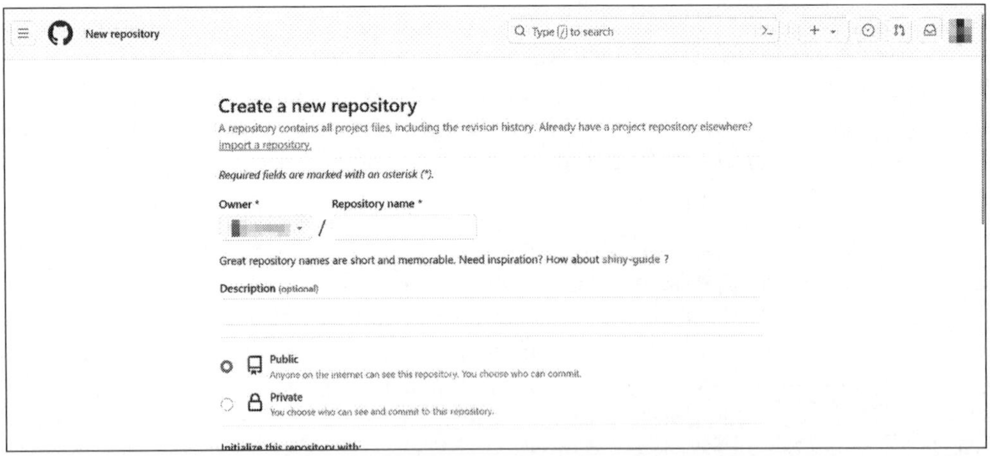

Figure 2.9: *Creating a new repository on GitHub*

2. **Syncing your Azure environment with the created Git repository:**

   You can do this by creating a connection via the Azure portal

   a. Open Azure DevOps or Azure portal and navigate to Project settings or Repo settings.

   b. Under the Git Repositories, click **`'New repository'`**. Fill the necessary fields such as the name of the repository, which is usually the name of the project. Leave the Add a **`.gitignore`** checkbox marked **`None`** and create the repository.

   c. After creating the repository, navigate back to the homepage of your Azure project environment. Click on **`Repos`** from the left panel and select **`'File'`** then **`'Clone'`** in the upper-right corner.

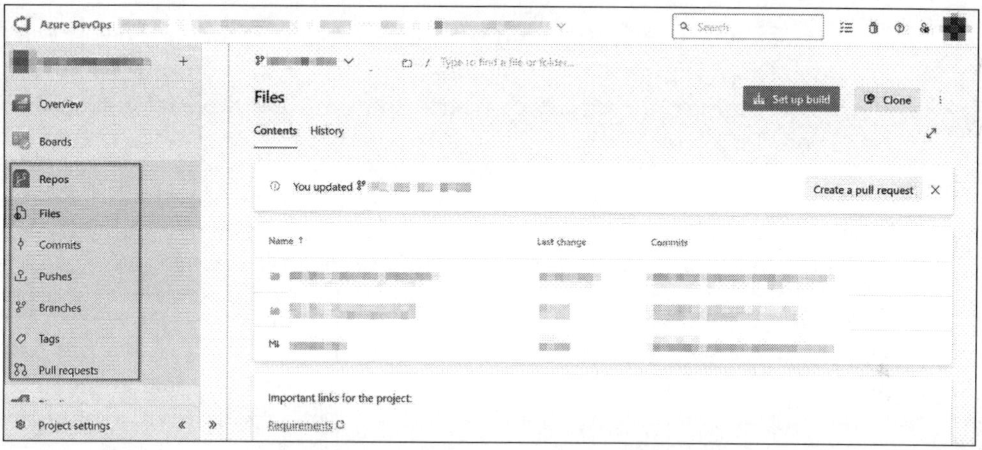

Figure 2.10: *Repository on Azure DevOps*

   d. A Clone Repository dialog box will appear containing the Git repository URL and two authentication methods – **`'Generate Git Credentials'`** and **`Personal Access Token`** (PAT). Choose the relevant authentication and copy the URL.

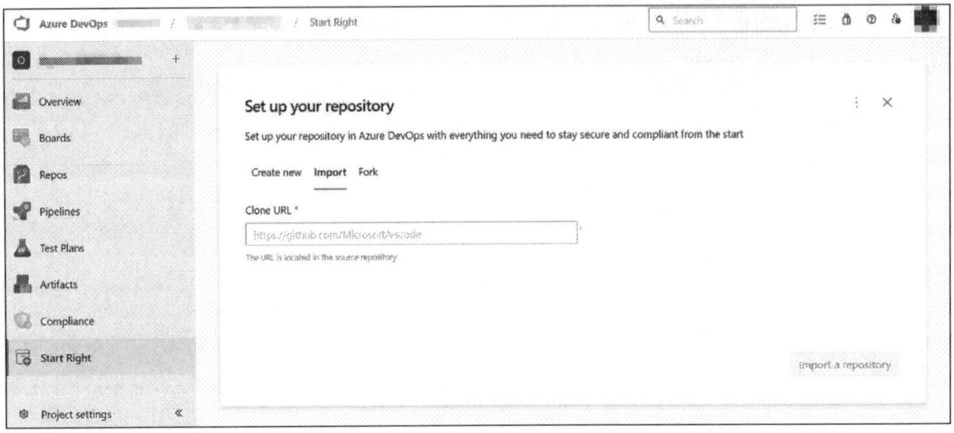

Figure 2.11: *Importing repository on Azure DevOps*

e. Open your local development environment (for example, Visual Studio Code). Open the terminal (Command Line Interface) and navigate (using cd command) to the directory where you want the repository files to live on your local machine.

f. In your terminal, enter the command `'git clone'` followed by the URL you copied from Azure (for example, git clone https://exampleurl.com). Enter your chosen authentication when requested.

This step will create a local copy of your Git repository that is in sync with your Azure environment. Any changes made can now be pushed (uploaded) to the Azure environment, or pulled (downloaded) from it, to keep everyone's local copies up to date with the latest changes. This synchronization forms the crux of how version control and effective collaboration are achieved within the Azure environment.

3. **Setting up a workflow:**

   This entails defining rules and expectations for the Git operations such as commits, pushes, and merges.

4. **Training team members:**

   Every member of the project team must understand Git operations such as committing, pushing, merging, and resolving conflicts.

Collaboration Features in Azure

Azure does an excellent job of providing comprehensive features to foster collaboration in data science projects. Let us take a closer look at some of these features:

Azure DevOps

Azure DevOps is a suite of collaborative tools that caters to every stage of a project's life cycle. This means your team can use it to plan their data science projects, manage their codes, and even deploy their projects. It also comes with a robust tracking system that allows you to monitor the progress of your projects. A key element of Azure DevOps is its integration with Git repositories, which allows for version control, code reviews, and history tracking.

Azure Notebooks

Azure Notebooks is another excellent collaborative tool in Azure. It runs Jupyter Notebook, a popular open-source web application that allows users to create and share documents with live code, equations, visualizations, and explanatory text. With Azure Notebooks, data scientists can collaborate on the same document, thereby encouraging knowledge sharing, code reviews, and refining of methodologies. Additionally, Azure Notebooks provide an integrated, secured, and simplified workspace for interactive data explorations, model training, and deployment.

Azure Boards

Azure Boards allow you to track and manage all aspects of your data science project in a visual and intuitive manner. With Azure Boards, you can create work items for tasks, features, bugs, or ideas, which can then be assigned to different team members. This way, you can ensure that everyone stays on task and no detail gets overlooked. Features like Kanban boards, dashboards, and reporting tools aid in visualizing progress, managing workflow, and keeping track of project performance.

Azure Pipelines

An essential for DevOps and version control, Azure Pipelines is a cloud service that can automatically build, test, and deploy your code project to any platform. Data scientists can collaborate to create robust multi-platform applications with data pipelines, set up continuous integration and continuous delivery (CI/CD) to automate tests and ensure faster, more reliable updates to end-users. Furthermore, with Azure Pipelines you can implement strategies like A/B testing and canary releases, giving you more control over feature rollouts.

These features, along with the integration of Git, make Azure's environment a highly conducive platform for teams working on data science projects. They streamline workflows, foster efficient task tracking, and facilitate effective version control, which are all crucial in maintaining high-quality data science projects.

By integrating Git and leveraging the collaboration features of Azure, data scientists can enhance the effectiveness and efficiency of their projects. Adopting these tools as part of your Azure environment setup is sure to give you the upper hand in managing your data science operations.

Conclusion

In this chapter, we saw a roadmap on how to effectively establish and manage your Azure environment, a key step towards a successful data science project. A concise introduction to Azure and its role in data science set the scene, followed by an elaborate guide on account creation and subscription choice. A thorough overview of Azure services pertinent to data science was then presented, including instructions on their optimal utilization and the benefits of setting up an Azure Machine Learning workspace.

We went through the structure of Azure Machine Learning Studio Interface by exploring its tools and functionalities and highlighted the importance of compute resources and their efficient management. Introductions to Azure notebooks and their role in executing data science experiments were given. We also emphasized the importance of version control and collaboration in data science, detailing how to integrate Git within the Azure platform.

In the ensuing chapter, *Data Preparation and Exploration*, we will delve into the quintessential steps of cleaning, transforming, reshaping your data, and subsequently exploring it with Azure's suite of tools to reveal patterns, insights, and trends. By the end, you will learn how to transform raw data into a format suitable for analysis and gain preliminary insights, paving the way for informed decision-making and creation of new features for more intricate analysis or modeling.

Questions

- Does subscribing to Azure require any specific documents or identification?
- Can you explain how Azure services relevant to data science can optimize the efficiency of a project?
- Are there any limitations on the compute resources that one can configure in Azure?
- Can you detail the process and benefits of using Azure Notebooks for running data science operations?
- Why is it vital to integrate Git for version control in Azure, and how does it facilitate collaboration for data science projects?
- What are some essential features and benefits of Azure Machine Learning workspace that can enhance data science experiments?

- Is Azure Machine Learning Studio Interface user-friendly for beginner data scientists?
- Does Azure Notebooks support Python for executing data science experiments?
- How can efficient management and configuration of compute resources improve the performance of data science experiments in Azure?
- Is it possible to collaborate externally with non-Azure users with Git Integration in Azure?

Multiple Choice Questions

1. Which of these Azure Services is relevant in Data Science?
    a. Azure DevOps
    b. Azure Storage
    c. Azure Event Hubs
    d. All of the above
2. What is Azure Machine Learning Studio used for?
    a. Web Development
    b. Data Science Operations
    c. Network Security
    d. Cloud Computing
3. Which of these compute resources cannot be configured in Azure?
    a. CPU
    b. GPU
    c. Disk Storage
    d. None of the above
4. Azure Notebooks primarily supports which programming language for executing data science experiments?
    a. R
    b. Python
    c. C++
    d. Both a and b

5. Git Integration in Azure is used for:
    a. Version Control
    b. Collaboration
    c. Both a and b
    d. Neither a nor b
6. Which of these Azure services does not directly contribute to data science experiments?
    a. Azure Machine Learning
    b. Azure Databricks
    c. Azure SQL Database
    d. Azure Active Directory
7. What is the Azure version control system?
    a. Azure Repo
    b. Git integration
    c. Both a and b
    d. None of the above
8. Which of these is not a component of Azure Machine Learning Workspace?
    a. Compute Instances
    b. Data Stores
    c. Training Jobs
    d. Azure Maps
9. What language do Azure Notebooks primarily support for executing data science operations?
    a. Java
    b. Ruby
    c. Swift
    d. Python

10. What are the main considerations while choosing an Azure subscription for data science applications?
    a. Cost
    b. Scalability
    c. Specific services required
    d. All of the above
11. Azure is:
    a. Infrastructure as a Service (IaaS)
    b. Platform as a Service (PaaS)
    c. Both a and b
    d. None of the above
12. What is the first step to set up Azure Machine Learning Studio?
    a. Manage Compute Resources
    b. Creating a Workspace
    c. Git Integration
    d. Creating an Azure account
13. Azure Notebooks are essential for data science operations for:
    a. Experimentation
    b. Collaboration
    c. Both a and b
    d. None of the above
14. What does Git Integration provide in Azure?
    a. Collaboration
    b. Version control
    c. Ability to roll back changes
    d. All of the above

15. In the context of Azure for data science, compute resources refer to:
    a. Software applications available
    b. Hardware abilities like CPU capacity, memory, storage, and more
    c. Collaboration tools available
    d. None of the above

Answers

1. d
2. b
3. d
4. d
5. c
6. d
7. c
8. d
9. d
10. d
11. c
12. b
13. c
14. d
15. b

CHAPTER 3
Data Ingestion and Storage in Azure

Introduction

In this intriguing chapter, we will embark on a journey to explore the exciting realm of Data Ingestion and Storage with Azure. We will delve deep into the nuances of how information flows into systems and the vital role this plays in formulating business intelligence and data analytics strategies. You'll gain an understanding of the Azure landscape, including its storage and management services.

We'll explore in-depth the various storage options and techniques that Azure offers, with a focus on Azure Data Lake Storage, Azure SQL Database, Azure Blob Storage, and Azure Data Factory. You'll learn about their key features, advantages, practical use-cases, and the appropriate scenarios to choose each of them. The chapter also covers important aspects such as data security, access, governance, and compliance in Azure. So, buckle up, as we unpack the potentials of Azure in revolutionizing your approach to data management!

Structure

In this chapter, the following topics will be covered:

- Introduction to Data Ingestion in Azure
- Azure Data Storage Options
- Data Ingestion Techniques in Azure
- Introduction to Azure Data Lake Storage Gen2
- Data Access and Security in Azure
- Data Governance and Compliance in Azure

Introduction to Data Ingestion in Azure

In today's digitally fueled business environment, data is an invaluable asset. The way data is ingested – or brought into a system – can have a significant effect on the integrity, usefulness, and overall quality of the data. This chapter introduces you to the concept of data ingestion and its significance in transforming businesses.

Explaining Data Ingestion and Its Significance

Data ingestion is a fundamental aspect of any data-driven operation, serving as the method through which raw data is imported from various sources and readied for further processing, be it immediate analysis or storage for future utilization. At its core, data ingestion describes the journey of data from its source, no matter its nature - structured or unstructured - or quantity, to a destination where it's accessible and usable.

For instance, consider a vast global business that accumulates data from multiple origins - be it customer databases, insights from social media, industry sources, or IoT devices. Each of these sources can generate data vastly differing in formats, structure, speed, and size. The function of data ingestion, therefore, entails synchronizing these distinct aspects for a streamlined data flow into the system. When executed aptly, this opens doors for both real-time analytics, which necessitates on-the-spot ingestion and analysis, and batch processing, which allows data collection over time periods, followed by scheduled analysis.

The significance of data ingestion comes to light when we contemplate the criticality of data as a spine for decision-making in contemporary businesses. The ability to swiftly and accurately ingest datasets the stage for seamless analytics processes, ultimately painting a comprehensive, accurate, and timely picture of business insights. It is these insights that enable strategic, well-informed decision-making, helping businesses stay agile in response to market dynamics, customer preferences, and emerging opportunities or threats.

For instance, a quick ingestion of customer data can enable real-time personalization, sharpening customer experiences, and potentially leading to superior customer engagement and conversions. Alternatively, efficient ingestion of operational data can pave the way for identifying performance bottlenecks, leading to timely interventions to enhance functional efficiency.

Thus, data ingestion operates as the wiring behind solid analytics, creating a stepping stone to gain a competitive edge in today's data-centric business ecosystem. It's not hyperbolic to assert that a firm's ability to ingest data accurately and expediently can be a critical determinant of its business agility, customer-centricity, operational efficiency, and market victories.

Overview of Azure Data Storage and Management Services

Microsoft's Azure provides an extensive suite of data storage and management services that cater to a variety of data needs - from structured SQL databases to unstructured big data lakes. These services help businesses store, manage and analyze data with optimal efficiency, speed, and insight.

Azure offers a variety of storage options such as Azure Data Lake Storage, Azure SQL Database, and Azure Blob Storage, designed to provide affordable, reliable, scalable and secure cloud storage solutions. Each of these services has unique benefits and is suitable for different types of data and scenarios.

In terms of data management, Azure provides services like Azure Data Factory and Azure Stream Analytics. These help in creating robust data pipelines and real-time analytics.

Through this chapter, you'll gain a detailed understanding of these Azure services, their applications, and best practices to use them. Effectively managing data with Azure means making the most of your data, powering your business towards data-driven excellence.

Azure Data Storage Options

Microsoft Azure offers a robust selection of versatile data storage services. Whether you're dealing with structured or unstructured data, need to have something scalable for big data or require something transactional for an application, Azure has got you covered. Let's begin by exploring three key data storage options:

Azure Data Lake Storage (ADLS) Gen2

Azure Data Lake Storage Gen2, or simply ADLS Gen2, is a cutting-edge offering from Microsoft that combines the best elements from two generations of Azure data lakes. It is designed to deliver sophisticated solutions for big data and analytics needs.

One of the main advantages of ADLS Gen2 is the capability for Hadoop-compatible access. If your business already uses Hadoop for big data analytics, then ADLS Gen2 will seamlessly integrate with your existing setup. It supports so-called Hadoop Distributed File System (HDFS) APIs, which allow Hadoop applications to treat data in ADLS Gen2 as they would data stored in an on-premises Hadoop environment. This compatibility means that shifting from traditional big data platforms to Azure-based AI and analytics projects can be done with minimal hiccups.

Notably, ADLS Gen2 provides a hierarchical directory structure, in contrast to the flat namespace usually seen in Azure Blob storage. This hierarchical structure allows for the creation of a more organized directory that can be optimized for specific use cases. Data can be stored in hierarchical namespaces, enhancing data organization and operational efficiency. These hierarchical namespaces can improve data access performance for certain workloads and allow for more efficient directory manipulations, such as renames or deletes.

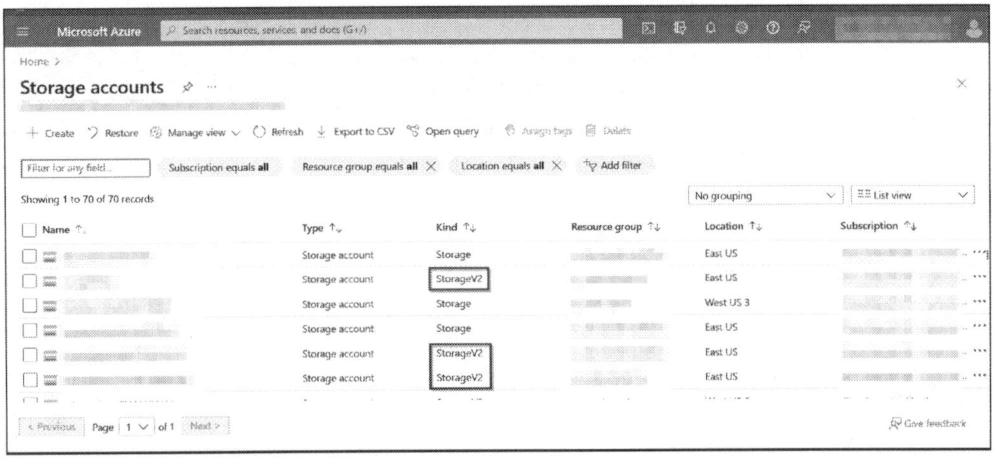

Figure 3.1: *Storage account dashboard. The marked Storage V2 shows the accounts having ADLS Gen2*

ADLS Gen2 is deftly engineered to deliver optimized cost and performance, incorporating the cost-effectiveness of object storage with the low latency and high throughput of file systems. By retaining large datasets in lower-cost tiers and frequently accessed items in higher-performance tiers, Azure Data Lake Storage Gen2 ensures your workloads perform optimally.

When ensuring security, ADLS Gen2 uses a finer-grained security model. It employs Access Control Lists (ACLs) at the file and folder levels, enabling more granular control over data and better compliance with data protection regulations.

When it comes to scalability, ADLS Gen2 truly shines. It inherits the massive scalability from Azure Blob storage, which means it can handle exabytes of data – a scale suitable for the biggest big-data use cases. The scalability is not limited to size but extends to handling high volumes of small writes quickly and cost-effectively as well.

ADLS Gen2 provides a robust, scalable storage solution that sets a new standard for data lakes. Its capabilities in creating a hierarchical file structure for improved data organization, compatibility with Hadoop for easy integration, access controls for enhanced security, alongside considerable cost optimization and performance benefits render it a powerhouse for any firm aiming to supercharge its big data analytics.

Steps to create an ADLS Gen2 resource

Here are the general steps to create Azure Data Lake Storage Gen2:

1. Sign in to the Azure portal.
2. In the left menu, click **`Create a Resource`**.
3. In the new window, search for **`Storage account`**.

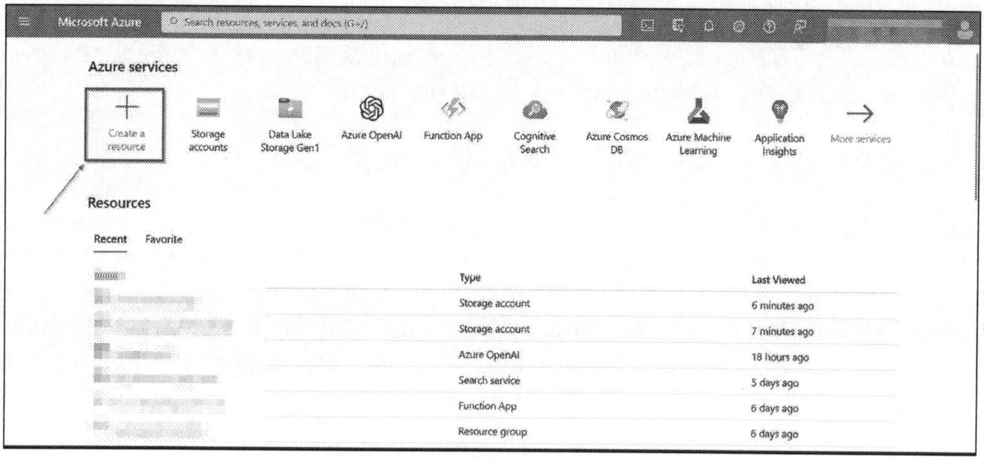

***Figure 3.2:** The create resource in Azure portal's home page*

4. In the search results, select **`Storage account`** and then click **`Create`**.
5. Select your **`Azure Subscription`**.
6. Choose or create a new **`Resource Group`**. This group will contain your ADLS Gen2 account.
7. Enter a name for your **`Storage account`**. Azure will check the name's availability.
8. Select the **`geographical Region`** where you want your service to reside.
9. For **`Performance`**, choose **`Standard`** as it supports all storage tiers and replication options.
10. For Account kind, choose **`StorageV2`** (general-purpose v2) because the v2 accounts deliver the latest Azure storage capabilities including Blob Storage integration and tiering.
11. Ensure that Replication is set to **`Read-access geo-redundant storage`** (RA-GRS) or **`Geo-redundant storage`** (GRS) for higher durability.
12. Under the **`Advanced`** tab, make sure that Data Lake Storage Gen2 and Hierarchical namespace are both enabled.

13. For Security + networking or other settings, choose the options that suit your requirements.

14. Review the account settings on the next screen, if they are all right, hit the `Create` button.

15. Azure will now allocate the resource. The deployment process may take a few minutes. Once the deployment is complete, you can access the newly created Azure Data Lake Storage Gen2 from the Storage Account window.

Please note that while these are general steps, certain options might vary based on the specific needs and restrictions of your project or organization.

Azure SQL Database

Azure SQL Database is a dynamic, fully managed relational database service provided by Microsoft Azure. It is built upon the solid foundation of SQL Server, known industry-wide for its strong relational database capabilities, and thus already synonymous with efficient, reliable, and powerful data manipulation and management. What makes Azure SQL Database unique is its added intelligence, with functionalities that learn and adapt to the specific patterns of your databases, outstandingly serving in a multi-tenant environment.

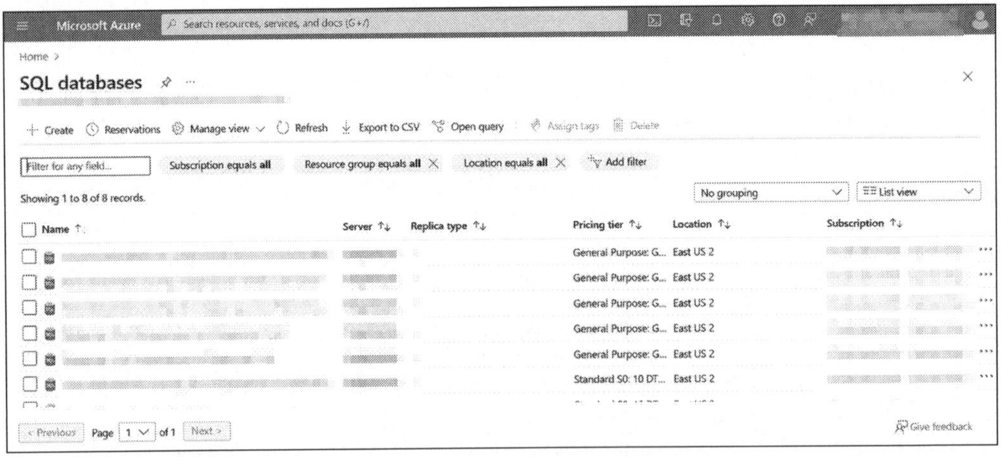

Figure 3.3: *List of SQL databases created, as seen in SQL databases dashboard*

In Azure SQL Database, both the infrastructure and database management functions are automated. This built-in intelligence significantly enhances its performance, coupled with guaranteed reliability and data protection. It learns from your unique database patterns and the rich telemetry of the service, and it automatically tunes performance by adjusting database resources commensurately. The robust automated backup system is another feature that ensures data protection even in unforeseen circumstances, making data loss concerns a thing of the past.

The service offers some key advantages that render it a top choice for businesses of all kinds. It boasts of automatic scaling capabilities that accommodate and instantly adapts to your changing business requirements – permitting you to dynamically adjust resources to match the demands of your workload. Intelligently optimizing itself for better performance, Azure SQL Database ensures your data operations are always at their prime. One key aspect is its capacity for high availability. It offers several architectures aimed at different requirements and price points, making it the suitable service for hosting applications imperative to your business, which require relational data storage.

Steps to create an Azure SQL database

Here's a step-by-step guide to create an Azure SQL Database:

1. Sign in to the Azure portal.
2. In the left-hand menu, select **`Create a resource`**.
3. In the **`New`** window, search for **`SQL Database`**.
4. In the search results, select **`SQL Database`**, and then click **`Create`**.

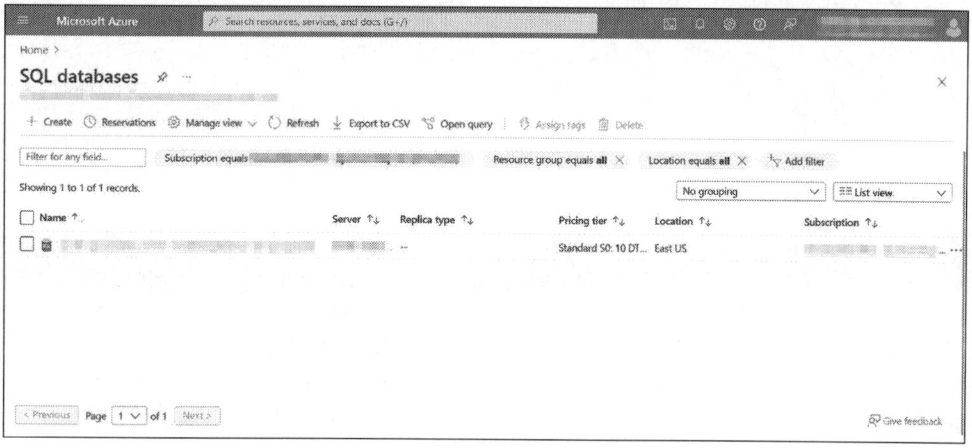

Figure 3.4: *Click Create in the SQL dashboard*

5. In the New SQL Database' form, fill in the details of your new database - the subscription, the resource group under which you want to create the database, the database name, and the server. You may choose to **`Create a new`** server if required.

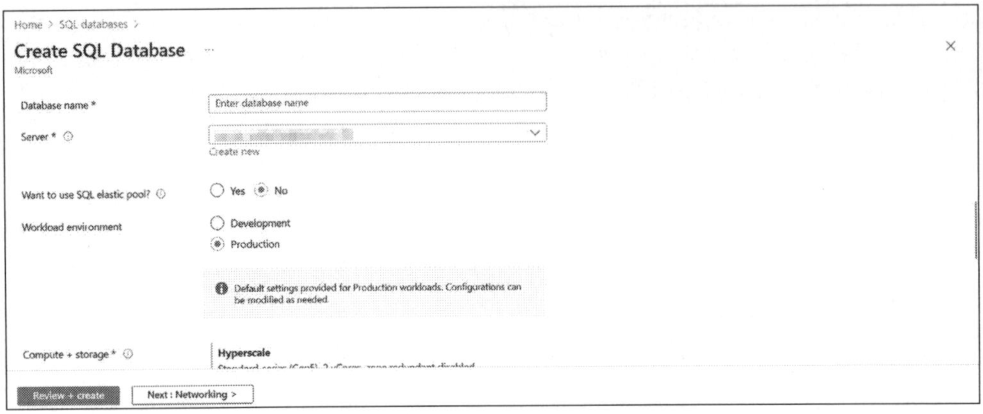

Figure 3.5: *Fill up the details required*

6. Choose the **`Compute + Storage`** option that suits your needs. You can either choose a pre-configured bundle or customize based on your workload.
7. Click **`Next`** to configure networking, security, and additional settings as per requirements.
8. Review your settings for the new database. Once you are satisfied, click **`Create`**.

Azure will now create your SQL database. Once the deployment is complete, it becomes available for use. As always, the specific settings may vary based on the specific needs and restrictions of your project or organization.

Azure Blob Storage

Azure Blob Storage is a versatile, cloud-based storage solution offered under Azure's vast array of services. With its impressive ability to handle unstructured data such as text or binary data, it is an ideal choice for organizations dealing with large volumes of data. Whether you need to serve images or documents directly to a browser, store files for distributed access, or occasionally stream video and audio content, Azure Blob Storage is equipped to handle all these tasks with exceptional efficiency.

One of the key attractions of Azure Blob Storage is its massive scalability. As your data needs grow, this service can effortlessly upscale to accommodate more data, without compromising on accessibility or performance. It eliminates the need for substantial upfront investment in storage infrastructure, thus providing a cost-effective solution for enterprises dealing with voluminous data.

Moreover, geographically dispersed replication options enhance data resilience. Azure Blob Storage ensures the safety of your data by maintaining multiple copies of each blob in different locations. These locations can be either within the same region or cross-regional, providing a reliable safeguard against potential data loss.

Another commendable feature is its on-demand, pay-as-you-go pricing model. This ensures you only pay for the storage you use and aids in effectively managing storage costs. You can easily scale up or down based on requirement and save on capital expenditure. In terms of capabilities, Azure Blob Storage can handle varying types of blobs or Binary Large Objects, which includes Block Blobs for handling large files, Page Blobs suitable for frequent read/write operations, and Append Blobs which are great if you need to append additional information.

Azure Blob Storage offers a robust, affordable and flexible storage solution for businesses, seamlessly handling large dynamic volumes of unstructured data. It is a boon for organizations needing secure, scalable and resilient cloud storage.

Steps to create a Azure Blob Storage

Creating Azure Blob Storage is a fairly straightforward process:

1. First, log in to your **`Azure account`** and navigate to the Azure portal.
2. Click **`Create a Resource`** and search for **`Storage Account`**.
3. Click **`'Create'`** and fill in the necessary details, such as the subscription, resource group, storage account name, and location.

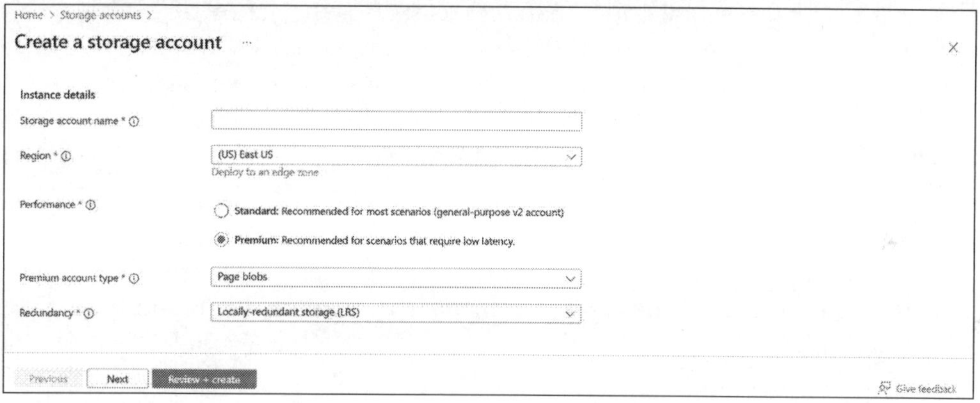

Figure 3.6: *Fill up the details required*

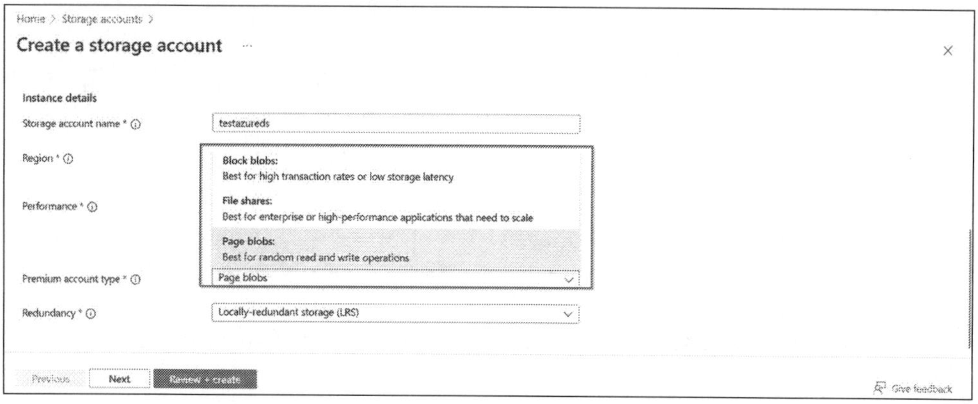

Figure 3.7: *Select the appropriate account type required*

4. Choose **`Blob Storage`** under the **`Account kind`** dropdown.
5. Configure the remaining settings as per your requirements, including replication, performance, and access tier details.
6. Finally, review your choices and click **`Create to have your Blob Storage`**.

Following are the values that are to be filled:

`Deployment model` ⇒ **`Resource Manager`**

`Performance` ⇒ **`Standard`**

`Account kind` ⇒ **`StorageV2 (general-purpose v2)`**

`Replication` ⇒ **`Locally redundant storage (LRS)`**

`Access tier` ⇒ **`Hot`**

Choosing the Right Azure Storage for Your Needs

Deciding on the most suitable Azure storage for your needs isn't a one-size-fits-all decision. It hinges on several critical parameters such as the nature of the data you are handling, the requirements of your specific application, scalability needs, performance targets, and cost considerations. By carefully evaluating these aspects, you can align your choice with your intended outcomes, laying a solid foundation for effective and efficient data processes.

Azure proposes a diverse array of data storage options, each with its unique set of capabilities and advantages. For instance, when it comes to handling analytic and big data operations, Azure Data Lake Storage often emerges as a preferred choice. This is thanks to its exceptional ability to manage large file systems and supercharge analytic performance. On the flip side, when working with relational data or when high availability is a key requirement for mission-critical applications, Azure SQL Database often comes into the spotlight. It offers enterprise-grade SQL capabilities, automatic backups, high availability, and scalability; making it a strong choice for such scenarios.

Azure Blob Storage offers advantageous solutions for scenarios that deal primarily with unstructured data or require worldwide accessibility due to its inherently global infrastructure. Its massive scalability and diverse data type accommodation make it a favored choice of businesses with voluminous and varied data.

The key to unlocking the true potential of these storage options lies in understanding their inherent strengths and assessing how these align with your data needs and business contexts. In doing so, the decision-making process shifts from being a technical selection to becoming a strategic resolution, empowering the businesses to optimally utilize their data while enhancing productivity and insights generation.

Data Ingestion Techniques in Azure

For dealing with the complexity and diversity of data ingestion processes, Azure platforms deliver advanced, reliable, and strongly integrated services. Let's delve into two significant Azure services that facilitate seamless data ingestion - Azure Data Factory and Azure Stream Analytics.

Azure Data Factory

Azure Data Factory (ADF) is designed as a cloud-based, scale-out data integration service. It allows you to conceive and manage data-driven workflows, thereby orchestrating and automating data movement and transformation. ADF empowers you to construct pipelines that can not only ingest data from various data stores but also leverage diverse transformations and direct the data to different data storage destinations. This versatility turns ADF into a central hub for data management tasks, providing a consolidated platform to seamlessly transform raw data inputs into meaningful insights.

Figure 3.8: *Data factory dashboard*

Among the robust features of Azure Data Factory is a visual interface that supports the building, debugging, and managing stages of pipelines. This visual environment simplifies pipeline creation and eliminates the need for complex coding, promoting user-friendly experiences. Accompanying this is ADF's capability to ingest and prepare data for machine learning. It helps to streamline the machine learning process, enabling seamless integration of data processing and machine learning workflows. Another noteworthy feature is the in-built monitoring and management capacities. This encourages proactive troubleshooting and ensures your pipelines are always performing optimally. Featuring a wide array of applications, ADF plays a critical role in areas ranging from data warehousing, where it supports large-scale data ingestion in batches, to real-time analytics, facilitating immediate data processing.

Steps to create a Data Factory

Following are the steps to create a Data Factory:

1. **Create a new Data Factory:** Start by launching the Azure portal. Look for Data Factories and then click **+** add. Proceed by filling in the fields including name, subscription, resource group, and location.

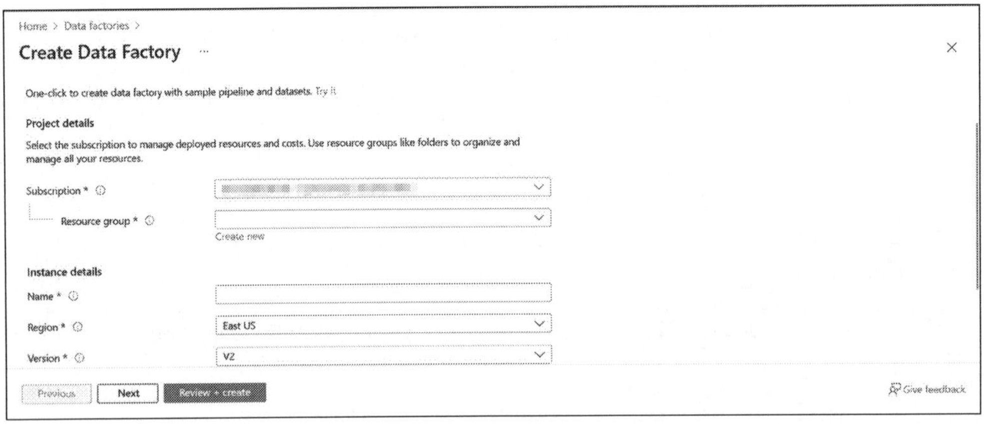

***Figure* 3.9:** *Creating a data factory*

2. **Use the Copy Data Tool**: Once the Data Factory is created, inside the **`Data Factory`** screen, click **`Author and Monitor`**. This will open a new window, here select the **`Copy Data`** option to start configuring your pipeline.

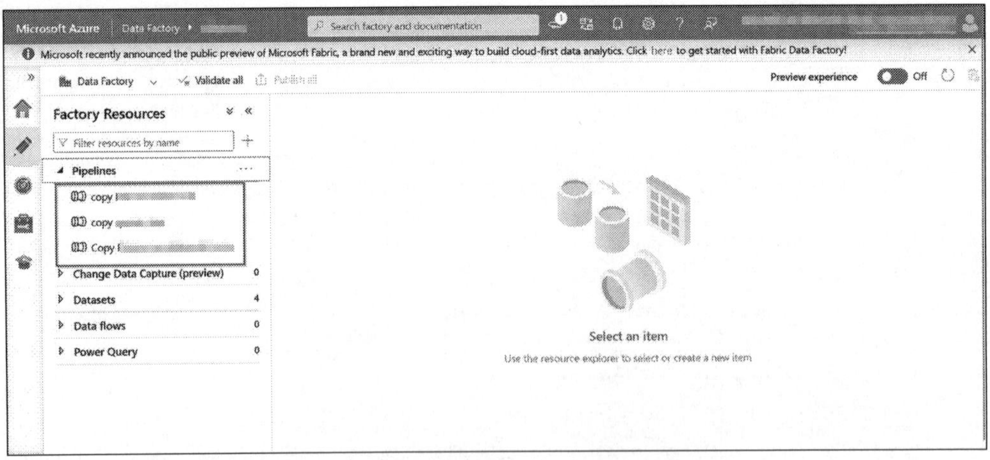

***Figure* 3.10:** *Copy pipelines in Data Factory*

3. **Configure the input and output data stores**: Here, specify the source (input) from where the data will be copied and the sink (output) where the data will be loaded. This can be any supported data store.

4. **Specify transformations:** If needed, define the transformations which need to be applied to the data while being transferred from the source to the sink.

5. **Set a schedule:** You can define how often and when the data should be copied from the source to the sink. This could be on a one-time basis, on schedule, or in real-time.

6. **Deploy the pipeline**: After all configurations are done, click **`Next`** on each screen and finally on **`Finish`** to deploy the pipeline.

7. **Monitor the pipeline**: Once the pipeline is deployed, monitoring its performance and data flow is critical to ensure everything is working as expected. The Azure Data Factory's monitoring tools provide visuals and statistics to assist with this.

Remember, these steps are applicable for a straightforward data copying pipeline. Customizing pipelines for more complex scenarios involving multiple transformations or different kinds of data stores might require additional steps and configurations.

Azure Stream Analytics

Azure Stream Analytics is a real-time analytics and complex event-processing engine that is designed to analyze and visualize streaming data from various sources such as devices, sensors, websites, and social media feeds.

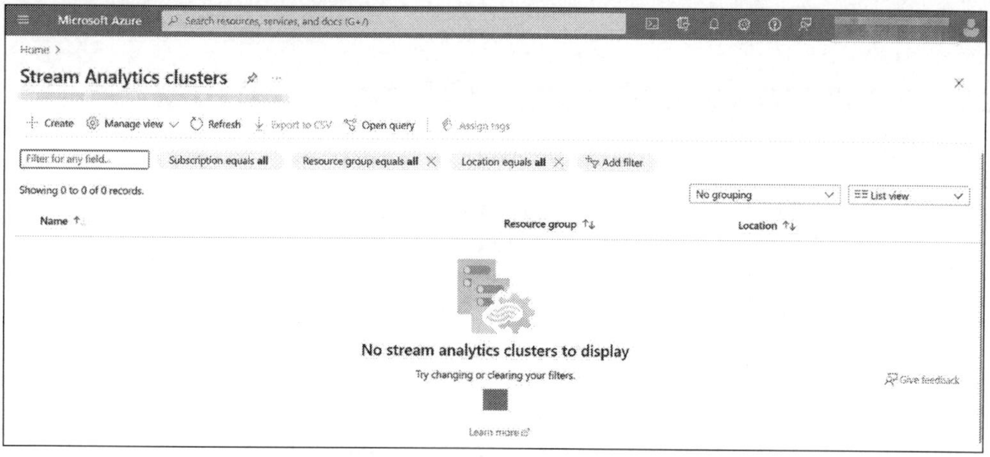

Figure 3.11: *Azure Stream Analytics dashboard*

Some key benefits offered by Azure Stream Analytics include the ability to process data from many sources in real-time, low-latency response times, and a SQL-based language for quick development. Azure Stream Analytics is commonly used in real-time dashboarding, real-time metrics and analytics, IoT scenarios, and in response to remote changes in real-time.

Building Azure's Data Ingestion Pipeline

Azure Data Factory and Azure Stream Analytics together form a comprehensive data ingestion pipeline in Azure, supporting both batch and real-time streaming. The pipeline starts with the data sources, which can be anything from SaaS applications to on-premises SQL Servers.

Azure Data Factory is used to extract the data from these sources, transform it (if necessary), and load it into a destination data store. If working with real-time data, instead of ADF, you would use Azure Stream Analytics to ingest, process, and analyze the streaming data in real-time.

Thus, by using services like Azure Data Factory and Azure Stream Analytics, you can build efficient data ingestion pipelines, facilitating robust data flows from multiple sources to your key data storage and analysis platforms.

Introduction to Azure Data Lake Storage Gen2

Azure Data Lake Storage Gen2, or simply ADLS Gen2, is a highly scalable and secure data lake that combines the best elements of the first-generation Azure Data Lake Storage and Azure Blob Storage. It offers a high-quality hierarchical file system with the benefits of low-cost, tiered storage facilities, and global scalability provided by Azure Blob Storage.

Elucidation of the Azure Data Lake Gen2 Services

Data Lake Storage Gen2 allows you to perform big data analytics on data of any size, type and ingestion speed in one single place. It takes advantage of Azure Blob Storage capabilities, bringing in features like a hierarchical namespace that allows the organization of datasets in a hierarchical file and folder structure. It works seamlessly with Hadoop and Spark, enabling you to process and analyze large amounts of data with ease.

Highlighting the Distinguished Features and Advantages

One of the most significant features of ADLS Gen2 is its ability to support both object and file system APIs. This ensures that your data solutions built on object storage can continue working when you migrate to the hierarchical namespace of Data Lake Storage.

Its benefits include high-performance analytics that help in accelerated decision making. Other attributes include security and ease of management; data in ADLS Gen2 is encrypted and you can use Azure Active Directory to control access. Seamless integration with analytics frameworks and data pipeline tools like Azure Databricks and Azure Data Factory make it a valuable tool for businesses handling vast quantities of data.

Real-World Applications of Azure Data Lake Storage Gen2

Azure Data Lake Storage Gen2 (ADLS Gen2) offers exemplary flexibility, scale, and capabilities to fulfil a broad scope of real-world applications across multiple industries. One of its core applications is functioning as a comprehensive data lake wherein businesses can store and analyze colossal amounts of big data, structured or unstructured, without any performance sacrifices. The scalability of ADLS Gen2 allows organizations to manage big data and facilitates immediate analytics or future batch processing. Businesses can take advantage of the high-throughput data streaming and data analytics provided by this service, as it can help in delivering real-time insights, thus aiding in faster and more accurate decision-making processes.

Furthermore, ADLS Gen2 plays a pivotal role in advancing scientific fields like precision medicine and genomic research, both of which necessitate the secure storage and efficient analysis of massive volumes of data. For instance, genomic sequencing outputs extensive datasets and employing ADLS Gen2 enables researchers to securely store petabytes of genomic and medical data. Not only can this empower scientists with the ability to perform exhaustive analyses, but it can also drastically toe the line of scientific and medicinal breakthroughs by enhancing research processes.

On a similar note, in the realm of IoT, ADLS Gen2 can serve as the ideal repository for sensor data. In the age where billions of IoT devices are generating continuous streams of data, ADLS Gen2 can efficiently handle these massive volumes. Whether it's data from temperature sensors in a weather monitoring system or readings from Industrial IoT devices, ADLS Gen2's scalability can immensely support the storage and consecutive analysis of the data. This could, sequentially, boost IoT deployments' efficiency by providing valuable insights and streamlining IoT data management. These scenarios illustrate the vast-ranging applications of ADLS Gen2, reinforcing its position as a vital component in modern-day data strategies.

Data Access and Security in Azure

Data is the lifeblood of any business, and its security is of paramount importance.

Microsoft Azure provides comprehensive security measures that ensure your data is protected at all times. From advanced access controls to data encryption, Azure offers various tools and features to safeguard your data.

Understanding Azure's Data Security Measures

Understanding Azure's security measures is a fundamental step in ensuring your data's safety and integrity, particularly when operating within the digital realm of the Azure cloud. The Azure environment is architected with multiple layers of security, enveloping every aspect of its structure to create a sphere of protection around the data it hosts. This approach ranges from safeguarding its physical data centers - stringent control measures for unauthorized access, consistent monitoring, and advanced disaster recovery systems - to securing its expansive network - intrusion detection, DDoS attack prevention, and isolation of storage accounts.

This particular focus on layered security extends to access control and data protection mechanisms. Access controls in Azure are about ensuring that only authenticated and authorized parties can access the resources. This goes hand in hand with Azure's data protection mechanisms which are aimed at safeguarding the data when at rest, in transit, or in use. Azure's encryption protocols, for instance, serve to shield data at rest, while secure transport channels like HTTPS and TLS safeguard data when in transit. Besides, Azure's role-based access control and multi factor authentication adds an extra layer of security by validating the privileges of users and restricting unauthorized access to data.

Additionally, what sets Azure a class apart is its robust compliance offering. With over 90 compliances, Azure has one of the most comprehensive compliance portfolios in the industry, designed to help users adhere to privacy and compliance requirements that pertain to their geographic region, industry, and data type. Furthermore, there's Azure Security Center - a unified infrastructure security management system that provides advanced threat protection across hybrid workloads in the cloud. Azure Security Center uses advanced machine learning algorithms to detect and block malicious activities, offering capabilities such as Just-In-Time access control to prevent unauthorized access and adaptive threat protection to constantly monitor and eliminate potential threats before they inflict any serious damage. In essence, Azure's manifold security measures and strategies together create a well-guarded, secure, and compliant environment for your data to reside.

Encryption Types and Data Protection Tactics

One of the mainstays of data protection in Azure is its robust encryption offerings. Encryption is an essential pillar of data security, transforming information into an unintelligible format that can only be deciphered with the right keys or credentials. In Azure, two broad types of encryptions are used to safeguard data - Transport Layer Security (TLS) for data in transit, and Advanced Encryption Standard (AES) for data at rest.

In-transit data refers to data being transferred over a network, such as from a user's device to Azure's cloud or between Azure data centers. Transport Layer Security (TLS) is employed for this, providing robust security that keeps malicious agents at bay. On the other hand, data at rest refers to inactive data stored physically in any digital form in databases, data warehouses, spreadsheets, archives, tapes, off-site backups, mobile devices, and more. This is where Azure uses the industry-standard AES, providing robust security to your data when it's most vulnerable.

Azure also hosts supplemental security measures that further enhance data protection efforts. One such additional security feature is Azure Storage Service Encryption (SSE), responsible for automatically encrypting data prior to storing this information within Azure Storage. Given it is an automatic process, it singularly reduces the user burden of maintaining and managing encrypted data. Furthermore, Azure incorporates Transparent Data Encryption (Azure TDE), a real-time I/O encryption and decryption system. It is designed to analyze databases, backups, and transaction log files at the page level. Yet another vital tool in Azure's security suite is Azure Key Vault, handling cryptographic keys and other secrets including tokens, passwords, database credentials, and API keys used by cloud applications and services. This enables a secure storage of these cryptographic keys and facilitates a stringent access control over storage and retrieval of keys. Overall, these flairs of Azure not only render a multifaceted encryption strategy but also ensure a stringent access control mechanism, elevating its data protection regime to an industry-leading standard.

User Authentication and Access Control in Azure

Authentication and access control mechanisms are crucial facets of any cloud ecosystem, and Azure is no exception. An essential component of Azure's data security strategy is Azure Active Directory (Azure AD). It is essentially an identity and access management service which provides seamless access to your applications through a safe and secure universal platform. Azure AD is responsible for managing user identities, providing various options for authentication, such as multi-factor authentication (MFA) and single sign-on (SSO), to validate identities before granting access to resources.

Azure AD is vital in the grand scheme of Azure's access controls. It provides the basis for managing and controlling who can access your data, and what actions they can perform with it. The primary objective is to ensure that only authorized individuals or systems access critical pieces of information. It's not just about validating individuals; Azure AD can also authenticate application services and devices. Whether it's a developer requiring access to a database, an IoT device sending data, or an AI service processing data, Azure AD facilitates secure and seamless access.

Adding to Azure's access control arsenal is the Role-Based Access Control (RBAC), designed to enforce organizational control while leveraging Azure's resources. RBAC works by assigning resources to roles and then associating these roles with users, groups, service principals, or managed identities. Users only gain access to the resources their role is authorized to access and can only perform specific actions their role is assigned to. Predesigned roles such as Owner, Contributor, and Reader come with a select set of permissions, or you can create custom-designed roles that perfectly match your business needs. This granular level of control with RBAC adds an extra layer of security, ensuring both operational efficiency and robust governance with minimal risk of unauthorized access.

Importance of Data Security in Cloud Storage

The increasing adoption of cloud storage solutions by businesses across all sectors, driven by the necessity of digital transformation, has underscored the criticality of data security in cloud storage. It has become an essential and non-negotiable aspect of not just IT policy, but of business strategy itself. The shift to the cloud has expanded the threat landscape, making data more susceptible to breaches and attacks. This, coupled with the increase in the volume and complexity of data, mandates the need for robust, reliable, and evolving cloud security measures to safeguard sensitive data.

To meet this need, Azure stands as one of the market leaders in providing strong cloud storage security. Azure's robust infrastructure for data protection is designed to prevent unauthorized access to data, secure information no matter where it resides, and resist attacks from various threats. Azure's security measures range from data encryption, threat detection, and multi-factor authentication mechanisms, to access controls, and regular security audits. Adherence to these security measures guarantees the protection of sensitive and confidential data, including customer information. Furthermore, it plays a crucial role in preventing detrimental data breaches that could result not only in financial losses but also in a significant setback to the organization's reputation and customer trust.

Investing time and resources in understanding and implementing Azure's data security measures is a worthwhile venture for organizations handling critical data. Prioritizing data security is essential, not just for risk mitigation but also forms the foundation for building customer trust and ensuring business continuity amidst threats and vulnerabilities. With increasingly sophisticated cybersecurity threats, Azure's data security offers a proactive and resilient approach to securing data in the cloud, providing businesses with the confidence to operate securely whilst reaping the benefits of digital transition.

Data Governance and Compliance in Azure

One of the significant aspects of successful data management in Azure is ensuring effective data governance and adherence to compliance regulations. Data governance refers to the organizational bodies, rules, policies, and procedures enforced by a company to manage, use, and protect its data.

Understanding the Role and Principles of Data Governance in Azure

Understanding the structure, functioning, and the lifecycle of data within an organization is critical for data governance. This understanding aids in creating informed policies that help in managing data effectively, supporting key business objectives, and ensuring compliance. Microsoft Azure provides an extensive suite of sophisticated capabilities and services that support effective data governance.

Azure acknowledges that data governance extends beyond securing stored data and enters the realm of managing that data throughout its lifecycle – right from the time of creation until it is archived or deleted. Such management entails controlling how the data is created, accessed, used, classified, and deleted. It helps establish the necessary checks and balances to maintain the consistency and reliability of the data, minimize the risks associated with it, and ensure proper alignment with regulatory requirements.

Helping organizations gain a holistic understanding of their data, Azure introduces Azure Purview, a unified data governance service. Azure Purview provides a bird's eye view of an organization's data landscape, enabling them to map, catalogue, comprehend, and control data, regardless of where it resides. Concurrently, Azure Policy aids in establishing and enforcing various policies to ensure compliance with both corporate and regulatory standards. Azure Policy assesses the state of your resources for non-compliance with assigned policy definitions and provides a detailed compliance assessment for each applicable policy. Together, Azure Purview and Azure Policy act as cornerstones for effective data governance in Azure, ensuring organizational data is not only well-understood and utilized effectively but also secured and compliant.

Compliance Policies as per Different Jurisdictions

The aspect of compliance is a crucial parameter in cloud services, and Azure takes it very seriously. Compliance refers to adhering to predetermined regulations, standards, and practices that are typically set in accordance with data protection, security, privacy, and other critical areas of concern. The realm of these regulations is vast and depends on several factors such as geographic location, the nature of the industry, the specific type of data, and more. Each of these aspects has its set of norms formulated by different jurisdictions, thereby creating a multi-dimensional compliance landscape.

Azure sets itself apart by offering an unprecedented level of compliance coverage in the industry. Azure's compliance portfolio is comprehensive, boasting over 90 compliance certifications. The range is global and includes specific certifications for different regions like the United States, Europe, Asia Pacific, and the Middle East. This variety ensures that Azure is equipped to handle and meet regulatory requirements from different corners of the world, adhering to the distinct laws and standards set by different regions and countries. Furthermore, Azure also provides industry-specific certifications, ensuring adherence to detailed and stringent regulations set forth by industries including finance, health, education, and government.

By providing such extensive compliance coverage, Azure aims to foster trust with its customers by demonstrating its commitment to data protection and privacy. This comprehensive approach to compliance also simplifies the path to meeting regulatory obligations for Azure users. It ensures that businesses operating in multiple jurisdictions can rely on Azure's services without worrying about meeting varying compliance needs. Thus, Azure's holistic approach to compliance enables organizations to focus on their core business operations while ensuring that their data protection and privacy obligations are expertly managed.

Azure's Support Tools for Governance and Compliance

Microsoft Azure provides an abundance of tools and services designed to assist businesses in implementing and maintaining strong governance and compliance strategies. Effective data governance and compliance protocols are critical for any organization, and Azure makes it easier to realize with its comprehensive suite of support facilities. From creating data management policies to tracking compliance, Azure's services are available to guide companies every step of the way.

The Azure Policy is a core service that aids businesses in creating data management policies, which are fundamental building blocks of a strong data governance strategy. These policies can define the types of resources to be used, the location of these resources, and also put restrictions on naming conventions. Such rules help to maintain consistency, clarity, and control over the data, which is vital for effective governance. Another tool, Azure Blueprints, brings automation to the governance processes, enforcing organization-wide compliance in a unified, scalable manner. It helps with correct resource setup, delivering a way to orchestrate the deployment of various other Azure services, such as Resource Groups, Policies, Role-Based Access Control and more. Azure Monitor plays its part by helping track compliance at scale. It collects, analyses, and acts on telemetry data from your cloud and on-premises environments, helping to maintain visibility across applications, infrastructure, and network.

Azure also provides specific tools geared towards data security, forming a multi-layered defense against potential threats. Azure Security Center is a pivotal asset in this context, providing unified security management and advanced threat protection across hybrid cloud workloads. It helps in detecting and blocking malicious activities and aids in addressing potential security vulnerabilities in a timely manner, thereby reducing the surface area of attacks. Furthermore, another essential aspect of governance is cost management. Azure Cost Management provides businesses with the tools necessary to track cloud spending effectively, helping you get the most value out of Azure cloud resources.

The core tools that Azure provides for governance and compliance include:

- **Azure Policy**: For creating and managing data policies.

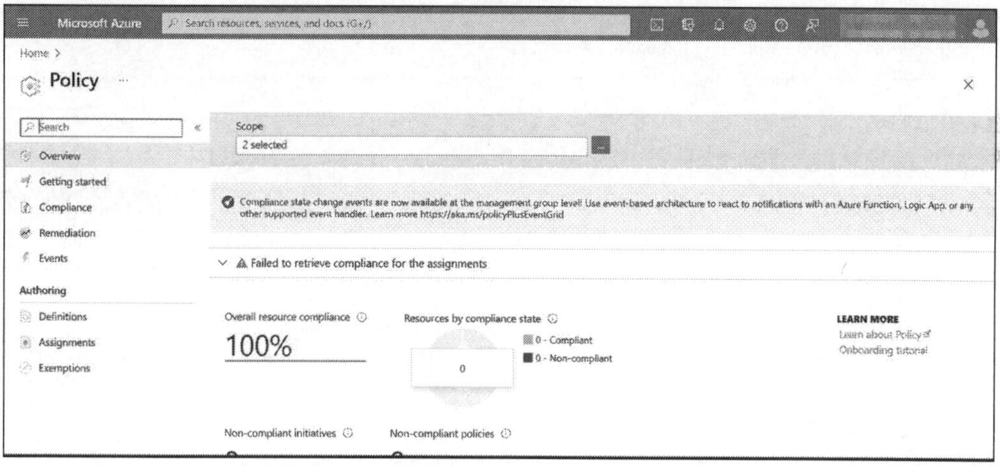

Figure 3.12: *Azure Policy dashboard*

- **Azure Blueprints**: To automate governance processes.

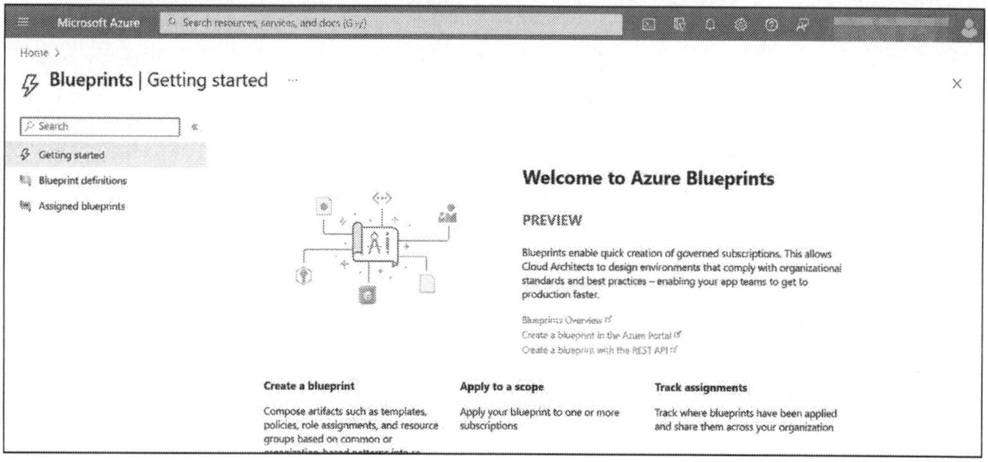

Figure 3.13: *Azure Blueprints dashboard*

- **Azure Monitor**: To track compliance.

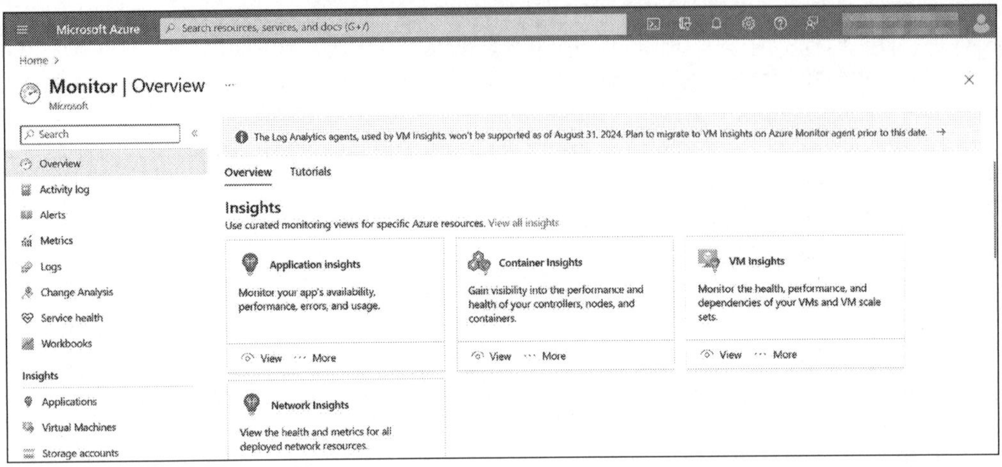

***Figure 3.14:** Azure monitor*

- **Azure Security Center:** For unified security management.

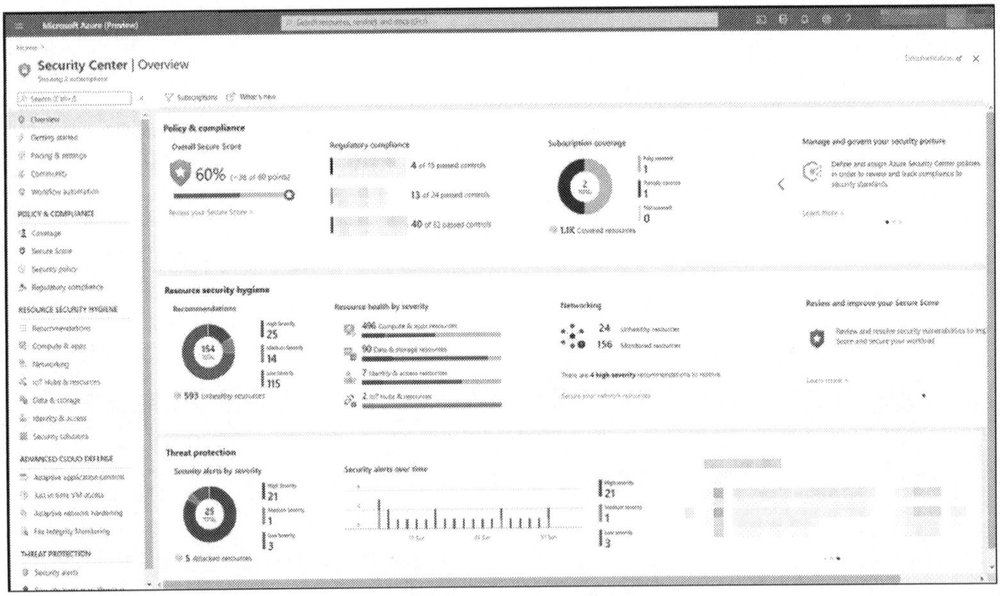

***Figure 3.15:** Azure security center*

- **Azure Cost Management:** To track and optimize cloud spending.

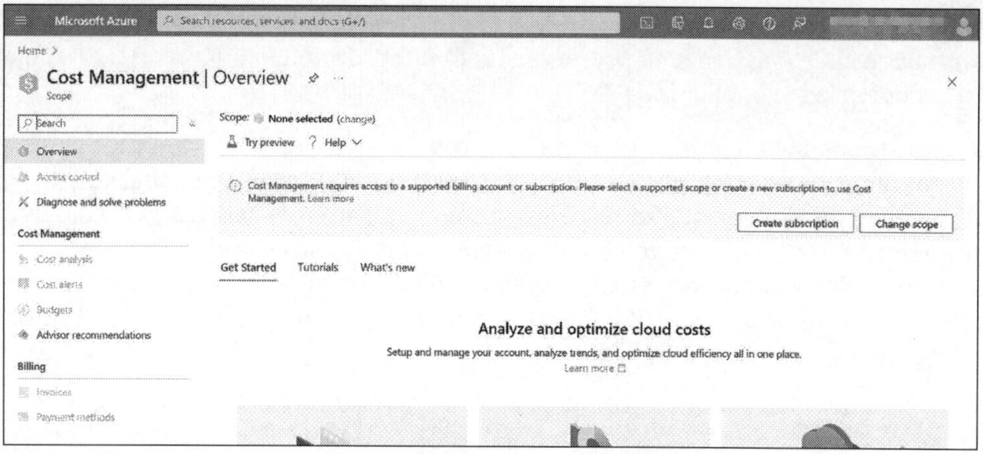

Figure 3.16: *Azure cost management*

By leveraging these tools effectively, businesses can build a robust governance and compliance strategy in Azure, ensuring data integrity, security, and value optimization.

Role of Governance and Compliance in Data Trustworthiness

Governance and compliance play a vital role in upholding data integrity and trust. Good governance ensures the availability, usability, consistency, data integrity, and data security, including protection of sensitive data. Adhering to compliance regulations not only prevents legal repercussions but builds customer trust and establishes business reputation.

Failing to properly govern data and comply with industry regulations can lead to loss of customer trust, legal problems, and financial penalties. Therefore, understanding and implementing data governance and compliance techniques is pivotal for successful data management in Azure.

Conclusion

In this chapter, we uncovered the diverse and rich landscape of data ingestion, storage, and management within Azure. We initiated our exploratory journey by understanding the critically foundational aspects of data ingestion and Azure's powerful storage options, which include Azure Data Lake Storage, Azure SQL Database, and Azure Blob Storage. Delving into the technical intricacies of Azure Data Lake Storage Gen2, we outlined its functionalities, the benefits it offers, and its comprehensive use-cases.

We shifted gears to focus on crucial and inseparable aspects of data management - data security and governance. We uncovered the multi-layered security features Azure possesses to fortify data protection, including encryption types, user authentication mechanisms, and access controls. Moreover, we addressed the critical role of governance and compliance in preserving data integrity and maintaining trust amidst various compliance stipulations.

In the forthcoming chapter, we will prepare ourselves to dive into another essential element of the data lifecycle with Azure. Data transformation and cleaning ensure that the raw data harvested to Azure is sifted, refined, error-free, and ready for analytics, paving the road to highly accurate and reliable insights. Azure continues to underscore its pivotal role in sound data management – ensuring an inclusive and robust data strategy – as we progress in this data-driven journey. Buckle up, as we continue to explore the vast universe of Azure's capabilities.

Questions

- Discuss the significance of data ingestion in the process of data analysis and business intelligence in today's digital landscape.
- How would you compare Azure SQL Database and Azure Blob Storage? Discuss their advantages and suitable use cases.
- Can you elaborate on the security measures that Microsoft's Azure provides to safeguard data?
- In the context of cloud storage, illustrate the role of RBAC (Role-Based Access Control) as a security measure in Azure?
- How does Azure address data governance and compliance with regard to different jurisdictions and industry-specific regulations?
- Does Azure Data Lake Storage Gen2 support both object and file system APIs?
- Is Azure Blob Storage suitable for storing large volumes of unstructured data?
- Does Azure use Transparent Data Encryption (TDE) to perform real-time encryption and decryption of databases?
- Is Azure Policy used in creating and enforcing policies to ensure compliance with corporate standards?
- Does Azure offer tools and services that assist in maintaining governance and ensuring compliance?

Multiple Choice Questions

1. Which Azure service is ideal for storing and analyzing petabyte-size files?

   a. Azure SQL Database

   b. Azure Blob Storage

   c. Azure Data Lake Storage

   d. Azure Data Factory

2. What does Azure Active Directory (Azure AD) handle?
   a. Authentication
   b. Data Storage
   c. Data Encryption
   d. Data Governance
3. Encryption type used for data at rest in Azure is?
   a. TLS
   b. Advanced Encryption Standard (AES)
   c. RSA
   d. None of the above
4. What does Azure Purview primarily help with?
   a. Data Analysis
   b. Data Governance
   c. Data Encryption
   d. Data Compression
5. Azure Security Center provides unified security management and _____.
   a. Disaster Recovery
   b. Advanced Threat Protection
   c. Encryption Management
   d. None of the above
6. Which of the following is NOT a data storage option in Azure?
   a. Azure Data Lake Storage
   b. Azure SQL Database
   c. Azure Blob Storage
   d. Azure Data Divide
7. What is Azure Cost Management primarily used for?
   a. Managing cloud spending
   b. Organizing data in the cloud
   c. Encrypting data
   d. Storing data

8. Which Azure service uses machine learning to detect and block malicious activities?
    a. Azure Blob Storage
    b. Azure Data Lake Storage
    c. Azure Security Center
    d. Azure SQL Database
9. Which Azure tool aids in creating data management policies?
    a. Azure Blueprints
    b. Azure Policy
    c. Azure Monitor
    d. Azure Key Vault
10. Which Azure service provides managed relational database service?
    a. Azure Blob Storage
    b. Azure Data Lake Storage
    c. Azure SQL Database
    d. Azure Data Factory
11. Which Azure service is a fully-managed cloud service that lets you run the Apache Hadoop ecosystem in the cloud?
    a. Azure Databricks
    b. Azure SQL Database
    c. Azure HDInsight
    d. Azure Machine Learning
12. Which service in Azure acts as a safeguard for cryptographic keys and other secrets used by cloud applications and services?
    a. Azure Active Directory
    b. Azure Key Vault
    c. Azure Policy
    d. Azure Monitor
13. What is Azure Blob Storage best suited for?
    a. Storing relational data
    b. Running high-performance databases

    c. Storing large volumes of unstructured data
    d. All of the above

14. Which service in Azure is used for creating data pipelines for orchestrating and automating data movement and data transformation?
    a. Azure Machine Learning
    b. Azure Stream Analytics
    c. Azure Databricks
    d. Azure Data Factory
15. Which layer of Azure infrastructure is responsible for access and control management?
    a. Physical data center
    b. Network security
    c. Identity and Access
    d. None of the above

Answers

1. c
2. a
3. b
4. b
5. b
6. d
7. a
8. c
9. b
10. c
11. c
12. b
13. c
14. d
15. c

CHAPTER 4
Data Transformation and Cleaning

Introduction

In this chapter, we will unravel the hidden science behind effective data preprocessing and cleaning techniques. Expect to explore a range of fundamental concepts, from understanding the importance of accurate data cleaning to implementing advanced data transformation techniques using Azure Data Factory. As we navigate through this chapter, we equip ourselves with the tools and the know-how to deal with the complexities of both structured and unstructured data, thus breaking barriers between raw information and insightful analysis.

We will also plunge into the intricacies of data wrangling with Azure Databricks, unraveling its powerful ability to transform and shape data. Brace yourselves to decode data transformation pipelines and learn orchestration using Azure's state-of-the-art tools. By shining the spotlight on practical applications of Azure in data preprocessing, we put theory into practice, bringing abstract concepts to life. So, get ready to dive into a whirlpool of knowledge that will prepare your data for thorough and accurate analysis.

Structure

This chapter explores the following key themes:

- Overview of Data Transformation and Cleaning
- Understanding Data Preprocessing and Cleaning
- Azure Data Factory for Data Transformation
- Data Wrangling Using Azure Databricks
- Dealing with Structured and Unstructured Data
- Focus on Data Transformation Pipelines and Orchestration

Overview of Data Transformation and Cleaning

Data transformation refers to the process of modifying data into a format that allows for better analytics and effective decision-making. This procedure may involve several operations such as scaling, rotating, aggregating data, or even incorporating advanced mathematical transformations. It's a critical step in data preprocessing as it ensures the data complies with the algorithm's prerequisites, thereby improving machine learning models' effectiveness and accuracy.

On the other hand, data cleaning constitutes the process of identifying and correcting or removing errors, inconsistencies, duplicates, or inaccuracies in datasets. With data being sourced from various platforms, including web scraping, databases, or IoT devices, it is bound to possess irregularities. Data cleaning helps in maintaining the sanctity, reliability, and precision of the data. This cleaning process, quite often, is a tremendous task in itself, consuming approximately 80% of a data scientist's time. However, it is an investiture that's worth every minute, as the conclusions derived are as good as the data fed.

In conclusion, the process of data transformation and cleaning is crucial in the lifecycle of data analysis. By adequately cleaning and transforming data, we can ensure the generality and accuracy of models and insights that are generated. Although the responsibility is vast and sometimes complex, the development of various tools and platforms, such as Azure Data Factory and Azure Databricks, have significantly simplified the process, thus aiding data scientists immensely in their journey of uncovering hidden patterns and relationships within data. Let's explore more about these tools in upcoming sections of this chapter.

Understanding Data Preprocessing and Cleaning

The art of data analysis starts with pristine data gathering and treatment. Within this treatment phase, two integral elements come to the fore: data preprocessing and data cleaning. These procedures lay the foundation for quality analytical outcomes.

Definition and Importance

Data preprocessing is essentially the transformation phase, where raw data gets converted into a comprehensive format. This phase is characterized by data cleaning, data transformations, data integration, and data reduction. Each of these tasks amplifies the quality of the data, which assists in enhancing the structure and potency of the models generated.

Meanwhile, data cleaning operates as an error-rectifying cell within preprocessing. It's primarily fixing or removing the inconsistencies and errors in the datasets. These discrepancies can spring from numerous sources, like human errors, system-related inconsistencies, or mismatches during data integration with varying formats.

The role of data preprocessing and cleaning is significant in the world of data science. Since high-quality, clean data facilitates accurate analysis, it is revered by analysts and organizations alike. These preliminary steps serve as a guarantee of trustworthiness in the data. They enable better decision-making capabilities since the predictions depend heavily on these initial processes. According to experts, data scientists expend up to 80% of their time on data preprocessing and cleaning.

Basic Techniques of Data Cleaning

Data cleaning is brought to action through a connected series of techniques. To begin with, data auditing works on the principle of employing statistical methodologies to discover anomalies in the data. It is invaluable in spotting operational mistakes, inconsistencies, or unusual entries. Various data profiling tools can provide solid support in this stage of auditing, especially marking values that appear suspiciously apart from the norm.

The next step is implementing data cleaning via workflows, which involve detecting, categorizing, and rectifying errors as defined during the data auditing process. A manageable form of this is stating constraints that the data must align with and performing checks accordingly.

Data imputation adds another layer of refinement as it focuses on filling missing values through reasonable approximations, often derived through statistical models. Common imputation methods utilize tactics such as mean/median/mode, regression models, or even advanced machine learning algorithms to fill the gaps.

The Outlier detection technique scans for data points that tend to differ unusually from the rest of the dataset. These outliers can either be genuine data inconsistencies or just statistical anomalies. Based on the cause and the nature of the anomaly, a decision is made to correct or ignore the outlier.

Finally, the cleaning process also includes data transformation and data reduction stages. While in transformation, data is morphed to fit the requirements of the investigation method or model, whereas data reduction employs dimensionality reduction techniques to create an accurate representation of the data with significantly fewer variables.

Undoubtedly, data preprocessing and cleaning play a fundamental role in data science, paving the way for a meticulous treatment of the data and a cognizant understanding of the area of study. The employed methods can range from simple statistical ones to complex machine learning algorithms, but the common objective rings loud - achieving quality data for intelligent and accurate decision-making.

Azure Data Factory for Data Transformation

In this section, we shift our focus towards another important tool for data transformation in the realm of data science - Azure Data Factory. Serving as a core data integration service, Azure Data Factory simplifies the process of data transfer and transformation, making it a valuable tool for data scientists globally.

Introduction to Azure Data Factory

Azure Data Factory (ADF) is a sophisticated, cloud-based data integration tool provided by Microsoft, specifically designed to simplify the process of transforming and loading data from a myriad of sources to a singular, refined format. This comprehensive tool plays a crucial role in the daily routines of data engineers and data scientists, enabling them to handle data more efficiently in an era where *'data is king'*.

The Azure Data Factory operates with compute services such as Azure HDInsights, Azure Data Lake Analytics, Hadoop, and Spark to process and modify data. It means that data engineers and data scientists can leverage the significant computation power of ADF to make data compatible to their specific requirements and manipulate it with great efficiency. Consequently, the actual value of the data can be efficiently harnessed.

A salient feature of the Azure Data Factory is its ability to automate data transformation procedures. This critical function eliminates the necessity of repetitive and supererogatory tasks and provides a highly convenient option to data engineers and data scientists focusing on other crucial aspects of their jobs instead. Automation in today's world is vital as it significantly reduces the chance of errors.

The second pivotal element in the Azure Data Factory service portfolio is the ETL (Extract, Transform, Load) operations. With these operations, you can define specific conditions and steps for extracting data from various sources, transforming it to conform to a particular, consistent format and finally loading it into an endpoint (such as a database) for further analysis or visualization. This function represents the essence of most data-related tasks and is vital in successfully completing many data-centric projects.

Azure Data Factory excels when handling big volumes of data. In our data-driven world, the ability to manage large amounts of data efficiently is a crucial advantage, as it often directly correlates with the success of the business. The scalable nature of

ADF means that irrespective of the size of your data, ADF can adjust itself to deal with any level of demand optimally.

The Azure Data Factory, with its impressive arsenal of features, is a formidable tool for managing and manipulating data. Its various aspects, such as the automation of data transformation processes, defining ETL steps, and handling big data, make it a valuable asset for any data engineer or data scientist. Overall, it is an indispensable tool, making life easier for those involved in the data management and analysis process.

Benefits of Using Azure Data Factory in Data Transformation

Azure Data Factory offers plentiful benefits in data transformation, making it an asset in a data scientist's toolkit. One primary advantage is its scalability and performance when dealing with big data. It supports a wide range of data sources, extending from SQL Data Sources to NoSQL and even social media platforms.

Another key benefit of ADF resides in its ease of transformations. With ADF, you can clean and transform unstructured data into insights that drive business decision-making. These transformations take place in a secure and compliant manner, adhered to by Azure's security measures.

Moreover, it makes it easier to construct ETL and ELT processes without the need for coding, which saves time and enhances efficiency. Finally, the built-in dashboards and management tools of ADF bring visibility and monitoring to your pipeline runs and performance.

Step-by-Step Guide to Using Azure Data Factory

So, let's dive deeper into understanding how to utilize this invaluable tool for data transformation. Keep in mind, mastering Azure Data Factory can dramatically enhance a data scientist's ability to seamlessly manipulate and transform data. Now, here's a more detailed, step-by-step guide on how to use Azure Data Factory:

1. **Create a Data Factory**

   Log in to Azure Portal, and in the left-hand menu, select ***Create a Resource***. In the new window, search for ***Data Factory*** and select it. Click the **Create** button to start the process. You'll need to provide some specifics for your data factory, such as the name, subscription, resource group, region, and version. After filling in the information, click ***Review + Create*** to finalize the creation of your data factory.

2. **Create a data pipeline**

   Data pipelines are logical groupings of activities that perform a unit of work together. First, open your Azure Data Factory instance, and in the overview section, click **`Author and Monitor`**. This will open the Azure Data Factory interface. In this interface, click **`Author`** on the left-hand navigation bar. Now, click the three-dot button (...) and then click **`Pipeline`**. Give a name to your pipeline and hit **`OK`**.

3. **Create activities in the pipeline**

   Activities are the actions or units of work to be performed, like data movement activities or data transformation activities. For example, you can have an activity to copy data from blob storage to Azure SQL. Click the **`Move and Transform`** category and drag the CopyData activity to the central panel, linking it to the pipeline. In the new screen, select your source and destination datasets.

4. **Configure control flow settings**

   These include pipeline parameters, variables, and annotations that influence data flow execution. You can also add control flow activities which include conditions, switches and loops, and so on.

5. **Run the data pipeline**

   Once all the activities are created in the pipeline, you can publish your changes and run your pipeline. Click the **`Validate`** button to check for errors in the pipeline before publishing.

6. **Monitor the data pipeline**

   Azure Data Factory lets you monitor your data pipeline through Azure Monitor and Azure Log Analytics. You can view the status of pipeline runs, activity runs, trigger runs, and more. Data Factory provides visuals to understand the data lineage and system health. You can use in-built alerts for proactive monitoring.

7. **Debug and troubleshoot pipelines**

   Azure Data Factory provides capabilities such as breakpoints for debugging and logs for troubleshooting issues in the pipeline.

Through these steps, users can not only create and manage their data pipelines within Azure Data Factory, but also monitor the health and status of their operations to ensure the accurate transformation and integration of their data.

Data Wrangling Using Azure Databricks

One of the most crucial steps in data preprocessing for data scientists is Data Wrangling, which involves the process of transforming and mapping data from its raw form into another format with the purpose of making it more suitable and valuable for a variety of downstream purposes such as analytics.

Data Wrangling entails numerous operations including cleaning, normalizing, and transforming data; plotting diagrams; and computing statistics. As a complex and time-consuming aspect of data science, this is where Azure Databricks comes into play, adding real value with its advanced features for data wrangling.

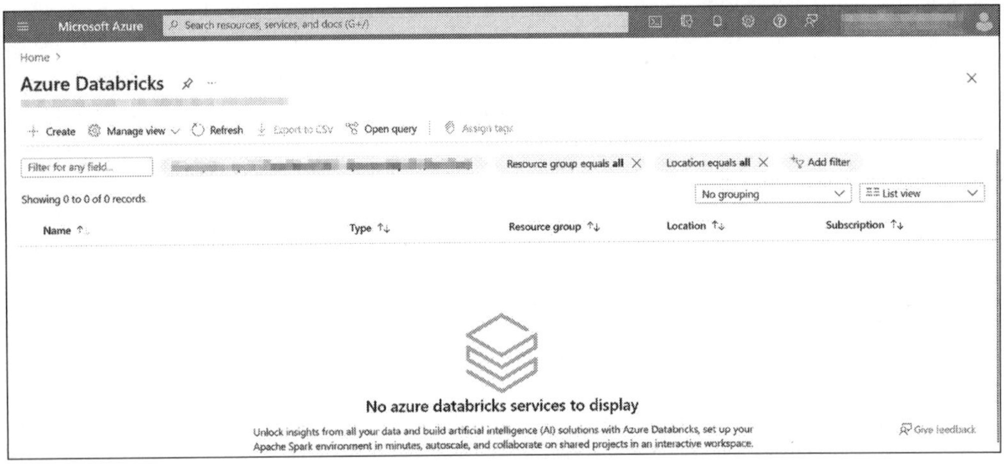

Figure 4.1: *Azure Databricks dashboard*

Introduction to Data Wrangling

Data Wrangling, colloquially known as data munging, is a crucial data processing technique within the field of data science and analytics. This method entails a meticulous transformation and mapping process that restructures unrefined, raw data into a form that is more suitable, meaningful, and ultimately more valuable to users.

At its core, data wrangling emphasizes three essential tasks: the cleaning, structuring, and enriching of raw data. Cleaning or cleansing the data involves sifting through the multitude of data to detect and correct, or remove, any errors or discrepancies. This could include anything from dealing with missing or incomplete data, irrelevant data, or even correcting erroneous entries. Cleaning data enables the analyst or the system to focus only on the data that is relevant and accurate.

Structuring data, on the other hand, involves organizing the raw data in a manner that makes better sense to both the end-user and the system interpreting it. When working with large volumes of raw data, the data comes in various disparate formats, which may not necessarily be cohesive or compatible with one another. To make this data usable, it needs to be formatted or restructured to fit into a consistent format which the analyzing system can comprehend.

Enriching data is the final step of data wrangling. This process involves augmenting the existing data by incorporating additional information or context. This could mean adding more attributes or dimensions to the data or linking different datasets together to create a singular, consolidated, and comprehensive record of data.

The ultimate goal of data wrangling is to empower the ability for better decision-making in less time. It is aimed at breaking down complex, turbulent heaps of uncertain data into comprehensible, reliable insights that can be used to drive strategic business decisions.

The benefit of data wrangling comes not only from the improved quality and structure of the data but also from the deeper insights it provides. The process of wrangling allows for the identification of key patterns and revealing of hidden trends within the data, which, in turn, can lead to more effective and insightful analysis. These insights can guide businesses in making more informed decisions, reducing risks, and identifying new opportunities.

In summary, data wrangling is a significant preliminary step in the data processing pipeline. It emphasizes the conversion of raw, crude data into a more organized, meaningful, and insightful format, which in turn, amplifies the effectiveness of the subsequent data analysis.

Introduction to Azure Databricks

Azure Databricks is an analytics platform powered by Apache Spark, it provides a seamless experience for managing, structuring, and analyzing big data. It has built-in capabilities to prepare and clean massive volumes of data most efficiently and effectively. With its user-friendly, collaborative workspace, Azure Databricks allows data scientists to create, explore, and automate data pipelines, reducing the data wrangling time substantially.

Azure Databricks integrates beautifully with various Azure services providing a unified platform for data warehousing, machine learning, and advanced analytics. Moreover, Azure Databricks offers a host of features including easy-to-use notebook workflows, readily available scale-outs, and data exploration tools that make it a desired platform by data scientists across the globe.

Step-by-Step Guide on Implementation of Data Wrangling with Azure Databricks

Implementing data wrangling with Azure Databricks involves a few key steps:

1. **Import Your Data:**

   In Azure Databricks, you may start importing the data by reading it into a

DataFrame. For example, to load a CSV file from Azure Blob storage, following is a sample code snippet:

```
storage_account_name = "<Your-Azure-Storage-Account-Name>"
storage_account_access_key = "<Your-Azure-Storage-Account-Access-Key>"
file_type = "csv"
file_location = "wasbs://<Your-Blob-Container>@{}.blob.core.windows.net/<Path-to-Your-File>".format(storage_account_name)

spark.conf.set(
  "spark.hadoop.fs.azure.account.key."+storage_account_name+".blob.core.windows.net.",
  storage_account_access_key)

df = spark.read.format(file_type).option("inferSchema", "true").option("header", "true").load(file_location)
```

Figure 4.2: *Importing data using Python*

2. **Explore Your Data**

   You can use the `` `display(df)` `` function for visual inspection of the imported dataset or `` `df.describe().show()` `` to get the statistical summary of numeric columns.

```
display(df)
df.describe().show()
```

Figure 4.3: *Commands to describe the data*

3. **Clean Your Data**

   The data cleaning step uses multiple functions to remove null values, duplicates, and any inconsistencies in the dataset.

```
#Drop rows with null values
df = df.dropna()

#Remove duplicates
df = df.dropDuplicates()

#To replace inconsistent entry
df = df.replace("Old_Value","New_Value")
```

Figure 4.4: *Cleaning data*

4. **Normalize Your Data**

   To normalize numeric columns, you can use the `MinMaxScaler` function from `pyspark.ml.feature`.

```
from pyspark.ml.feature import MinMaxScaler
from pyspark.ml.linalg import Vectors

# Assuming your DataFrame has a column named "Feature_Col" to be normalized
assembler = VectorAssembler(inputCols=["Feature_Col"], outputCol="Feature_Vector")
df = assembler.transform(df)

scaler = MinMaxScaler(inputCol="Feature_Vector", outputCol="Normalized_Feature")
scaler_model = scaler.fit(df)
df = scaler_model.transform(df)
```

Figure 4.5: *Normalizing data*

5. **Transform Your Data**

   Depending on your use case, you might have to transform your data. For example, if you want to create a new column based on the existing column.

```
from pyspark.sql.functions import udf
from pyspark.sql.types import IntegerType

# Assuming your DataFrame has a column to be transformed named "Existing_Col" and
# you want to transform this column to an integer type
udf_func = udf(lambda x: int(x) if x else None, IntegerType())
df = df.withColumn("Transformed_Col", udf_func("Existing_Col"))
```

Figure 4.6: *Transforming data*

6. **Export Your Data**

   Once you have cleaned and transformed your data, you can write it back to Blob storage or any other storage platform that Azure supports.

```
output_location = "wasbs://<Your-Blob-Container>@{}.blob.core.windows.net/<Output-
Path>".format(storage_account_name)

df.write.format(file_type).save(output_location)
```

Figure 4.7: *Exporting the data*

7. **Automate Your Data Pipeline**

   Finally, Azure Databricks enables automating the data wrangling process via job scheduling. The scheduling can be done using Databricks' UI in the Jobs tab or using Databricks' REST API.

   This guide, while simple, can form the backbone of any data wrangling process you ought to undertake in Azure Databricks. These steps can be expanded and customized to fit specific project requirements.

   By following these steps, data scientists can leverage Azure Databricks to perform efficient and effective data wrangling, saving them precious time and resources.

Dealing with Structured and Unstructured Data

In the world of big data and machine learning, data comes in various forms. As data scientists, you'll have to deal with a wide range of data types. Primarily, we divide data into two types - structured and unstructured. This section will delve into the differences between structured and unstructured data, the challenges associated with both, and useful techniques for dealing with them.

Differences Between Structured and Unstructured Data

Structured and unstructured data are two fundamental types of data that organizations encounter while dealing with multiple data sources. Recognizing the difference between these two types of data will not only enhance our understanding of data analysis but also enable us to comprehend and utilize the data effectively (see *Table 4.1*).

Structured	**Unstructured**
Structured data adheres to a specific model that governs its organization and arrangement.	Unstructured data doesn't neatly fit into traditional row-and-column databases or prespecified models.
This data is clean, easy to search, and usually stored in a conventional database.	This data is non-uniform and its analysis and interpretation are time-consuming.
It follows a specific format and pattern that aids easy searching.	Unstructured data can be found in varied formats, including text files, emails, videos, and more.

Structured data is easier to analyze and organize due to its structured nature.	It can also be generated through mobile activity, social media, and websites, and is hard to categorize.
Commonly stored in Relational Database Management Systems (RDMS) such as SQL databases.	The variety in its formats and speed of creation makes handling unstructured data more complex than structured data. Processing this data requires different kinds of analytical methods and tools, such as NLP and text analytics.
An example is a 'Customers' table in SQL where each row is a customer and columns represent specific customer information.	An example is data harvested from social media sites such as Twitter and Facebook, which is extremely diverse.

Table 4.1: *Difference between structured and unstructured data*

Understanding the Challenges

Structured data refers to any type of data that resides in a fixed field within a database or record. This type of data is straightforward and easy to analyze due to its organized nature. However, this structured data framework can pose complex challenges, including:

- **Inflexibility**

  The major problem associated with structured data is its lack of flexibility. The rigid structure, which makes it easy to input and analyze data that perfectly fits into the prescribed format, poses a significant problem when the data deviates from the standard model. A change in a single field would require modification in the whole structure of the database, making it a daunting task. This inability to easily accommodate varying data types for storage and retrieval can create significant barriers to effective data use.

- **Cost and Time**

  Implementing changes to structured data can be expensive and time-consuming. Including new, unexpected, or differently formatted data might necessitate an overhaul of the existing database system. This process, apart from being labor-intensive and requiring specialized technical expertise to implement, can also cause considerable downtime in accessing the information.

Unstructured data, on the other hand, refers to information that doesn't reside in a traditional database. Unstructured data can be textual or non-textual, and includes data including emails, videos, photos, social media posts, surveillance video footage, transaction receipts, web pages, and much more. While its format offers a lot of flexibility, it comes with its own set of challenges.

- **Data Extraction**

Due to its lack of a predefined structure, it can be complex to extract meaningful information from unstructured data. Traditional data mining tools might prove ineffective when it comes to handling this type of data since it can take varied forms and structures. This in turn creates a need for sophisticated artificial intelligence algorithms and expert human intervention to extract cogent insights.

- **Analytical Difficulties**

Making an effective analysis and interpretation from a vast pool of unstructured data is another significant obstacle. Unlike the structured data where tools can easily crunch numbers, unstructured data does not always follow the same luxury. The analysis can often seem like finding a needle in a haystack due to the vast volume and varied formats of unstructured data.

- **Volume and Storage**

The explosion of digitization has led to an avalanche of unstructured data. Blogs, tweets, emails, videos, audios, and many other digital content forms produce terabytes of unstructured data daily. Storing this vast data requires significantly more storage space, increasing the infrastructure costs. This huge volume of data poses a significant computational challenge and raises concerns over data safety and redundancy.

- **Computational Exhaustion**

The process of sorting, processing, and analyzing unstructured data requires substantial computational resources. As data size grows, so does the computational effort needed to manage and process the information. This can overtax system resources and potentially degrade system performance, which would impact all users in an organization. Therefore, effective data management strategies must be in place to ensure that unstructured data can be handled without negatively affecting system performance.

To sum up, both structured and unstructured data come with their own unique set of challenges. While structured data struggles with flexibility and adaptability, unstructured data proves challenging in terms of extraction, analysis, volume, storage, and computational needs. That's why an optimum approach often involves adopting a hybrid data management system that combines the best of both structured and unstructured data. This allows the system to offer rigid, easy-to-manage tables for rapidly processing certain types of data while also supporting flexibility for evolving data needs.

Techniques to Deal with Structured and Unstructured Data

Working with varied types of data, such as structured and unstructured data, is an integral part of a data scientist's job profile. Each type of data brings its unique characteristics that require a distinct way of handling and processing to extract valuable information.

Structured Data

Structured data essentially refers to the data that is organized in a uniform manner across rows and columns. Examples of structured data might include PostgreSQL databases, Excel spreadsheets, or any other source of tabular data. This kind of data is easier to handle as the format, and the schema of data is consistent throughout. Following are some techniques to manage structured data efficiently:

- **Database and SQL Queries**

  As the traditional method for managing structured data, relational databases offer excellent capabilities for storing and manipulating structured data through SQL (Structured Query Language) queries. SQL allows deep-dive analysis by enabling operations such as filtering, sorting, joining, and managing tables, and so on. For example, one can use SQL queries to filter out particular information from the database.

- **Statistical Analysis**

  Structured data, being quantitative by nature, can be subjected to in-depth statistical analysis to extract meaningful insights. Software solutions including R and Python libraries, such as pandas, NumPy, and SciPy, are commonly used for this purpose.

- **Machine Learning Algorithms**

  Machine learning can be extremely powerful when applied to structured data. Predictive models, such as Random Forests, Logistic Regression, Neural Networks, and so on, can be used to predict outcomes based on historical data.

Unstructured Data

Unstructured data is the kind of data that doesn't follow a specific format or schema. Specific examples of unstructured data include emails, audio files, video files, social media posts, and more. Owing to its non-uniform nature, dealing with unstructured data can be complex and challenging. Here are some techniques to use when handling unstructured data:

- **NoSQL Databases**

  NoSQL databases provide a way to store and retrieve data that is modeled in ways other than the tabular relations used in relational databases. NoSQL databases are becoming increasingly popular for working with unstructured data due to their scalability and flexibility. Leveraging NoSQL databases, such as MongoDB, Couchbase, and so on, one can store data with dynamic or flexible schema.

- **Big Data Processing Frameworks**

  When dealing with a large amount of unstructured data, big data processing frameworks, such as Hadoop, Spark, and so on, can be extremely beneficial. These tools provide distributed and parallel processing capabilities to handle vast volumes of data efficiently.

- **Natural Language Processing (NLP)**

  NLP is a subset of AI that deals with the interaction between computers and humans. Using NLP techniques, one can perform sentiment analysis on social media text data, spam detection in emails, chatbot development, and so on.

- **Image/Video Analysis Techniques**

  Today, there are various advanced techniques like Convolutional Neural Networks (CNN), object detection algorithms, and so on, which can effectively analyze images or videos and extract valuable information. For instance, using these techniques, companies can perform tasks such as face detection, medical image analysis, vehicle detection, and many more.

In conclusion, while each type of data presents its unique set of challenges, understanding their nature and knowing the appropriate techniques to handle them can help data science professionals extract maximum value from the data. It is crucial to understand and adapt to the ever-evolving landscape of data analysis to uncover meaningful insights effectively.

Focus on Data Transformation Pipelines and Orchestration

The importance of data pipelines and orchestration in the flow and management of information cannot be overstated. As the world is becoming more digitalized, an increasing amount of data is generated for various levels of analysis. This information needs to be processed and transferred from one point to another efficiently and effectively. This critical task is performed by data pipelines and choreographed by orchestration. It's through these that raw and unprocessed data is structured into understandable formats, allowing it to be analyzed and transformed into valuable insights.

The data pipeline refers to the series of processes and steps that allow the movement and transformation of data from its raw state to a more usable format. Fundamentally, it is a set of actions that extract data from various sources, transform it according to business rules or user needs, and then load it into a data warehouse for storage or further processing. The pipeline can perform these actions at great speed and on a massive scale, thereby ensuring a constant flow of transformed data. Its services prove critical in big data analytics, real-time streaming applications, and many other areas where speedy and reliable processing of large datasets is crucial.

Orchestration, on the other hand, is what ties together these processes into a single, harmonious workflow. It coordinates the execution of the tasks within the workflow, responsible for managing the allocation and scheduling of resources. Orchestrated processes are designed to be fault-tolerant and resilient, meaning they can recover smoothly from failures and ensure the reliable operation of the overall process. Orchestration tools are essential in automating repetitive tasks and reducing errors, thereby saving time and efforts in managing complex workflows.

The integration of data pipelines and orchestration is essential to ensure the right data is available at the right time and in the right form. This precondition is crucial to the delivery of accurate and timely analysis. It's like setting the stage for a performance: the data pipeline is the script that outlines what needs to happen when, while orchestration is the director making sure that everything happens smoothly and as per the script.

Data pipelines and orchestration offer a powerful solution for handling and managing an organization's data, facilitating a smooth path from raw data to actionable knowledge. As they continue to evolve, they will fundamentally shape the future of business intelligence and data analytics.

Understanding Data Transformation Pipelines

A data transformation pipeline refers to the series of steps involved in moving data from the source to a data storage or analysis system. Each step in the pipeline denotes an individual job that forms part of the whole process. Steps may involve such processes as extraction, cleaning, transformation, and loading (ETL), which can be as simple as extracting data from a source and loading it into a data warehouse to complex sequences of data manipulations involving various tools and languages.

Data transformation pipelines are essential, as they convert data into a usable format that can be easily analyzed. They enable organizations to handle large volumes of data in real-time. Working with a well-defined and effective data transformation pipeline means efficiently translating raw and messy data into insightful information for data-driven decision making.

The Role of Orchestration in Data Transformation Pipelines

Orchestration in data transformation pipelines refers to the automated configuration, coordination, and management of complex computer systems and services. In the context of data pipelines, orchestration is responsible for coordinating the automation of the data pipelines process, ensuring each job in the pipeline is successfully completed before the successive job begins.

Orchestration aids in streamlining the pipeline processes, reducing the risk of errors, and enforcing data integrity. It also helps in scheduling and monitoring data pipelines, allowing for proactive troubleshooting of any issues that arise in the transformation process.

Orchestration engines often come with data pipeline tools to handle dependencies between jobs, scheduling, and error handling. This leads to more reliable data delivery and allows data engineers and data scientists to focus more on data transformation and analysis processes.

Use of Azure Features in Pipeline Orchestration

Azure is one of the industry-leading cloud computing platforms that provide several essential services that cater to pipeline orchestration. Azure Data Factory and Azure Logic Apps are primary examples.

Azure Data Factory is a cloud-based data integration service that orchestrates and automates the transformation and movement of data from various sources. It allows you to construct data-driven workflows for orchestrating and automating data movement and data transformation.

On the other hand, Azure Logic Apps provide a user-friendly platform to build integrated solutions, automating workflows and business processes.

Both of these provide powerful connectivity across various data sources and have robust monitoring and management capabilities, assisting in creating, scheduling, and orchestrating data flows effectively.

To sum up, the smooth functioning of your data transformation pipelines and orchestration processes is critical for effective data analysis. A platform like Azure brings the required efficiency, accuracy, and scalability to your data processing tasks.

Conclusion

This chapter provided an in-depth understanding of data transformation and cleaning, explaining their importance in data science. We delved into various aspects of data preprocessing and explored basic techniques related to data cleaning.

We introduced Azure Data Factory as a powerful tool for data transformation and discussed its numerous benefits, in addition to a detailed guide on how to use it. We highlighted the practical applications of data wrangling using Azure Databricks and walked through a step-by-step process of implementing it.

Recognizing the diversity in data types, the chapter also covered how to handle both structured and unstructured data, their concise differences, challenges that come with each and practical techniques to effectively deal with such variances.

Lastly, we explored the concept of data transformation pipelines and the role of orchestration in it. A closer look at Azure's features in the orchestration of these pipelines offered a comprehensive understanding of how data can be efficiently transformed and managed.

As we progress to the upcoming chapter, we will step into the intriguing world of Machine Learning. Leveraging the knowledge gained in this chapter about data preprocessing, transformation, and management, we will delve into how these processed data can be used for predictive analyses and modeling in machine learning.

Questions

- Can you elaborate on the step-by-step guide to using Azure Data Factory in data transformation?
- How do you define Data Wrangling, and what are its notable features?
- How might you handle the challenges of structured and unstructured data?
- Discuss the role of orchestration in data transformation pipelines.
- Is there a simple solution to dealing with both structured and unstructured data?
- Does Azure Data Factory simplify the process of data transformation?
- Can basic techniques of data cleaning handle all types of datasets?
- How do Azure Databricks and Azure Data Factory differ in functionality and application?
- Given the option, would you prefer to use Azure Databricks for data wrangling over any other tool? Why or why not?
- Do you consider it essential to have orchestration in data transformation pipelines?

Multiple Choice Questions

1. Which tool is particularly suited for data transformation?

   a. Azure Databricks

   b. Azure Data Factory

   c. AWS Lambda

   d. Google Cloud Datastore

2. What is a major difference between structured and unstructured data?

   a. Volume

   b. Complexity

   c. Organization

   d. Source

3. Why is data cleaning necessary before any data transformation process?

   a. To simplify the data

   b. To remove redundancies

   c. To ensure accurate results

   d. All of the above

4. What is the main task of Data Wrangling?

   a. Data storage

   b. Data transformation

   c. Data visualization

   d. Data security

5. Which Azure feature is specifically designed for pipeline orchestration?

   a. Azure Functions

   b. Azure Logic Apps

   c. Azure DevOps

   d. Azure Active Directory

6. An orchestration plan in the data transformation pipeline is meant to ________.

   a. Reduce data volume

   b. Increase processing speed

   c. Manage resources and dependencies

   d. Enhance security

7. Azure Databricks is primarily used for...
   a. Data visualization
   b. Data storage
   c. Data Wrangling
   d. Data security
8. True or False: All data needs to be cleaned before being processed.
   a. True
   b. False
9. What is the main advantage of using Azure Data Factory in data transformation?
   a. Increased speed
   b. Reduced cost
   c. Integrated environment
   d. Enhanced security
10. Is it possible to handle both structured and unstructured data using Azure Databricks?
    a. Yes
    b. No
11. Which feature distinguishes Azure Data Factory from other data processing tools?
    a. Scalability
    b. Visual interface
    c. High cost
    d. Limited functionality
12. True or False: Data wrangling and data cleaning are the same.
    a. True
    b. False

13. What is the primary benefit of data preprocessing?
    a. Data reduction
    b. Cost saving
    c. Time-saving
    d. Improved accuracy
14. True or False: Orchestration in data transformation pipelines is about managing the order of operations.
    a. True
    b. False
15. Which of the following is NOT a basic technique of data cleaning?
    a. Missing value treatment
    b. Outlier detection
    c. Noise removal
    d. Data visualization

Answers

1. b
2. c
3. d
4. b
5. b
6. c
7. c
8. a
9. c
10. a
11. b
12. b
13. d
14. a
15. d

CHAPTER 5
Introduction to Machine Learning

Introduction

Machine learning, a critical component of artificial intelligence, is no longer an elusive concept; it is incredibly significant in our daily lives. This chapter seeks to help you unravel the world of machine learning by providing you a firm grounding in its basics.

Starting with the fundamentals, we describe the majortypes of machine learning – supervised, unsupervised, and reinforcement learning. We delve into their principles, applications, and the differentiation among them. Following this, we explore the crux of machine learning algorithms such as classification, regression, and clustering. This segment presents a comprehensive view of how these algorithms operate and their real-life implications.

Subsequently, we focus on feature engineering and selection, integral processes in machine learning for the creation and optimization of features that feed into learning models. In the subsequent section, we switch gears to discuss evaluation metrics, providing you with the tools to assess the performance and accuracy of your machine learning models.

Finally, the chapter concludes with a deep dive into bias, fairness, and ethics in machine learning. An understanding of these aspects is invaluable as the consequence of their neglect can yield misleading and divisive outcomes.

By the end of this chapter, you will establish a solid understanding of the core principles, tools, and ethical implications of machine learning, preparing you for further exploration of this thrilling field.

Structure

In this chapter, you will learn the following:

- Fundamentals of Machine Learning
- Overview of Machine Learning Algorithms
- Feature Engineering and Selection
- Evaluation Metrics for Machine Learning Models
- Bias, Fairness, and Ethics Considerations in Machine Learning

Fundamentals of Machine Learning

This section aims to lay the foundational understanding of the significant components of machine learning – Supervised Learning, Unsupervised Learning, and Reinforcement Learning. Each provides distinct learning methods, offering different ways to look at and solve problems.

Supervised Learning

Supervised learning is a form or method of artificial intelligence (AI), more specifically, a type of machine learning algorithm. The method uses labelled training datasets to instruct, teach, and educate the machine learning algorithm. In this type of learning scenario, both the input and the output variables are provided. The algorithm is then guided to map a function that establishes a link between these input and output variables. This learning method is often referred to as the teacher-student model, as the algorithm continuously learns from the training dataset similar to how a student learns from a teacher.

Let us understand in detail through an example. Let us assume there are two types of fruits – an apple and an orange – that we need to identify using a machine learning model. In the supervised learning method, we provide labeled data such as images of apples and oranges to the model. With powerful analytic capabilities, the model learns to discern the unique characteristics of each fruit (like color, size, shape, and so on) from the provided labeled examples. Over time, when this model is given a new image of either fruit, it would be able to identify whether it is an apple or an orange, based on its learnings.

Unsupervised Learning

Unsupervised learning is another form of Machine Learning which relies on pattern recognition and deriving structures from data. Here, unlike in supervised learning, the algorithm works on its own to discover information that is not provided with any labels or categorizations. The focus is more on finding the underlying structure and patterns in the data rather than predicting output for a specific input.

Let us consider an example to illustrate this concept further. Let us take a basket of various fruits – apples oranges, strawberries, and bananas. In unsupervised learning, the machine learning model is merely provided with this data, without any labels. The model might not initially know what an apple or banana is, but it will learn to differentiate and cluster these fruits based on specific patterns and similarities like size, color, shape, and texture. The machine thus learns to identify different groups, without prior knowledge about these fruits.

Table 5.1 shows the difference between Supervised and Unsupervised algorithms:

Supervised Algorithm	**Unsupervised Algorithm**
Labeled Data Supervised learning relies heavily on labelled data. The quality and quantity of this data can significantly impact the model's performance. Thus, the labeled data must be accurate and relevant to ensure the model makes precise predictions.	**Labeled Data** Unlike in supervised learning, the datasets used in unsupervised learning are unlabeled. This makes unsupervised learning less complex and time-consuming as the tedious task of data labeling is not required.
Training and Testing The labeled data is split into two portions – one for training and the other for testing. The training set is to teach the model, while the testing set is used to evaluate the model's performance.	**Training and Testing** Since there is no output to be predicted, the concept of splitting the dataset for testing and training purposes does not apply in unsupervised learning.
Algorithms Popular algorithms in supervised learning include ***Support Vector Machines, linear and logistic regression, neural networks, decision trees, and Naive Bayes classifiers.***	**Algorithms** Common unsupervised learning algorithms include ***clustering methods (like k-means, hierarchical clustering) and association rules (such as Apriori, Eclat).***
Uses Supervised learning is frequently used in various fields like healthcare for predicting diseases, in finance for credit card fraud detection, in marketing for customer segmentation and targeting, in sales for predicting future sales based on historical data, and many other applications.	**Uses** Unsupervised learning is widely used in various sectors. For example, in marketing, it is used for customer segmentation. In social media, it is used for friend suggestions on platforms like Facebook. And in finance, it can be used to spot unusual transactions that could indicate fraud.

Limitations	**Limitations**
While supervised learning has its merits, it comes with its limitations. The model is only as good as the data it is trained on. So, if the data lacks diversity, the model will be biased. Also, procuring and labeling large datasets can be time-consuming and costly.	Some challenges with unsupervised learning include its difficulty in validating the results because the outcomes are unpredictable. It is also difficult to handle and manage if the dataset is vast and complex.

Table 5.1: *Supervised vs. unsupervised*

Reinforcement Learning

Reinforcement learning is another major type of machine learning that works in noticeably different ways from supervised and unsupervised learning methods. This method is focused on making strategic decisions, and it provides the model an ability to interact with its environment by producing actions and discovering errors or rewards. The goal of reinforcement learning is to find the most effective strategy, known as the policy, to yield the greatest possible cumulative reward.

To understand it better, let us use an example. Consider a self-learning robot trying to navigate a maze. The robot does not have any prior understanding of the environment. In reinforcement learning, the robot learns from its actions. Each wrong action (like hitting a wall) would result in a negative reward ('*punishment*'), and each correct move (like moving closer to the exit) would result in a positive reward ('*reward*'). Over time, by using the algorithm, the robot learns the most effective way to navigate the maze to achieve the highest cumulative reward (reaching the exit).

Some Key Pointers about Reinforcement Learning

With the broad understanding of reinforcement learning in place, let us venture into the fine details that make this learning path distinctly effective.

Reward System

Reinforcement learning operates on a reward system. Each correct action is rewarded, while each wrong action is either not rewarded or penalized, guiding the model towards the most effective operations.

Trial and Error

Unlike supervised and unsupervised learning, reinforcement learning is not trained on data but relies heavily on the trial and error method where the agent learns from its past experiences.

Algorithms

Common reinforcement learning algorithms include ***Q-Learning, Deep Q Network (DQN), State-Action-Reward-State-Action (SARSA), and Monte Carlo methods.***

Uses

Reinforcement learning is generally used in areas where making a sequence of decisions is crucial. This includes areas like robotics (for process automation), gaming (strategy formation), recommendation systems (user-behavior learning), and in computer system's resource management.

Challenges

The primary challenges of reinforcement learning include the need for lots of data and computation. Also, it may become less efficient in situations where instant feedback is not feasible.

In conclusion, Reinforcement Learning is a potent mechanism in the field of machine learning. It is well-suited to problems that include long-term sequential decision-making and when the data is highly uncertain. It is a continual learning process where learning is a by-product of experiencing and interacting, eventually leading to improved decisions over time. The key to reinforcement learning is leveraging the power of exploration, trial and error, and adaptation.

Overview of Machine Learning Algorithms

Algorithms are the backbone of machine learning. They form the basis for training the model and provide the path to learning from the data. In this section, we will delve into the core machine learning algorithms – Classification, Regression, and Clustering.

Classification

Classification is a key concept in machine learning, a subfield of artificial intelligence, where computer systems are trained to perform tasks by 'learning' from data. The primary goal of these methods is to predict and categorize different labels or classes within a dataset. In this context, a class refers to a particular group of data within a dataset, and labels are the identifiers for those classes. Thus, classification models learn from previously labeled data to classify new unseen data into these categories.

Types of Classification Algorithms

Let us delve deeper into the various classification algorithms used in machine learning:

- **Logistic Regression**

  Despite its name suggesting otherwise, logistic regression is a classification algorithm. It uses a logistic function to describe the relationship between the categorical dependent variable and the independent variables. The logistic function, often referred to as the sigmoid function, is an S-shaped curve that maps any real-valued number onto a value between 0 and 1 but never exactly at those limits. The sigmoid function is given by the formula:

$$S(x) = 1/(1+e^{\wedge}-x)$$

Here, S(x) represents the probability estimate. These values are used to predict the binary output, classifying data as 0 or 1 - akin to true/false, yes/no, or spam/not spam.

- **Decision Trees**

  A decision tree is a flowchart-like structure where each interior node denotes a test on an attribute, each branch represents the outcome of this test, and each leaf node is a class label. Starting from the root, data is divided based on attribute values, and this process continues recursively. Decision trees are intuitive and simple yet powerful tools for classification and even regression. The 'information gain' formula is central to decision tree algorithms:

$$IG(S,a) = H(S)- \Sigma (|Sv| / |S|) * H(Sv)$$

Here, IG(S, a) is the information gain after splitting set S based on attribute a, H(S) is the entropy of set S and Σ (|Sv| / |S|) * H(Sv) is the sum of entropies for each subset Sv.

- **Random Forest**

  Random forest, as the name indicates, consists of a large number of individual decision trees that operate as an ensemble. Each individual tree in the random forest brings out a class prediction, and the class with the most votes becomes the model's prediction. Random forest helps in attaining robustness against overfitting which decision trees are prone to.

- **Support Vector Machines (SVM)**

  This classification algorithm is best suited for binary classification but can also handle multi-class problems. SVM finds a hyperplane in N-dimensional space that distinctly classifies the data points, where N is the number of features. It selects the hyperplane that results in the maximum margin between classes. The formulation for SVM is often represented as a quadratic programming problem.

- **Naive Bayes Classifier**

  It is a simple but powerful classification algorithm that uses principles of probability based on Bayes' theorem along with an assumption of independence among predictors (features). The underlying principle implies that every feature contributes independently to the probability of the target outcome. This assumption is called 'class conditional independence'. The formula used in the Naive Bayes classifier is Bayes' Theorem:

$$P(A\backslash B) = [P(B\backslash A) * P(A)] / P(B)$$

Here, P(A|B) is the posterior probability of class A given predictor B. P(B|A) is the likelihood of predictor B given class A. P(A) and P(B) are the prior probabilities of class A and predictor B, respectively.

These classification algorithms, alongside others like K-nearest neighbors (KNN), Linear Discriminant Analysis (LDA), Gradient Boosting, and more, provide the foundation for creating intelligent systems capable of categorizing and making predictions from complex data. The model selection depends on the nature and complexity of the task at hand, the size of the dataset, the dimensionality of the features, and the computational resources available.

Regression

Regression is another prominent subfield in supervised machine learning. The primary goal in regression analysis is predicting and understanding the relationship between a dependent variable (also referred to as the target variable) and one or more independent variables (also known as predictors). Unlike classification, the target variables in regression are continuous in nature, such as age, income, sales, or house price.

Types of Regression Algorithms

Let us discuss some common regression algorithms used in machine learning:

- **Linear Regression**

  Linear Regression tries to fit a linear equation (Y = a*X + b, where 'Y' is the dependent variable, 'X' is the independent variable, 'a' is the slope, and 'b' is the y-intercept) between the observed data. The predictive capability is derived from the '*best fit line*' represented by this equation. The '*best fit*' is calculated by minimizing the sum of squared residuals (the difference between the actual and predicted value).

  - ***Simple Linear Regression***

    It involves a single independent variable

    The formula is $Y = a + b * X1$

- ***Multiple Linear Regression***

  It includes multiple independent variables.

  The formula is $Y = a + b1 * X1 + b2 * X2 + b3 * X3 + ... + bn * Xn$

- **Polynomial Regression**

  In Polynomial Regression, the relationship between the dependent variable and the independent variable is modeled as an nth degree polynomial. Polynomial regression can model relationships where the dependent variable and the independent variable have a nonlinear relationship.

  The general equation of a polynomial regression is:

  $Y = a + b1 * X + b2 * X^2 + b3 * X^3 + ... + bn * X\text{^}n$

- **Ridge Regression**

  Ridge regression is a method of estimating the coefficients of multiple-regression models in scenarios where independent variables are highly correlated. Ridge regression aids in analyzing multiple regression data that suffer from multicollinearity (high correlation among predictor variables). It adds a degree of bias to the regression estimates, which reduces the standard errors.

- **Lasso Regression**

  Least Absolute Shrinkage and Selection Operator (LASSO) is a type of regression that uses shrinkage. It performs both variable selection and regularization to enhance the prediction accuracy and interpretability of the statistical model it produces.

- **Elastic Net**

  Elastic Net is a regularized regression method that linearly combines the penalties of the lasso and ridge methods to handle multicollinearity, outlier effects and to achieve variable selection.

- **Logistic Regression**

  Despite its name, logistic regression is a fundamental classification method. It estimates the parameters of a logistic model and is generally used for binary classification problems.

- **Poisson Regression**

  Poisson Regression models are best used for modeling count data, that is, when the dependent variable has non-negative integer values representing counts, and our data is likely to follow a Poisson process.

- **Bayesian Linear Regression**

  Bayesian linear regression methods provide a probabilistic framework for making predictions. Using Bayesian methods, we can quantify the uncertainty of our predictions.

  The selection of a regression algorithm depends upon the problem at hand, the nature of the input and output variables, the computational efficiency required, and the level of precision required in the prediction. The more sophisticated methods, such as Lasso, Ridge, and Bayesian linear regression, provide additional layers of complexity and nuance, but they may also be computationally demanding. For a simpler problem with fewer variables, a standard linear or polynomial regression might suffice.

Clustering

Clustering is an unsupervised machine learning technique used to group unlabeled data together based on their inherent similarities. These similarities are quantified using measures such as distance, connectivity, and intensity. The aim is to segregate data into different groups so that the data points in the same group are more similar to each other than the points in other groups.

Key Clustering Algorithms in Machine Learning

Let us discuss some of the most prominent clustering algorithms often employed in the field of unsupervised machine learning:

- **K-Means Clustering**

  K-Means clustering is an iterative algorithm that divides a group of n datasets into k non-overlapping subgroups or clusters, where each dataset belongs to the cluster with the nearest mean. The number of clusters, K, is user-defined. The algorithm begins by randomly initializing 'K' centroids, and data points are clustered based on the minimum distance from these centroids. An iterative process of recalculating centroids and re-clustering data continues until centroid locations stabilize.

- **Hierarchical Clustering**

  In hierarchical clustering, the data is not partitioned into a particular cluster in a single step. Instead, a series of partitions takes place, which runs from a single cluster containing all objects to n clusters that each contain a single object. Hierarchical clustering can be classified into two types – Agglomerative and Divisive. In Agglomerative, the process starts with each object forming a separate group. It keeps on merging the objects or groups that are close to one another until all of the groups are merged into one or until the termination condition holds. In Divisive, the process is exactly the opposite of Agglomerative clustering.

- **DBSCAN (Density-Based Spatial Clustering of Applications with Noise)**

  This algorithm uses the concept of density to form clusters. It groups together points with many nearby neighbors. It is robust to outliers and can even find clusters of various shapes, unlike K-Means, which can only find convex clusters. This algorithm depends heavily on the distance measure (Euclidean distance is very commonly used), and its parameters include the radius of the neighborhoods and the minimum number of points needed to form a dense region.

- **Spectral Clustering**

  Spectral Clustering performs clustering using the spectrum (eigenvalues) of similarity matrices. It uses the top eigenvectors of a matrix derived from the distance between points to possible axes. It considers each data point as a graph-node and performs graph partitioning. This approach is particularly powerful for identifying clusters that, geometrically, are non-convex.

- **Mean-Shift Clustering**

  Mean-shift clustering is a sliding-window-based algorithm that aims to discover "*blobs*" in a smooth density of samples. It is a centroid-based algorithm that works by updating candidates for centroids to be the mean of the points within a given region. These candidates are then filtered in a post-processing stage to eliminate near-duplicates, forming the final set of centroids and hence cluster centres.

- **Affinity Propagation**

  This algorithm uses a message passing approach to clustering. Unlike other clustering methods, Affinity propagation chooses the number of clusters based on the data, and this number can also be manually adjusted with a preference parameter.

  Choosing an appropriate clustering algorithm typically comes down to the needs of your application, the nature of your data, and the context in which the clustering model will be deployed. Each method has its own strengths and weaknesses, and so the decision should be made considering these factors.

Feature Engineering and Selection

The success of a machine learning model heavily relies on the quality of data fed into it, and this is where feature engineering and selection play a critical role. This section will discursively explore what these steps involve and their significance in building a machine learning model.

Steps in Feature Engineering

Feature engineering is the process of creating, modifying, and selecting features that are fed into machine learning algorithms. This can greatly enhance the predictive performance of these models by assisting them in understanding patterns better. Feature engineering requires an extensive understanding of the data and is often domain-specific.

The feature engineering process comprises several steps:

Variable Transformation

Variable transformation entails altering the variables to make them fit the assumptions of the machine learning algorithms better. In many instances, ML algorithms necessitate input data to be Gaussian, normal or scaled from 0 to 1. Variable transformation assists in satisfying these assumptions.

Example: For instance, some algorithms like SVM and KMeans operate better when data variables are on the same scale. Thus, it is necessary to transform all the variable values from different ranges to the same range. This can be achieved using techniques such as normalization and standardization. Another example can be implementing log transformations on skewed data to achieve a more normalized distribution.

Some of the common transformations include:

- **Scaling:** Scale data to standardize their range by subtracting the mean and dividing by the standard deviation.
- **Normalization:** Change the values so that they fall within a smaller, specified range.
- **Binning:** Classify data into specified groups or ranges.
- **Logarithm:** Apply the logarithm function to compress large-scale data.

Variable Creation

This involves creating new features from the existing ones or even from external sources. These features will help the machine learning model to understand the signals better and enrich the features with additional relevant information.

Example: Let us assume that you are working with a dataset containing information on houses including their sizes (in square feet) and prices. A new feature could be created using '**price per square foot**'. This new feature may provide the algorithm with significant information that it may not have picked up from the individual '**size**' and '**price**' features.

Sometimes, variable creation could be used to introduce a higher dimension of complexity into a machine learning model. For instance, it can be used when trying to improve the accuracy of the model by modifying existing features. Moreover, variable creation might require significant computational resources, time, and expertise in the specific field and the data.

Another example is considering external factors such as holidays or special events to create a new feature. If the dataset is related to store sales, an additional feature could be created indicating whether a sale event, such as Black Friday, has happened in that period. While this new feature may not be directly correlated to the previous features, it might play a significant role in predicting the trends in the data.

Together, variable transformation and creation can significantly improve the results of machine learning models, enhancing their accuracy, robustness, and generalization capabilities. However, it is crucial to carefully consider the implications of each transformation or creation task. Irrelevant or redundant features might lead to overfitting or underfitting. Therefore, it is essential to experiment with different strategies and validate their performance before making final decisions. Hence, feature engineering is an iterative process, characterized by constant back and forth adjustments until the model achieves satisfactory performance.

Strategies for Attribute Selection

Just as feature engineering is important, feature selection is equally essential in building an efficient and accurate machine learning model. Feature selection is important to remove any unnecessary noise in the data, reduce overfitting, enhance model accuracy, and improve computation speed.

Methods for Feature Selection

Here are different methods used for feature selection:

Univariate Selection

Univariate selection is a statistical technique used to select the features which have the strongest relation with the target variable. This method uses statistical tests to select such features.

Assume we have a dataset with features X1, X2, ..., Xn and the target variable Y. In univariate selection, we will individually evaluate the relationship of X1, X2, ..., Xn with Y using a statistical test like the Chi-Squared test, ANOVA F-test, and more.

For instance, the Chi-Squared test calculates the Chi-square statistic, which follows a Chi-squared distribution when the null hypothesis is true, giving us a p-value. The features with lower p-values are considered more significant and thereby selected.

Recursive Feature Elimination (RFE)

This method works by fitting the model, evaluating it, and then discarding the least important feature. This process is repeated iteratively until all unimportant features are eliminated.

Conceptually, RFE is pretty simple:

- Initially, the model is trained on all available features and the importance of each feature is obtained. This is typically determined by either the coefficient values (absolute value) of the linear model or feature importance in tree-based models.
- The least important features are then removed from the current set of features. This subset is then used to train the model.
- The steps above are recursively repeated until a specified stopping criteria is reached, such as a designated number of features to select.

Principal Component Analysis (PCA)

PCA is a dimensionality reduction technique which also doubles as a feature selection method. It works by generating a new set of features called principal components. Each principal component is a linear combination of the original features and are oriented orthogonal to one another.

Mathematically, PCA translates the original coordinates of data points (features) to a new set of coordinates such that the greatest variance lies on the first coordinate (first principal component), second greatest variance on the second coordinate (second principal component), and so on.

This is achieved by computing the covariance matrix of the data, then performing eigen-decomposition on the covariance matrix to obtain the eigenvalues and the eigenvectors. The eigenvectors that correspond to the largest eigenvalues (the principal components) can be used to reconstruct a large fraction of variance of the original data.

In conclusion, feature engineering and selection processes make a machine learning model more efficient, accurate, and reliable, and thus it is an essential process in machine learning model creation. It underscores the importance of thoroughly understanding your data and being aware of what you are trying to predict.

Evaluation Metrics for Machine Learning Models

Evaluation metrics are essential tools to measure the overall performance and effectiveness of machine learning models. These metrics guide the development of a model by highlighting areas where improvements can be made. They can also be used to compare and contrast different machine learning models, to determine the best fit for a particular problem.

Classification Metrics

Classification metrics are quintessential in evaluating the performance of a machine learning model, especially when dealing with imbalanced class problems.

We will use Confusion Matrix, a fundamental matrix to understand classification metrics. In the confusion matrix, we have four terms:

- **True Positives (TP)**

  Observation is positive, and is predicted to be positive. If an email is a spam and the model correctly identifies it as a spam, it is considered as a True Positive. This means the model correctly identifies positive instances.

- **False Negatives (FN)**

  Observation is positive, but is predicted negative. If an email is spam but the model incorrectly identifies it as not-spam, it is considered as a False Negative. This means the model incorrectly identifies positive instances.

- **True Negatives (TN)**

  Observation is negative, and is predicted to be negative. If an email is not spam and the model correctly identifies it as not spam, it is considered as True Negative. This means the model correctly identifies negative instances.

Positive		**Actual Values**	
		Positive	**Negative**
Predicted Values	**Positive**	True Positive	False Positive
	Negative	False Negative	True Negative

***Table* 5.2:** *Confusion Matrix*

It is helpful to remember that "*True*" refers to the model's predictions matching the actual results, "*False*" refers to mismatches. "*Positive*" and "*Negative*" correspond to the model's actual predictions (spam or not spam, in this example).

- **False Positives (FP)**

  Observation is negative, but is predicted positive. If an email is not spam but the model incorrectly identifies it as spam, it is considered as False Positive. This means the model incorrectly identifies negative instances.

Accuracy

This is the ratio of the total correctly predicted cases over the total cases. It is ideal when target classes are balanced. For imbalanced classes, accuracy is not a good measure. For instance, if we have a dataset with 95 negatives and 5 positives, a model that always predicts negatives will have high accuracy (95%), but it fails to capture the positive class, which might be our main interest.

$$Accuracy = (TP+TN) / (TP+FP+FN+TN)$$

Precision

This is the ratio of correctly predicted positive cases to the total predicted positive. Precision answers the question, '*Out of the positive predictions, what portion is truly positive?*'. It is a good metric when the cost of False Positive is high, for instance, email spam detection.

$$Precision = TP / (TP+FP)$$

Recall (Sensitivity)

This is the ratio of correctly predicted positive cases to the actual positive. Recall answers the question, '*Out of the actual positives, how many did we predict correctly?*'. It is a good measure when the cost of False Negative is high, for instance, in cancer detection.

$$Recall = TP / (TP+FN)$$

F1 Score

Sometimes, we want a balance between Precision and Recall. We calculate an F1 Score, the weighted average of Precision and Recall. F1 Score is best if there is uneven class distribution. It is a better measure than accuracy when the False Negatives and False Positives are crucial.

$$F1\ Score = 2*(Precision*Recall) / (Precision+Recall)$$

Specificity (True Negative Rate)

This is the ratio of correctly predicted negative cases to the actual negatives. When the cost of a false positive is high, specificity is a key measure. For example, in a pregnancy test, a false positive (saying someone is pregnant when they are not) could have serious implications.

$$Specificity = TN / (TN+FP)$$

Receiver Operating Characteristic (ROC) Curve

This is a fundamental way to evaluate binary classification models, plotting the True

Positive Rate (Recall) against the False Positive Rate (1 - Specificity). The area under this ROC curve (known as AUC) gives the performance measure. An AUC near to 1 signifies better performance. It is widely used when we need to assess the model's performance over variable threshold points.

In conclusion, the choice of the evaluation metric entirely depends on the business problem we are trying to solve. Depending on the cost of errors (False Positives, False Negatives), we may want to optimize for a specific metric over the others.

Regression Metrics

In Machine Learning, regression metrics are used to measure the performance of regression models. Regression models are machine learning models that output a numerical or continuous value – like predicting the temperature for the next week or predicting house prices.

Such numeric predictions can rarely be perfect due to the uncertainty and randomness present in our data. Therefore, we need to quantify the difference between the predicted numeric output and the actual numeric output. This quantified difference is what we call error.

Regression metrics, thus, give us an indication of how well our regression model is predicting. The smaller the error, the better our model is performing.

Let us discuss some commonly used regression metrics:

Mean Absolute Error (MAE)

This is the simplest regression metric, and it indicates the average absolute difference between the actual and predicted values. MAE gives equal weight to all errors, unlike Mean Squared Error. MAE is a linear score which means all the individual differences are weighted equally in the average. For example, the MAE term would be the same if the model missed a single 3 unit prediction and if it missed three 1 unit predictions.

$$MAE = sum(|Actual - Predicted|) / n$$

Mean Squared Error (MSE)

This is the average of the squared differences between the actual and predicted values. Squaring the differences (actual - predicted) penalizes the model more severely for bigger errors and less for smaller ones, as opposed to MAE. Hence, MSE is popularly used when we are concerned about significant deviations. On the downside, MSE is sensitive to outliers, as the squaring will exaggerate the effect of those outliers.

$$MSE = sum((Actual - Predicted)^2) / n$$

Root Mean Squared Error (RMSE)

This is the square root of the mean square error. RMSE measures the average magnitude of the error, giving a sense of how much error the system typically makes in its predictions, with higher weight given to large errors. It is more preferred than MSE because it scales the error back to the original units, which is easier to interpret.

$$RMSE = sqrt(sum((Actual - Predicted)^2) / n)$$

R-squared (Coefficient of Determination)

This is a statistical measure that represents the proportion of the variance for a dependent variable explained by an independent variable or variables in a regression model. R-squared value ranges between 0 and 1 where a higher value is better. A high R-squared indicates that the data fits the regression model well.

$$R^2 = 1 - (SS\_res / SS\_tot)$$

Here `SS_res` is the sum of squares of the residual errors and `SS_tot` is the total sum of errors.

In conclusion, the choice of the error metric depends on the context and the specific application. For instance, if we care more about large errors, we might prefer MSE or RMSE. However, if all differences are equally important, MAE might be preferred.

Understanding these metrics helps in the process of model selection and optimization, helping you choose the model that best aligns with your project objectives. Evaluating machine models is just as important as developing them since this evaluation leads to model refinement and drives the accuracy of the predictions that the model is making.

Bias, Fairness, and Ethics Considerations in Machine Learning

Bias, fairness, and ethics considerations in machine learning have become critical topics in today's technological landscape. As machine learning algorithms increasingly influence decision-making processes, it is essential to address the potential biases they may perpetuate and ensure fairness in their outcomes. Moreover, ethical considerations help mitigate the unintended consequences that arise from machine learning models, prompting thorough examination of the impact on individuals and society as a whole.

Understanding Bias in Machine Learning

Bias in machine learning refers to the tendency of a model to prioritize certain data points or variables, based on the disproportionate weight given during the learning process. This usually results from the preference, assumptions or prejudices inherent in the dataset on which the model was trained.

Biased data, in turn, originates from data that is incomplete, mis-representative or outdated. For example, if a bank's historical lending data is used to train a loan approval model, and this data shows a preference for a certain race, gender, or income group, this bias would be passed on to the model. Thus, individuals from these groups will have higher odds of loan approval compared with their counterparts. This could be an issue, especially in regulated industries that prohibit discrimination based on certain demographic features.

Another example could be in hiring processes. If a company's hiring data displays preference to candidates from a particular institution, region, or age group, and this data is used to train a candidate screening model, the model may also replicate this bias. For example, if the bias in data favors individuals under 30 years old from Ivy League institutions, the machine learning model might unfairly reject qualified candidates who do not fall into these categories.

Furthermore, consider a healthcare industry example. If a dataset used to train a diagnostic model contains mostly data points for one demographic, such as Caucasian males, it could lead to significant inaccuracies when trying to diagnose diseases in a different demographic group such as Asian females. This bias would likely produce inferior results leading to poor patient outcomes for the underrepresented groups.

In the retail and advertising sector, an algorithm that is trained on biased data might disproportionately target certain groups with specific product recommendations or adverts. For example, if a machine learning algorithm is trained on data suggesting women mostly buy beauty products, and men buy auto parts, the model could carry on this bias by recommending beauty products to all females and auto parts to all males. This simplifies and generalizes consumer behavior, thus missing out on broader and more diversified marketing opportunities.

Therefore, to prevent this systematic bias, it is essential that the datasets used to train these algorithms are diverse, balanced, and representative of all possible scenarios and variables. If not, the bias within these datasets could lead to unfair and incorrect outcomes.

Types of Bias

There are various types of bias that can affect machine learning models:

Sample Bias

Sample bias is a form of systematic bias that has a significant impact on the reliability of machine learning models due to the unrepresentative nature of the training dataset.

The basis of the problem lies in the fact that the data used to train the model does not adequately typify the entire population that it is intended to represent.

For instance, if a machine learning model tasked with predicting cardiovascular disease rates is trained using a dataset exclusively obtained from high-income countries, this model's effectiveness may drop significantly when applied to low-income countries. This difference in performance may surface due to variations in lifestyle, dietary habits, access to healthcare services, and even genetic variances across diverse socio-economic groups. Thus, sample bias restricts the predictive capability of a model by hindering its capacity to generalize well.

Prejudice Bias

Prejudice bias in machine learning arises when a model generates prejudiced outcomes owing to discriminatory data used in training. It is predominantly a product of inherent biases in the data which are inadvertently propagated through to the model's predictions.

Consider a scenario where an organization trains a machine learning model to shortlist candidates for a job using its historical hiring data. If, traditionally, males have been selected more frequently for a particular position, the dataset used for training will reflect this bias. Consequently, the machine learning model, without any understanding of fairness or equity, will absorb this prejudice, leading it to favor male candidates unfairly, regardless of their skills or qualifications compared to female applicants. Hence, prejudice bias can perpetuate and augment inequality embedded in the past and present data, narrowing the opportunities for diverse groups.

Measurement Bias

Measurement bias refers to a systematic error that leads to incorrect data collection owing to faulty measurement techniques or instruments. In machine learning, it can influence the model's learning process, affect its prediction, and limit its reliability.

For instance, if a machine learning model has been trained to predict weather conditions using a dataset that consistently captures temperature with a faulty thermometer reading always 5 degrees higher, the model will integrate this discrepancy into its learning process. As a result, the weather predictions produced by the model will consistently deviate from the actual conditions, reflecting the inherited inaccuracy. Therefore, measuring bias does not mean a model is being prejudiced towards any subclass of population; instead, it refers to a model being trained on incorrect data due to flaws in measurement techniques or tools.

Exclusion Bias

This occurs if certain data are systematically excluded during the data gathering phase, leading to an incomplete representation of the population in the dataset. For instance, a model trained to predict TV viewership may be skewed if it does not account for those who watch TV programs using streaming platforms.

Confirmation Bias: This refers to giving more importance to data that supports existing beliefs while disregarding conflicting information. For example, if during a flood prediction model's development, the developers could disregard previous instances where heavy rainfall did not result in floods, leading the model to over-predict floods.

Selection Bias

This type of bias occurs when samples are selected or rejected based on certain attributes. For instance, a sensor might malfunction only for high temperature readings, causing high temperature readings to be underrepresented in the data.

Outlier Bias

Some learning algorithms are sensitive to outliers in the training data, which can influence the model's outcomes. For example, a housing price prediction model may be skewed by a few extraordinarily high or low values.

Algorithmic Bias

This type of bias arises from the structures and rules within the machine learning algorithm itself. For instance, some machine learning algorithms are more susceptible to over-fitting or under-fitting, which could result in bias in their predictions.

All these biases can lead to inaccurate predictions and results, ultimately affecting the performance and fairness of a machine learning model. Therefore, it is crucial to carefully select and preprocess the training data to ensure it is representative and maintain a transparent and fair machine learning process.

Importance of Fairness in Machine Learning

The increasing integration of machine learning models into our society's fabric comes with the vital responsibility of ensuring fairness in their operation. Regardless of their application – from screening job applicants to approving loans or powering facial recognition technology, these models must be careful not to discriminate or favor certain demographics over others. Leveraging machine learning technologies brings substantial benefits, but we must be equally mindful of the ethical implications, especially when it comes to fairness.

Fairness in machine learning is a cornerstone of ethical AI development. Algorithmic bias, a condition wherein an algorithm systematically produces results favoring a particular group over others, can inadvertently perpetuate existing inequalities, and at times introduce new ones. This results in unbalanced outcomes that deviate from the ideal of fairness. Situations where the algorithm's decisions have severe social consequences, such as approving a loan or selecting candidates for a job, heightens the urgent need for impartial algorithms. Leaving unchecked, these biases can have lasting impacts on individuals belonging to certain demographic groups, further perpetuating societal inequalities.

Examples of the dramatic consequences of unfair machine learning algorithms abound. A notable case is that of an AI system used in the US to predict future criminals, which was found to unfairly target people of color. Such a system not only reproduces existing societal biases but can also exaggerate them and legitimize unfair practices.

The path to fairness in machine learning involves a suite of strategies at each stage of the machine learning pipeline. To start with, data preprocessing requires the collection of a diverse and representative dataset. Adequate care must be taken to remove irrelevant features, deal with missing values, and conduct a meticulous statistical analysis of the data used for training. These steps ensure that the model's predictions are a true reflection of reality rather than a warped representation skewed by systematic errors or bias.

Additionally, techniques like algorithm modification, stratified sampling, and continuous evaluation can be adopted to mitigate bias and ensure the model's decision-making process remains fair. Post-processing techniques, including adjusting prediction thresholds and enhancing transparency around algorithmic decision-making, can help correct bias even after the model is trained.

Thus, ensuring fairness in machine learning models is not just an afterthought but a deliberate action taken throughout the learning process, complemented by several methods to ensure just and unbiased results. A focus on fairness in machine learning not only makes for ethical AI but also fosters trust in these systems and encourages wider adoption. Fairer machine learning algorithms lead to better, more inclusive solutions that reflect the world's diversity more accurately and advance equality within our global society.

Techniques to Ensure Fairness

In pursuit of ensuring fairness in machine learning, several techniques can be employed at various stages of the machine learning process. These techniques work towards alleviating biases, minimizing discrimination, and promoting equal treatment across all demographic and social groups. The ultimate goal of these strategies is to align the outcomes of machine learning applications with ethical standards and principles of fairness, ensuring their broader acceptance and beneficial impact within society. So, let us delve into some of the ground-breaking techniques to ensure fairness in Machine Learning.

Data Preprocessing

This involves collecting a diverse and representative dataset, removing irrelevant features, handling missing values, and performing rigorous statistical analysis. By making sure the data is well-distributed and representative of various scenarios and demographics, we reduce bias and ensure equal representation of all subclasses in the data.

Stratified Sampling

Stratified sampling involves dividing the population into homogeneous subgroups and taking a balanced sample from each subgroup. This method ensures a representative dataset across all determined groups, effectively reducing bias by ensuring all groups within the data are adequately represented in your sample.

Feature Selection

This process involves selecting the most relevant variables for model training and discarding the irrelevant or redundant ones that might introduce bias. By focusing solely on features directly relevant to the problem in question, we can minimize the scope for biased influence on the model's predictions.

Algorithm Modification

Adjusting the learning algorithm reduces the impact of bias. For instance, using a cost-sensitive learning algorithm assigns higher costs to biased predictions, thereby encouraging the model to avoid such biased outputs. These adjustments can guide the learning process to make more equitable predictions.

Post-processing

This involves adjusting the model's predictions retrospectively. Techniques like threshold adjusting, where different thresholds are set for different groups, can ensure fairness by counteracting any bias. This aids in offsetting any existing bias that might exist after a model is trained.

Evaluation Metrics

By using evaluation metrics that consider fairness, we can help to identify and quantify bias, guiding the machine learning models during development and tuning to avoid biased outcomes effectively.

Bias-Awareness Training

Including a bias-awareness component in machine learning training programs helps in recognizing and correcting biases that may be inadvertently built into the models. This underlines the biases in the model and prompts the algorithm to correct the course accordingly.

By employing these strategies, we can reduce the likelihood of bias and ensure that our machine learning models deliver accurate, representative, and more equitable predictions.

Ethics in Machine Learning

Ethics in Machine Learning is an emerging field that acknowledges and addresses the ethical implications and challenges that come with the developing technology of machine learning. It revolves around the principles of transparency, fairness, non-malfeasance, and accountability, which together form the basis of ethical behavior in these intelligent systems.

Transparency in machine learning refers to the ability to understand and interpret how a model makes its decisions. An ideal system is explainable and its workings can be easily understood by humans. However, many advanced machine learning models, such as deep learning neural networks, are often termed as '*black boxes*' due to their complex and inscrutable nature. For example, in healthcare, a system that predicts certain diseases must be transparent about the factors leading to its conclusions since the consequences of its decisions could be life-altering.

Fairness is another crucial aspect where machine learning models should not discriminate against certain groups. A case that stirred extensive debate was the use of predictive policing algorithms. These algorithms were scrutinized when they were found to disproportionately target certain ethnic groups over others, thereby producing biased outcomes and perpetuating existing societal inequalities.

Non-malfeasance, doing no harm, requires that machine learning systems function as they are intended without causing detriment to users or society. For example, a machine learning model that allows a self-driving car to identify pedestrians, signals, and other vehicles must perform accurately, as any errors could result in catastrophic outcomes.

Accountability implies that the developers, users, and regulators of machine learning models are held responsible for the behavior of these models. When Microsoft's AI chatbot, Tay, began producing offensive tweets due to its learning from the interactions with users on Twitter, the organization had to take responsibility for not foreseeing and preventing such an event.

In conclusion, with the increasing application of machine learning models in sensitive areas like finance, healthcare, and criminal justice, it is essential to understand and address ethical considerations. This recognition leads us not only towards the development of better machine learning models but also towards creating a more just and equitable society.

Ethical Considerations

As machine learning models continue to gain prominence across various sectors, the ethical considerations linked to their development and deployment grow more significant. With the facility of handling vast data and influencing decision-making in key domains like healthcare, finance, and law enforcement comes the responsibility of ensuring the judicious use of such technology. Failure to address these ethical considerations can lead to severe consequences, including legal repercussions, loss of public trust, and societal harm. Consequently, the development of machine learning systems must incorporate the following critical ethical aspects – informed consent, transparency, and privacy protection. Each of these dimensions forms a crucial cornerstone of ethical AI, ensuring its responsible and beneficial application in society.

Informed Consent

Informed consent in machine learning refers to the ethical necessity of obtaining explicit approval from users before collecting and using their data. Given the vast amounts of data that machine learning models often require, informed consent is an essential step in validating the use of this data and assuring the users that their information is being used ethically.

The General Data Protection Regulation (GDPR) in the European Union sets strict rules on how the consent of users must be obtained, stipulating that consent must be freely given, specific, informed, and unambiguous. A violation of these rules can result in heavy fines.

An example where this came into play was when the United Kingdom's NHS (National Health Service) came under scrutiny for sharing patient data with Google's DeepMind. The collaboration aimed to develop an AI system that would help with early detection of kidney injuries. However, the lack of explicit consent from patients led to criticism and strained public confidence.

Obtaining informed consent not only ensures legal compliance but also helps build trust in the organization's AI initiatives, thus enhancing its reputation and potential for success.

Transparency

Transparency in machine learning refers to the clear understanding of how a model makes decisions. Transparent AI systems allow users and regulators to understand and trace how a decision was arrived at.

Transparency is an essential element of the EU's GDPR. According to Article 22, individuals have rights concerning decisions based purely on automated processing. This includes the right to understand the logic behind the decision, and to contest and seek human intervention in such decisions.

One groundbreaking example of transparent AI is IBM's AI OpenScale. It provides insights into AI-based decisions, makes bias transparent, and ensures that the AI's behavior aligns with human values and business requirements.

Transparency in machine learning can not only help avoid regulatory fines but also fosters trust among users, potentially leading to wider adoption of AI technologies.

Privacy Protection

Privacy protection is another significant ethical aspect in machine learning. It requires treating sensitive user data with extreme caution and care, particularly given the vast amounts of data collected and processed by machine learning systems.

In the context of law, GDPR again plays a critical role, requiring organizations to implement adequate safeguarding measures to protect data and report any breaches within 72 hours.

A stark reminder of the importance of privacy protection was the Facebook-Cambridge Analytica scandal. Cambridge Analytica collected personal information from Facebook users without their consent for political advertising, affecting millions of users and leading to a huge global outcry.

Upholding privacy protection not only prevents potential legal ramifications but also builds and maintains trust among users, rendering a competitive advantage for businesses in the data-driven digital space.

In conclusion, dealing with bias, maintaining fairness, and considering ethics are integral to responsible machine learning. By respecting user's data rights and ensuring that algorithms reflect the diversity of the society in which they operate, more robust, equitable, and resilient machine learning systems can be created.

Conclusion

Throughout this comprehensive chapter on machine learning, we delved deep into its fundamentals, including supervised, unsupervised, and reinforcement learning. We also walked through various types of machine learning algorithms, such as classification, regression, and clustering, and clarified how they function in different settings. Furthermore, we introduced the important aspects of feature engineering and selection that are crucial steps for creating a robust machine learning model. Evaluation metrics that truly reveal the performance of your model were also discussed in great detail. Lastly, we concluded the chapter by understanding the significance of bias, fairness, and ethical considerations in the sphere of machine learning. This knowledge helps in developing not just technically sound, but also ethically responsible machine learning models.

In the upcoming chapter, we will be exploring new territories of machine learning through a detailed exploration of Azure Machine Learning Studio. The next chapter focuses on how all the principles and concepts we have learned in this chapter can be actualized using Azure's dedicated platform for machine learning – Azure Machine Learning Studio. We will learn about building, training, and deploying machine learning models in a scalable end-to-end manner. It will be an exciting journey that will complement the theoretical knowledge we gained in this chapter with practical, hands-on experience.

Combining the insights gained from this chapter with the practical learning from the next, you will be well positioned to effectively develop, evaluate, and deploy your own machine learning models!

Questions

- What are the ethical considerations we need to keep in mind while designing and implementing machine learning solutions?
- True or False: Unsupervised learning models cannot accept input data (close-ended).
- Can we use every type of machine learning algorithm in all kinds of problems?
- How can reinforcement learning be applied in the healthcare industry?
- Do evaluation metrics affect the performance of machine learning models?
- Could you discuss some advanced strategies for feature selection?
- Is supervised learning more effective than unsupervised learning?
- Explain the concept of bias in machine learning and its potential impacts on model performance.
- Describe the differences between principal component analysis and clustering.
- True or False: Fairness has no importance in machine learning models.

Multiple Choice Questions

1. Which type of machine learning algorithm would you generally use for predicting future prices in a stock market?

    a. Supervised Learning

    b. Unsupervised Learning

    c. Reinforcement Learning

    d. None of the above

2. In machine learning, SVM stands for?

    a. Secure Virtual Machine

    b. Support Vector Machine

   c. Simple Vector Machine
   d. Scaled Vector Machine
3. Which of the following methods is used to find groups of similar data points in unlabeled data?
   a. Classification
   b. Regression
   c. Clustering
   d. None of the above
4. Which of the following statements is true about feature engineering?
   a. Feature engineering is used after the model training
   b. Feature engineering is limited to creating new features
   c. Feature engineering includes selecting high-quality, relevant features
   d. All of the above
5. What does recall as an evaluation metric depict in a machine learning model?
   a. It is the ratio of correctly predicted positive instances to the total instances
   b. It is the ratio of correctly predicted positive instances to the total number of negatives
   c. It is the ratio of correctly predicted positive instances to the total predicted positives
   d. It is the ratio of correctly predicted positive instances to the actual positives
6. Which of the following is not a bias in machine learning?
   a. Confirmation Bias
   b. Sampling Bias
   c. Algorithm Bias
   d. Halo Bias
7. Which of the following is a machine learning based Recommendation System?
   a. Popularity Model
   b. Content-Based Filtering

   c. Collaborative Filtering
   d. All of the above
8. Reinforcement learning involves an agent, an environment, and what else?
   a. Actions
   b. Rewards
   c. States
   d. All of the above
9. Which of the following is not a type of cluster analysis?
   a. Hierarchical Clustering
   b. K-dimensional Clustering
   c. Centroid-based Clustering
   d. Density-based Clustering
10. In regression evaluation, if the RMSE (Root Mean Square Error) is 0, then it denotes?
    a. Perfect Prediction
    b. Terrible Prediction
    c. Model is overfitting
    d. Model is underfitting
11. Which of the following is not a method for dimensionality reduction?
    a. Principal Component Analysis (PCA)
    b. Linear Discriminant Analysis (LDA)
    c. Feature Extraction
    d. Random Forest
12. Which of these is not a parameter of K-means clustering?
    a. The initial position of the centroids
    b. The number of centroids (K)
    c. The actual data points
    d. K-dimensional labeling
13. Wrangling is a method used in:
    a. Feature Engineering

   b. Preprocessing Data
   c. Evaluating Machine Learning Models
   d. Predicting Results

14. In a binary classification problem, which of the following metrics can be used?
    a. Accuracy
    b. Precision and Recall
    c. F1-Score
    d. All of the above

15. What conversational context is generally used in the final model phase of a machine learning project?
    a. Bias
    b. Fairness
    c. Generalizability
    d. Ethics

Answers

1. a
2. b
3. c
4. c
5. d
6. d
7. d
8. d
9. b
10. a
11. d
12. d
13. b
14. d
15. d

CHAPTER 6
Azure Machine Learning Studio

Introduction

In this chapter, we will explore the powerful capabilities of Azure Machine Learning Studio, a leading tool for building, training, and deploying machine learning models. From a detailed introduction to Azure Machine Learning Studio, we will understand its integral role in model development and deployment. We will delve into creating and managing experiments within the platform, discussing accessing and importing data for training and evaluation along with preprocessing techniques. Next, we will discuss how to construct machine learning models using Azure Machine Learning SDK and cloud resources for training these models. Furthermore, we will explore in-depth hyperparameter tuning and strategies for model selection. We will also discuss methods for evaluating your models, understanding evaluation metrics, and strategies for model validation and cross-validation. Knowing how to deploy models is key. We will study how to prepare a model for deployment, create real-time prediction endpoints, and set up an environment necessary for deployment. In addition, managing and monitoring deployed models will be presented as part of the learning journey.

Lastly, we will touch upon best practices for model reproducibility and version control, security and compliance considerations, and strategies for cost management and optimization in Azure Machine Learning. By the end of the chapter, key takeaways will be summarized, and resources for further learning will be mentioned, encouraging readers to dive deeper into their journey with Azure Machine Learning. Whether you are a novice data scientist or an expert looking for a refresher, this comprehensive guide addresses each step of the machine learning process using Azure Machine Learning Studio.

Structure

Let us delve into the topics we are going to explore:

- Overview of Azure Machine Learning Studio
- Creating and Managing Experiments in Azure Machine Learning Studio
- Preparing Data for Training and Evaluation
- Building and Training Machine Learning Models Using Azure Machine Learning SDK
- Hyperparameter Tuning and Model Selection
- Model Evaluation Techniques and Metrics
- Deploying Models and Real-time Prediction
- Managing and Monitoring Deployed Models
- Best Practices and Considerations

Overview of Azure Machine Learning Studio

Azure Machine Learning Studio, a pivotal choice for data scientists and analysts, is a cutting-edge technological solution in the world of cloud-based analytics. Promising simplicity and integration, it aims to consolidate and streamline your machine learning tasks into an interactive, visual workspace, thus providing you with a comprehensive platform to plan, develop, test, and deploy machine learning models.

Introduction to Azure Machine Learning Studio and Its Capabilities

Azure Machine Learning Studio, or simply Azure ML Studio, is an innovative cloud-based service designed by Microsoft that enables us to build powerful machine learning models with ease. As a browser-based tool, it provides a rich and interactive drag-and-drop user interface that eliminates the necessity to write complex lines of code.

The sterling capabilities of Azure ML Studio are comprehensive. Primarily, it provides robust support for a wide variety of pre-built machine learning algorithms that can be easily deployed for model building. Importantly, Azure ML Studio stands out for its feature, which allows users to export their models as web services that can be easily integrated into any application or system, regardless of whether it is on-premises or cloud-based.

Navigating the Azure Machine Learning Studio Interface

Azure Machine Learning Studio, right off the bat, presents a well-orchestrated user interface to its users upon login. Even before entering a specific workspace, users are presented with a myriad of options that set the tone for an intuitive and navigable journey into the world of machine learning.

At the core of the interface is the option to `'Select Workspace'`. A workspace in Azure is a comprehensive environment where users can manage all their machine learning operations. These include creation, coordination, and management of machine learning artefacts such as experiments, jobs, datasets, models, components, and inference endpoints. Workspaces, in essence, are collaborative grounds for teams to undertake group-related work and jointly build machine learning solutions.

On the left navigation pane, a hub of various options meticulously categorized to facilitate user interactions. Each category is designed to direct users to specific features of Azure ML Studio.

`'Workspaces'` category aids in managing various workspaces wherein individual or collaborative projects can be undertaken.

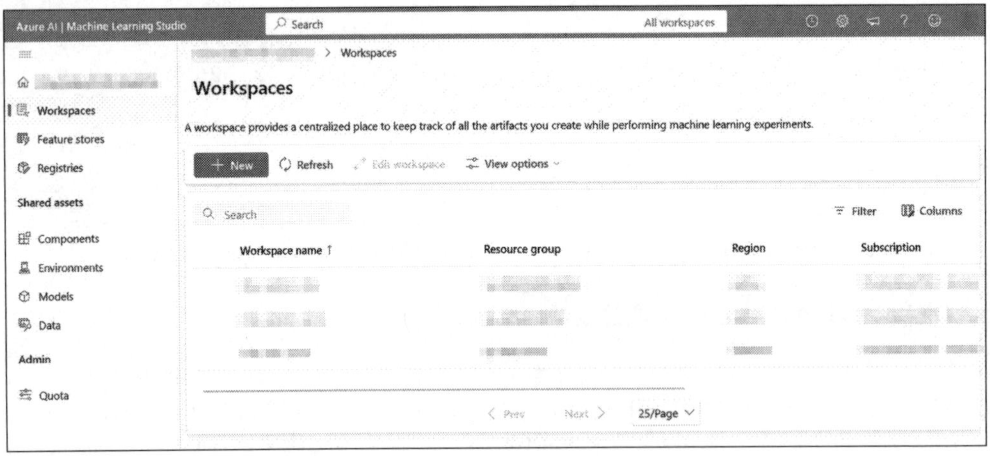

***Figure 6.1**: Workspaces in Azure ML Studio*

The `'Feature stores'` option allows users to manage reusable features in a central repository, streamlining the process of building machine learning models.

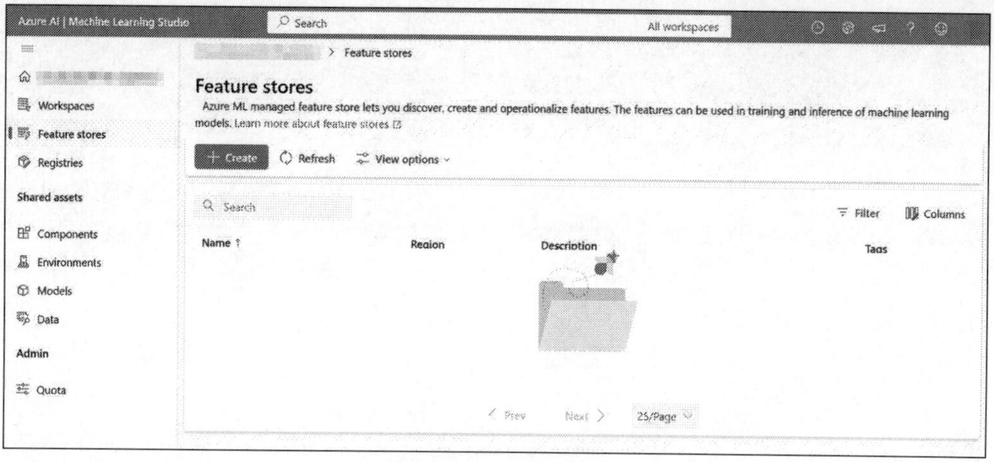

Figure 6.2: *Feature Stores*

The **'Registries'** section is designed for efficient management of various ML resources like ML models, transformation pipelines, and so on.

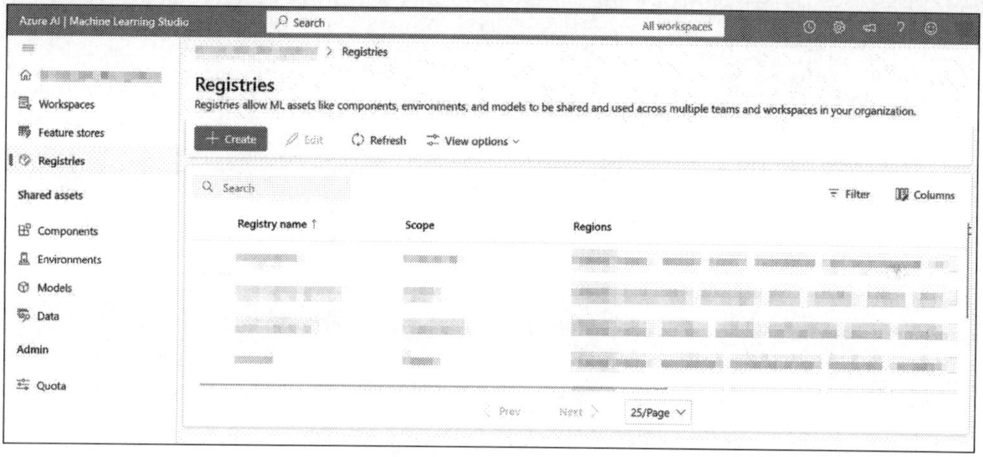

Figure 6.3: *Registries*

Under the **'Shared Assets'** category, users can find a roster of sub-categories. The **'Components'** sub-category contains predefined or custom components that quicken the ML pipeline creation.

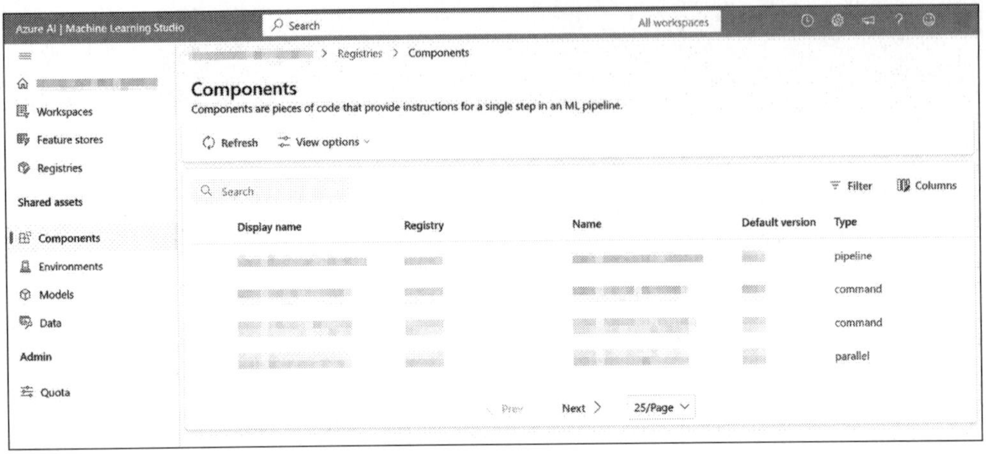

Figure 6.4: Components

The **'Environments'** section provides a space for managing reusable, versioned machine learning environments, promoting consistency across experiments. The **'Models'** and **'Data'** sections house all related resources and assets, allowing for efficient management and tracking.

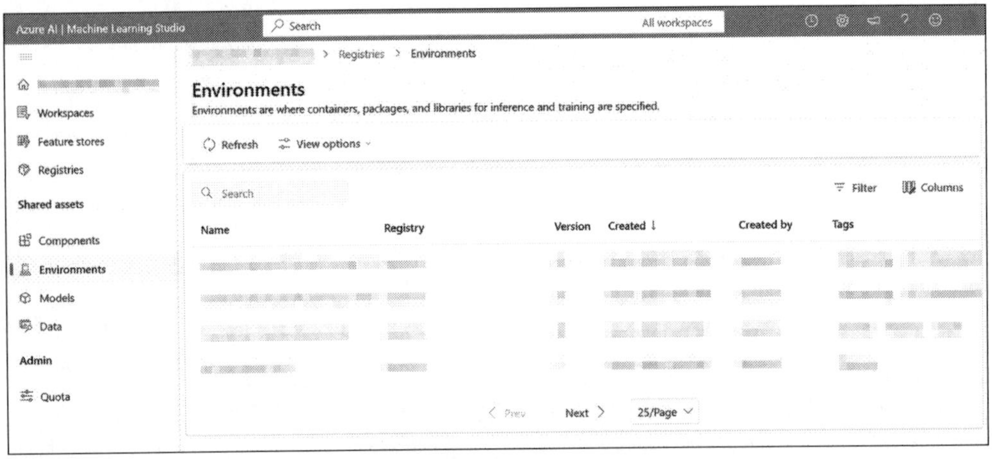

Figure 6.5: Environments

Lastly, the **'Admin'** section, particularly designed for administrators, includes features like **'Quota'**. This tool helps manage assigned resources to a workspace or a subscription effectively, keeping a balance between cost and performance optimization.

Thus, the Azure Machine Learning Studio's user interface, with its thoughtful design, ensures a seamless and hurdle-free journey into creating, managing, and deploying machine learning solutions.

Our initial dive into the Azure Machine Learning Studio interface here provides a broad overview of how to get started with the platform. However, it is important to remember that this robust tool offers much more once a workspace is selected, opening up a range of options to handle all aspects of machine learning projects efficiently. This deeper exploration into the Azure Machine Learning Studio interface, after the selection of a workspace, is extensively laid out in a previous chapter. You will find this discussed in detail in *Chapter 2, "Setting Up Your Azure Environment"*. Specifically, the sub-section titled "*Understanding Azure Machine Learning Studio Interface*" further elaborates on the various tools and features and how best you can leverage them in your machine learning projects.

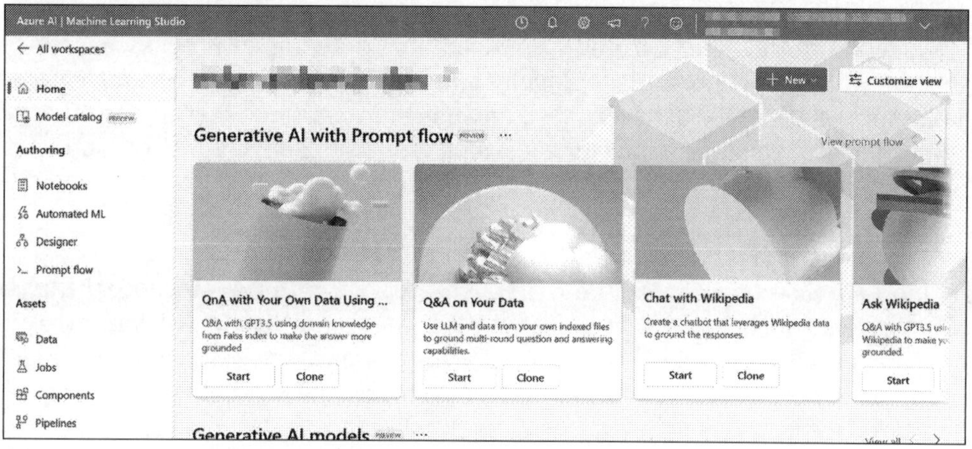

Figure 6.6: *Azure Machine Learning Studio*

Role of Azure Machine Learning Studio in Model Development and Deployment

Azure Machine Learning Studio plays a pivotal role in model development and deployment in different ways. It is a cloud-based, browser-based tool that provides an interactive and user-friendly canvas for constructing and executing machine learning workflows. With its drag-and-drop interface, it simplifies the process of building machine learning models.

In the development of a machine learning model, Azure Machine Learning Studio offers a rich set of pre-built AI algorithms and data manipulation modules that eliminate the need for writing code. It allows users to design and construct complex machine learning models with high efficiency. During the model development phase, Azure Machine Learning Studio provides access to an array of machine learning algorithms, tools, and utilities that support processes like data preprocessing, feature extraction, and feature selection. These capabilities speed up the model development process and facilitate the creation of robust, reliable models. They also allow users to experiment with various algorithms and parameters to find the one that works best for their specific requirements.

For model deployment, Azure Machine Learning Studio provides a seamless, easy-to-use mechanism. Once a model is fully trained and validated, it can be converted into a web service within minutes. Azure ML Studio automatically generates API endpoints for the deployed model, which can be accessed and consumed by client applications. It also provides tools for facilitating batch scoring and real-time scoring.

Additionally, Azure Machine Learning Studio supports the monitoring and managing of deployed models. It allows users to track their model's performance over time and provides opportunities for cyclical model retraining and updating as necessary.

In essence, Azure Machine Learning Studio simplifies the complex processes associated with model development and deployment. Its interactive interface and extensive utilities make it easier for data scientists and machine learning practitioners to create, validate, deploy, and manage machine learning models effectively in the cloud.

Practical Application

It is time we transition from theory to practical application. As we step into the hands-on part of our journey, we will actively utilize the Azure Machine Learning Studio to implement what we have learned so far. This will enrich our learning experience, allowing us to better understand the tool's intricacies and strengths. So, roll up your sleeves and prepare to dive into the exciting world of Azure Machine Learning Studio as we gear up to predict house prices! Let us demonstrate the power of machine learning, one step at a time.

Introducing Our Project: Predicting House Prices

As we delve into the functionalities and capabilities of Azure Machine Learning Studio, we will be working on a practical case scenario – a project on predicting house prices. This project involves utilizing machine learning models to forecast house prices based on specific features like location, number of rooms, area in square feet, among others. Our goal is to guide you in understanding how to approach a real-world machine learning problem using Azure Machine Learning Studio.

Setting Up the Project on Azure Machine Learning Studio

Now that we have a clear understanding of what our project is about, let us start by setting up the project on Azure Machine Learning Studio.

Step 1

Log in to Azure Machine Learning Studio: Navigate to the Azure Machine Learning Studio web page and log in using your credentials.

Step 2

Create a New Workspace: Once logged in, create a new workspace. Click `"+ Create a resource"` > `"AI + Machine Learning"` > `"Machine Learning"`. Fill in the necessary details including the unique name for your workspace.

Step 3

Create a Datastore: We first need to configure a Datastore to point to your Azure storage where your dataset is stored. Simply navigate to `"Datastores"` in your workspace, then click `"+ New datastore"`. Choose the type of Azure storage that contains your housing dataset. Provide the necessary details and credentials, then click `"Create"`.

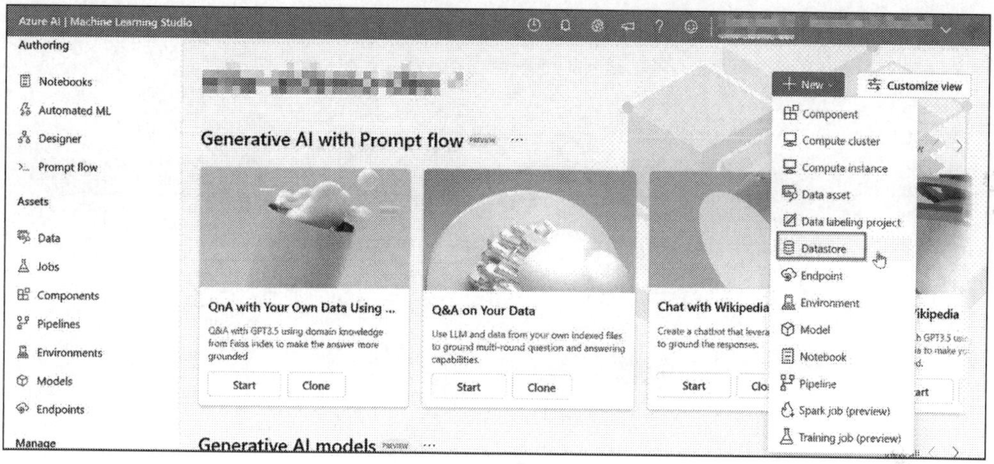

Figure 6.7: *Creating New Datastore*

After clicking on the `Datastore` option from the dropdown, we will be directed to the Datastore portal, where we will fill in the details.

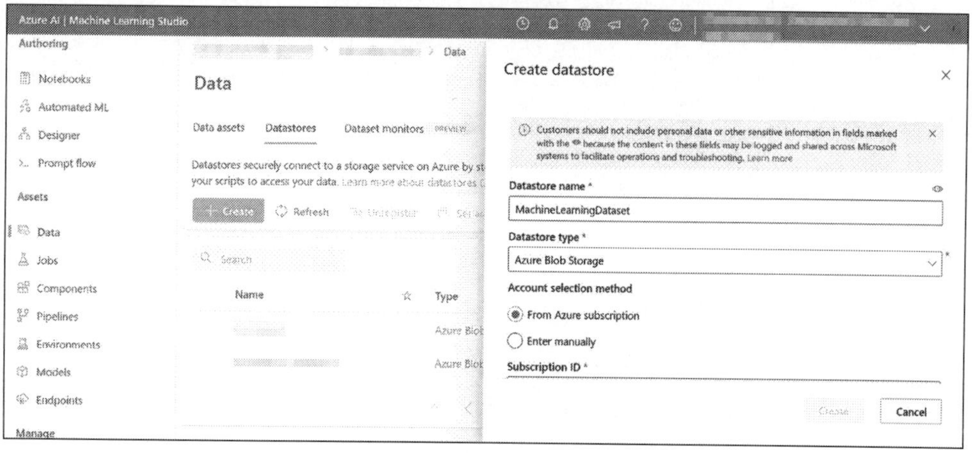

Figure 6.8: *Creating New Datastore*

Step 4

Register Dataset: With the datastore connected, you can now proceed to create a dataset. Click **"+ New Data Assets"** under the **"Data Assets"** option, then select **"From datastore"**. Choose the datastore configured in the previous step. Specify the format and path of your data. Provide the necessary settings, then click **"Next"**. In the settings and preview pane, you can modify how your dataset is imported. Confirm the settings, then click **"Next"**. In the schema pane, confirm the automatically detected dataset schema or modify it as needed. Click **"Next"**. Finally, provide a name and description for your dataset, and click **"Create"**.

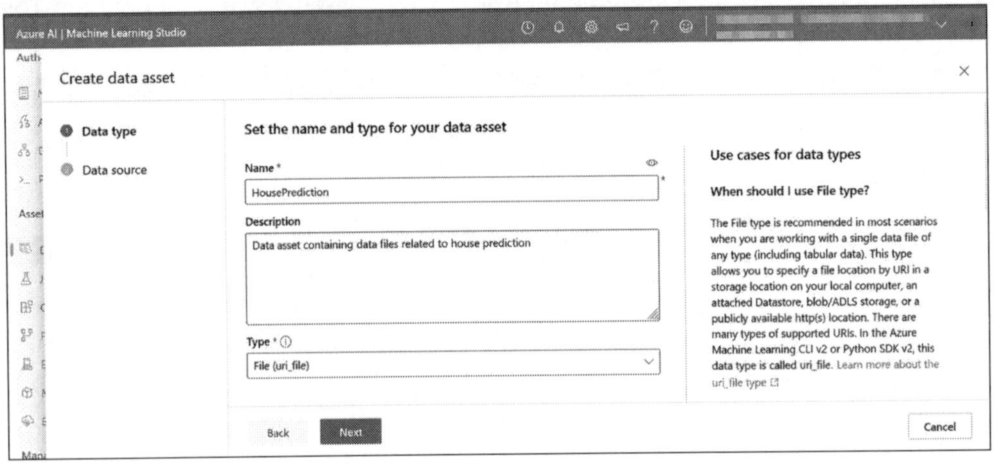

Figure 6.9: *Creating Data Asset*

After adding the name, select the source of the data.

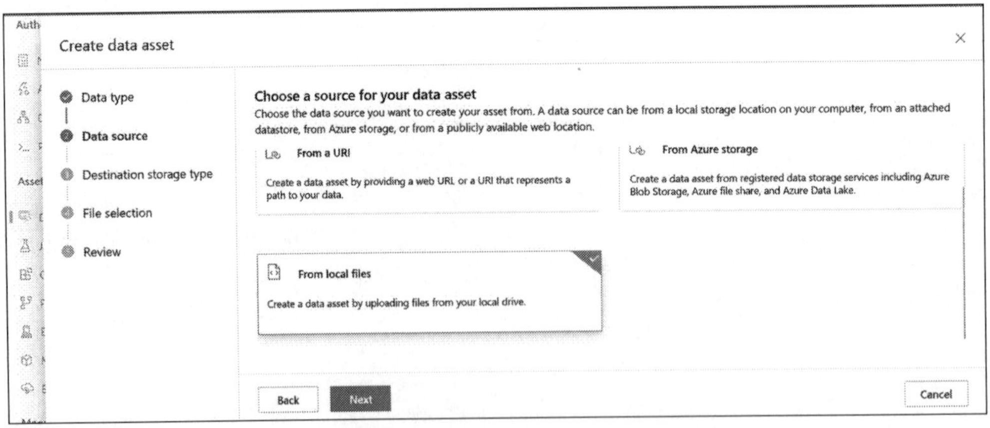

Figure 6.10: *Selecting Data Store*

Next, specify the format and path of your data. Provide the necessary settings and then click **"Next"**:

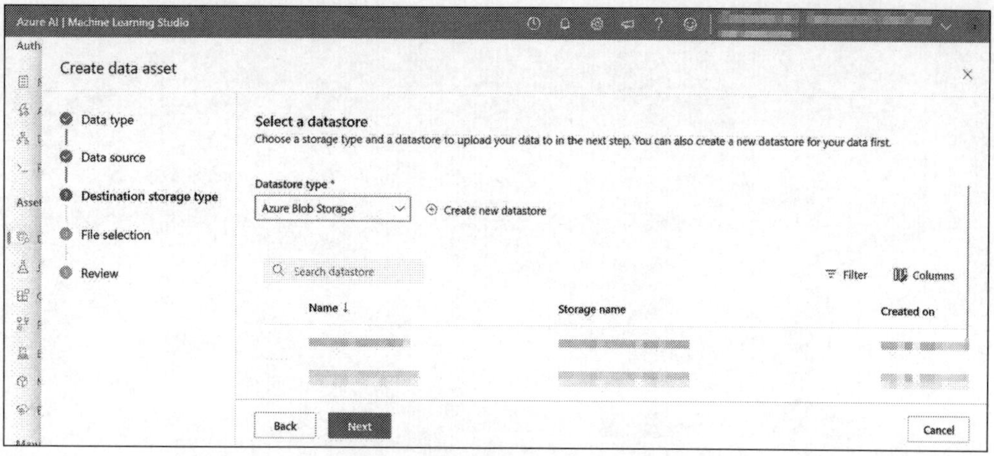

Figure 6.11: *Attaching Datastore*

Add the path of your data source and click **`Next`**.

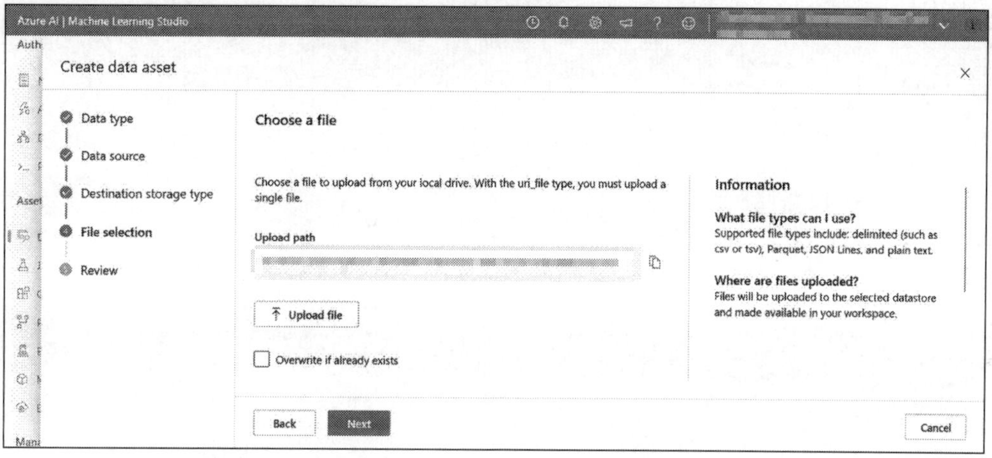

Figure 6.12: *Selecting the File from Local and Uploading*

Review the data asset.

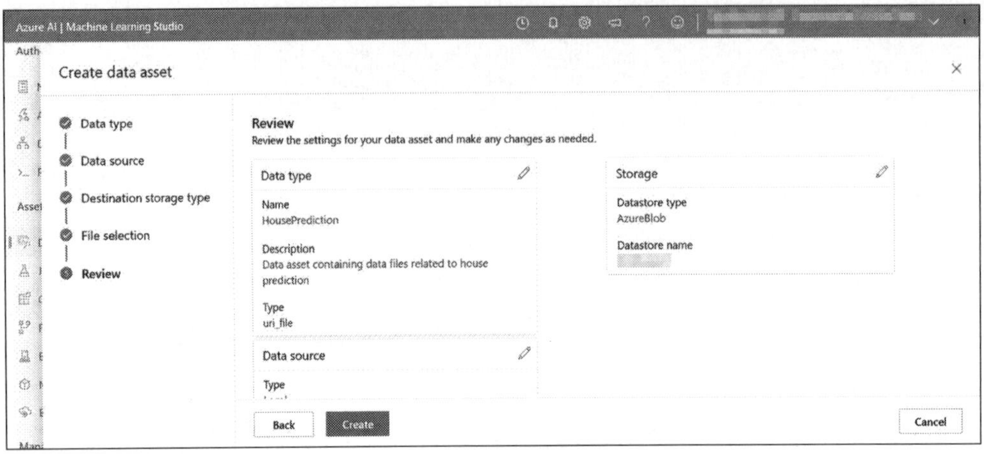

Figure 6.13: *Check Setting*

Once the data asset is created, you will see all the details of the asset as follows:

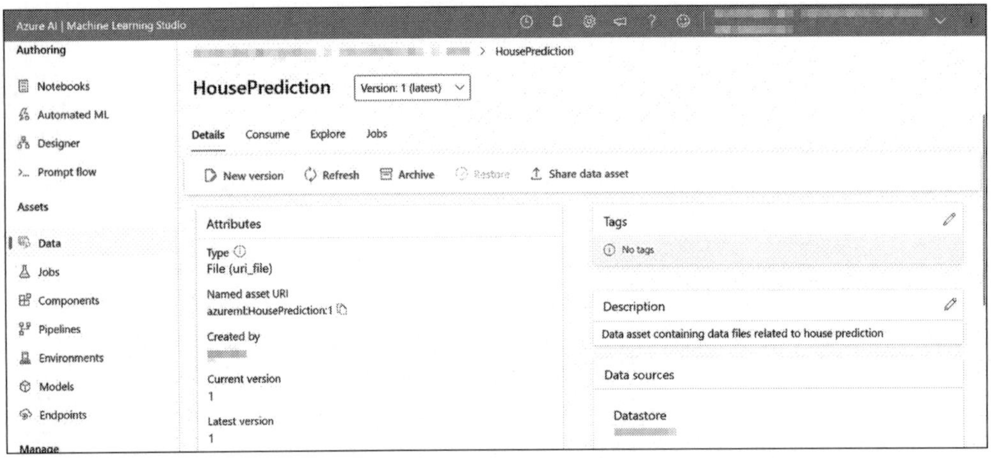

Figure 6.14: *Upload is Done*

Step 5

Prepare Data: Once your dataset is ready, you can prepare it for machine learning by performing data transformation tasks, feature engineering, handling missing values, and other necessary steps for our specific problem.

Step 6

Create a Compute Instance: Instead of an experiment, we now create a compute instance for running our machine learning model. Navigate to "`Compute`" and select "`+ New`" under "`Compute Instances`". Provide the necessary settings and click "`Create`".

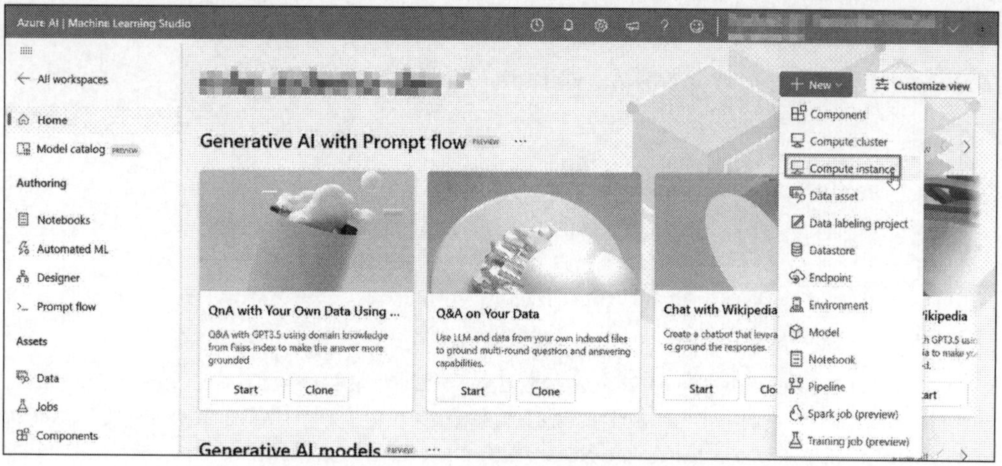

***Figure 6.15**: Creating Compute Instance*

In the next sections of your Azure Machine Learning pathway, you will be using this computer instance to run Python notebooks for building, training, and evaluating your house pricing prediction model.

Creating and Managing Experiments in Azure Machine Learning Studio

Data science and machine learning involve running several experiments to explore data, build models, and make evaluations. In the Azure Machine Learning workspace, an experiment is a named process that involves running a script or a pipeline to generate metrics and outputs, which can be tracked. Each experiment can be run multiple times with different data, code, or settings, with each run being tracked by Azure Machine Learning. This section will discuss creating and managing such experiments in Azure Machine Learning Studio.

Setting Up a Workspace and Creating New Experiments

A workspace in Azure Machine Learning Studio is a virtual environment where you can create, manage, and organize all the resources related to your machine learning project. This essentially includes datasets, models, computations, and experiments that are essential to your project.

Steps to set up a workspace:

Step 1

Launch Azure portal at portal.azure.com and login to your Microsoft account.

Step 2

Use the search bar at the top to navigate to "`Machine Learning`."

Step 3

Click on "`Create`" to establish a new workspace.

Step 4

Fill in the details required, including the unique name for the workspace, subscription, resource group, and location.

Once a workspace has been created, new experiments can be created within. You can navigate to the "`Experiments`" tab on your workspace and select "`+ New Experiment`". Here, you can name your experiment and configure the settings as per the requirements of your machine learning project.

Organizing Resources Within the Azure Machine Learning Studio Environment

When working on machine learning projects, you might end up dealing with a multitude of resources including datasets, scripts, trained models, and computational resources like storage and compute instances. Effectively managing all these resources is no small feat, and the Azure Machine Learning Studio provides various features to simplify this task, keeping your workspace organized and efficient.

Azure Machine Learning Studio implements a hierarchical structure within your workspace to systematically organize your resources. At the top level of this hierarchy is your workspace itself, followed by the resource groups that you can create to group related resources together. Within these resource groups, you can further classify your resources into various types – datasets, models, experiments, pipelines, and more. This way, related resources stay within their groups, making it easier to navigate and manage your workspace.

Firstly, datasets can be imported from multiple sources and organized within your workspace. Once a dataset is uploaded to Azure, it can be accessed and shared across different experiments and models within the same workspace.

Scripts and Notebooks can be managed using Git-based versioning, allowing you to keep track of changes made across different versions of your scripts. You can create a repository and link it up with Azure Machine Learning Studio for seamless version control.

When it comes to computational resources, Azure supports a spectrum – from powerful virtual machines and clusters for training heavy machine learning models to low-profile instances for lightweight tasks. You can create and manage these resources as per your requirement.

The models you train are crucial resources in your machine learning projects. Azure allows you to track all the models you have trained, including model parameters and performance metrics. Not just that, you can also version your models, allowing you to revert to a previous version if needed.

In essence, Azure Machine Learning Studio provides you with a comprehensive and organized control over all resources involved in your machine learning projects. With its capabilities, you can focus on building and refining your models, while Azure takes care of efficiently managing the resources.

Monitoring Experiments and Logging Runs

As you dive into the world of machine learning, one of the most important aspects is to systematically observe and record the course of your experiments. This involves closely monitoring each experiment run and meticulously logging those runs for onwards analysis.

Monitoring Experiments

In Azure Machine Learning Studio, a unique feature known as the Experiment Run Context is at play. This Run Context mainly represents the running of your experiment, and two of its most fundamental functions are initializing and wrapping up the experiment run.

As you proceed with your experiments, the Run Context gauges the runtime and denotes the beginning and end of experiment runs for tracking in Azure Machine Learning. This means that each experiment you run, no matter the different data, code, or settings you apply, is persistently tracked. This convenient feature lets you view the run history and compare the results for each run.

Logging Runs

While monitoring gives you the run-time attributes of every experiment keystroke, logging methods allow you to keep track of informative metrics that can dramatically aid in more accurate analytical reviews.

Azure Machine Learning Studio offers several functionalities, specifically designed for logging runs. You can record a single value through the '**`log`**' function, or a whole array of values through '**`log_list`**.' If you have multiplexed data, '**`log_row`**' enables you to record a row with multiple columns, and '**`log_table`**' can record the dictionary as a table. Even images and plots can be logged through '**`log_image`**.'

These metrics are crucial for comparing different models and doing an in-depth analysis of the experiment. By recording experiment progress, log files enhance reproducibility and help in diagnosing and understanding model behaviors. You can view logged metrics through Azure Machine Learning studio, or use the `'get_metrics'` method to obtain a JSON representation of the metrics.

Output Files

Apart from the logged metrics, your experiments will also generate output files. These could range from machine learning models, analysis results, graphs to any other file that you intend to save as an output from your experiment. All such files of an experiment are saved in a dedicated `'outputs'` folder.

This systematic approach to monitoring experiments and logging runs ensures that your workflow of running experiments remains organized, making it easier for you to review results and make improvements in your models.

Preparing Data for Training and Evaluation

In any machine learning process, the quality of data is paramount. High-quality data boosts the prediction accuracy of a model. As such, data preparation is a critical step and entails selecting the appropriate data, pre-processing it, and splitting it into training and test sets. Azure Machine Learning Studio facilitates this process through its user-friendly interfaces and pre-built machine learning algorithms, making it suitable for developers, irrespective of their coding expertise.

Accessing and Importing Data into Azure Machine Learning Studio

Azure Machine Learning Studio simplifies data access and importation. It enables easy data importing from various sources, including local files, HTTP(s), SQL databases, Azure Blob Storage, and others. On importing into Azure Machine Learning Studio, data exists either as datasets – which are references to the original data source or as datastores – which are abstractions over an Azure storage account.

To import data, we need to do the following:

Step 1

Go to **`Data`** from the left navigation panel:

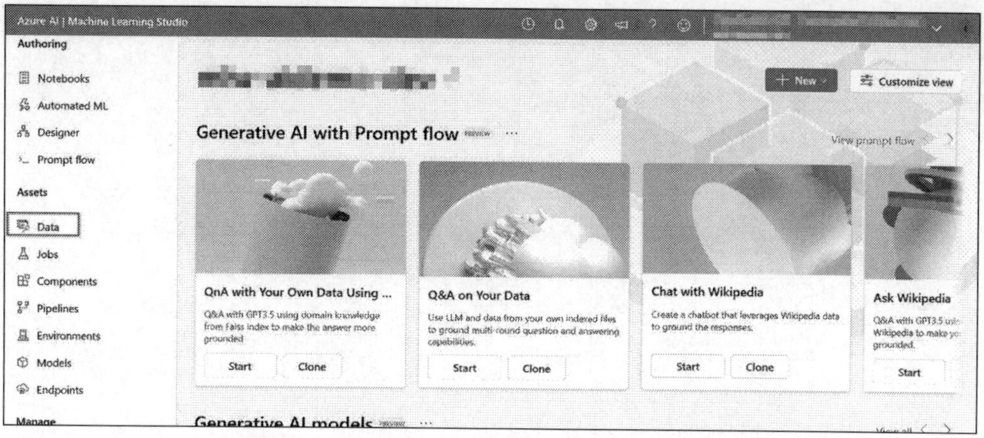

Figure 6.16: *Navigate to Data Section from Left Pane*

Step 2

Select the `Data assets` that was created previously:

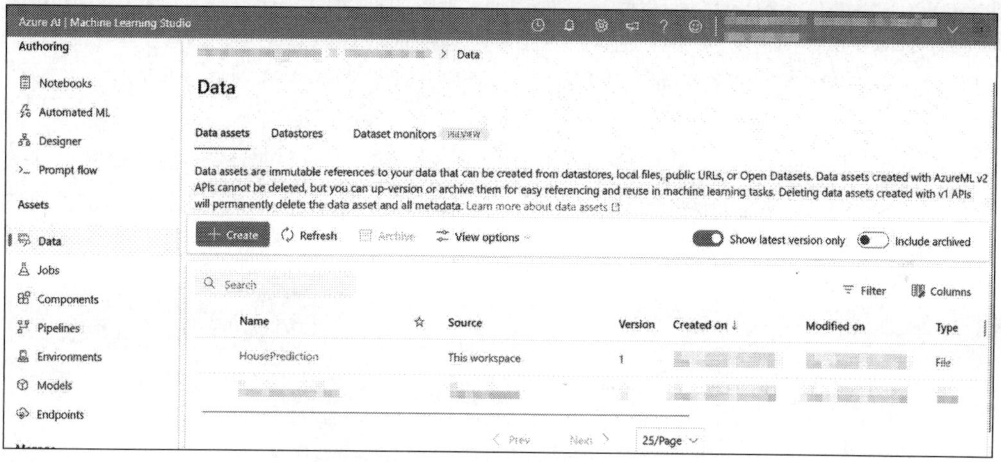

Figure 6.17: *The Data Dashboard*

Step 3

Go to `Consume` tab and copy the code:

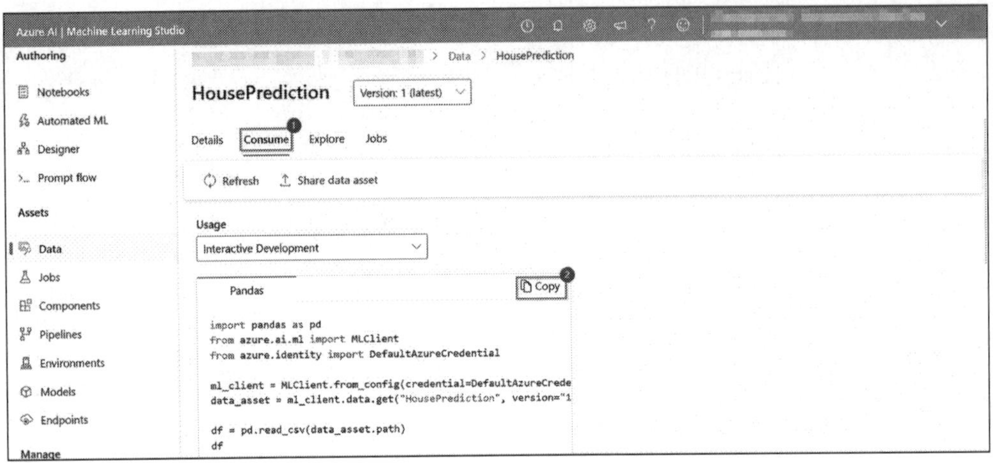

Figure 6.18: *Go to Consume Tab and Copy the Code*

This will let you easily use the data asset in the notebook.

Next, we will navigate to Notebooks from the left navigation pane. Create a new file and give an appropriate name. This will create your notebook.

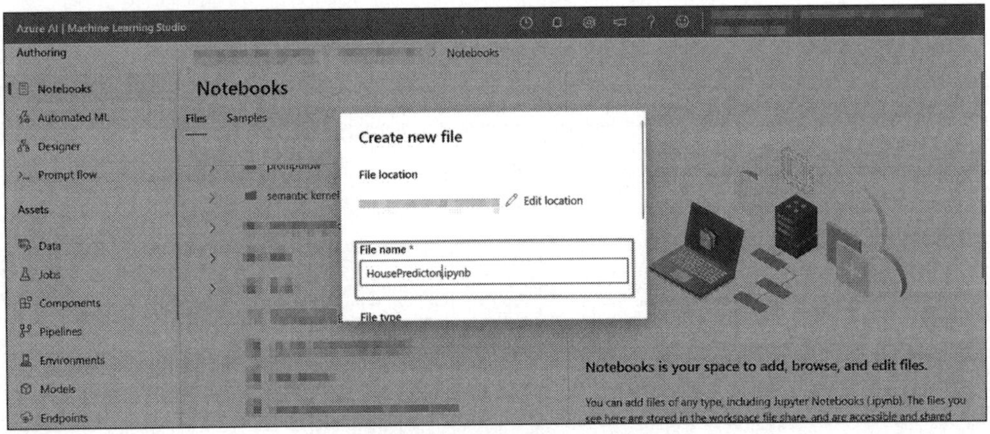

Figure 6.19: *Creating New Notebook*

From the compute section, select the compute that was created in the previous step.

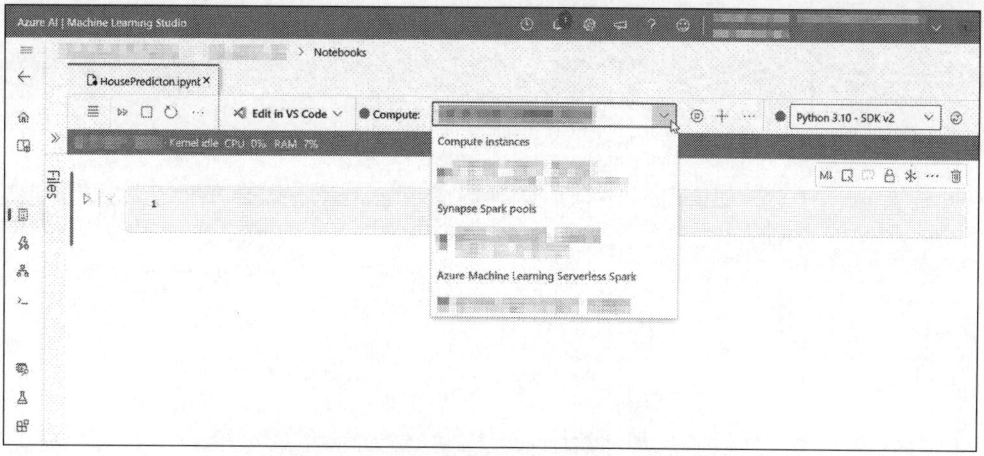

Figure 6.20: *Selecting the Compute Created*

Data Pre-processing Techniques Supported by Azure Machine Learning

After importing the data into Azure Machine Learning Studio, pre-processing is the next fundamental step. It is in this step that the data is cleaned and transformed to ensure optimal suitability for the machine learning model.

Azure Machine Learning supports different pre-processing techniques such as filling missing values, selecting essential features, adjusting the scale of values for numeric columns, and various data transformation modules. Moreover, Azure Notebooks allows the use of Python for data preparation tasks including data exploration and cleansing using the robust Pandas library.

Here are the steps elaborated with further details and Python code:

Loading the Data

This is the first step where data is loaded into a DataFrame from a specified source. A DataFrame provides a flexible data structure for data manipulation, similar to a spreadsheet or SQL table.

```
import pandas as pd
data = pd.read_csv('data.csv')
```

Figure 6.21: *Loading Data*

To load from a data asset, follow the aforementioned steps.

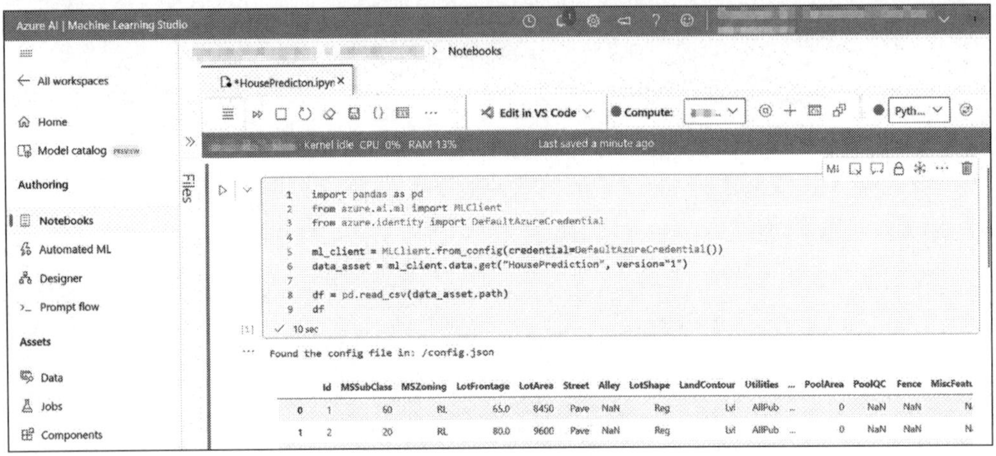

***Figure 6.22**: Importing Data (code copied from Consume tab)*

This Python code snippet is for importing a specific dataset from Azure Machine Learning Studio using the Azure SDK and loading it into a pandas DataFrame for further usage.

Here is a step-by-step explanation of the code:

```
import pandas as pd
```

This line is importing the pandas library as `**pd**`. Pandas is a software library used for data manipulation and analysis. It provides data structures and functions needed to manipulate structured data.

```
from azure.ai.ml import MLClient
```

This line is importing the **`MLClient`** class from the azure.ai.ml module. The **`MLClient`** class provides methods for managing machine learning resources on Azure.

```
from azure.identity import DefaultAzureCredential
```

This line is importing the **`DefaultAzureCredential`** class from the **`azure.identity`** module. This class provides a simple way to get a token from Azure Active Directory using the default credentials available on your system for the authenticated session.

```
ml_client = MLClient.from_config(credential=DefaultAzureCredential())
```

Here, we are creating an instance of **`MLClient`** using the **`'from_config()'`** function. This function creates an **`MLClient`** instance with the specified Azure credentials.

```
data_asset = ml_client.data.get("HousePrediction", version="1")
```

This line of code uses the `'get'` method to fetch the specific data (here, `"HousePrediction"` with version `"1"`) from Azure Machine Learning Studio. The fetched data is assigned to the variable `'data_asset'`.

```
df = pd.read_csv(data_asset.path)
```

Finally, the data is loaded into a DataFrame `'df'` using the `'read_csv'` method in Pandas. The `'read_csv'` function reads a comma-separated values (csv) file into DataFrame. The `.path` attribute of the data asset gives us the location of the csv file in the filesystem or url of the source.

The purpose of this code is to extract data from Azure Machine Learning Studio and load it into a Pandas DataFrame for further analysis or pre-processing. The DataFrame is a two-dimensional labeled data structure with columns of potentially different types. It is generally the most commonly used pandas object.

Inspecting the Data

Observing the data helps to understand its content and context. Getting an overview of its structure, features, and initial patterns would guide further data cleaning and processing strategy.

```
data.shape  #returns the number of rows and columns in your data
data.head() #returns the first few rows in your data
data.describe() #provides statistical insight into your numerical columns
```

Figure 6.23: *Inspecting Data*

Handling Missing Values

Missing values in the data can lead to misleading statistics and can cause algorithms to malfunction or produce faults. Hence, it is crucial to handle them correctly. Replacing these missing values with column mean, median, mode, or a specific value, or entirely dropping those values are few ways commonly used. The strategy depends on the nature of the data.

```
# Fill NaNs with the mean of the column
data['column_name'].fillna(value=data['column_name'].mean(), inplace=True)

# Replace all NaNs with a specified placeholder
data.fillna(-99999, inplace=True)

# Or drop rows with any empty cells
data.dropna(inplace=True)
```

Figure 6.24: *Handling Missing Values*

In this project, we are doing the following:

Step 1:

Printing the nulls present in each column:

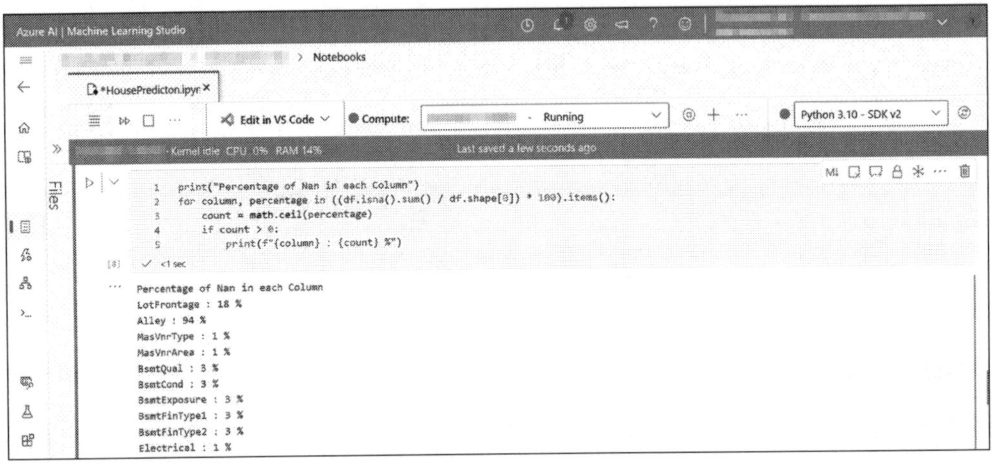

***Figure 6.25**: Calculating Null Percentage*

The null here means absence of a feature. Hence, we will fill the null values and drop the columns having extremely large null percentages.

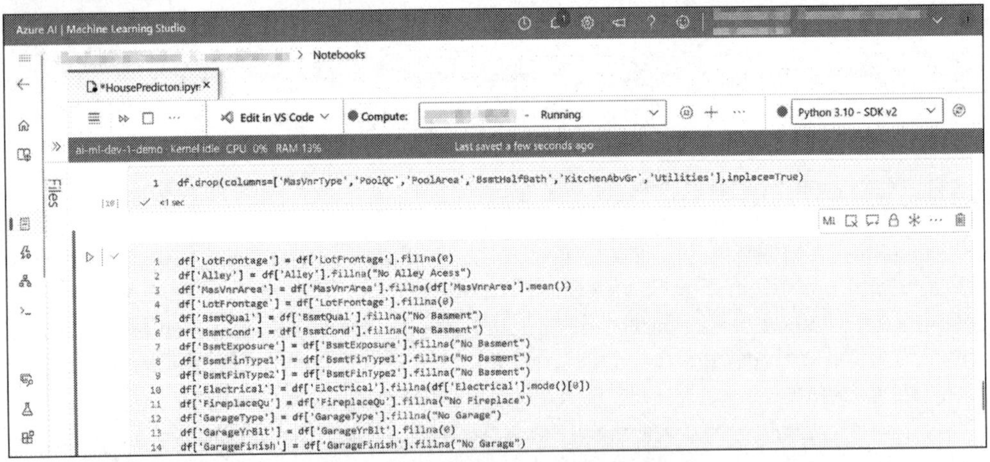

***Figure 6.26**: Filling Null Values*

Handling Duplicates

Duplicate entries could manipulate the model by creating a bias during training. Therefore, it is crucial to detect and delete any duplicate values to achieve a more accurate model.

```
data.drop_duplicates(inplace=True)  #removes all duplicate rows based on all columns
data.duplicated().sum()   #detecting duplicates
```

Figure 6.27: *Handling Duplicates*

Handling Outliers

Outliers represent data points that are significantly different from the others. These can occur due to variability in the data or experimental errors. They can substantially skew or bias our statistical analyses and hence need to be identified and handled.

One common method to detect and remove outliers is the **Z-Score method**. The Z-score is a measure which conveys how many standard deviations an element is from the mean. If the Z-score of a data point is greater than a threshold (commonly a Z-score of 3 or -3), it is considered an outlier.

Let us see how to implement the Z-score method using Python:

```
from scipy.stats import zscore

# Calculate Z-scores
z_scores = zscore(data['column_name'])

# Assume that we choose our threshold to be 3, Identifying outliers
outliers = np.where(z_scores > 3)[0]

# Removing outliers
data_clean = data.drop(outliers)
```

Figure 6.28: *Handling Outliers*

The preceding code calculates the Z-score for each data point in the `'column_name'` column. It then identifies the data points that have a Z-score greater than 3. These are considered outliers and are dropped from the DataFrame.

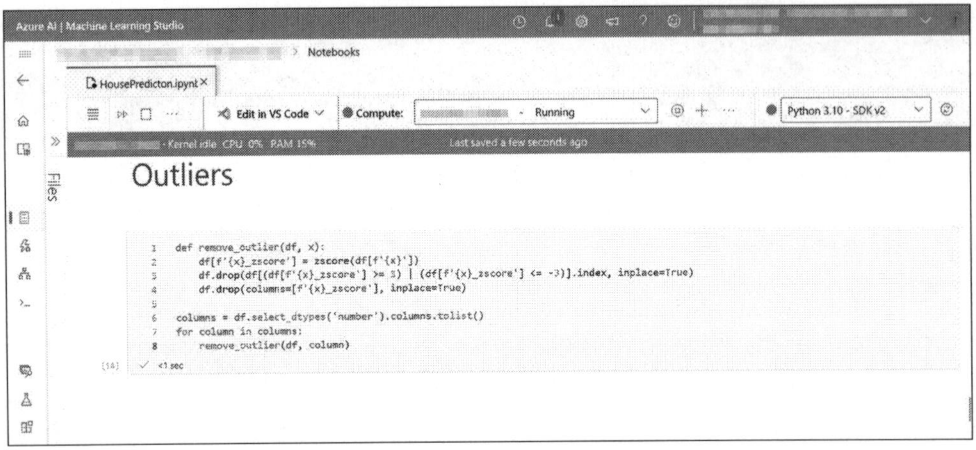

***Figure 6.29**: Handling Outliers Using Z-score*

This step is integral in data pre-processing as it helps refine our dataset by removing anomalous observations, which can drastically affect our model's accuracy and performance. Always remember that not all outliers are bad and dropping them all might lead to underfitting. Hence understanding the data well and basing your decisions on that is extremely essential.

Converting Data Types

The values could be numerical, categorical, date, or text. Each data type requires specific treatment and is used differently by machine learning algorithms. Some algorithms only accept numeric values, hence necessitating the need to convert categorical data into a numerical format (a process known as encoding).

```
data['some_column'] = data['some_column'].astype('category')
```

Data Transformation

Distinct features in a dataset can often have different scales. Suppose one feature measures in kilometres, and other measures in centimetres. These dissimilar scales can create complications for certain machine learning algorithms (like Support Vector Machine SVM, Linear Regression) as they measure distances between different data points. Therefore, scaling features to the same range can prevent this issue. Scaling can be performed in numerous ways, including Normalization(0-1 scaling), Standardization(mean=0, variance=1), and so on.

```
from sklearn.preprocessing import StandardScaler, MinMaxScaler,
RobustScaler

sc = StandardScaler() #instantiate the StandardScaler

data['column_name'] = sc.fit_transform(data['column_name'])
```

Encoding Data

Encoding is a process of converting categorical data into a format that can be easily understood by machine learning algorithms. Some algorithms can directly handle categorical data, but many require numerical inputs.

One encoding method often used is the Creation of Dummy Variables. This method converts a categorical variable into a series of zeros and ones, which makes them easier to quantitatively measure.

Let us see how to create dummy variables using Python's pandas library:

```
encoded_data = pd.get_dummies(data, columns=['categorical_column'])
```

This code takes the categorical column **`'categorical_column'`** and creates a new binary column for each unique category in the original column. If **`'categorical_column'`** had three categories (**`A`**, **`B`**, **`C`**), it would create three new columns (**`categorical_column_A`**, **`categorical_column_B`**, **`categorical_column_C`**). Each row in the dataset would have a 1 in the column that matches the original value and 0 in the other dummy columns.

The choice of encoding method depends on the categorical data's attributes (ordinal or nominal) and the specific algorithm you are applying. While dummy variables are great for linear regression models, other encoding methods like ordinal encoding or one-hot encoding might be more suitable for tree-based models. Encoding enhances the expressiveness of the dataset, allowing machine learning algorithms to interpret the data better and create more accurate models.

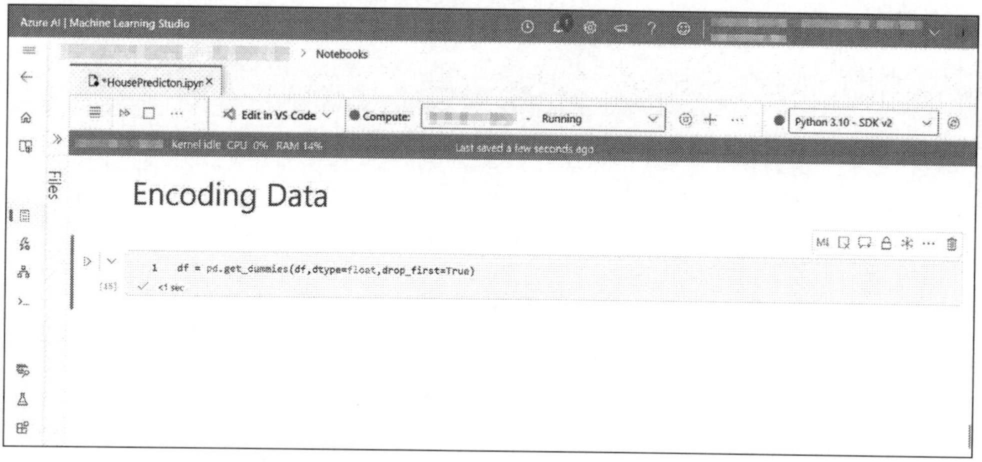

***Figure 6.30**: Encoding Data*

Implementing these pre-processing steps in Azure Machine Learning using Python provides an understanding and expertise to handle any kind of data and improve its quality, consequently enhancing the performance of your machine learning model.

Splitting Data into Training and Test Sets

Once data is pre-processed, it is divided into two sets – training dataset and test dataset. This split is essential for model evaluation in Azure ML.

The **'train_test_split'** function from the sklearn library in Python offers a quick and easy way to split the data.

```
from sklearn.model_selection import train_test_split

# Assume 'Feature' as independent variables and 'Target' is the dependent variable
X_train, X_test, y_train, y_test = train_test_split(data['Feature'], data['Target'], test_size=0.2,
random_state=42)
```

***Figure 6.31**: Splitting the Data*

The **'test_size'** parameter in the function represents the proportion of the dataset to include in the test split. Another parameter **'random_state'** is used for initializing the internal random number generator, which decides the splitting of data into train and test indices.

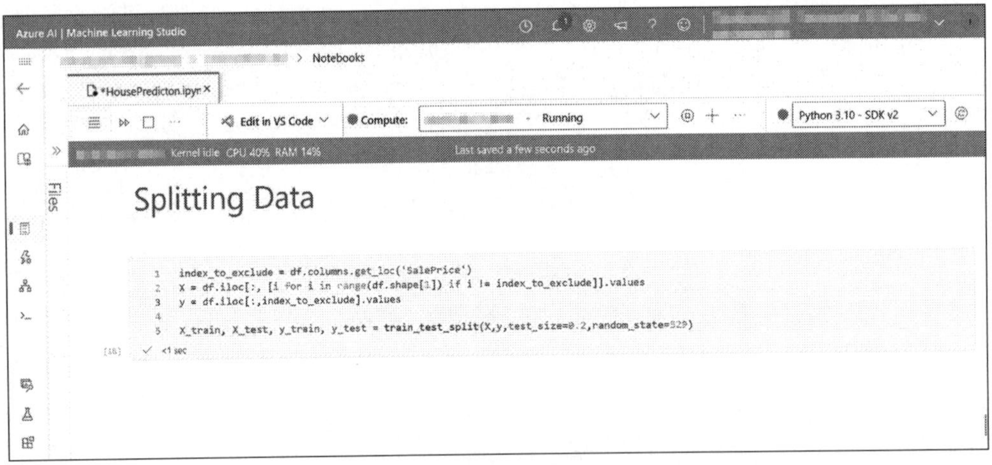

***Figure 6.32**: Splitting into Train and Test Dataset*

These steps, including training and testing data, data pre-processing, and data importing, all come together to create an effective process for preparing data in Azure Machine Learning.

After we are done with the splitting, we will scale the data.

Data Scaling

Scaling adjusts the range or distribution of feature values in your data to ensure that they can be compared on a common scale. Some machine learning algorithms, like K-Nearest

Neighbours (KNN) and Support Vector Machine (SVM), use distance-based calculations, while others like gradient descent benefit from faster convergence with scaled data. Machines can find it harder to learn from features that have a wide range of values. Hence, data scaling is performed to bring all the features to the same level of magnitudes.

The most common types of scaling are Standardization and Normalization. Standardization adjusts the features so they have a mean of 0 and a standard deviation of 1, while normalization scales features from 0 to 1. The choice of scaling technique depends on your data and the machine learning algorithm you are using.

Reasons to Scale Data After Splitting

The main reason to scale data after splitting into train and test sets is to avoid data leakage. When you are training a model, you should only use the training data. This applies to preprocessing steps like scaling as well. If we scale our data before splitting it, we are using information from our future test set (mean and standard deviation) to scale the entire dataset.

This could lead to overly optimistic results during the evaluation step, as we are artificially lowering the dataset's complexity based on the knowledge from the test set. In real-world scenarios where test data is unseen data, using data from the test set to influence the training set destroys the whole purpose of the test-train split.

So, it is recommended to fit the scalar to the training data only, then standardize both the training and test sets using this scaler. This way, we are not `'cheating'` by using information about our test data in the pre-processing step; hence, it helps us make a reliable estimate of how our model will perform on unseen data. Here is an example:

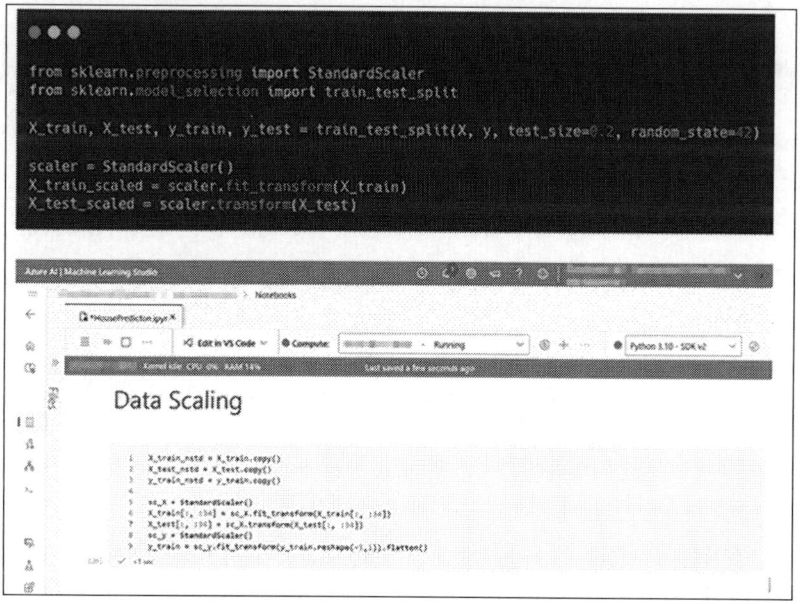

Figure 6.33: *Scaling Data Using Standard Scalar*

In the above case, note that we used `fit_transform` on the training data but only `transform` on testing data. This process maintains the integrity of the testing set and provides a realistic evaluation of the model's performance on unseen data.

Building and Training Machine Learning Models Using Azure Machine Learning SDK

With the advent of powerful cloud computing resources, it has become more feasible to train sophisticated machine learning models that require substantial processing power and memory. One such tool that has facilitated this change is Azure Machine Learning SDK. The Azure Machine Learning SDK is a Python-based, open-source library that enables data scientists to effectively train, test, and deploy machine learning models using the vast resources offered by Microsoft's Azure machine learning service.

Enhancing the working capability of Python, the feature-rich Azure SDK offers several utilities and classes to streamline machine learning workflows. The main topics discussed below will provide a comprehensive understanding of using the Azure Machine Learning SDK, specifically focusing on selecting and constructing models and training them using cloud resources.

Overview of the Azure Machine Learning SDK for Python

Azure Machine Learning SDK is an effective tool designed to leverage cloud computing resources for machine learning. It offers a wide range of services from model training to deployment and management. Azure ML SDK is a reflection of Microsoft's commitment to bring machine learning to every developer across different industries.

The Azure Machine Learning SDK operates with the following primary components.

Workspace

The Workspace class represents an Azure Machine Learning resource on the cloud. It holds all the key details associated with your machine learning experiments. Its core function is to act as the central hub where various components such as shared resources, connection settings, credential details, and high-level features like datastores and compute targets are associated and managed.

Each workspace is tied to a single Azure subscription and resource group, which is a collection of resources that share the same lifecycle, permissions, and policies.

Workspaces are crucial in handling the security and compliance of resources used in machine learning workflows.

```
from azureml.core import Workspace
ws = Workspace.create(name='myworkspace',
                      subscription_id='<azure-subscription-id>',
                      resource_group='myresourcegroup',
                      create_resource_group=True,
                      location='eastus2'
                      )
```

***Figure 6.34**: Initiate Workspace*

Experiment

An Experiment in Azure ML represents a series of runs, usually aimed at achieving a single comparable outcome. It is essentially a naming scope to organize various runs. The series of runs under an experiment may correspond to tuning hyperparameters of a model, iterating over data, testing different model types, or any other variations imposed on the model in the ML process.

Each run in an experiment logs metrics and outputs to get insights into the results during or after the run. This information is stored in the Azure cloud and is accessible even after the run is complete. You can compare the results of different runs in an experiment and choose the best performing model for your requirement.

```
from azureml.core import Experiment

experiment = Experiment(workspace=ws, name="myexperiment")
```

Run

A Run in Azure refers to the execution of a script or a piece of code. The **Run** class lets us monitor the asynchronous execution of a trial, log metrics, and store output of the trial, and analyze results. Each Run instance is a child of an Experiment.

When working on complex machine learning tasks, you might initiate multiple runs. It could either be for data preprocessing, model training, model validation, or model deployment. Each run records the information it generates, including both the metadata like start time, end time, status, and so on, and the metrics, which allows you to audit and reproduce your work later.

```
run = experiment.start_logging()

run.log("trial", 1)

run.complete()
```

Model

A Model is a fundamental part of machine learning. It is the outcome of a machine learning algorithm run on data. A model represents what was learned by a machine learning algorithm. Azure Machine Learning keeps track of all trained models, their versions, their performances, and the run that created the model.

In Azure ML, you can manage (register, version, retrieve, and deploy) models using the **`Model`** class. You register a model when you want to track and manage the model including deploying it, or when you want to share the model with others. Azure Machine Learning supports tracing models not just from training runs, but from anywhere, helping to manage models and facilitating easy comparisons across models based on a range of metrics.

```
from azureml.core.model import Model
model = Model.register(workspace = ws,
                       model_path ="./model.pkl",
                       model_name = "mymodel",
                       tags = {"version": "1.0"},
                       description = "model description")
```

***Figure 6.35**: Registering model*

Selecting and Constructing Machine Learning Models Using SDK

When selecting a machine learning model using Azure Machine Learning SDK, the choice is largely driven by the nature of the problem at hand. The SDK provides a vast range of machine learning algorithms for tasks such as regression, classification, clustering, anomaly detection, and others.

For choosing the appropriate algorithm, Azure also offers automated machine learning (AutoML) which includes automated model selection and hyperparameter tuning to optimize model performance.

Here is an example of how to use automated machine learning to select and construct a model using the SDK:

```
from azureml.train.automl import AutoMLConfig

automl_config = AutoMLConfig(task='classification',
                             iterations=10,
                             primary_metric='AUC_weighted',
                             training_data=data_train,
                             label_column_name='label',
                             n_cross_validations=5)
from azureml.core.experiment import Experiment
experiment = Experiment(ws, 'Automl_experiment')
local_run = experiment.submit(automl_config, show_output=True)
```

Figure 6.36: *Training*

When constructing models, Azure Machine Learning SDK gives the flexibility to define and train models using popular libraries such as Scikit-learn, TensorFlow, or PyTorch, among others. For instance, you can use Scikit-learn to define and train a model then use SDK to log metrics or save the model:

```
# Importing Required Libraries
from sklearn.linear_model import LogisticRegression
from sklearn.metrics import roc_auc_score
from azureml.core.run import Run

# Getting The Current Run
run = Run.get_context()

# Defining and Training Logistic Regression Model
clf = LogisticRegression().fit(X_train, y_train)

# Making Prediction on validation data
y_hat = clf.predict(X_validation)

# Calculating the AUC score
auc_score = roc_auc_score(y_validation, y_hat)
run.log('AUC', auc_score)

# Saving The Model
import joblib
joblib.dump(value=clf, filename='model.pkl')

run.upload_file(name = 'outputs/model.pkl', path_or_stream = './model.pkl')

run.complete()
```

Figure 6.37: *Predicting and saving the model*

After training, the resulting trained model can be easily registered into the workspace.

The registered model then can be deployed on a local machine for testing or on cloud-based resources for large-scale, real-time inference.

```
from azureml.core.model import Model
model = Model.register(model_name='classification_model',
                       model_path='outputs/model.pkl',
                       tags={'Area': 'diabetes', 'Type': 'Logistic Regression'},
                       description='A model to predict diabetes',
workspace = ws)

Where, workspace, can be registered as follows:

ws = Workspace.get(name="myworkspace",
               subscription_id='<azure-subscription-id>',
               resource_group='myresourcegroup',
location = 'location')
```

Figure 6.38: *Registering model to workspace*

With automated machine learning and support for popular libraries, Azure Machine Learning SDK simplifies both model selection and construction.

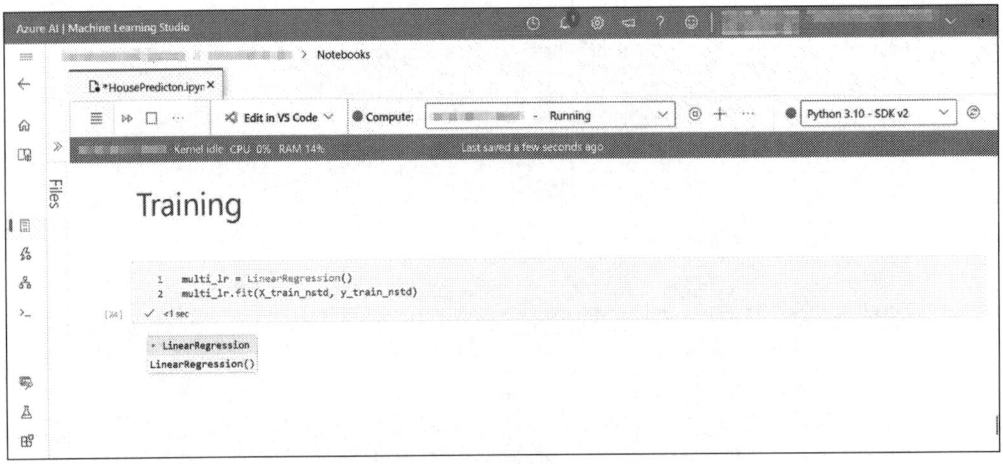

Figure 6.39: *Creating and training the model*

After training is done, we need to evaluate how well our model is performing.

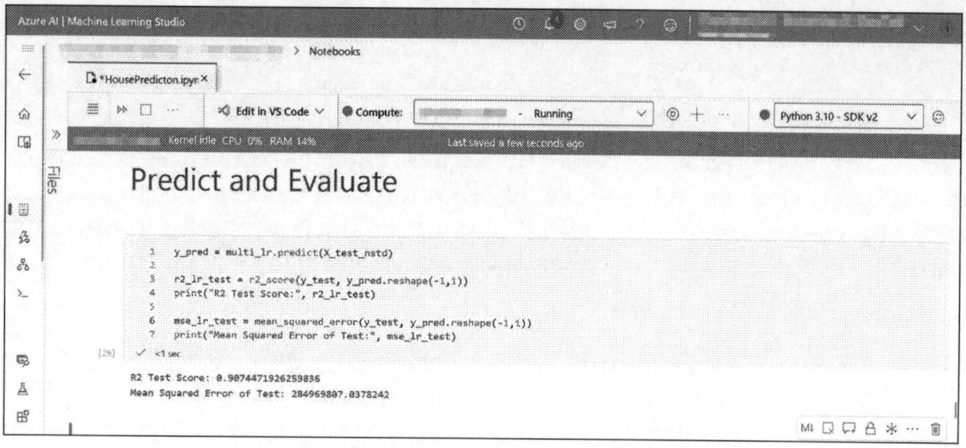

Figure 6.40: *Predict and evaluate the model*

Next, we log in the metrics of the model.

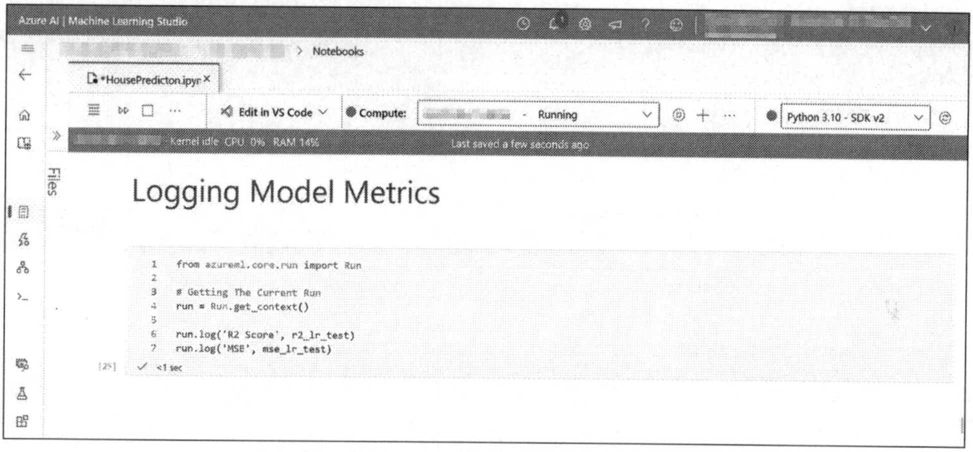

Figure 6.41: *Logging the metrics using Run*

The preceding code is logging metrics for a machine learning model in the Azure Machine Learning workspace.

Here is a breakdown of what is happening:

```
from azureml.core.run import Run
```

This line imports the `Run` class from the Azure Machine Learning SDK. The `Run` class provides methods for managing and tracking the progress of your model training scripts.

```
run = Run.get_context()
```

In this line, the `get_context` method is used to retrieve the current service context for the `Run`. The `Run` context is a way to interact with the Azure ML workspace that the current script is being run in. It allows you to log metrics and upload/download files to/from the workspace.

```
run.log('R2 Score', r2_lr_test)
```

Here, the `log` method is being used to track a metric named **'R2 Score'** in the current `Run`. `r2_lr_test` is the value of the R2 Score for this model run. The R2 Score is a statistical measure that represents the proportion of the variance for a dependent variable that is explained by an independent variable or variables in a regression model.

```
run.log('MSE', mse_lr_test)
```

Similarly, the Mean Squared Error (MSE) of the model is being logged here. `mse_lr_test` is the value of the MSE for this model run. The MSE measures the average squared differences between the observed and predicted values.

These logged metrics will appear in the Azure Machine Learning Studio, where you can monitor the performance of your machine learning models and experiments. They are particularly useful when you need to track operation results or model performance during training, especially when performing hyperparameter tuning or model comparison.

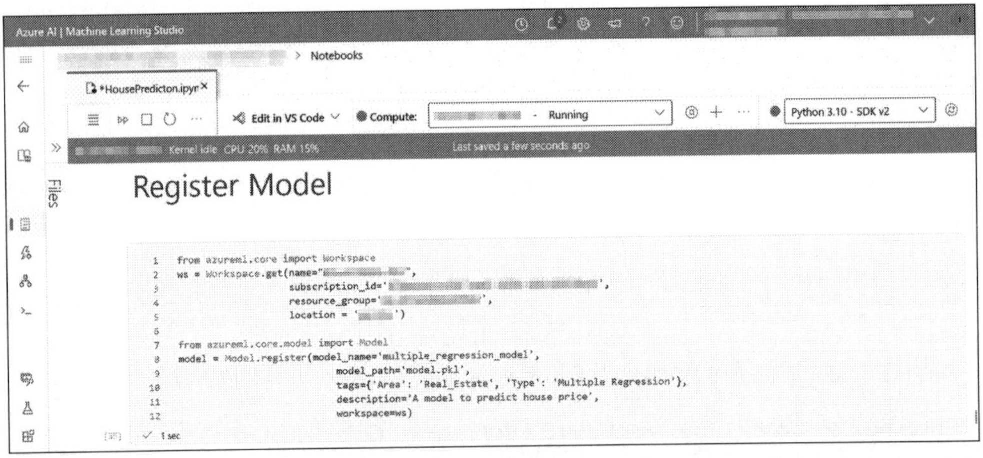

***Figure 6.42**: Register Workspace and Model*

Training Models on Cloud Resources

Training a machine learning model can be resource-intensive. However, cloud resources provide scalable computing power which can be customized based on the requirements. Azure Machine Learning service provides a range of options on which to train your model, from your local machine to a single cloud-based Virtual Machine, to a GPU cluster in Azure.

Azure Machine Learning SDK includes features for managing compute targets – cloud-based resources for training models which abstract the raw hardware. It allows you to easily scale up and out from your local machine to powerful cloud-based computing resources without needing to manage the hardware. The training tasks are sent to these compute targets from the SDK and queued up centrally in the workspace, providing robust management of training resources.

In summary, the Azure Machine Learning SDK provides powerful, streamlined tools for managing the full lifecycle of machine learning models. Its support for an extensive range of machine learning tasks, from model construction and training to deployment and management, makes it a valuable tool in any data scientist's toolkit.

Hyperparameter Tuning and Model Selection

Building robust and effective machine learning models is not a one-shot deal; it is an iterative grind, where data scientists repeatedly tweak and test various aspects of the model to find the optimal version. This process, known as model development, is essential because a machine learning model is not just slapped together – it is carefully crafted and adjusted for best results.

This development-focused iteration involves a lot of trial and error with different model architectures and algorithms, each with its unique characteristics and settings. The options could range from simple decision trees to sophisticated neural networks, each bringing something different to the table. With these choices in hand, data scientists must also navigate the world of hyperparameters – these are settings that are not learned from the data but are set before the learning process begins. They can dramatically affect how well a model learns and performs.

However, tuning these hyperparameters is no walk in the park, especially because there is usually no clear formula for setting them. Choosing the right configuration often involves searching through a massive number of possibilities to find the best combination. This can be done either exhaustively, by trying out many combinations (like with grid searching), more randomly (like with random searching), or by using advanced methods such as Bayesian optimization that cleverly pick hyperparameters based on past outcomes.

With each iteration, models are compared against performance metrics that make the most sense for the problem at hand. These could include common measures such as accuracy, precision, and recall. But picking the winner is not just about finding the model with the best metrics – it is also about ensuring it will work well in the real world. Considerations like how easy the model is to understand, how costly it is to run, and whether it will scale to handle large amounts of data all matter.

In short, creating great machine learning models is a repetitive and detail-oriented process. It is about testing different options, fine-tuning settings, and carefully balancing the many factors that contribute to a model's success, from performance to practical deployability.

Introduction to Hyperparameter Tuning

While developing machine learning models, the term "*hyperparameters*" refers to the configuration variables that govern the model construction process. Unlike regular parameters, which are learnt from the data during the training phase, hyperparameters are predefined. They guide the overall structure and performance of the model.

Consider the example of a neural network. The number of hidden layers, the number of neurons in each layer, the type of activation function, the learning rate – all these are examples of hyperparameters. They are not directly learnt within the estimator, and yet they significantly influence the model's performance.

Hyperparameter tuning, thus, is a crucial step in the process of building machine learning models. It involves selecting the right set of hyperparameters to optimize the model's performance. If you think of the model as a car, then hyperparameters are like the settings you adjust to make your car run smoothly and efficiently. Just as you might adjust your car's suspension or tyre pressure to improve its performance, in machine learning, you tweak the hyperparameters of your model to enhance its predictive accuracy and efficiency.

However, hyperparameter tuning poses a challenge, and here is why – The set of possible hyperparameters can be enormous, and each combination will lead to a unique set of model performances. The sheer number of possibilities makes it computationally expensive (both in terms of resources and time) to perform hyperparameter tuning.

This process becomes an optimization problem – You want to find a set of hyperparameters that will minimize (or maximize) a predefined objective function (which could be a loss function, accuracy score, F1-score, and so on). As this function is often described as a complex multi-dimensional space, hyperparameter tuning involves navigating this space in such a way that we reach the **`'valley'`** (minima) or **`'peak'`** (maxima) efficiently.

The most basic technique for hyperparameter tuning is Grid Search, where you define a set of possible values for each hyperparameter and test out every possible combination. This process, though simple, can be incredibly time and computation consuming. Another technique is Random Search, where random combinations of hyperparameters are chosen and used to train the model, and the model's performance is noted. While less exhaustive than Grid Search, it can be faster and more efficient.

More sophisticated techniques include Gradient-based optimization and Bayesian Optimization. Bayesian Optimization is a highly effective technique in which the next set of hyperparameters to evaluate depends on the results of the previous ones. This strategy aims to minimize the number of steps.

Clearly, hyperparameter tuning is as much art as it is science, requiring a balance between computational efficiency and a thorough search for optimized settings. The best set of hyperparameters often depends on the specific task and the nature of the data. Hence, machine learning practitioners often begin with standard settings, refine these using their understanding of the data and the problem at hand, and then rely on automated hyperparameter tuning techniques to further fine-tune the model.

Azure Machine Learning SDK Hyperparameter Tuning

Azure Machine Learning SDK provides comprehensive support for hyperparameter tuning in Python and simplifies a lot of the process. It first starts with generating a workspace, which is an environment for experimentation within Azure. The workspace maintains all resources under one cloud-based application, making it neat and easy to manage.

```
from azureml.core import Workspace
ws = Workspace.create(name='myworkspace',
                      subscription_id='my-subscription-id',
                      resource_group='myresourcegroup',
                      create_resource_group=True,
                      location='eastus2')
```

Figure 6.43: *Creating workspace*

Then, you can create a specific experiment within this workspace. An experiment acts like a repository where you can store multiple related `'runs'`.

```
from azureml.core import Experiment
exp = Experiment(workspace=ws, name='myexperiment')
```

Figure 6.44: *Creating experiment*

A `'run'` in Azure Machine Learning world is essentially a single execution of a script or method as part of your experiment. It is within these runs that the magic of hyperparameter tuning takes place.

```
run = exp.start_logging()
run.log("Experiment start time", str(datetime.datetime.now()))
```

Figure 6.45: *Using the run command*

Azure uses an approach of automated ML for hyperparameter tuning with a module called **HyperDrive**. You will need to define the search space for hyperparameters and a known performance metric for your model. This performance measure helps to compare and select the best model and hyperparameters.

```
from azureml.train.hyperdrive import RandomParameterSampling, PrimaryMetricGoal, HyperDriveConfig
param_sampling = RandomParameterSampling( {
    'learning_rate': normal(0.1, 0.05),
    'batch_size': choice(16, 32, 64, 128)
})

hyperdrive_config = HyperDriveConfig(run_config=src,
                                     hyperparameter_sampling=param_sampling,
                                     primary_metric_name='accuracy',
                                     primary_metric_goal=PrimaryMetricGoal.MAXIMIZE,
                                     max_total_runs=50,
                                     max_concurrent_runs=4)
```

Figure 6.46: *Using hyperdrive config*

Once the model training and optimization is completed, you save it with a name for future use and reference.

```
model = run.register_model(model_name='mymodel', model_path='outputs/model.pkl')
```

Figure 6.47: *Save the model*

Strategies for Selecting the Best Model

Choosing the best model for your machine learning problem can be a daunting task, especially as the number of potential models and model configurations can be vast.

Once the models have been trained through different runs with a variety of hyperparameters, it is crucial to select the one that promises the best predictive performance.

The model selection process involves comparing the evaluated metrics of the created models. These metrics can include common performance measures such as accuracy, precision, recall, F1 score, Mean Squared Error (MSE), Root Mean Squared Error (RMSE), Mean Absolute Error (MAE), and more sophisticated measures like the area under the ROC Curve (AUC-ROC). However, it is essential to remember that no single metric can encompass a model's desirability, and the selection will depend on the specifics of the problem at hand.

It is also important to verify that the model performance on the training data translates to similar performance on unseen data, ensuring that the model is robust and not overfitting. This verification is often done using cross-validation techniques, where the data set is split into several subsets. The model is trained on a combination of these subsets and tested on the remaining ones. Through cross-validation, the selected model's performance can be reasonably assured before deploying it to production.

Azure Machine Learning offers useful tools to make this process efficient. The **HyperDrive** module, for example, logs all the metrics from each run during the hyperparameter tuning process. This feature allows for easy comparison of the different models and hyperparameters configurations. Once the models have been ranked by their performance, the top-performing models can be further scrutinized by their performance on a hold-out validation set.

Other considerations for selecting the best model might include the complexity of the model, the interpretability of its predictions, and its computational resource requirements.

In theme with Azure Machine Learning's emphasis on the full machine learning lifecycle, the service also enables model management to ease updating models in production, versioning, and monitoring.

```
from azureml.core import Model

# List registered models
for model in Model.list(ws):
    print(model.name, 'version:', model.version)
    for tag_name in model.tags:
        tag = model.tags[tag_name]
        print ('\t',tag_name, ':', tag)
    for prop_name in model.properties:
        prop = model.properties[prop_name]
        print ('\t',prop_name, ':', prop)
    print('\n')
```

***Figure 6.48**: List down registered models*

In summary, selecting the best model involves evaluating each trained model's performance using appropriate metrics, ensuring the chosen model's generalizability through cross-validation, and considering computational and practical constraints. Tools provided by Azure Machine Learning greatly streamline this process, supporting clear and organized experimentation and decision-making.

Model Evaluation Techniques and Metrics

In the realm of machine learning, creating a model is just half the battle. The other critical aspect revolves around evaluating the effectiveness of the models. The evaluation process involves various techniques and metrics that ascertain whether a model is performing well, needs improvement, or is generally poor.

Different Evaluation Metrics for Various Machine Learning Tasks

Deploying the appropriate evaluation metrics is crucial for measuring a machine learning model's performance accurately. However, these metrics can vary significantly according to the task at hand. Here, we delve into some detailed examples of specific metrics utilized for various types of machine learning tasks.

Regression Task Metrics

Regression tasks entail the prediction of continuous values. Metrics employed for these tasks centre on determining the disparity between the model's predicted values and the actual outcomes. A few of the most applied regression evaluation metrics include the following.

Mean Absolute Error (MAE)

It calculates the average absolute difference between the predicted and actual values. The smaller the MAE, the better the model.

Mean Squared Error (MSE)

It calculates the average of the squares of the errors between the predicted and actual values. The smaller the MSE, the better the model. It is more sensitive to outliers compared to MAE.

Root Mean Squared Error (RMSE)

This is the square root of MSE. It has the advantage of expressing error in the same units as the original values, which aids interpretability.

Classification Task Metrics

In classification tasks, the aim is to predict discrete categories or classes. The most prevalent evaluation tools are as follows.

Accuracy

It indicates the proportion of correct predictions made by the model out of all predictions.

Precision

Focusing on the prediction of positive classes, precision calculates the percentage of correct positive predictions out of all predicted positives.

Recall (Sensitivity)

It identifies the percentage of actual positives the model accurately catches.

F1 Score

The F1 Score is the harmonic mean of precision and recall, providing a balance between them. It is particularly useful in cases of imbalanced class distribution.

Confusion Matrix

A '`Confusion matrix`', providing a tabulation of True Positives, True Negatives, False Positives, and False Negatives, can offer a comprehensive representation of the model's performance.

Clustering Task Metrics

Unsupervised learning tasks, such as clustering, demand another set of metrics. These metrics, like Silhouette Coefficient, Davies-Bouldin Index, and Mutual Information, are used to evaluate the quality of clustering achieved by the model.

Ranking Task Metrics

Ranking tasks involve the prediction of the ordering of examples. In these tasks, metrics like the Mean Reciprocal Rank, Normalized Discounted Cumulative Gain, and Precision at K are employed to quantify model performance.

Azure ML SDK v2 provides a built-in approach to these metrics, allowing the evaluation metrics to be integrated into the model with few lines of code. This greatly simplifies the model evaluation process and ensures an efficient and comprehensive analysis of the machine learning models in various tasks.

Visualizing and Interpreting Evaluation Results

Visualizing and interpreting evaluation results is vital to understand how a model performs. It helps in identifying the shortcomings of a model and provides a path for improvement.

Visualizing evaluation results in Azure can be done using assorted charts and diagrams using Python libraries such as Matplotlib and Seaborn. For instance, a Confusion Matrix can be visualized for classification tasks, while a scatter plot can illustrate prediction versus actual results for regression tasks.

Azure ML SDK v2 provides various methods that make it easy to interpret ML models. Model interpretability in Azure Machine Learning aids in understanding the model's overall global behavior, or understanding the reasons behind individual predictions.

Model Validation and Cross-Validation in Azure Machine Learning Studio

Model validation involves the splitting of the given dataset into a training set and a test set. The training set is used to train the model while the test set is used to evaluate the model's performance on unseen data.

Cross-validation is another technique to validate a model's performance. In this, the data set is divided into K "`folds`," where K-1 folds are used for training, and the last fold is used for testing. This process is repeated K times, each time with a different fold used as the testing set.

In the context of Azure Machine Learning Studio, both validation and cross-validation techniques are available. For cross-validation, Azure ML provides a module named "*Partition and Sample*" that enables a user to split the data into the desired number of partitions. It also provides an inbuilt cross-validation module, making it straightforward for users to perform cross-validation.

To summarize, the model evaluation process plays a crucial role in the development of a reliable and efficient machine learning model. It involves selection and application of the right evaluation metrics, visualization and interpretation of results, and validation of the model using suitable techniques. Azure Machine Learning Studio, with easy-to-use libraries and modules, empowers users to perform all these steps with ease and precision.

Deploying Models and Real-time Prediction

Whenever a machine learning model is trained and ready, the next step is to deploy it for practical use. This involves preparing the model for deployment, setting up a suitable deployment environment, and finally establishing a system for real-time predictions. Throughout this process, tools like Azure ML SDK v2 and ML Studio can simplify and streamline each step.

Preparing a Model for Deployment

Preparation of your machine learning model for deployment is the bridge between the development phase and the operational phase. This process is primarily directed towards ensuring that your model performs optimally in a live environment.

When we say preparation, a key fraction of this process is to finalize the model's parameters. This is necessary to optimize prediction accuracy in a production environment. The Azure ML SDK v2 provides a flexible platform for testing out various combinations of parameters using techniques like Grid Search and Random Search. You can select the combination of parameters that gives the highest accuracy or performance based on your designated criteria.

Next, you come to the part of training your algorithm with the complete dataset. While during the initial phases of model development, developers partition the dataset into smaller lots for training and testing purposes, this step ensures the model is exposed to the maximum variant of data points, thus helping improve its learning.

Evaluating the precision of your model is the following crucial step. Azure's ML SDK v2 offers a wide range of tools designed to measure model performance through various metrics such as confusion matrix, receiver operating characteristic (ROC) curve, Mean Absolute Error (MAE), Mean Squared Error (MSE), among others. These metrics give a quantitative basis to help understand how well your model has learnt from the data and predict future outcomes.

Finally, saving your model in an appropriate format that can be recognized and interpreted by the deployment environment is the final step in preparing your model. In Python, one of the commonly used formats for this purpose is `'.pkl'` (pickle), which is a serialized format for storing python objects, including the machine learning models. By employing the Azure ML SDK v2, you can easily pickle the model and unpickle it in the deployment environment, ensuring seamless integration.

In the same context, ML Studio, with its graphical interface, makes the process even more intuitive. The trained model details, along with the respective parameters, are encapsulated as a module that you can use with `'Train Model'`. The performance can be evaluated graphically using `'Score Model'` and `'Evaluate Model'`.

In conclusion, preparing a model for deployment is a meticulous process, as this will determine how the model performs in real-time. However, with tools such as Azure ML SDK v2 and ML Studio, this process is simplified and efficient, enabling developers to transition their models smoothly from the training phase to the production-ready phase.

Setting Up a Deployment Environment

Setting up a successful deployment environment for a machine learning model involves intricate stages, including deciding on a suitable deployment platform, configuring the necessary tools and resources, provisioning the computational resources, and finally deploying the model.

A deployment platform can be a local server, cloud platform, or an edge device depending upon your requirement. The platform should be capable of running the model and catering to the expected demand for model predictions. Ideally, the platform should be scalable to handle increasing data inputs and should provide low latency for prediction responses.

Azure ML SDK v2 offers a host of services and functionalities to easily set up a deployment environment for your models. One compelling feature is Azure's compatibility with Docker containers, which can package the model and its dependencies into a standardized unit for software development. These containers can be deployed on Azure's cloud platform, effectively encapsulating and isolating the model implementation.

For larger-scale deployments, Azure ML SDK v2 provides integration with Azure Kubernetes Service (AKS). AKS is a fully managed container orchestration service. It makes it effortless to deploy, scale, and manage distributed applications. AKS abstracts the underlying infrastructure, manages the orchestration of containers, and handles tasks like scaling and health monitoring. By using AKS, you can focus solely on the application logic and not get side-tracked with managing server infrastructure.

In Azure ML Studio, setting up a deployment environment is a user-friendly process. You can utilize the array of tools and modules provided by ML Studio to configure your environment without much technical knowledge. After creating and training your model, you can directly proceed to the **`"Setup Web Service"`** button. Here you have options to deploy your model as a classic web service or a new web service. Classic web services deploy machine learning models as web services hosted on Azure Cloud. New web services, on the other hand, grant access to even more extensive scalable solutions, including desirable features such as autoscaling and higher fault tolerance.

Both Azure ML SDK v2 and ML Studio support deploying your models for real-time predictions or batch predictions, depending upon your needs. The deployment process involves creating compute resources, deploying your model, and testing the endpoint of the deployed model.

Once your deployment environment is set up correctly, you can ensure seamless integration with your existing applications and services, coupled with the reliability and scalability of Azure's environment, which is critical for production-grade deployments of machine learning models. These tools not only reduce the complexity of the deployment process but also reduce time to market for the developed models.

Creating and Consuming Real-Time Prediction Endpoints

Creating and consuming real-time prediction endpoints involves generating an interface that can be accessed over the web to make real-time predictions based on your deployed model. This usually implies setting up an Application Programming Interface (API) endpoint that can accept and process input data, utilize the deployed model to yield predictions, and then return these prediction outcomes.

With tools like Azure ML SDK v2 and ML Studio, the process of generating prediction endpoints is highly simplified. These host your models as web services and automatically provide you with a unique URL (the endpoint) after deployment.

In Azure ML SDK v2, creating a prediction endpoint begins with the use of the '`deploy`' function, where you specify the model, inference configuration (which consists of the scoring script and environment), and the deployment configuration (which comprises the target compute). An inference pipeline is created and registered in your workspace and deposited in the target compute resource. A REST endpoint becomes active and ready to receive web service requests after successful deployment. Azure automatically generates the necessary Python, C#, or R code snippets that your client application needs to consume the deployed service.

ML Studio, on its part, once again proves its user-friendliness. After deploying the model as a web service, you are presented with an API key and the HTTP endpoint. This web service can consume the inputs through REST API calls and return responsive real-time predictions in either JSON or CSV format.

Consuming the endpoint goes beyond just sending requests to it. It includes structuring your data correctly in your POST request and ensuring your application can appropriately handle and interpret the model's response. Usually, input data is sent to the model as an array in a JSON format, gets processed by the model, and the prediction result is returned in the response.

Handling real-time predictions correctly and efficiently is essential for maintaining an effective application. Therefore, ensuring proper communication between your application and your model's endpoint is crucial. This involves implementing error checking on your POST requests to handle any potential errors that may occur, such as input data that cannot be processed by the model, or issues with the model's availability.

In conclusion, creating and consuming real-time prediction endpoints forms an integral part of deploying machine learning models, as this enables the user or client applications to access and interact with the models. Azure ML SDK v2 and ML Studio provide robust and reliable capabilities for managing these processes, from the initial creation of the prediction endpoints to their final consumption. They significantly alleviate the complexities involved in setting up real-time prediction functionalities, thereby making machine learning models more accessible and utilizable in real-world applications.

Managing and Monitoring Deployed Models

Deploying machine learning models into a production environment is just the initial step. Once the models are in production, their performance needs to be monitored and managed consistently. Regular monitoring and management ensure that the models continue to serve their purpose effectively without any lapse in quality. This is possible using Azure Machine Learning SDK V2 and ML Studio which allows efficient and effective monitoring and managing of deployed models.

Techniques for Managing Deployed Models

Managing deployed Machine Learning models is crucial to ensure that the models continuously deliver accurate predictions. Azure ML Studio and Azure ML SDK v2 offer technologies that make this process more streamlined.

Azure ML Studio provides an intuitive graphical interface for managing the lifecycle of machine learning models, from training and optimization to deployment and management.

Sample steps with Azure ML Studio can be viewed in the following sequence:

1. Selection of a workspace.
2. Choosing a compute target.
3. Creating, configuring, and running experiments.
4. Visualizing the results and selecting the best model.
5. Deploying the selected model.

Azure ML SDK V2 enables developers to manage models programmatically. It provides mechanisms to register, version, track, and query models. Here is a simple Python code using Azure ML SDK to register a machine learning model:

```
from azureml.core import Model

model = Model.register(workspace=ws,
                       model_name='my_model',
                       model_path='./model.pkl', # local path
                       description='A classification model')
```

Figure 6.49: *Register model*

You can view all versions of a registered model using:

```
model = Model(workspace, 'my_model')
model.list(ws, 'my_model')
```

Figure 6.50: *See versions of model*

In order to deploy a particular version of your model, you can use:

```
model = Model(workspace, 'my_model', version=2)
```

Figure 6.51: *Deploy specific version of model*

Azure ML Studio also allows you to organize, monitor, and manage all registered models from a single centralized location. You can compare different model versions, track the model status, and view any information related to the model such as when and by whom the model was deployed.

It is also worth noting Azure allows for deprecating older, no longer needed model versions. Updating and managing the lifespan of your models becomes a lot less tedious, thanks to Azure's automated lifecycle management.

In conclusion, Azure ML Studio, and Azure ML SDK provide valuable toolkits for data scientists and AI developers to manage their models efficiently, ensuring consistent performance, and solution delivery. These tools simplify the complex processes involved in model management, allowing scientists and developers more time to focus on creating powerful machine learning solutions.

Monitoring Model Performance and Data Drift

Monitoring the performance of deployed machine learning models is an integral part of the model management process. It helps ensure that the model is working as expected and allows for early identification of any potential issues.

Azure ML Studio and SDK V2 facilitate automatic data drift detection in machine learning models. This helps to track and identify any changes in patterns of the incoming data. When data drift is detected, it can mean that the model may no longer be accurate due to the shift and thus requires updating.

Azure also includes the ability to monitor models using the Azure Application Insights, which logs the model's key metrics like inputs, outputs, and latency, and so on. These metrics can be tracked in near-real-time to provide insights into the model's performance.

Strategies for Model Retraining and Updating

Machine learning models can fall victim to data drift over time. This phenomenon occurs due to the non-static nature of real-world data. The patterns and trends in incoming data often change, which makes the machine learning model built on previous data less effective. To tackle this potential issue, models need periodic updating or retraining. Azure ML Studio and SDK v2 provide a suite of capabilities that address this need.

Automated Retraining

Azure provides the feature to trigger retraining of models automatically. This can be scheduled based on different criteria like time intervals or a specified level of data drift. Once the criteria are met, the data pipelines automatically fetch the new batch of data, retrain the model, and deploy the updated model. This ensures your predictive models remain contemporary and relevant, enhancing their usefulness.

Validation Process

Azure includes features to validate a model before it is deployed. This means, after retraining a model, Azure automatically performs a series of rigorous tests and validations to ensure its performance surpasses the current model's. This evaluation ensures that only models with enhanced performance are deployed, thereby minimizing any risk of degradation in the model's performance.

Champion-Challenger Framework

Azure supports a Champion-Challenger testing framework where the existing model (the "`champion`") is tested against a new model (the "`challenger`"). The challenger model is the model retrained on new data. If the challenger model offers better performance than the champion, the system automatically promotes it to the status of the new champion. This approach guarantees that you are always using the best performing model based on the most recent data.

Seamless Model Updates

Azure seamlessly updates the models on detecting an improved version. There is a smooth transition with negligible interruptions, ensuring continuous service.

Model Version Control

Azure tracks and manages version histories of models. It logs each retraining instance, tracks the performance changes, and provides an easy rollback option to a previous version if needed. This feature aids in maintaining an ordered summary of updates and contributes to better reproducibility and auditability of machine learning solutions.

In essence, the strategies for model retraining and updating are foundational in maintaining the relevancy and accuracy of machine learning models over time. Leveraging Azure ML Studio and SDK v2 for these tasks ensures that your models are always adept in addressing your unique business challenges.

Best Practices and Considerations

Azure Machine Learning (AML) is a comprehensive framework developed by Microsoft to develop, train, and deploy machine learning models. With it, developers and data scientists can efficiently prepare data, conduct experiments, manage and optimize models, ultimately deploying a model as a web service. With the array of cloud resources offered by Azure, it is crucial to follow best practices for model reproducibility, security, compliance, and cost management amongst others. The details are pertinent to both the Azure Machine Learning SDK v2 and Machine Learning Studio capabilities.

Ensuring Model Reproducibility and Version Control

When developing machine learning models, creating a setup that can be reliably reproduced across different environments keeps your results consistent and accurate. This is what reproducibility means in the context of ML. In particular, version control is incredibly important for reproducibility, as opposed to starting anew with every iteration of model training. With Azure Machine Learning, this aspect is taken care of effectively.

Azure Machine Learning SDK v2 provides an efficient way to manage model versions. Every time a model is registered or re-registered in the workspace, it creates an iteration of the model. During this process, Azure ML automatically adds to the version number of the model, helping users keep track of its evolution.

In an era where small changes can significantly impact machine learning models, it is crucial to manage multiple iterations with minor differences. For this reason, Azure

ML's ability to archive different versions of the same model becomes instrumental. It not only allows you to try out various versions for the best results, but it also ensures an easy transition between the different versions based on performance without repeating the entire development process.

Another integral facet contributing to reproducibility is Azure ML pipelines. These pipelines document and automate each step – from data gathering and pre-processing to model training and validation, all the way to deployment. Every time a pipeline is run, an experiment is created in ML Studio documenting these details, which can be referred to or rerun later. This way, even complex workflows with several data processing and modeling steps can be easily replicated and versioned.

To further aid in keeping a track of the performance across several runs, Azure Machine Learning offers efficient experiment tracking abilities. On setting up an experiment and beginning the run, you can start logging metrics using Azure ML's logging functions. This allows you to capture essential aspects like hyperparameters used, algorithms chosen, and various performance metrics like accuracy, precision, and more, to a workspace. This information aids in comparing different experiment runs and easily finishing tasks like model validation.

Therefore, Azure ML makes a significant contribution to facilitating version control and reproducibility in machine learning projects – these two aspects immensely boost the accuracy and efficiency of results, ensuring the reliability and credibility of your data science projects.

Security and Compliance Considerations in Azure Machine Learning

In the realm of data science and machine learning, security and compliance are quintessential. They safeguard critical information and ensure that the organization maintains its ethical, legal, and regulatory obligations. Azure Machine Learning (AML), with its robust security architecture and comprehensive compliance standards, proficiently addresses these aspects.

Access Control and Identity Management

Azure Machine Learning implements a granular access control mechanism. It integrates with Azure Active Directory (Azure AD) for identity and access management. Azure AD helps manage and secure identities for specific roles that can access Azure ML workspaces, experiments, pipelines, models, and more. Roles like Owners, Contributors, Users, and so on, are distinguishable, with the capabilities of each role thoroughly pre-defined to reduce the risk of unauthorized access and misuse.

Encryption and Isolation

AML moves beyond simple access control measures. The platform provides end-to-end encryption of data – be it at rest or in transit, thereby ensuring its protection. The `"at rest"` data is encrypted using Azure Storage Service Encryption, while the data `"in transit"` is protected via SSL encryption.

Network isolation is another critical aspect that Azure addresses. Features like Virtual Networks (VNet) and Private Link permit private and secure connections to Azure ML services, isolating the traffic flow within Azure's infrastructure and strengthening the network's security perimeter.

Compliance

Compliance forms the cornerstone of any business today, more than ever when data handling is involved. Azure extends its support by acknowledging a broad set of international and industry-specific compliance standards like General Data Protection Regulation (GDPR), Health Insurance Portability and Accountability Act (HIPAA), and ISO 27001, amongst others. It helps organizations maintain and demonstrate compliance within the Azure ML environment with pre-configured settings, built-in controls, and shared responsibility across the service provider and the organization itself.

AML also supplies an audit trail for traceability and accountability. It logs and stores each user's actions using Azure Monitor and Azure Log Analytics, allowing administrators to keep an eye on the workspace and conduct forensic analysis if necessary.

Protections Against Threats

AML comes built-in with Azure Security Center, uncovering vulnerabilities and threats to reduce the overall security risks. The Security Center provides alerts on unusual activities, suspected attacks, and even recommends remediation steps.

By incorporating these robust security and compliance practices, AML provides a secure environment for constructing, deploying, and managing machine learning models, thus reassuring users of the system's integrity and trustworthiness.

Cost Management and Optimization for Machine Learning Projects in Azure

Cost management in machine learning projects on Azure can be a critical factor when dealing with extensive experiments and large datasets that require high-compute resources. The primary way to control costs in Azure is through effective management and optimization of the resources used.

One way Azure supports cost management is through its Cost Management and Billing service. This service gives to the users a centralized view of the resources they are using and the expenses associated with each one. It visualizes the data in a digestible manner, providing a better understanding of where costs originate, and therefore help to make informed decisions on resource allocation and cost management.

Additionally, the Cost Management and Billing service provides cost analysis tools offering detailed breakdown of resources used. You can create and manage various budgets at different levels (resource group, subscription) accordingly. Alerts can also be configured to notify users when costs exceed a certain threshold, further enabling cost control.

To ensure that you are only paying for what you use, Azure has a resource optimization advisor who gives recommendations based on your usage. For example, if you are working with virtual machines, the optimization advisor may suggest deallocating some resources when the machines are idle, which would significantly reduce costs.

When running machine learning experiments, compute resources are a significant part of the costs. Azure Machine Learning provides options like low-priority VMs and spot pricing for compute clusters that can significantly reduce costs. Choosing the right VM size tailored to your model's requirement prevents overpaying for un-utilized resources.

Data storage costs can also be a significant part of the overall budget in a machine learning project, especially when dealing with large datasets. In Azure, you can manage and optimize this through the use of Azure ML datastores. With datastores, Azure provides a secure and simplified interface for uploading and downloading data, thereby optimizing data storage costs.

Another essential cost-friendly feature in Azure is elastic scaling. Auto-scaling feature adjusts resources based on the demand, therefore, during peak demand, resources are scaled up to maintain performance while they can be scaled down during low demand to save costs. This flexibility ensures that you only pay for what you use.

Combining all these features and techniques, organizations can effectively control and cut down unnecessary costs in their Azure ML projects, ultimately maintaining an efficient and cost-effective operation.

Conclusion

Throughout this comprehensive chapter, we explored the robust capabilities of Azure Machine Learning Studio, navigated its user-friendly interface, and looked at its central role in model development and deployment. We understood the process of setting up workspaces, creating experiments, organizing resources, and how to monitor and log runs. In preparing data for training and evaluation, we mastered the steps for accessing, importing, and pre-processing data in Azure ML Studio, and splitting it into training and test sets. We then dived into building and training machine learning models using the Azure ML SDK, utilizing cloud resources for training. In the hyperparameter tuning and model selection segment, we explored the strategies for selecting the optimal model and learnt about Azure ML's hyperparameter tuning benefits. These strategies were then complemented by our understanding of different model evaluation techniques, metrics, visualization and interpretation methods, model validation and cross-validation all using Azure ML Studio.

The later sections introduced us to the nuances of preparing a model for deployment, creating and consuming real-time prediction endpoints, and monitoring model performance and data drift. We also discussed techniques to manage deployed models, and strategies for model retraining and updating. Lastly, we discussed the best practices and considerations around model reproducibility, version control, security, compliance, and costs in Azure Machine Learning.

As we progress further, in the next chapter, '*Model Deployment and Monitoring*', we will delve deeper into the deployment domain. Here, we will discuss deploying machine learning models using Azure Kubernetes Services (AKS) and Azure Container Instances (ACI). We will also cover practices of setting up Continuous Integration and Continuous Deployment (CI/CD) pipelines for model management and make use of Azure's services to monitor deployed models. This next step would solidify our comprehension about the end-to-end journey of machine learning models, from ideation to deployment, making us proficient in Azure Machine Learning.

Questions

- Discuss the importance and role of Azure Machine Learning Studio in modern machine learning projects.
- Is Azure Machine Learning SDK used in the construction of machine learning models?
- What strategies can be employed for model selection in Azure Machine Learning?
- Can Azure Machine Learning Studio be used to monitor model performance and data drift?
- Elaborate on the various techniques that Azure Machine Learning Studio supports for data pre-processing.
- Is it possible to manage resources within the Azure Machine Learning Studio environment?
- Does Azure support hyperparameter tuning?

- How does Azure Machine Learning Studio aid in the management and monitoring of deployed models?
- Can Azure Machine Learning Studio be used to create real-time prediction endpoints?
- Describe the various security and compliance considerations one must take into account when working with Azure Machine Learning.

Multiple Choice Questions

1. What is the main purpose of Azure Machine Learning Studio?
    a. Data visualization
    b. Database management
    c. Developing and deploying machine learning models
    d. Web scraping
2. What forms an essential part of preparing data for training and evaluation?
    a. Data decryption
    b. Data pre-processing
    c. Data duplication
    d. Data translation
3. In Azure Machine Learning, model validation is achieved using what method?
    a. Cross-validation
    b. Stratified sampling
    c. Bootstrapping
    d. Independent sampling
4. What is one of the strategies for managing deployed models in Azure Machine Learning Studio?
    a. Ignoring model performance
    b. Not considering data drift
    c. Periodic model retraining and updating
    d. Not updating models

5. What is a major security and compliance consideration in Azure Machine Learning?
    a. Model reproducibility
    b. Version control
    c. Cost management
    d. Compliance with data protection regulations

Answers

1. c
2. b
3. a
4. c
5. d

Practical Exercise

Project Title

Building a Customer Churn Prediction Model using Azure Machine Learning

Objective

The goal of this project is to create a predictive model that can forecast customer churn based on historical data using Azure Machine Learning.

Materials

Customer churn dataset: This dataset can be downloaded from the UCI Machine Learning Repository or Kaggle. It contains historical data about customers, including various behavioral attributes and whether or not they churned.

Procedure

1. Register on Azure and set up a new workspace in Azure Machine Learning Studio.
2. Import your downloaded dataset into the Azure environment.
3. Pre-process your data by cleaning up incorrect entries, encoding categorical variables, filling missing values, scaling numerical values, and handling any imbalanced data.

4. Split the processed data into training and test sets.
5. Use Azure Machine Learning SDK to perform feature selection and construct your machine learning model. Opt for a classification model such as Logistic Regression, Decision Trees, or Random Forest, depending on the nature of your dataset.
6. Train your model using the provided training set.
7. Use Azure's hyperparameter tuning capabilities to optimize the predictive power of your model.
8. Evaluate your model's performance with the test set and visualize your evaluation results.
9. Once you are satisfied with your model's performance, prepare it for deployment.
10. Register the model in Azure Machine Learning Studio.
11. Set up a deployment environment and create a real-time prediction endpoint.
12. Test your endpoint with additional data to verify that it provides appropriate predictions.

In addition to the main tasks, throughout each step, take into account best practices and considerations such as ensuring model reproducibility, security and compliance considerations, and cost management.

Chapter 7
Model Deployment and Monitoring

Introduction

This chapter will take you through the pivotal process of deploying and monitoring machine learning models. These steps are integral to successfully integrating models into real-world applications. We will guide you in this journey using the robust capabilities of Azure services, ensuring you understand and are comfortable with every step involved. We will start by deploying models using Azure Machine Learning service, an essential tool for making your machine learning models operational.

In continuation, we sharpen our focus on setting up ideal deployment environments such as Azure Kubernetes Service (AKS) and Azure Container Instances (ACI), making sure your models have the perfect platform to operate from. We understand that deployment does not end with just launching the models. Hence, we will extend our discussion to monitoring and managing deployed models using Azure Monitor and Azure Application Insights. Furthermore, we will delve into the crucial aspect of continuous integration and deployment (CI/CD) for machine learning, exploring how these practices can refine your end product. Finally, we will cover model versioning, updates, and rollbacks, equipping you with the knowledge to effectively manage your models post-deployment.

Structure

We will be covering the following in this chapter:

- Introduction to Model Deployment and Monitoring
- Deploying Models with Azure Machine Learning Service
- Setting Up Deployment Environments
- Monitoring Deployed Models
- Continuous Integration and Deployment (CI/CD) in ML
- Model Version Control and Rollback

Introduction to Model Deployment and Monitoring

The field of data science and artificial intelligence has grown significantly over the years, opening up new avenues of opportunity and potential. A key part of leveraging these opportunities is through model deployment and monitoring. This not only ensures the successful application of a machine learning model but also maintains its efficiency and functionality over time. Leaving the controlled environment of testing and research to real-world implementation can pose various challenges. In order to reach a substantial and productive output, it is of utmost importance to have a streamlined, well-thought-out strategy for deploying and monitoring models.

Overview of Model Deployment and Monitoring

Model deployment is the process of incorporating a fair and unbiased data science model into a production environment where it can provide practical outputs based on the input data. After a model has been trained, validated, and tested, it needs to be deployed to start making predictions or judgments. The deployment of a model can be done in different ways, such as Predictive Model Markup Language (PMML), cloud solutions, or on-premises software.

The next step after deployment is model monitoring, which is essential for keeping track of model performance. It allows tracking changes in model metrics, data feeds, business performances, and other factors. Monitoring becomes crucial as models '*decay*' with time due to changing trends, new customer behaviors, adaptation to regulations, and so on. Therefore, an unmonitored and outdated model can generate inaccurate predictions, negatively impacting the business.

Importance of Model Deployment and Monitoring

Deployment and monitoring of models have significant importance in data science and AI. The primary benefit of model deployment is the actionable insights that a company can leverage to make informed decisions, improve their services, or launch new products to a segment identified by the predictive model. Without deployment, the model's potential cannot be fully utilized, as it will be confined to the lab or the testing environment. The model must become part of the company's ecosystem, impacting real-life decisions and strategies.

Model monitoring, on the other hand, is vital for ensuring the sustained relevance and accuracy of the model. With evolving trends and changing data patterns, it is likely that a model will start showing reduced performance or even faulty outputs over time. Regular monitoring can help understand the drift and degradation in model performance and enables timely calibration or retraining of the model before it drastically affects the business operation.

To conclude, model deployment and monitoring are not just the last steps in creating a machine learning model but are continuous processes that have to be carried out regularly to ensure its efficiency and optimality in a fast-paced business environment.

Deploying Models with Azure Machine Learning Service

The world of data-driven decision making calls for sophisticated platforms that not only offer a conducive environment for building models but also for their effective deployment. One standout platform that offers such a solution is Azure Machine Learning Service.

Gaining Insight into Azure Machine Learning Service

Microsoft Azure Machine Learning Service is a cloud-based service that provides a robust and efficient platform to build, train, and deploy machine learning models. It offers several tools and services that streamline the entire machine learning pipeline. One significant feature is the ease with which models can be deployed and hosted either in the cloud or on the edge. This flexibility gears businesses with the agility to operate seamlessly.

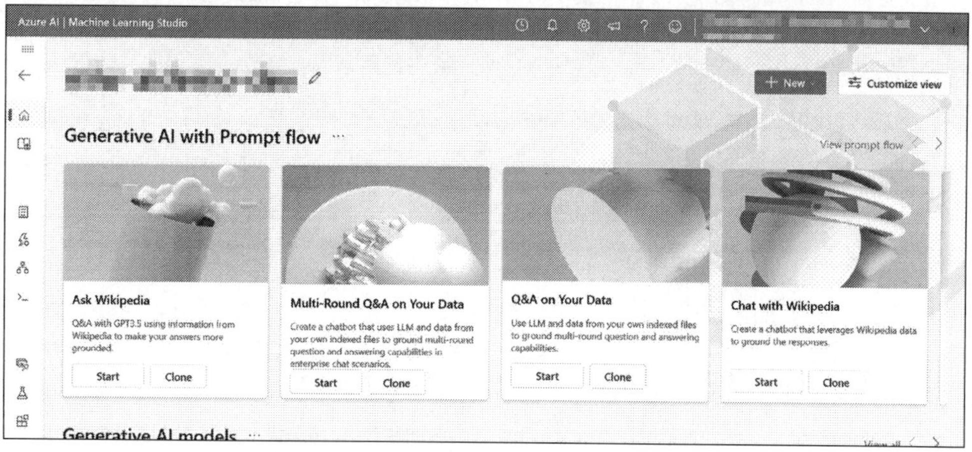

Figure 7.1: *Azure Machine Learning dashboard*

The service also provides high-end security measures to ensure the safety of your data and models. The usage of role-based access control (RBAC) lays down the ground rules for accessing the models, ensuring only authorized personnel can access or modify the models.

Navigating Through the Deployment Process

The process of deploying a machine learning model using Azure Machine Learning Service can be divided into several key steps, including:

1. **Model Registration:**

   Before deploying your model, registration is a necessity. It involves uploading the serialized model into the Azure Machine Learning workspace, which can be executed via Azure Portal, Azure Notebooks, or Azure Databricks.

2. **Creating Environment:**

   In this step, you need to specify the software dependencies needed to run your model. This can include specific Python packages, scoring scripts, and similar components.

3. **Configuring Deployment:**

   You need to choose your compute target. You could deploy it on Azure Container Instance (ACI), Azure Kubernetes Service (AKS), or an IoT Edge device. Depending on the type of compute, you need to design your inference configuration, as it describes how to set up the web service for predictions.

4. **Model Deployment:**

   Deploying the model is as simple as running a command. Once the deployment is successful, you get a REST endpoint that can be used for sending the data and receiving the prediction. You can deploy the model as a web service in a Docker container.

5. **Debugging and Testing the Model:**

   It involves sending the sample data to the deployed model and verifying the received response for its correctness.

6. **Monitoring the Model:**

   Once the deployment is tested, you should turn on data collection for model monitoring. For production-ready models, Azure Application Insights integration is recommended.

Each deployment takes a set of specific parameters that allow the service to create the runtime environment. Working through each step with precision ensures successful deployment, enabling your model to start giving actionable insights. Azure Machine Learning Service brings model deployment to your fingertips, making it a hassle-free and efficient process.

Setting Up Deployment Environments

Advanced analytics along with the deployment of machine learning models requires flexible and scalable environments. Azure offers two highly proficient services, Azure Kubernetes Service (AKS) and Azure Container Instances (ACI), that serve as excellent hosts for your machine learning models.

Preparing Azure Kubernetes Service

Azure Kubernetes Service (AKS) is a robust offering by Microsoft that provides serverless Kubernetes, simplifying containerized application deployment and management. AKS is an excellent choice for large-scale, high-demand applications owing to its capabilities of auto-scaling, self-healing, and load balancing.

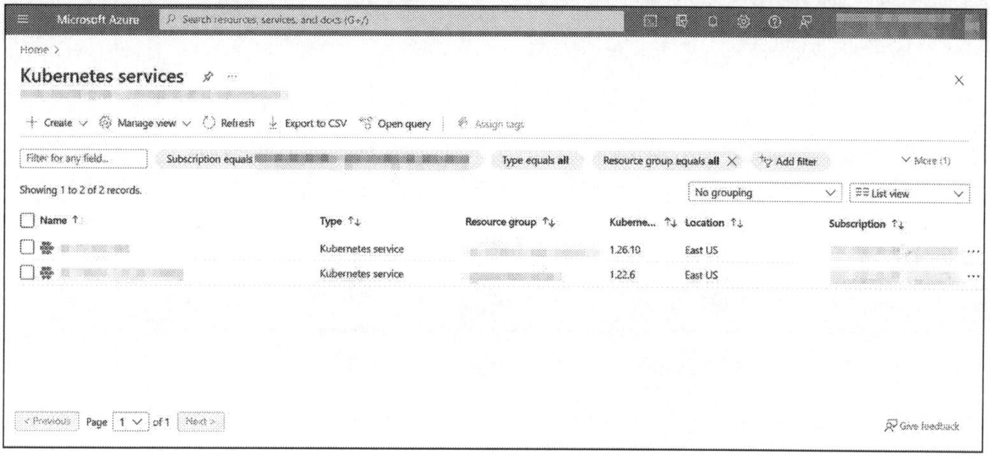

Figure 7.2: *Azure Kubernetes service dashboard*

Setting up an AKS environment includes the following steps:

1. **Creating an AKS cluster:**

   A Kubernetes cluster on Azure can be created through the Azure portal, Azure CLI, or Azure SDK's. Factors including location, resource groups, primary node pool, and networking must be taken into consideration while creating the cluster.

2. **Connecting to the cluster:**

   Once the cluster is created, you connect to it using the Kubernetes command-line client '`kubectl`'.

3. **Deploying your application:**

   After connecting to the cluster, you can deploy your application with the '`kubectl create`' or '`kubectl apply`' commands.

4. **Monitoring and troubleshooting the application:**

   Azure offers the Kubernetes dashboard, Azure Monitor, and Azure Log Analytics for monitoring and troubleshooting your applications.

Establishing Azure Container Instances

Azure Container Instances (ACI) offers an efficient solution to run containers without having to maintain servers. High speed and customizability, coupled with the per-second billing, makes ACI an ideal choice for short-term, data processing tasks.

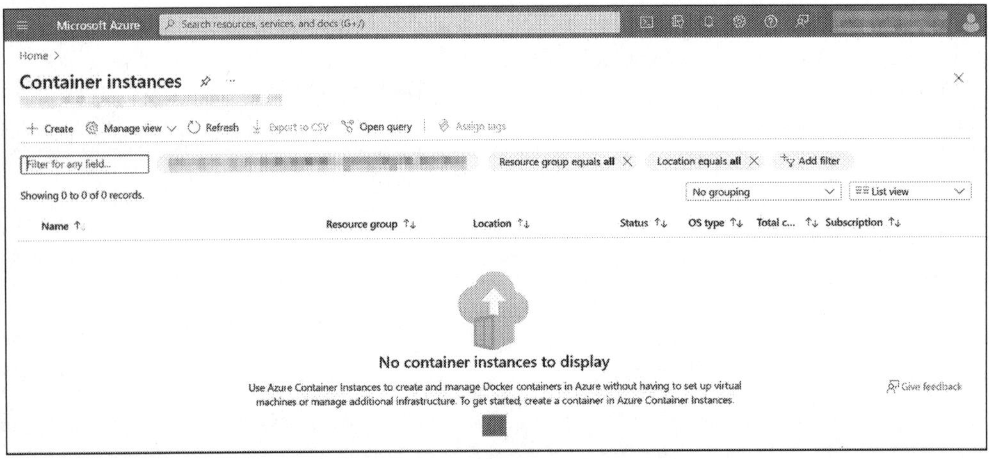

Figure 7.3: *Azure Container instance dashboard*

Creating an Azure Container instances environment involves:

1. **Creating a container instance:**

   This can be done via Azure portal, Azure CLI, or Azure SDKs. Configuration such as image source, container group, and restart policies must be specified during creation.

2. **Deploying the container instance:**

   Once the instance has been created, it can be deployed. It refers to the process of launching an instance of your container group in your Azure state.

3. **Accessing the container instance:**

   Once deployed, access your container via '`az container attach`' or '`az container exec`' commands. This gives you live access to your output console.

4. **Stopping/Deleting the container instance:**

   If you don't need the container instance, you can either stop it or delete it.

Hosting deployment environments with Azure affords users scalability, speed, and efficient handling of their models. By combining this hosting prowess with model monitoring, users have a robust framework for model deployment that promotes agility and operational efficiency.

Monitoring Deployed Models

After deploying machine learning models into production, it is crucial to monitor them effectively to ensure they continue to provide accurate and reliable predictions. Microsoft Azure provides robust monitoring tools like Azure Monitor and Azure Application Insights that help you track your model's performance and maintain its health.

Leveraging Azure Monitor for Model Monitoring

Azure Monitor is an Azure service that collects, analyzes, and acts on telemetry data from your Azure and on-premises environments. It allows you to deeply understand and improve the performance of your applications and ensure its smooth operation.

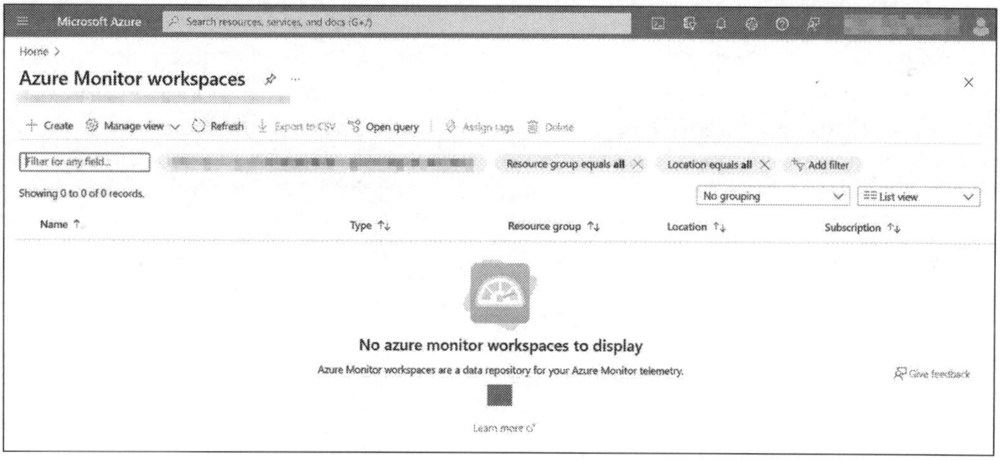

***Figure 7.4**: Azure Monitor dashboard*

Here are the steps to use Azure Monitor:

1. **Activating Azure Monitor:**

   Azure Monitor can be accessed through the Azure portal. Once in the portal, the user can navigate to `"Monitor"` to view and analyze the logs and metrics.

2. **Setting Up Metrics:**

   Azure Monitor uses metrics, which are numerical values that describes some aspect of a system at a particular point in time. This feature allows users to monitor real-time data, visualize it, and set alerts based on thresholds. You can customize your view by pinning valuable data to the dashboard or even integrating it with Grafana.

3. **Using Log Analytics:**

   Log data collected by Azure Monitor can be analyzed with queries to quickly retrieve, consolidate, and analyze collected data. It logs detailed information including the time an event occurred, the location, the type of issue, or even the aggregated statistics about a group of resources.

4. **Creating Alerts:**

   Alerts proactively notify you when issues are found with your infrastructure or application using your monitoring data in Azure Monitor. They allow you to identify and address issues before the users of your system notice them.

Implementing Azure Application Insights for Model Monitoring

Azure Application Insights is an extensible Application Performance Management (APM) service for developers and DevOps professionals. It allows you to monitor your live applications, automatically detect performance anomalies, and includes powerful analytic tools to help diagnose issues and understand usage patterns.

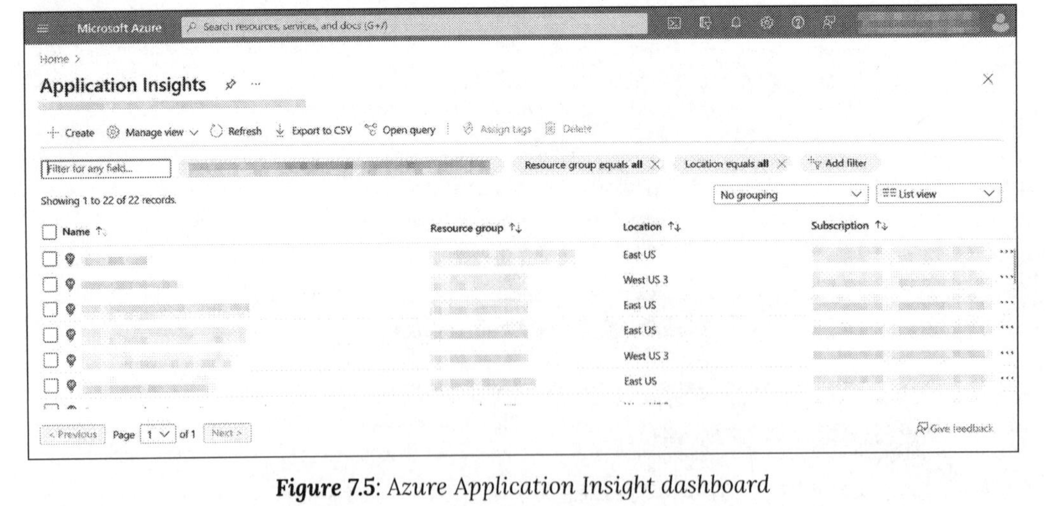

Figure 7.5: *Azure Application Insight dashboard*

Here are the steps to use Azure Application Insights:

1. **Setup Application Insights:**

   Set up Application Insights in the Azure portal while creating a new service or add it to an existing service. Add the Application Insights SDK suitable for the language and platform you're working with to your application code.

2. **Monitor Performance and Usage:**

   View a wealth of information about your application's performance and usage in Application Insights. It provides information about page views, server response times, and failure rates, which can help developers identify performance issues and trends in user behavior.

3. **Diagnostics Logs:**

   Application Insights also provides diagnostic logs, which allow you to see in-depth details about specific transactions, allowing you to trace activities through your application.

4. **Analysis with Machine Learning Algorithms:**

   Application Insights includes power analytics tools, which apply machine learning algorithms to your telemetry that help you detect performance anomalies and identify patterns.

Both Azure Monitor and Azure Application Insights are pivotal tools in ensuring your machine learning models continue to perform optimally, giving you proactive control over occurrences and potential issues that could hinder the real-world performance of your models.

Continuous Integration and Deployment (CI/CD) in Machine Learning

In the rapidly evolving sphere of machine learning, the necessity of efficient, consistent, and seamless software development practices is becoming increasingly pronounced. Continuous Integration and Deployment (CI/CD) practices play an indispensable part in modern machine learning operations, or MLOps, providing teams with the ability to consistently integrate, validate, and deliver valuable machine learning models.

Understanding and Highlighting the Importance of CI/CD in ML

In the context of machine learning, implementing Continuous Integration/Deployment has the potential to drive significant positive changes. It allows data scientists, ML engineers, and DevOps practitioners to seamlessly align their tasks, improving communication and efficiency in model development and deployment.

Continuous Integration ensures that changes and updates to a model or algorithm are continually merged and validated against the existing codebase. Instead of making big, occasional updates, the engineering team makes small and frequent changes, which are easier to manage and cause less disruption.

The main advantage of continuous integration is that it allows teams to identify and address issues of inconsistency or bugs immediately. This reduces the time taken to validate and review code and allows teams to respond rapidly to changes. It lowers the chances of complications due to integration, thereby reducing the time taken to release new model updates.

Continuous deployment, on the other hand, is the practice of automatically deploying the validated changes to the production environment. This not only accelerates the delivery speed but also ensures there is no 'down-time' in the model availability. Teams can roll out improved models and updates more quickly, ensuring end users or decision systems have access to the most up-to-date intelligence.

Moreover, using CI/CD in machine learning can also result in higher code quality since frequent integration means mistakes can be detected and dealt faster. It reduces the risks associated with manual deployments and makes the entire process more efficient and reliable.

In a nutshell, the principal benefit of implementing CI/CD in machine learning is the ability to automate repetitive tasks, react to new requirements, and maintain a consistent, high-quality machine learning system. By adopting CI/CD, organizations can achieve efficiency, rapidity, and reliability in their machine learning stack.

Implementing CI/CD in ML: A Step-by-Step Guide

Implementing CI/CD in ML may seem like a complex task, but breaking it down into step-by-step stages can simplify the process and help in efficient model building and deployment. Let's walk through the process involved in implementing CI/CD in ML.

Adopting CI/CD for ML involves several steps, which are as follows:

1. **Set Up a Version Control System:**

   Version control is the backbone of CI/CD. Services like GitHub or Bitbucket can be used to manage and track changes in the codebase.

2. **Automate Testing:**

   Implement automatic testing for each new code commit, checking for bugs and inconsistencies within the data and the model. This should include unit tests, integration tests, and validation of model performance metrics.

3. **Implement Continuous Integration:**

   Use CI tools, like Jenkins or GitLab CI, to trigger a sequence of actions on each new commit like running test cases, checking coding standards, or even alerting the team in case of breaking changes.

4. **Continuous Deployment/Delivery:**

   After the model has gone through all the CI stages, it's time to automatically deploy the changes using orchestration tools like Kubernetes or even cloud-based solutions like Azure Pipelines or AWS CodePipeline.

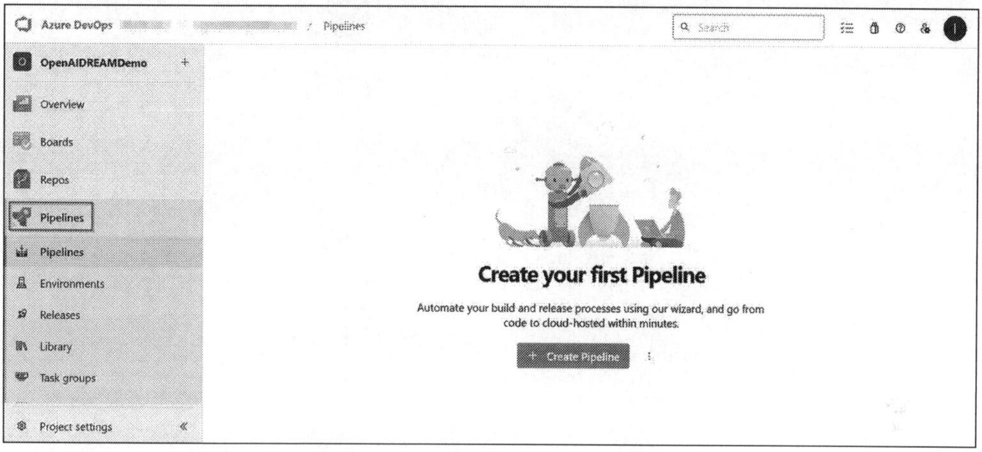

Figure 7.6: *Azure Pipelines Dashboard*

5. **Monitor Post-Deployment:**

   After successful deployment, continually monitor your model to ensure it continues to function well in the production environment.

CI/CD for ML incorporates the principles of reliability, consistency, and efficiency, principles that are most necessary in a field that is evolving as rapidly as ML. With the implementation of a proper CI/CD pipeline, ML teams can accelerate the lifecycle of their applications without compromising on the application quality.

Model Version Control and Rollback

In the realm of machine learning, models are constantly updated and improved upon with new data and iterations. This creates a need for effective management and control of different versions of these models, which introduces the concept of model version control and rollback.

Overview of Model Version Control and Rollback

Model Version Control is the task of managing and storing multiple versions of the same machine learning model, providing the flexibility to switch between different versions as required. As data changes over time, models also need to be updated to reflect these changes. With version control, you can try out different models and keep a record of what has changed in each version.

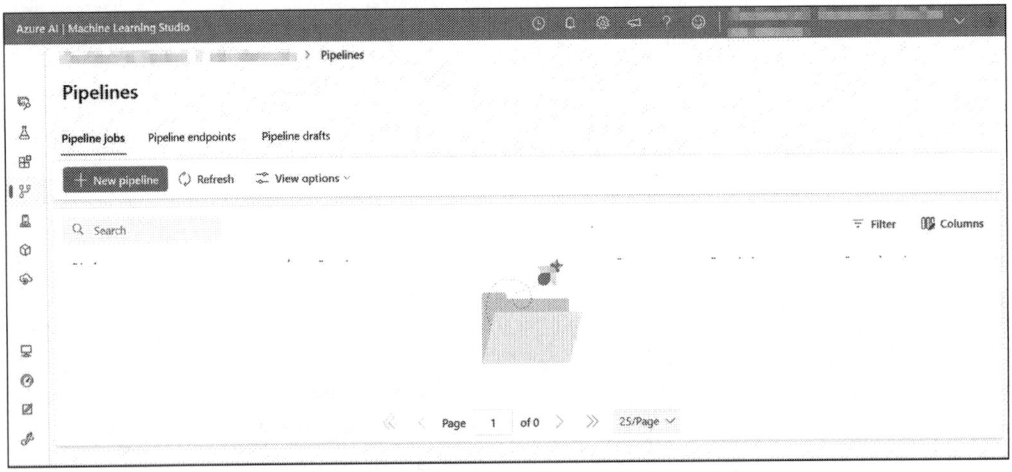

Figure 7.7: *Azure Machine Learning Studio Pipelines*

Rollback is the act of reverting to a previous version of the model. There are scenarios where recent changes to the model could lead to decreased performance or unforeseen errors, and in such events, rollback allows the model to be returned to a previous stable state.

Implementing version control and allowing for rollbacks are not only invaluable but arguably necessary for managing a production-grade ML system. They offer greater control and flexibility over the development process, enable quick recovery in case of errors, safeguard against data loss, and contribute to better collaboration within teams.

Process and Guidelines for Model Version Control and Rollback

Model version control and rollback can be orchestrated manually or with the help of tools such as MLflow or DVC. Here are some general steps and guidelines:

1. **Model Versioning:**

   This involves creating a unique identifier for each model version, which includes details about the code, data, and configuration used to produce that version.

2. **Tracking Model Performance:**

   Keep track of how each model version performs based on various metrics, and use a mechanism to capture this information alongside model metadata.

3. **Archiving Old Versions:**

   Retain old versions of a model to ensure you can resort to them if recent iterations are failing.

4. **Implementing Rollback:**

   If a deployed version of your model is causing errors or not performing as expected, use a rollback system to revert to a previous, more stable version.

5. **Automation:**

   Wherever possible, automate these processes. CI/CD pipelines are useful in managing version control and rollback procedure effectively, leading to increased efficiency and minimized manual errors.

In essence, model version control and rollback are integral parts of maintaining a healthy and agile Machine Learning system. This system enhances the iterative nature of machine learning, ensuring that developers or data scientists can confidently experiment, innovate, and deploy.

Conclusion

As we conclude this journey through the landscape of model deployment and monitoring, we aim to encapsulate the key learning points and takeaways and provide a glimpse into our next venture - Responsible AI.

Throughout this chapter, we delved into the essentials of model deployment and monitoring, understanding their importance in leveraging the benefits of machine learning models. We explored the powerful platform of Azure Machine Learning Service, taking a step-by-step journey through deployment environments like Azure Kubernetes Service (AKS) and Azure Container Instances (ACI).

We navigated the essential strategies for monitoring deployed models using Azure Monitor and Azure Application Insights, assessing the real-time status and performance of our models. We acknowledged the importance and implementation steps of CI/CD in machine learning for consistency and reliability. Finally, we addressed the need for model version control and rollback, making room for experimentation and quick recovery from errors.

The key takeaway from this discussion is the importance and necessity of robust deployment and monitoring strategies in the lifecycle of machine learning models. Without proper deployment, the potential of models stays untapped, and without effective monitoring, the consistency and reliability of model outputs could decline over time.

Looking ahead, the next chapter will explore an important dimension of AI - Responsible AI. As AI and ML technologies continue to evolve and proliferate in various sectors, ensuring the ethical and responsible use of these technologies is critical. The forthcoming chapter will delve into understanding Responsible AI, its principles and importance, as well as practical strategies to implement Responsible AI across organizations and projects.

Questions

- What potential challenges could you encounter when deploying a machine learning model, and how would you manage them?
- Discuss the potential risks of not monitoring a deployed machine learning model.
- Can you describe a situation where CI/CD was vital in your ML project and how it changed the outcome?
- How would you handle a situation where frequent model rollbacks are required? What steps would you consider to minimize such events?
- Considering tools like Azure Monitor and Azure Application Insights, explain your multi-level strategy for effective model performance monitoring.
- Is it possible to deploy your machine learning model without using platforms like Microsoft Azure Machine Learning Service?
- Can Azure Monitor and Azure Application Insights be used concurrently to monitor the same ML model?
- Is it necessary to always have a previous version of your ML model available in case a rollback is required?
- Do CI/CD practices always accelerate the machine learning lifecycle?
- Is it right that without a proper model version control system, the risk of data loss increases?

Multiple Choice Questions

1. What is the process of incorporating a machine learning model into a practical environment to make predictions known as?
   a. Model Control
   b. Model Configuration
   c. Model Deployment
   d. Model Development
2. Which Azure service is ideal for large-scale, high-demand applications due to its capabilities of auto-scaling, self-healing, and load balancing?
   a. Azure Container Instances
   b. Azure Kubernetes Service
   c. Azure Monitor
   d. Azure Databricks
3. In the context of Azure, when is it more ideal to use Azure Container Instances over Azure Kubernetes Service?
   a. For short-term, data processing tasks
   b. When auto-scaling is required
   c. When you have a large-scale application
   d. For long-term, data processing tasks
4. In the context of Azure Machine Learning services, what is the endpoint you get after successful model deployment used for?
   a. For sending the data and receiving the prediction
   b. For debugging the model
   c. For creating more instances of the model
   d. For registering the model
5. When implementing CI/CD practices in your ML project, why would setting up a Version Control System be a necessary first step?
   a. To manage and track changes in the codebase
   b. To monitor real-time data

   c. To ensure the model is free of bugs
   d. To deploy the model

6. Which Azure service is used for monitoring live applications, automatically detecting performance anomalies, and includes powerful analytic tools?
   a. Azure Container Instances
   b. Azure Kubernetes Service
   c. Azure Monitor
   d. Azure Application Insights

7. What is the term for going back to a previous version of an ML model due to reduced performance or unrecoverable errors in the current version?
   a. Rollback
   b. Backtrack
   c. Version control
   d. Debugging

8. Which step is NOT part of the CI/CD process in ML?
   a. Setting up a Version Control System
   b. Automating testing
   c. Implementing continuous integration
   d. Manually coding the entire application

9. Why is MLflow or DVC necessary in model version control and rollback?
   a. To implement new features in the model
   b. To manually upgrade the ML model
   c. To manage and store multiple versions of the same machine learning model
   d. To represent data in the model

10. Which of the following is NOT beneficial for ML teams implementing CI/CD?
    a. Accelerates the lifecycle of applications
    b. Increases the risk of bugs in the application

c. Enhances code quality
d. Reduces manual error

11. Which Azure service collects, analyzes, and acts on telemetry data from your Azure and on-premises environments?
    a. Azure Kubernetes Service
    b. Azure Monitor
    c. Azure Application Insights
    d. Azure Container Instances
12. What is the process of reverting to a previous version of your ML model through the version control system known as?
    a. Debugging
    b. Rollforward
    c. Tracking
    d. Rollback
13. What is Azure Monitor mainly used for?
    a. For managing versions of your ML model
    b. For deploying your ML model
    c. For tracking and improving your application's performance
    d. For automatically updating your ML model
14. Azure Container Instances is mainly used for...
    a. For diagnosing issues in your ML model
    b. For managing different versions of your ML model
    c. For running containers without having to manage servers
    d. For detecting performance anomalies in your ML model
15. In the realm of machine learning, why are CI/CD practices important?
    a. They reduce the necessity for manual testing
    b. They increase team reliance on automation tools
    c. They facilitate a more streamlined, reliable, and rapid release process
    d. They eliminate the possibility of errors in your ML model

Answers

1. c
2. b
3. a
4. a
5. a
6. d
7. a
8. d
9. c
10. b
11. b
12. d
13. c
14. c
15. c

CHAPTER 8
Embracing AI Revolution Azure

Introduction

This chapter takes a deep dive into the innovative realm of Generative AI and Large Language Models (LLMs). The chapter will provide a comprehensive exploration of Azure's advanced capabilities, such as OpenAI, and the Model Catalog. It will demystify the techniques for implementing Generative AI in a multitude of applications and explain how to engineer conversational experiences using Azure's PromptFlow. This chapter will also elaborate on how Azure's multi-modal AI services like Azure Speech and Vision can enhance the inclusivity of AI models. Concluding with a critical discussion on Responsible AI, the chapter addresses the necessity of designing ethical and unbiased AI models, and maintaining content safety. Expect a blend of theoretical, practical insight, and jargon-free explanations of these complex concepts.

Structure

We will be covering the following topics in the chapter:

- Introduction to Generative AI and Large Language Models
- Azure's Role in Advancing Generative AI
- Delving into Azure's PromptFlow for Creating LLM-Based Applications
- Working with Multimodal AI Services: Azure Speech and Vision
- Responsible AI in Azure: Creating Ethical and Unbiased AI Models

Introduction to Generative AI and Large Language Models

The advancements made in the realm of artificial intelligence have paved the way for significantly innovative systems such as Generative AI and Large Language Models (LLMs). These technologies have achieved remarkable milestones in artificial intelligence's rapidly changing landscape, indicating the leaps and bounds we have made in technological progressions. Generative AI can be regarded as an umbrella term that encompasses the different types of artificial intelligence models capable of creating original output. Essentially, these are models that have been programmed with the capacity to generate new information based on an array of inputs. They work by imitating their original dataset, learning its patterns, and making logic-based inferences to produce unique and creative outputs.

Practically speaking, this output could be anything from atmospheric prose to lyrical poetry, visually stunning paintings to rhythmically sound music and beyond. This array of artistic capabilities reflects the breadth and depth of Generative AI's potential. By providing an initial input, researchers essentially set a foundation or scaffold for the AI, which the system then utilized to produce a creative and unique output that resonates with its learned patterns. The ability to synthesize novel content demonstrates an impressive level of sophistication in Generative AI, brought about by its advanced learning capabilities. LLMs, on the other hand, form a specialized yet critical branch of Generative AI that focuses primarily on the understanding and generation of human-like textual content. These models are designed to perceive and interpret context, engage in dynamic conversation, and even spin narratives that resonate with the human experience. In essence, LLMs are capable of parsing through complex linguistic structures and generating human-like textual output that mirrors the richness and depth of human language.

The power of LLMs lies in their ability to understand and generate language that shares the complexity, subtlety and sophistication of human communication. This capability makes them an instrumental tool in the ongoing development of natural language processing technologies. The ability of LLMs to convincingly maintain a dialogue and generate narratives offer a compelling testimony to the progress that has been made in this field, as well as the promise it holds for the future of AI-based communication. Among the multitude of large language models, one particular system that stands out is the GPT-3 by OpenAI. As a testament to the potential of LLMs, GPT-3 has given impressive demonstrations of its ability to generate text that is remarkably indistinguishable from human-authored content, demonstrating a deep understanding of context and an uncanny knack for mimicking human-like conversation. This has created a buzz among the technology enthusiasts and research scholars, making it one of the most widely recognized LLMs in the world.

In conclusion, both Generative AI and LLMs represent significant milestones in the contexts of artificial intelligence and technological development, with their capabilities opening up new frontiers for academic research and practical applications alike.

Definition and Overview

The notation of "*Generative*" in the phrase "*Generative AI*," refers to the groundbreaking capacity of these types of artificial intelligence models to originate and produce unique substance or content. This capability does not only manifest in the form of concrete outputs, such as textual or image data, but also reflects on the AI's distinctive traits, including creativity, novelty, and self-sufficiency. The origins of the term "*Generative*," in this context, can be traced back to the domain of generative art, a medium that consists of artists implementing algorithms and elements of randomization to form works of art. This isn't produced in the conventional artist-controlled method, but rather generated through an unbiased, automatic process led by non-restrictive algorithms. They function as catalysts which trigger the creation of novel and unrepeated artistic manifestations. The artists set the primary parameters and conditions, but the final artwork is ultimately a result of the system's autonomous operations.

Generative AI operates on similar foundational principles. These models generate outputs that aren't strictly or explicitly programmed into the system. The concept of '*programming*' here is more nuanced than in traditional systems. While it's true that developers feed in algorithms and an initial set of data, generative AI goes a step beyond by learning, applying, and generating content based on that provided data. Conversely, LLMs are a specific breed of sophisticated deep learning models, designed with the unique capability of predicting the likelihood of a word within the context of a sentence. These AI models harness and process vast amounts of text data – often spanning multiple languages and domains – to develop a comprehensive understanding of language structure, syntax, and semantics.

LLMs are not merely predictive mechanisms. They contain within them the capacity for generation as well; the ability to produce human-speech-like text that captures the nuances and complexity of natural language. They can string words together to form coherent, contextually accurate sentences, thanks to their complex structure and in-depth training. Thus, they aren't limited to simple, direct responses, but rather, they can articulate comprehensive replies, thoughts, and even stories, much like a human would.

To sum up, both Generative AI and Large Language Models represent world-class technologies in the field of artificial intelligence. While they operate on different principles and focus areas, their foundations lie in the creation of novel, pertinent, and high-quality content, their methods of generating this content are what set them apart. Generative AI takes its cues from the artistic world of generative art while LLMs focus on the intricate world of language, underscoring the versatility and potential of AI technology.

Importance and Benefits

The importance and benefits of Generative Artificial Intelligence (AI) and Large Language Models (LLMs) in the ever-evolving technological landscape cannot be overstated. These powerful technological tools hold immense potential, significant implications, and transformative capacities across a multitude of industries and sectors. The advent of these AI models presents an intriguing range of possibilities and applications that were hitherto inconceivable. Generative AI and LLMs possess the ability to confer autonomous capabilities on systems, allowing them to execute a broad array of tasks. These tasks include drafting emails, composing literary outputs such as poetry, crafting stunning artworks, and even writing sophisticated code. Such dexterities point to unprecedented levels of automation that were previously deemed unattainable.

The ingenuity of these AI technologies can be harnessed by business enterprises for a diverse range of task executions. Businesses can tap into the potential of Generative AI and LLMs for customer service roles, where these tools can be configured into chatbots to handle customer enquiries effectively. They can also be utilized in the realm of content creation, where they can create engaging and original content tailored to a particular audience. Furthermore, marketing initiatives can benefit from the personalization capabilities of these AI technologies, resulting in uniquely crafted marketing strategies that resonate more effectively with targeted prospects. The versatility of Generative AI extends to disparate domains such as healthcare, design, and entertainment. In the healthcare industry, these AI models could expedite the process of drug discovery, thereby accelerating the deployment of novel treatments and therapies. The design sector can leverage Generative AI's prowess in creating digital assets thereby speeding up the design process. In the entertainment industry, the technology has the potential to revolutionize content generation by offering personalized and tailored content on viewers' preferences.

At the same time, LLMs carry with them the potential to revolutionize arenas such as data science. In this space, they can simplify convoluted data terminologies, converting them into plain language that is exceptionally more accessible to those without a deep knowledge of the area. This paves the way for democratizing data accessibility, culminating in the availability of valuable insights to a larger and less specialized audience. LLMs also have the potential to transform education. The interaction of students with AI language models can enrich their learning experiences and facilitate grasping new concepts with greater ease. Furthermore, LLMs, with their commendable language translation capabilities, can bridge language barriers. This allows for more effective communication and collaborations across geographic boundaries, thereby unifying the global community further.

In conclusion, Generative AI and LLMs are redefining the limits of what technologies can achieve. Their potential implications are vast, suggesting limitless possibilities within various industries. As we continue to unravel their capabilities, we embark further into an era of unprecedented technological advancements.

Applications

Generative AI and LLMs have a wide array of applications in different sectors. Here's a breakdown showing how various industries are leveraging these sophisticated technologies.

- **Digital Art and Design**

  Digital art relies heavily on Generative AI for creating captivating imagery. Applications such as Google's DeepDream, PaintsChainer, DeepArt, and Prisma are classic examples. Google's DeepDream uses the technology to produce hallucinogenic-like images, while PaintsChainer uses it to color artworks. DeepArt and Prisma take it further, converting everyday photos into works resembling those of celebrated artists. These applications demonstrate the potential of Generative AI in enhancing creativity and design.

- **Media and Entertainment**

  Generative AI is also having a significant impact on the media industry. The sophisticated technology is key in creating deep fakes – remarkably realistic, AI-generated audio, images, and video content. While this raises ethical questions, it also opens up opportunities for revolutionary filmmaking, advertising, and online content creation.

- **Translation and Language Services**

  Language Learning Models have propelled progress in tools such as Google Translate. They are instrumental in bridging language barriers and fostering global communication. By plumbing the depths of foreign languages and learning their intricate patterns, LLMs make accurate translation a reality.

- **Writing and Editing Technologies**

  Tools such as Grammarly use LLMs to improve language correction. They learn grammar regulations, punctuation necessities, and vocabulary usage from colossal text databases and use this knowledge to correct human-written text. LLMs can also generate creative content, such as poetry, demonstrating their scope beyond technical applications.

- **Customer Service and Communication**

  LLMs have become essential in developing advanced chatbots and virtual assistants. For example, Microsoft's Cortana and Amazon's Alexa rely heavily on these models. They empower these applications with the ability to understand and hold contextual human conversations, hence improving user engagement and satisfaction.

- **Future Potential**

  While the capabilities of Generative AI and LLMs have been put to use in various sectors, the true extent of their applicability remains under discovery and appreciation. There's fertile ground for future exploration, potentially birthing revolutionary applications in sectors yet untouched by these tech marvels.

These examples point to the immense potential of Generative AI and LLMs. By reaching into different areas, they're transforming how we create, communicate, and connect, shaping a future where AI becomes increasingly intertwined with human life.

Azure's Role in Advancing Generative AI

As an integral part of cutting-edge cloud computing technology, Microsoft Azure plays a pivotal role in advancing Generative AI. Generative AI encompasses machine learning technologies focused on generating novel output, whether it's images, text, or music. Azure caters to these needs with services including Azure OpenAI and Model Catalog. These robust tools and services significantly contribute to the expansion, application, and evolution of Generative AI.

Azure OpenAI

Azure OpenAI represents a remarkable initiative aimed at tapping into the inherent capabilities of OpenAI models and effortlessly incorporating them into a diverse array of applications. Such an undertaking signifies a radical exploration of the potential that AI models hold and an ambition to broadly diffuse them in a way that lead to substantial advancements in various domains. As a comprehensive managed service, Azure OpenAI quells the multitude of complications frequently associated with the imposition and application of artificial intelligence, ironing out the problems developers often encounter.

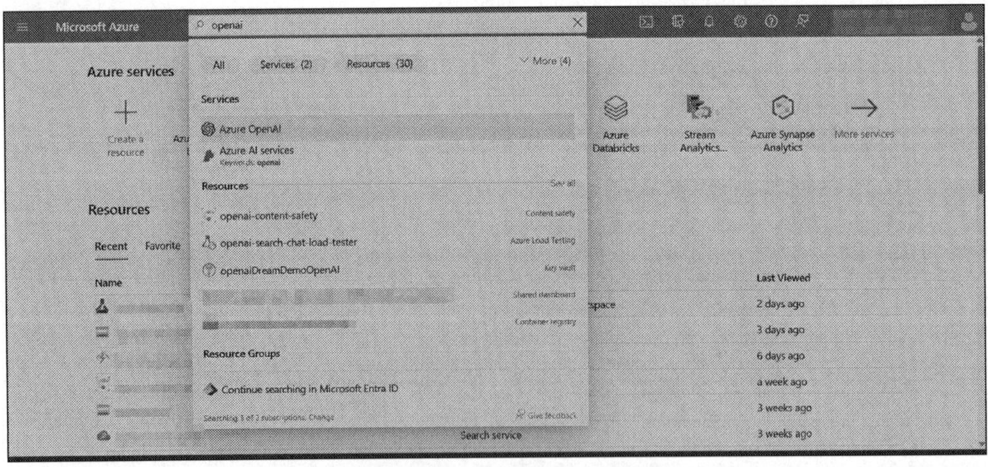

Figure 8.1: *Searching for OpenAI*

- In essence, Azure OpenAI paves a remarkably barrier-free pathway for developers to access a comprehensive array of AI models, covering an extensive spectrum from natural language processing to computer vision, and everything in between. These simplified integrational advancements programmed into Azure OpenAI are geared towards accelerating the adoption of AI technology in a diversity of applications. However, Azure OpenAI goes beyond simply providing a channel for AI integration. It represents the vast potential developers can unlock by strategically using artificial intelligence, such as enhancing user experiences or revolutionizing products and services.

Take, for instance, the practical implications of Azure OpenAI in the realm of natural language processing capabilities. Developers could integrate such capabilities into an application, essentially enabling it to comprehend, process, and react to human language. The end-result would be an application that is significantly more interactive and responsive, breaking down the barriers of communication between machines and humans, and creating a more seamless, intuitive user experience.

Furthermore, Microsoft Azure OpenAI offers an intuitive and user-friendly API that tremendously simplifies the process of integrating cutting-edge AI into applications. Imagine developing high-end voice-assistive technology; Azure OpenAI allows for access to top-notch speech recognition models, equipping you with the capacity to integrate them flawlessly into your application. This can potentially open up vast new possibilities, such as enabling recognition and responsive capabilities to voice commands, effectively creating an interactive and intellectual user interface.

In addition to its simplified integration and access to pre-trained models, Azure OpenAI also adds another layer of utility for developers in the form of customization. With Azure OpenAI, developers are not merely restricted to default models and interfaces. They also have the opportunity to tailor the AI models and tools according to their specific requirements, effectively resulting in a more adaptive and personalized development ecosystem that enhances the efficiency and effectiveness of the applications.

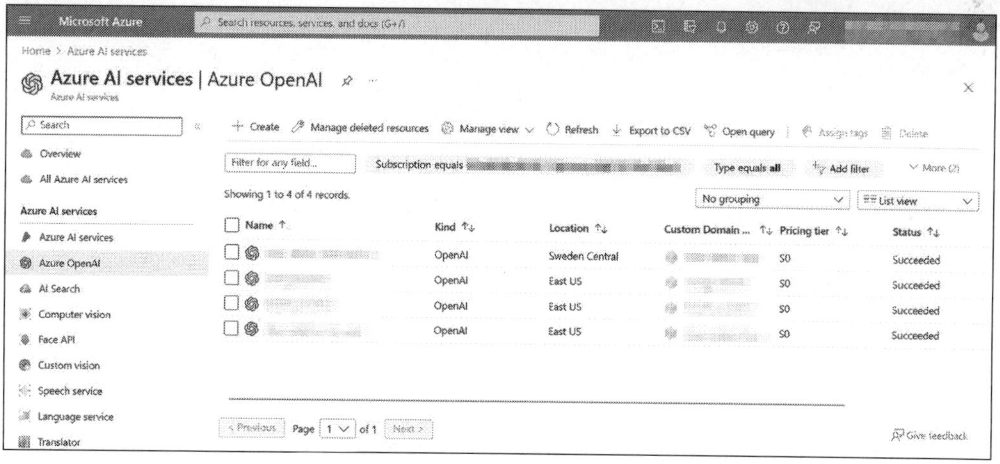

Figure 8.2: *Azure OpenAI dashboard*

Lastly, Azure OpenAI places a strong emphasis on responsible AI. In an era where ethical use of AI is a critical concern, Azure OpenAI ensures that developers have the power and accountability to create applications that leverage AI effectively, while ensuring fairness, transparency, and inclusivity. This fosters responsible AI use.

In doing so, Microsoft Azure OpenAI essentially empowers developers to mold the future of technology responsibly. Therefore, it plays a pivotal role in shaping a future where AI not only exists to serve humanity but does so in a way that respects the fundamental rights and freedoms of individuals as well.

Steps to Create an Azure OpenAI Resource

Here's a step-by-step guide to seamlessly create an Azure OpenAI resource:

1. Start by conveniently locating the OpenAI dashboard. Type **`"OpenAI"`** into the search bar and click the corresponding result to navigate to the dashboard.
2. Upon reaching the OpenAI dashboard, seek out the **`"Create"`** button. This button is usually evident on the screen, ready to guide you through the creation process.
3. As soon as you click **`"Create"`**, you'll be prompted to fill in some essential details. These include your Subscription ID, your desired Pricing Tier, and the Region you wish to create your resource in. Take your time to input these details accurately.

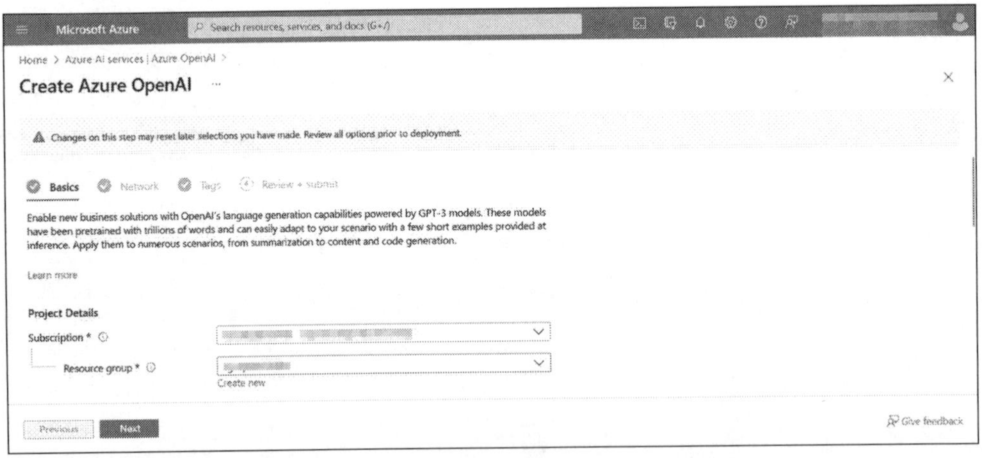

Figure 8.3: *Basic Information while creating Azure OpenAI resource*

4. After you have filled in the necessary details, look towards the lower portion of the dialog box and click **`"Next"`**. This action takes you to the next stage of creating your resource.

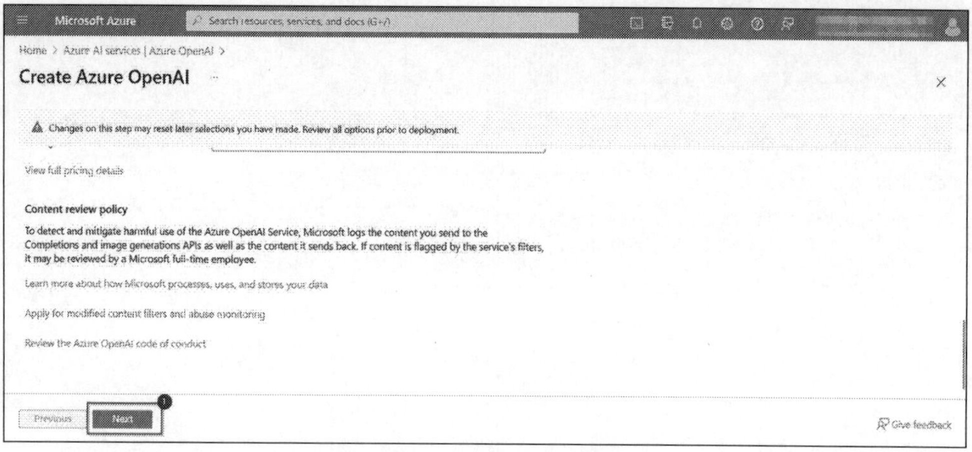

Figure 8.4: *Continuing the process*

5. The following screen prompts you to choose your Network Access configuration. There are usually three options. If you want to give all networks access to your resource, choose **"All Networks"**; for limited access, select **"Selected Networks"**; and if you do not wish any network to access your resource, choose **"Disabled for All Networks"**.

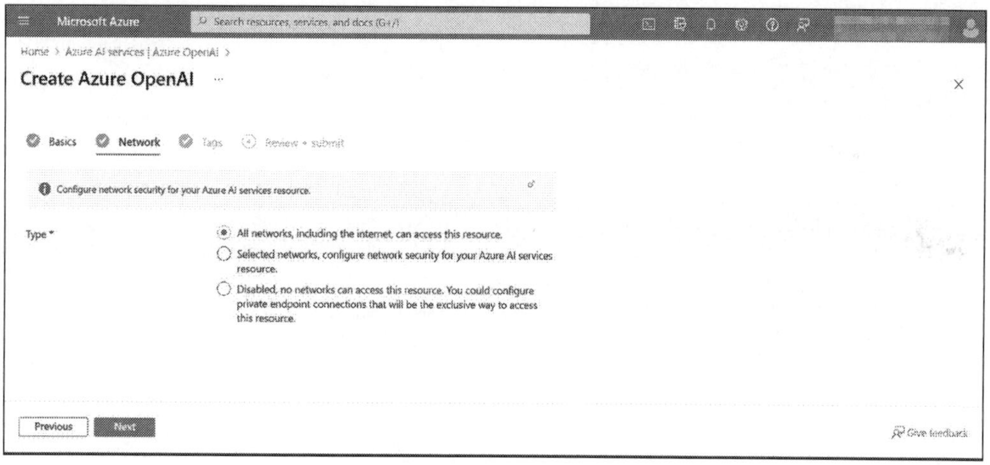

Figure 8.5: *Network security selection*

6. Once you've made your decision on the network access, click **"Next"** again to proceed to the subsequent stage.

7. The next step involves the application of appropriate tags. These tags help in categorizing and organizing your resources according to your preferences or the demands of the project.

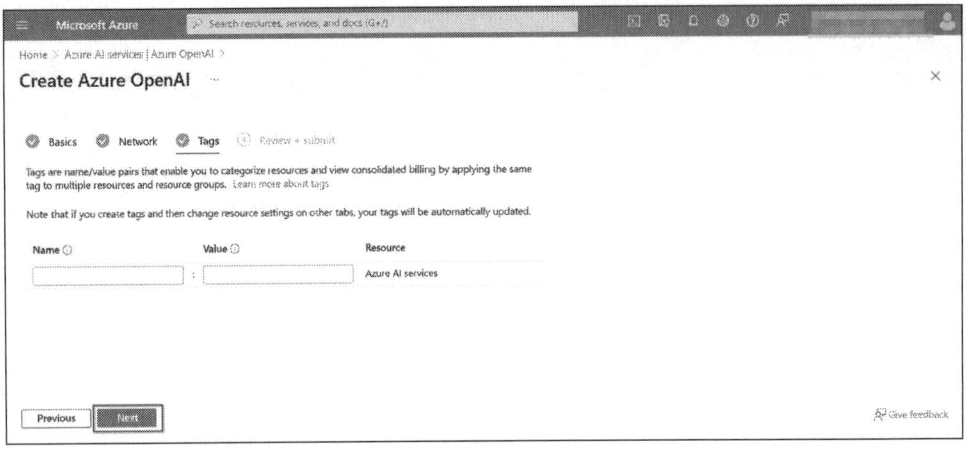

Figure 8.6: *Tagging resource*

8. After successfully adding the necessary tags, the final stage involves reviewing all your inputs and then submitting your information. Locate the "**`Submit and Create`**" button and click it to establish your Azure OpenAI resource.

   Take your time, be patient, and ensure every detail entered is as per your needs. This way, your new Azure OpenAI resource will be optimized for your development needs.

Model Catalog

Model Catalog in Azure forms the epicenter for a diverse array of open-source models, either developed by Microsoft or third-party entities. These pre-trained models are tailored for various language, speech, and vision use-cases.

Primarily, Model Catalog serves to acquaint users with the most appropriate pre-trained models for their unique requirements, thereby accelerating the AI integration process. Users can then customize and deploy these models using Azure's capabilities, ensuring their applications stay top-notch in terms of intelligence and functionality. A great example would be using a pre-trained vision model to detect objects in an image processing application.

Model Catalog's role doesn't end at discovery and deployment. It is the bridge linking Generative AI with practical applications. By contributing to fine-tuning, deploying, and importing pre-trained models, it creates a conducive environment for Generative AI to thrive. Suppose you're developing an AI chatbot application. Model Catalog hosts a multitude of pre-trained language models that could be enhanced using Generative AI to comprehend and generate human-like responses, making your chatbot sound real and more engaging. Conclusively, Azure's OpenAI and Model Catalog have carved out a significant role in advancing Generative AI, shaping a future where intelligent applications rule the roost.

Function and Usage

The Model Catalog hosts a diverse collection of AI models, making it an invaluable functionality of Azure for AI developers and data scientists. The catalog exhibits three main collections:

- **Open source models curated by Azure AI**

  The first collection comprises popular open source third-party models that have been curated by Azure Machine Learning. This provides a reliable, accessible set of models fit for various applications, enhancing the speed and ease of deploying AI applications on Azure.

- **Azure OpenAI models, exclusively available on Azure**

  The second collection houses models from Azure OpenAI. Azure platform users can directly fine-tune and deploy these exclusive models via the 'Azure Open AI' collection in the Model Catalog, thereby eliminating the need for sourcing and vetting third-party models.

- **Transformers models from the HuggingFace hub**

  The third collection grants access to thousands of models from the HuggingFace hub. These models are available for real-time inference with online endpoints, allowing AI practitioners to rapidly infer and apply machine learning techniques in real-world scenarios.

Relationship with Generative AI

The Model Catalog plays an integral role in advancing Generative AI through Azure. Generative AI models within the catalog can be directly utilized in the Azure platform to build sophisticated applications. By providing a vast range of pre-trained models, the catalog empowers developers to benefit from Generative AI without needing to build models from scratch.

For instance, if a user is working to develop a text-generation software, they could leverage a Generative AI model from the catalog, such as GPT-3, to quickly integrate generative capabilities into their application.

Additionally, the diverse collections within the Model Catalog– including Azure OpenAI models, curated open-source models, and HuggingFace models–offer developers myriad options for implementing Generative AI, making the catalog an imperative connection between Generative AI and its practical deployment.

Steps for Using Model Catalog

Navigating and harnessing Microsoft Azure's Model Catalog is straightforward, thanks to its user-friendly interface and systematic structure. The process of selecting, understanding, and deploying models from the catalog can be summed up in the following steps:

1. **Opening Azure Machine Learning Studio**

   The journey begins with accessing the Azure Machine Learning Studio. Azure Machine Learning Studio is essentially a workspace wherein you can create, manage, and deploy machine learning models.

2. **Navigating to Model Catalog**

   Upon landing in the Azure Machine Learning Studio, navigate to the Model Catalog via the side pane. The Model Catalog contains a plethora of pre-trained machine learning models ready for deployment.

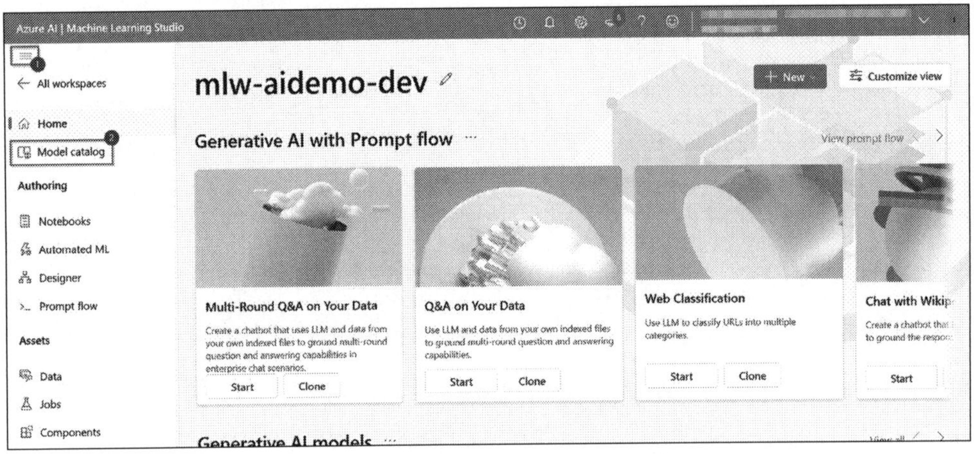

Figure 8.7: *Navigating to Model catalog*

3. **Selecting Models**

   Inside the Model Catalog, you can approach the model selection in three ways. You can either search for a specific pre-trained model using specific keywords, filter models based on desired tasks, or just casually browse through all available models to familiarize yourself with the options at hand.

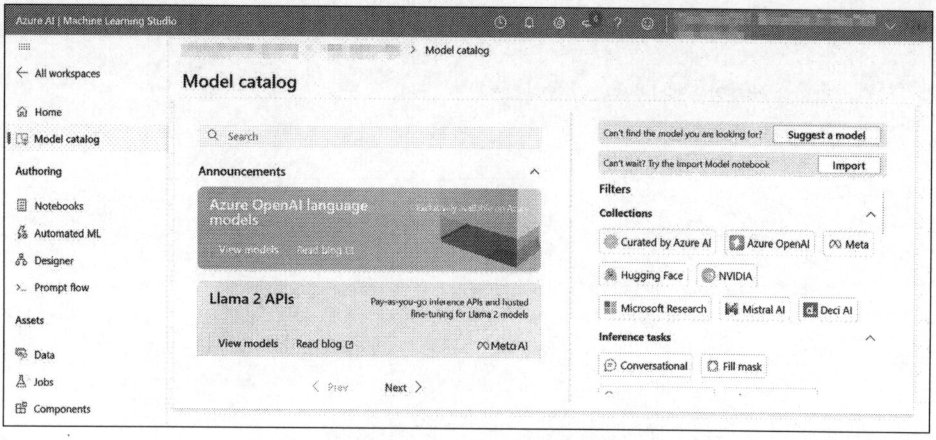

***Figure 8.8**: Model catalog page*

4. **Choosing the Desired Model**

   Once you have zeroed in on a model that suits your application's requirements, select it to progress to the next phase.

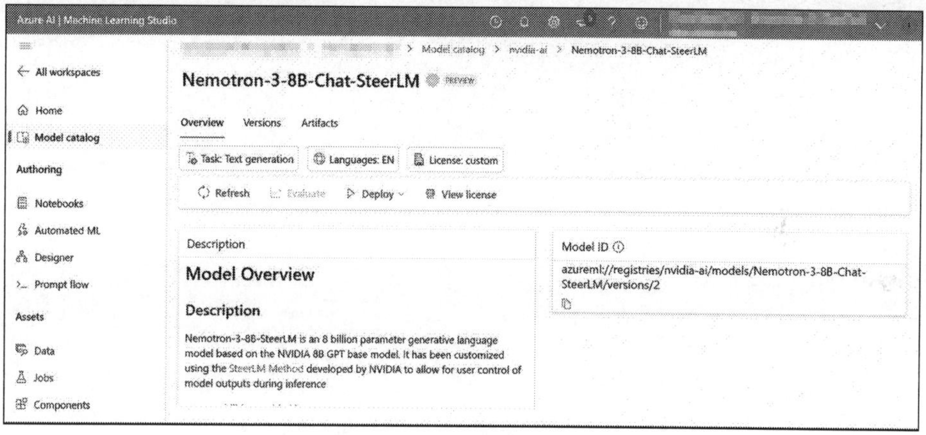

***Figure 8.9**: Model description page*

5. **Reviewing Model Information**

   After selecting a model, you will be directed to its dedicated page where you can comprehensively review its specifications. Here, you will find details like its description, ID, version, artifacts, and other relevant information that could help gauge its suitability for your needs.

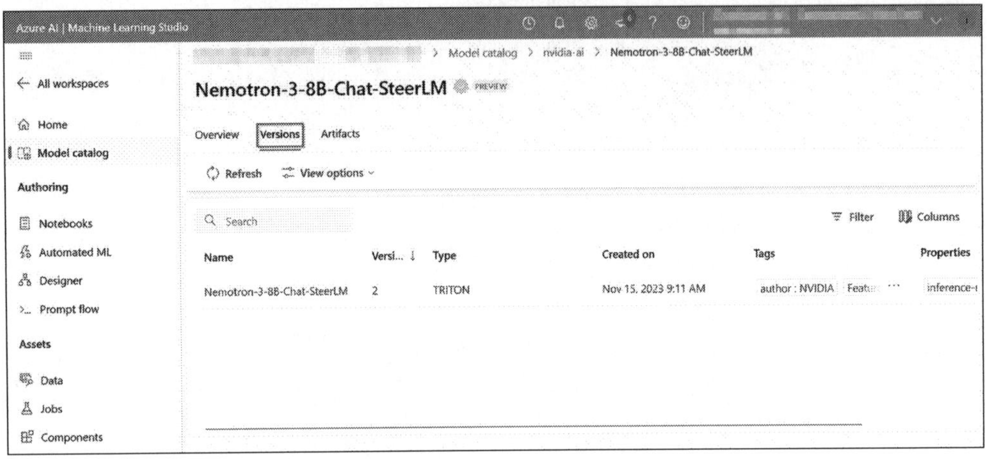

Figure 8.10: *Model Versions*

We can also look into the Artifacts of the model, which include the metadata for the given model.

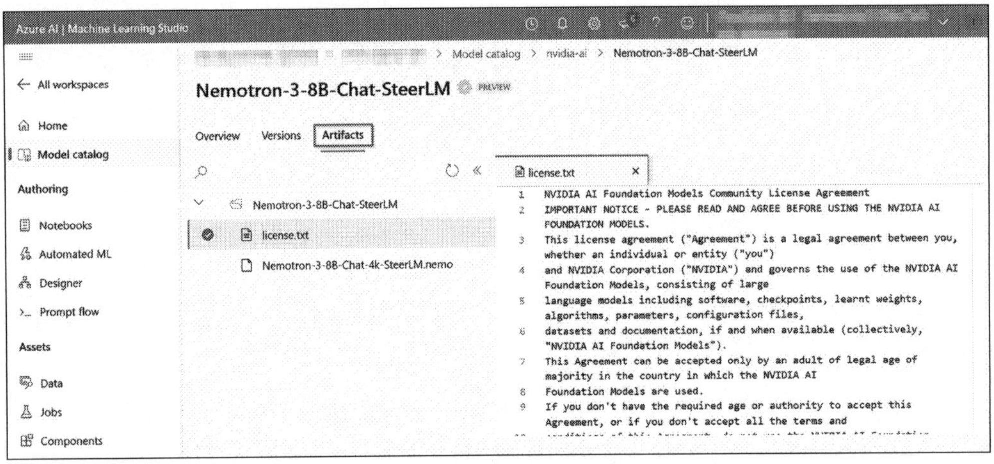

Figure 8.11: *Model artifacts*

6. **Deploying the Model**

   Next, you can proceed to deploy the model. Azure offers two methods of deployment: real-time endpoint and batch endpoint. The real-time endpoint allows immediate inference, ideal for time-sensitive applications, whereas the batch endpoint is suited for bulk processing.

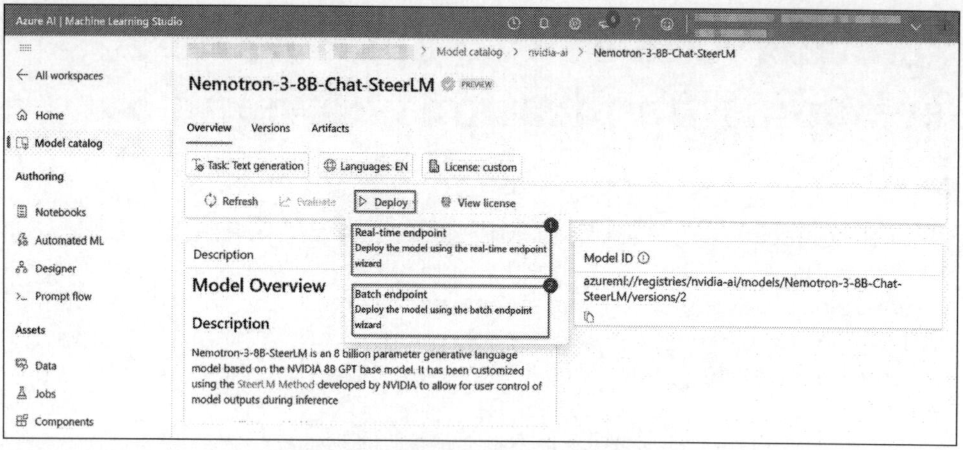

Figure 8.12: *Deployment options*

7. **Filling in Deployment Details**

   Depending on the method you choose, you will be prompted to provide specifics about where to deploy your model. Here, you'd need to provide information including the type of virtual machine to use, resource configuration, and more.

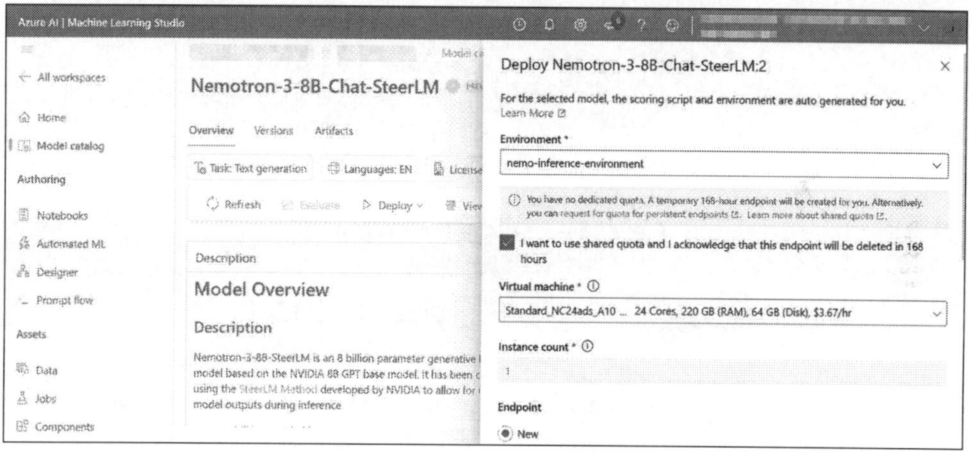

Figure 8.13: *Model Deployment Wizard*

8. **Model Deployment**

   After all the necessary details are keyed in, give your data one final review and hit **`'deploy'`**. Azure takes it from there by automating the rest of the process. In minutes you'll find your selected model up and running, ready to be integrated for intelligent operations in your desired application.

In a nutshell, Azure's Model Catalog provides a seamless pathway to the deployment of sophisticated, pre-trained AI models, thereby accelerating your application's journey towards smart operational capabilities.

Exploring Azure's PromptFlow for Developing Applications Powered by LLMs

In the cutting-edge world of artificial intelligence and machine learning, Microsoft's Azure PromptFlow for the development of LLMs applications takes center stage. It is meticulously designed to streamline and simplify the overall development process. From prototype to product deployment, Azure PromptFlow is the one-stop-shop for everything you need when using large language models to power your AI applications.

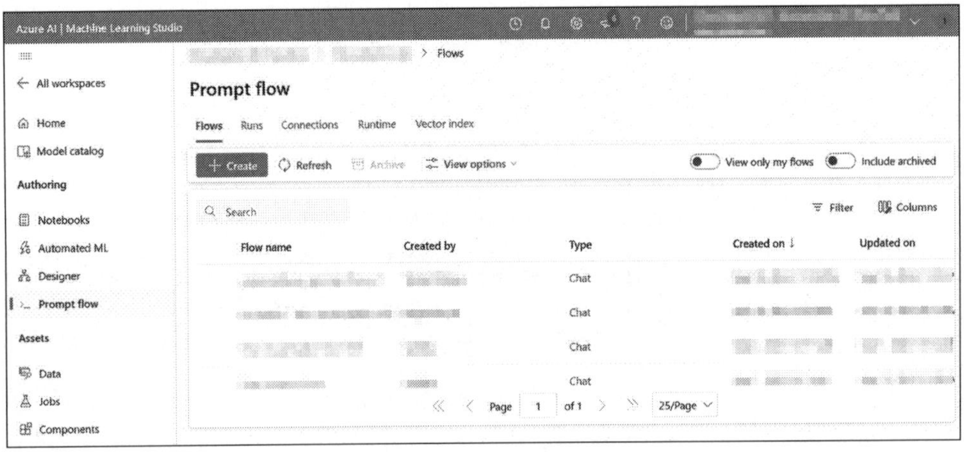

***Figure 8.14**: Prompt flow dashboard*

Understanding Azure's PromptFlow

Launched under the reliable banner name Azure, PromptFlow is an innovative tool for Machine Learning enthusiasts. Azure Machine Learning PromptFlow is essentially a game-changer that remarkably simplifies the entire process associated with developing AI applications powered through Large Language Models (LLMs). It unlocks new opportunities and potential for prototyping, experimentation, and iteration, accelerating the journey from the drawing board to application deployment. It not only eases the application development process but also broadens the horizons for AI applications that are based on LLMs. With PromptFlow, users can create effective and efficient executable flows while linking LLMs, prompts, and Python tools. It also offers debugging and iterative opportunities, creation and evaluation of variant prompts, and the deployment of a real-time endpoint, bringing an all-rounded development experience to the users.

Advantages of PromptFlow in LLM Application

PromptFlow brings to the table a range of compelling advantages that set it apart in the dynamic landscape of LLM application. It acts as a catalyst, enabling efficiency, and enhancing productivity in the development process.

Prompt Engineering Agility

PromptFlow, by design, supports an interactive authoring experience that helps users to–and comprehend projects seamlessly. Utilizing visual representation of the flow's structure, it allows users to navigate and understand the project structure effortlessly, all while providing a notebook-style coding experience that coders find both familiar and effective.

PromptFlow also brings to the fore the highly resourceful feature of prompt tuning. It fuels an iterative refinement process by allowing users to create and compare various prompt variants. In this way, it not just eases the developmental process, but also allows room for creativity and innovation.

One of the other distinctive advantages of using PromptFlow for LLM application development is that it allows the users to assess the effectiveness and quality of the prompts and flows with pre-built evaluation flows. This feature is extremely useful in finalizing the prompt and the flow that works best.

Enterprise Readiness

When it comes to working in an organization, collaboration is key. This seamless collaboration is promoted by PromptFlow as it enables collective work on prompt engineering projects. This not only improves knowledge sharing but also helps to maintain an effective version control.

Furthermore, PromptFlow can also be touted as an all-in-one platform that streamlines the entire prompt engineering process–from the initial development stages to evaluation, from monitoring to the final deployment.

Unveiling the LLM-based Application Development Lifecycle

The LLM-based application development lifecycle can be divided into following parts:

Initialization

Begin by identifying the requisite business use case and collecting data pertinent to it. This stage involves learning how to build a rudimentary prompt and further developing a flow to enhance its capabilities.

Experimentation

Proceed to execute the flow using the sample data collected, evaluating the performance of the prompts. If necessary, iterate upon the flow. Continuing experimentation is advised until satisfactory results are achieved.

Refinement and Evaluation

Utilize a larger dataset to gauge the performance of the flow. In this stage, assess the effectiveness of the prompt and make refinements as required. Progress to the next phase only after the results align with the desired criteria.

Production

Focus on optimizing efficiency and effectiveness at this movement. This includes deploying the developed flow and monitoring its performance in a real-life setting. Collect feedback and usage data which can be applied to enhance future iterations of the flow.

Creating an Azure's PromptFlow: A Step-By-Step Guide

Embarking on a journey of creating enterprise-level applications built on Large Language Models (LLMs) using Azure's PromptFlow might seem daunting at first. However, with the right guidance and understanding, the process can be as simple as a few strategic clicks. Let's break down the process of setting up your own PromptFlow:

1. **Launching the Platform**

   The first step toward creating your PromptFlow is accessing the Azure Machine Learning studio, the primary dashboard from where you manage all AI operations. This online portal is your workspace–where you will develop, run, manage, and track machine learning workflows.

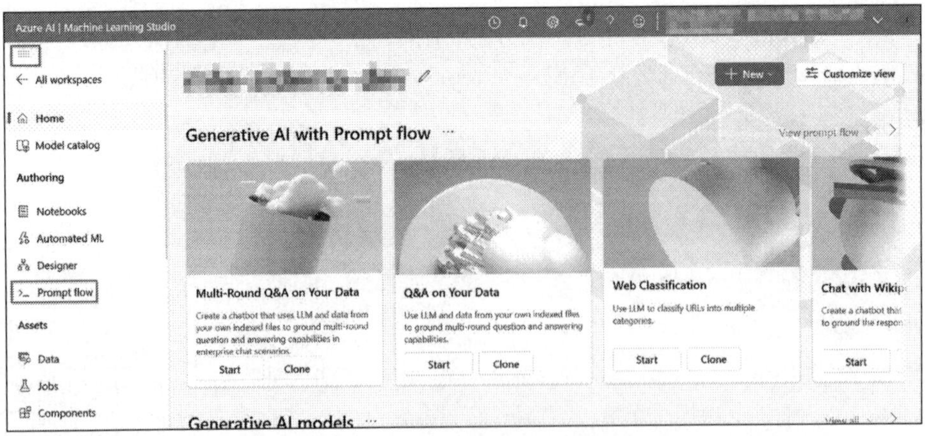

Figure 8.15: *Navigating to prompt flow*

2. **Accessing PromptFlow**

   Once you are in the Azure Machine Learning Studio, navigate to the left pane of the interface to locate and select `'Prompt flow'`. This is where the journey begins as you take your first step towards AI application development using LLMs.

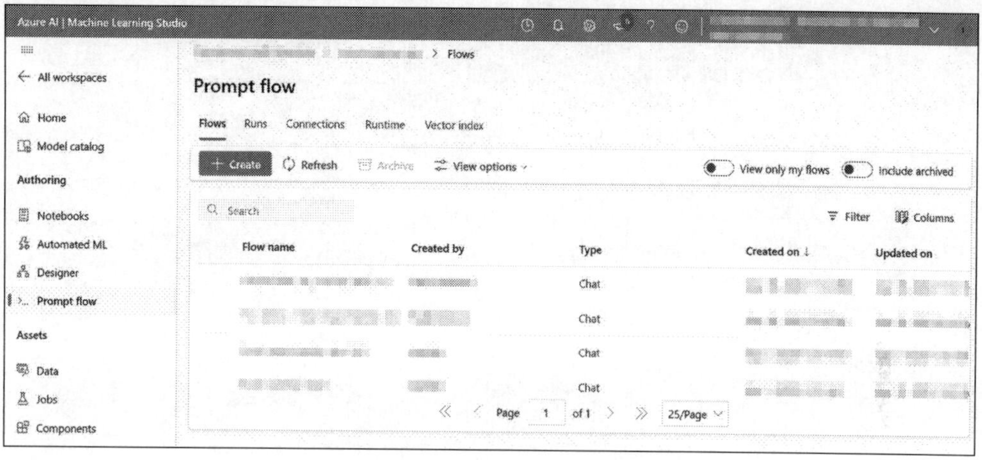

Figure 8.16: *The flows created*

3. **Managing Connections**

   At this stage, it is essential to set up `'Connections'`. Connections in Azure are a pivotal feature. They facilitate the secure storage and efficient management of sensitive credentials like secret keys, necessary for communicating with LLMs and other external tools such as Azure Content Safety.

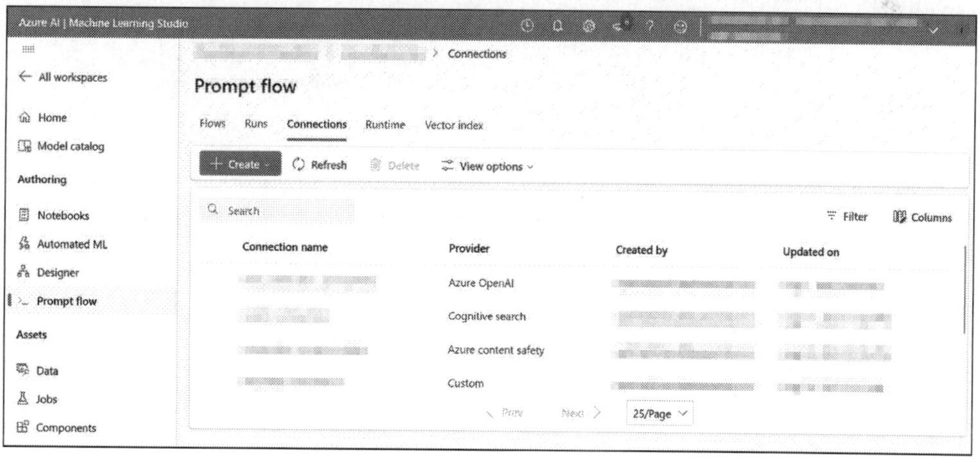

Figure 8.17: *Connections dashboard in prompt flow*

4. **Customizing Connections**

   Upon navigating to `'Connections'`, click `'Create'` and select the type of connection you want to establish. In our walkthrough, we will build an **`'Azure OpenAI'`** connection. You will be required to provide Azure OpenAI details related to your subscription. Provide the necessary details to continue with the process.

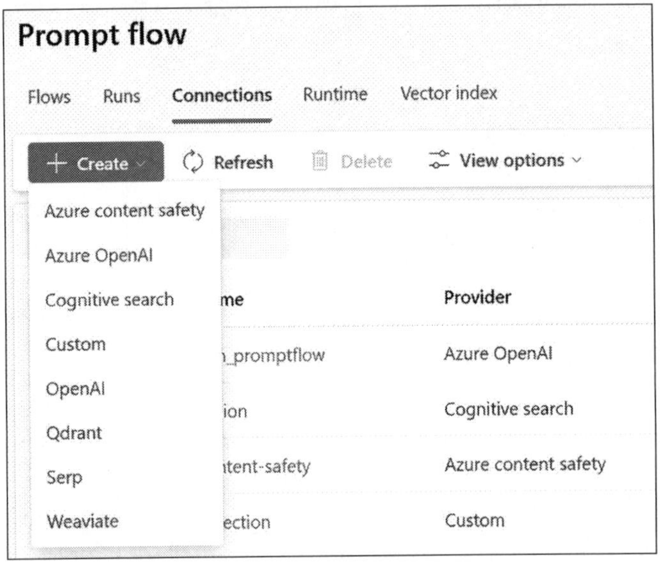

Figure 8.18: *Types of connections that can be made*

On selecting the option, it will ask you to enter the details.

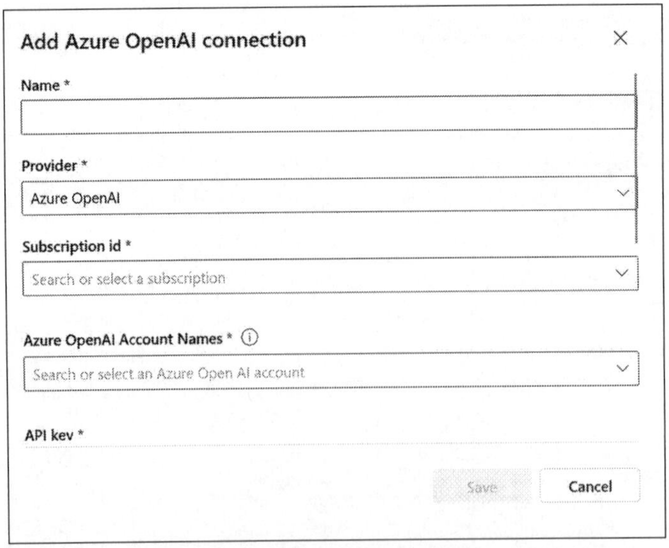

Figure 8.19: *Adding connection information*

5. **Switching to Flow Tab**

   After successfully establishing the connection, close the `'Connections'` tab and shift your attention to the `'Flow Tab'`.

6. **Initiating a New Flow**

   Find and click the `'Create Flow'` button, marking the beginning of your flow creation process.

7. **Choosing the Flow Type**

   Once the `'Create Flow'` button is clicked, you will be presented with several choices. You can either start with a blank canvas lending complete flexibility or kickstart your journey using a prebuilt flow template.

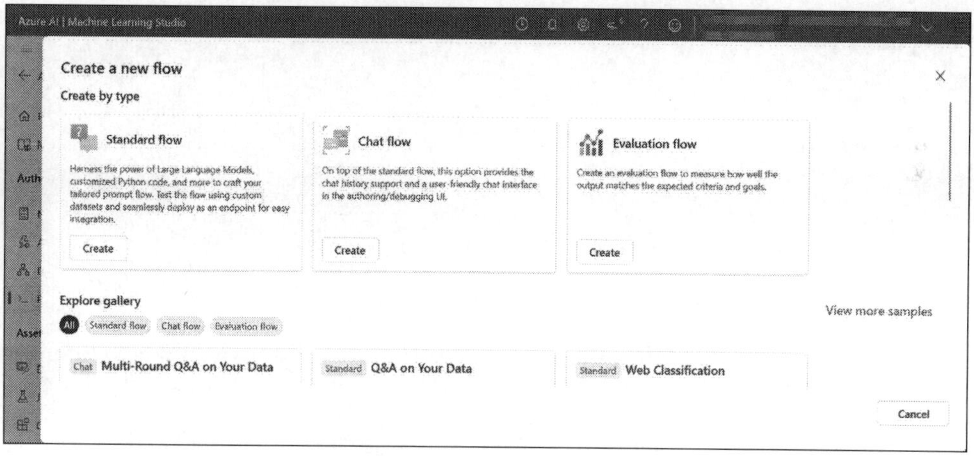

***Figure 8.20**: Creating new flow*

8. **Selecting a Prebuilt Flow**

   For this demonstration, we will be using a prebuilt flow. Scroll through the options and select the `'Web Classification'` flow, a popular starting point.

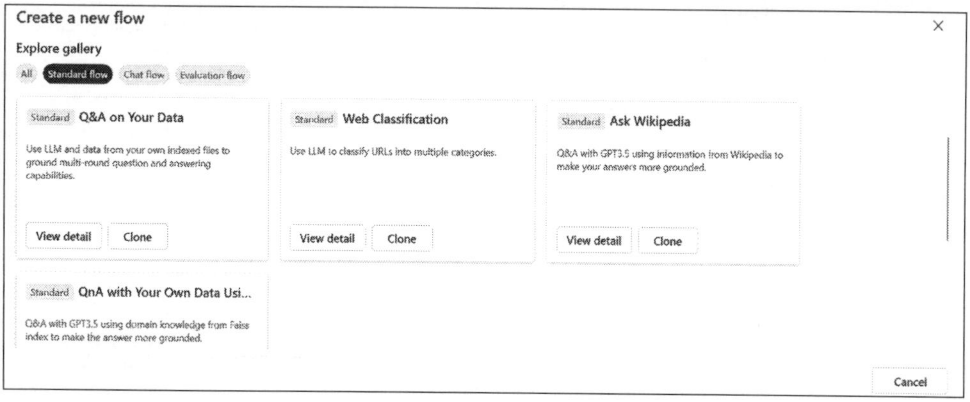

***Figure 8.21**: Selecting a prebuilt flow*

9. **Customizing the Flow**

   PromptFlow will prompt you for location details specific to your flow, an essential step to harmonize your operations with regional data regulations and latency considerations. Fill in the location details and click `'Create'`.

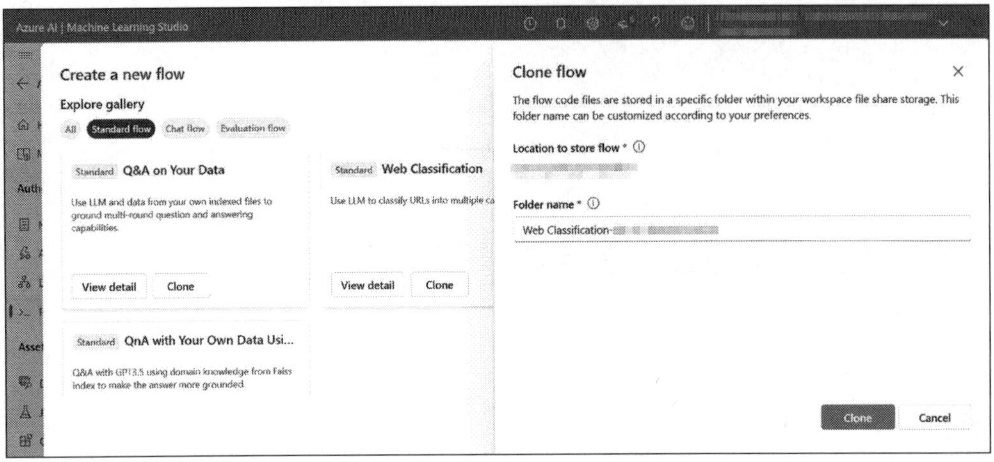

Figure 8.22: *Customizing the flow*

10. **Celebrating Your First Flow**

    There you go! Your first flow using Azure's PromptFlow is now live and ready for action.

    You will see that there are two columns in the prompt flow. The first one allows you to write, modify code. The `'Graph'` column gives a graphical view of the entire flow and makes it easy for the developer to understand, modify and create efficient applications.

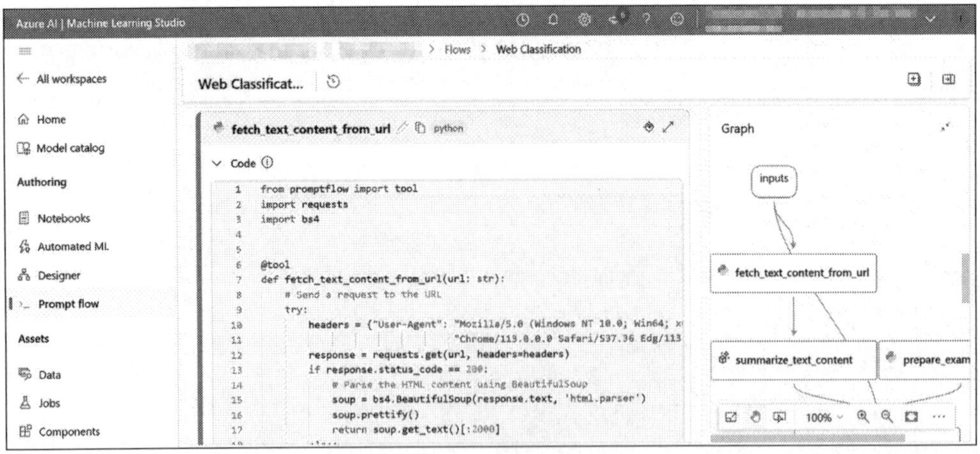

Figure 8.23: *New flow created*

Here is the graph:

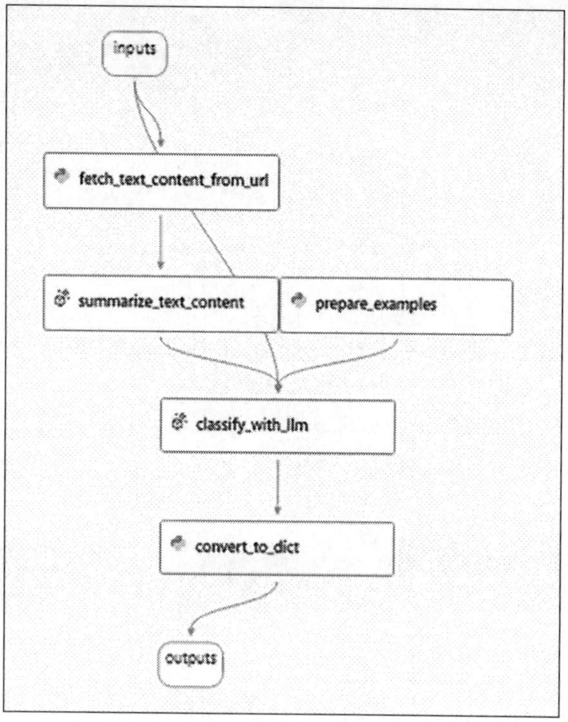

Figure 8.24: *The graph for the flow*

In these ten simple steps, we have demonstrated how to unlock the potential of Azure's Machine Learning studio in creating LLM-based AI applications using PromptFlow. Armed with this knowledge, you are now ready to take charge and commence creating revolutionary applications leveraging the power of Large Language Models.

Going in Depth

Let us look part by part at each node of the flow we just created.

- **Inputs**

  This node takes the input that will come in the flow. It has three information of the input variable, including:

  - Name: The name of the variable, in this case the '**url**'.
  - Type: Similar to programming languages, it needs to know whether the variable is string, numerical or any other type.
  - Value: The value which we are feeding. In single run it will take one url and run, when we do multiple runs, we can give a list of urls, and it will run for each url.

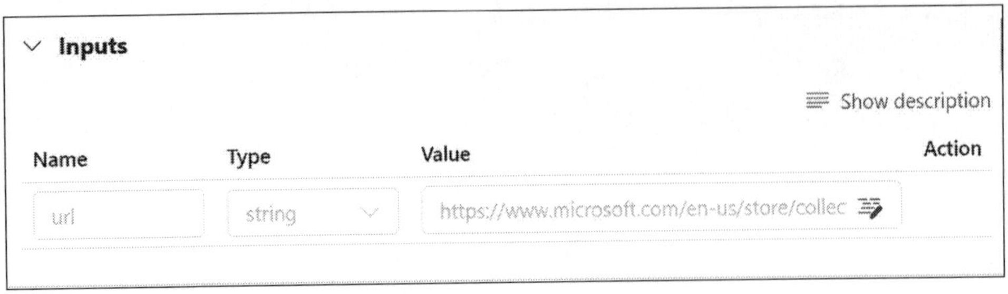

Figure 8.25: *Input parameters*

- Fetch content from url

  This is a python node. A python node means we can execute code inside it. Here we are scraping a website for analyzing.

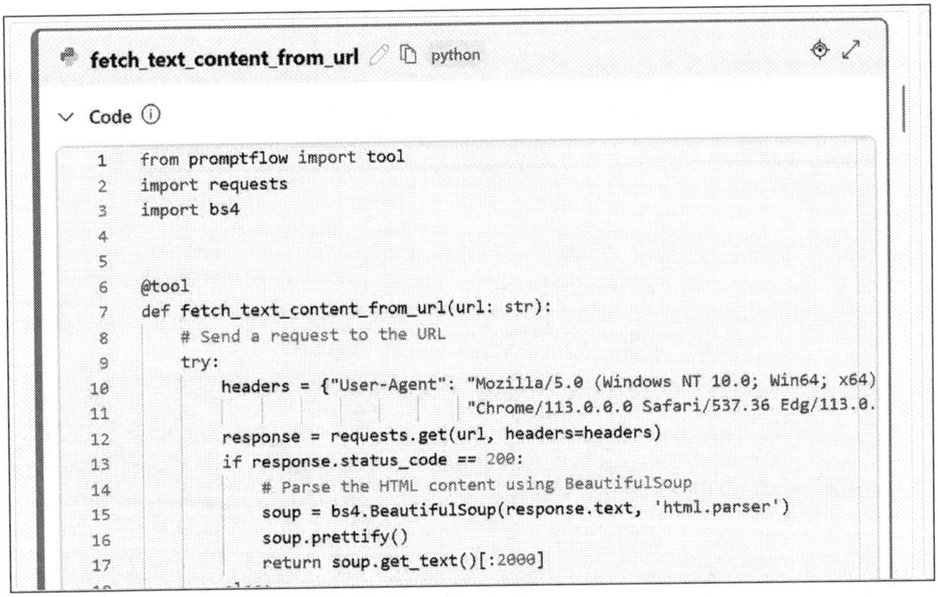

Figure 8.26: *Fetching content from URL*

- Summarizing content

  This node is an **llm** node, which means we can write the prompt inside it. Here you can see we are asking the LLM to summarize the text content that we received after scraping a website.

  You will notice that the input for this node is the output from the above-mentioned python node.

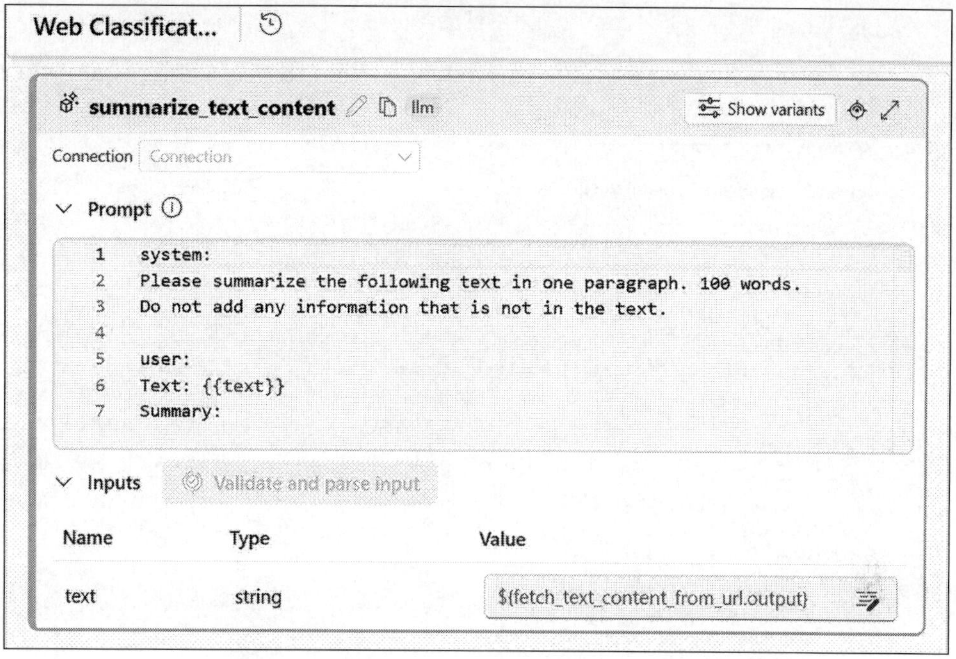

***Figure 8.27**: Summarizing the content received*

- Preparing examples

  This is to implement few shot prompting. We are giving it url, the content and what the content is. This helps LLM perform in a desirable and controlled manner.

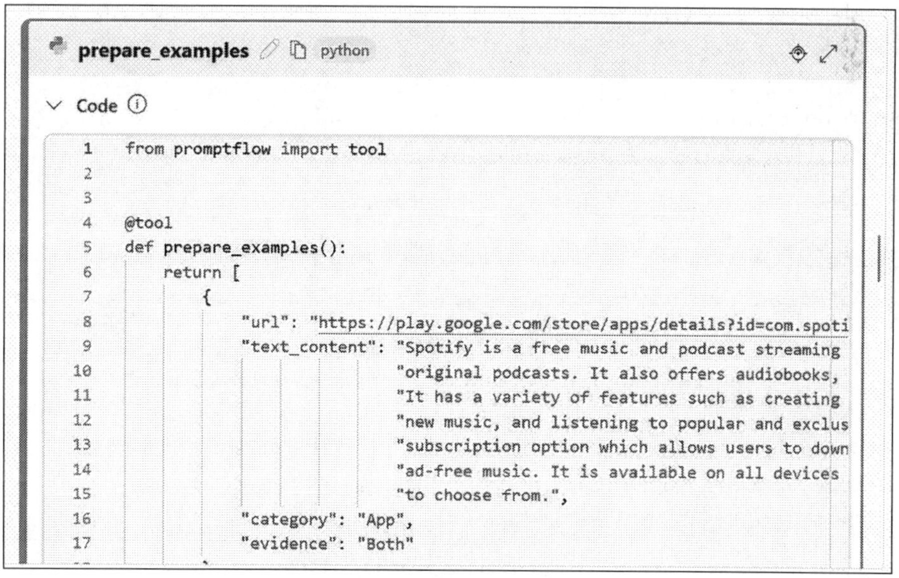

***Figure 8.28**: Preparing examples*

- Classification

  Now, we are ready to classify the websites. We are providing prompt for the task, and the required inputs.

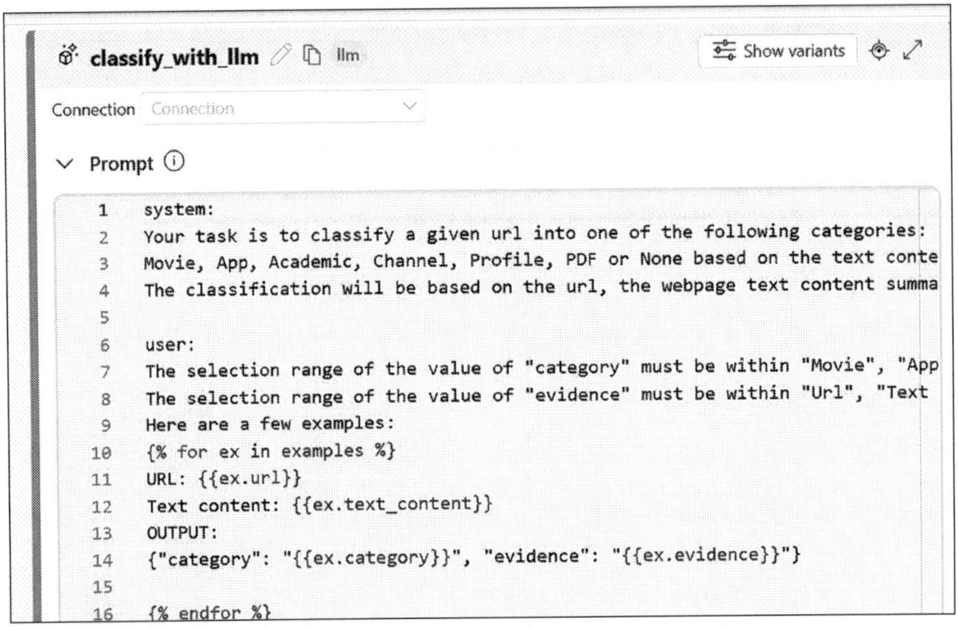

Figure 8.29: *Classifying the content*

The inputs are as follows:

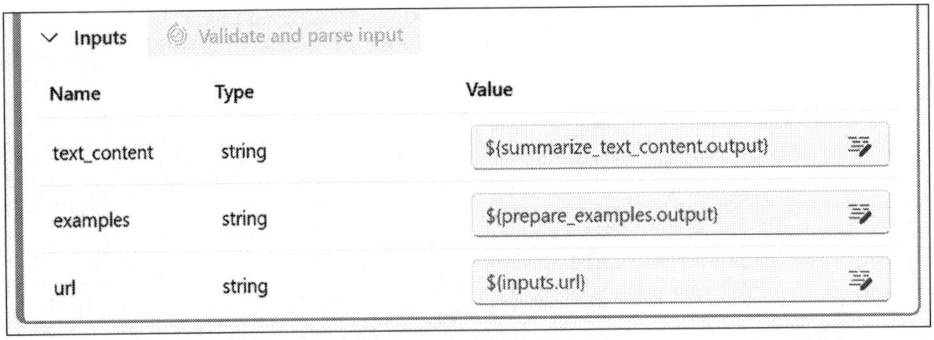

Figure 8.30: *Inputs for the classifying block*

- Converting to dictionary

  After the classification is done, we take the result and the url and convert it to a dictionary. This helps us in creating a json output which can be fed into evaluation tools to evaluate how accurate our flow is.

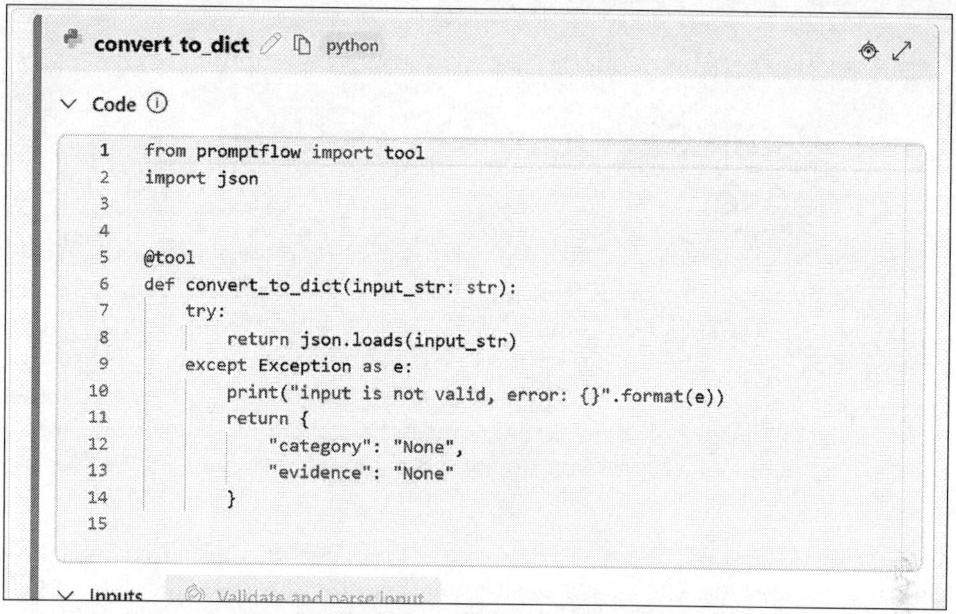


```python
from promptflow import tool
import json


@tool
def convert_to_dict(input_str: str):
    try:
        return json.loads(input_str)
    except Exception as e:
        print("input is not valid, error: {}".format(e))
        return {
            "category": "None",
            "evidence": "None"
        }

```

Figure 8.31: *Converting the output as dictionary*

Working with Multimodal AI Services: Azure Speech and Vision

The epoch of the technological revolution has ushered in a myriad of advancements, among which stands the advent of AI services. Multimodal AI services such as those provided by tech giant Microsoft's Azure represent the new phase of technological evolution, offering a comprehensive suite of Speech and Vision services. These services are critical tools that developers can harness to construct applications that possess the prowess to process and dissect data efficiently and effectively.

In the rapidly changing business landscape, these AI tools provided by Azure are not just path-breaking innovations; they are invaluable resources that can be employed to scale operations, drive innovation, and revolutionize the modus operandi of businesses. By embracing these services, businesses have the potential to make machines more adaptable, intuitive, and intelligent. This section delves into the practical implementation and utilization of Azure's Speech and Vision services, illuminating the pathways to achieving business transformation through AI.

Azure's Speech Services: The Voice of AI

In its essence, Azure's Speech services offer a monumental opportunity for developers to integrate speech processing capabilities into their applications. It does this by converting spoken language into written text and vice versa, thereby introducing a new level of interaction between the user and the application.

Azure Vision Services: AI's Optical Powerhouse

With Azure's Vision services, AI isn't just about providing intelligent responses but about venturing into the realm of visual perception. These services are all about giving the machines the capability to comprehend and interpret the world as we humans do, through our eyes. The Vision services provided by Azure entail a diverse range of functionalities from identifying and analyzing visual content to recognizing faces and emotions. The power of these services lies in their ability to transform raw visual data into meaningful insights which can fuel intelligent decision-making processes in businesses.

By integrating these state-of-the-art Speech and Vision services into their applications, businesses can leverage the power of AI to navigate the complexities of the modern business environment with ease and efficiency. The following sections provide an in-depth exploration of the functionalities, applications, and benefits of Azure's Speech and Vision services.

Azure Speech

Azure Speech is an array of services that provide speech recognition capabilities at par with humans, allowing businesses to transform spoken language into written text accurately. These services extract meaning from user inputs, making them essential in building AI models.

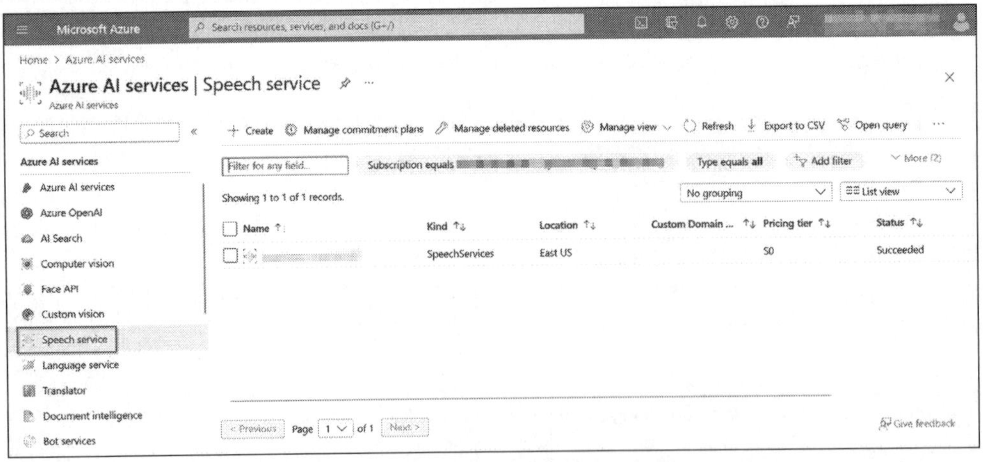

Figure 8.32: *Azure Speech Service dashboard*

Utilization in AI Models

Azure Speech is predominantly utilized in AI models to innovate communication mechanisms. For instance, it can be used in real-time transcription services, chatbots, and virtual assistants, amongst others. It performs tasks like speech recognition, text-to-speech, and speech translation, enhancing user interaction and making the models more intelligent.

It brings in a conversational intelligence aspect to AI models, allowing them to understand, interact, and respond with precision. The feature of continuous language understanding makes systems adapt and learn, thereby making AI models more compelling.

Practical Implementation

The practical implementation of Azure Speech involves integrating Speech APIs into the AI models. These APIs use robust algorithms that convert spoken language into written text and generate human-like synthesized speech. Also, they can recognize a broad set of speech across various languages and user scenarios.

These services can be used to build applications that respond to voice commands, transcription services, voice-enabled chatbots, and much more. The ease of integration of Azure Speech services into apps makes it even more user-friendly and adaptable to diverse businesses.

Azure Vision

Azure Vision is another crucial service provided by Azure, used for interpreting and analyzing visual cues.

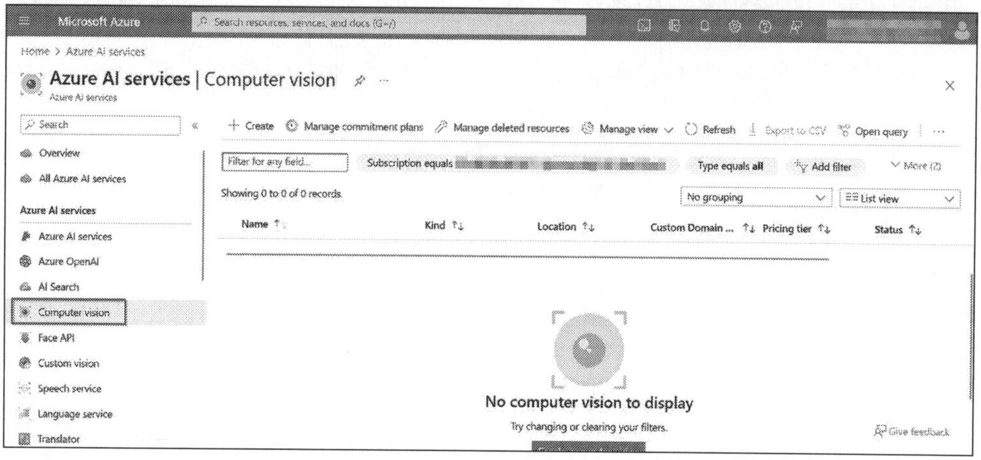

Figure 8.33: *Azure vision service dashboard*

Role in AI Models

The vision services play a crucial role in AI models as they leverage powerful image processing algorithms to build insightful and intuitive visual models. These services can analyze content, extract visual features, decipher handwriting or printed text, recognize celebrities, detect brand logos, and much more.

Azure Vision broadens the scope of AI models by recognizing patterns and making predictions, thereby enhancing the model's output and autonomous capabilities.

Walkthrough of Implementation

Implementing Azure Vision involves integrating Computer Vision APIs into the AI model. These APIs can analyze visual content in different ways based on the requirements.

For example, they can be used to generate thumbnails, recognize and analyze images, extract printed and handwritten text, or detect faces. Azure Vision's implementation improves the efficacy of AI models by giving them the capability to interpret, analyze, and react to visual data.

Thus, Azure Speech and Vision services play a vital role in enhancing AI models, allowing them to process and analyze data accurately, making machines more autonomous and capable of better decision-making.

Responsible AI in Azure: Creating Ethical and Unbiased AI Models

Artificial Intelligence (AI) in the contemporary modern era has become an integral component in decision-making processes spanning a multitude of industries. The implications it has on our daily lives are substantial, but there is an escalating concern surrounding the unintentional integration of bias and ethical discrepancies into these AI models. This concern is rooted in the potential for unfair or damaging consequences if these technologies are left unchecked.

In an attempt to counteract these challenges, Microsoft Azure has committed substantial resources into not only the development of AI models that are unbiased and adhere to ethical principles, but also in the promotion of safe AI practices. This illustrates their dedication to fostering an AI environment that is both trustworthy and fair, ensuring that their technologies are implemented responsibly and with accountability.

Importance of Ethical and Unbiased AI Models

AI systems essentially function as mirrors to the data they are trained upon. This implies that any biases present in the training data, regardless of whether they are overt or concealed, might result in the AI behaving in an unacceptable or erroneous manner. Therefore, it is crucial to develop AI models that are not only ethical but also devoid of any biases.

Models imbued with principles of fairness and inclusiveness, and a strong regard for reliability and safety, ensure that AI operates in a manner that respects human rights and values. Such models ensure a more equitable decision-making process, which is particularly important in fields such as criminal justice or employment where the consequences of unfair decisions can be severe.

Furthermore, AI models free from bias help to avoid unintentional discrimination, which is critical in fostering trust in AI technologies. This trust is integral to the successful adoption and integration of AI into our societies and industries. Ethical and unbiased AI models also play a significant role in promoting positive progress in technological sectors. They help to ensure that the benefits of AI such as improved efficiency, customization, and decision-making are not marred by the detrimental impacts of bias and discrimination. As such, the cultivation of ethical and unbiased AI models is a necessity as we continue to marry our lives and societies with these evolving technologies.

Azure's Approach to Responsible AI

Azure places a considerable focus on Responsible AI. It has established a detailed set of principles that governs its AI creation and use, including fairness, reliability and safety, privacy and security, inclusivity, transparency, and accountability. Azure's approach to Responsible AI promotes consistent implementation of these principles across all its AI products and services.

Azure AI Content Safety

Azure AI Content Safety aims to detect harmful user-generated and AI-generated content in applications and services, ensuring online spaces maintain safety and integrity.

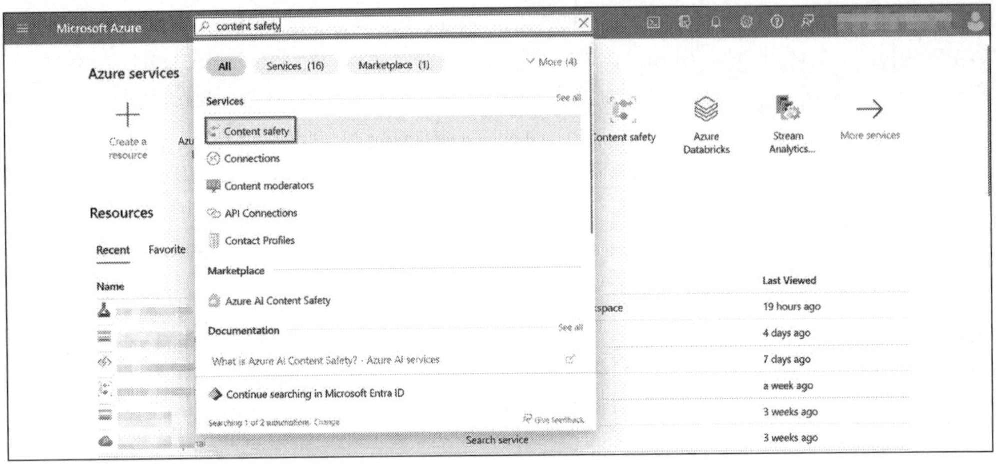

Figure 8.34: *Searching for Content Safety*

Steps to Create Content Safety Resource

To create a content safety resource, we need to do the following:

1. Go to Content Safety dashboard

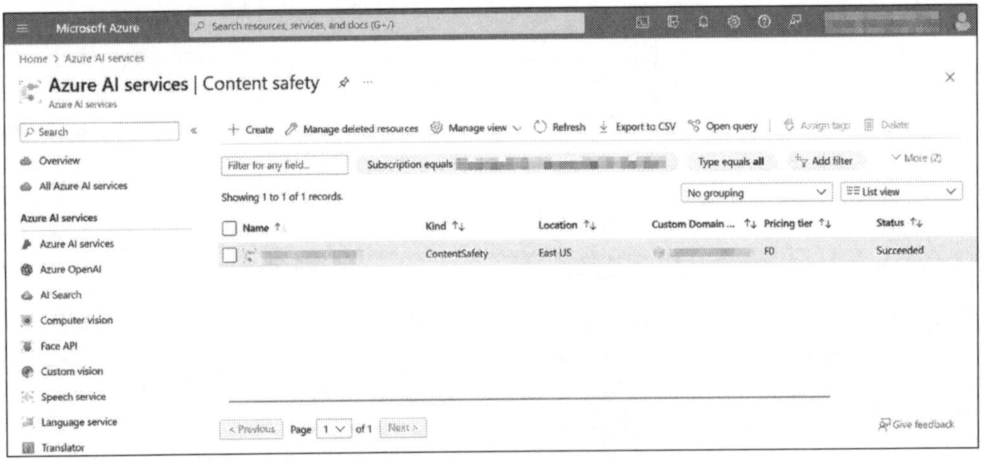

Figure 8.35: *Azure Content Safety dashboard*

2. Click "**Create**"
3. The resource creation wizard will open, here we will have to enter all the required details.

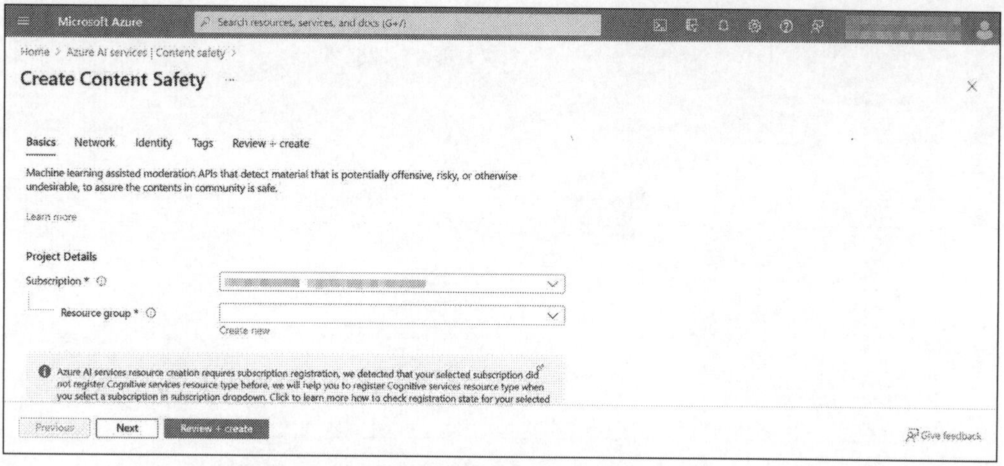

Figure 8.36: *Adding basic information for resource*

4. After giving all details, click **"Review + Create"** and yay! Your content safety resource is ready to use.
5. Now let's see how this works. Go to https://contentsafety.cognitive.azure.com/ which is the content safety studio.

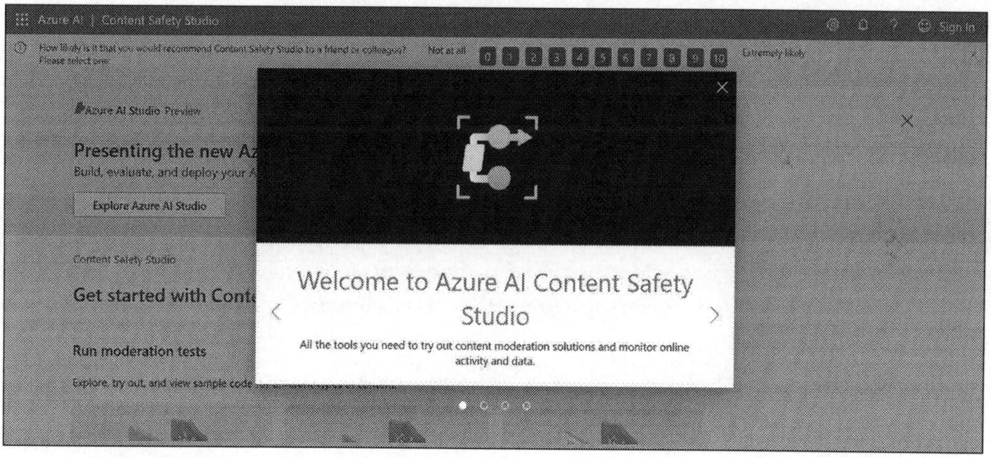

Figure 8.37: *Azure Content Safety Studio*

6. Let us see how text moderation works. Go to **"Moderate text content"**. You will be asked to enter your resource, select the resource you created. And you will be able to test your text inputs.

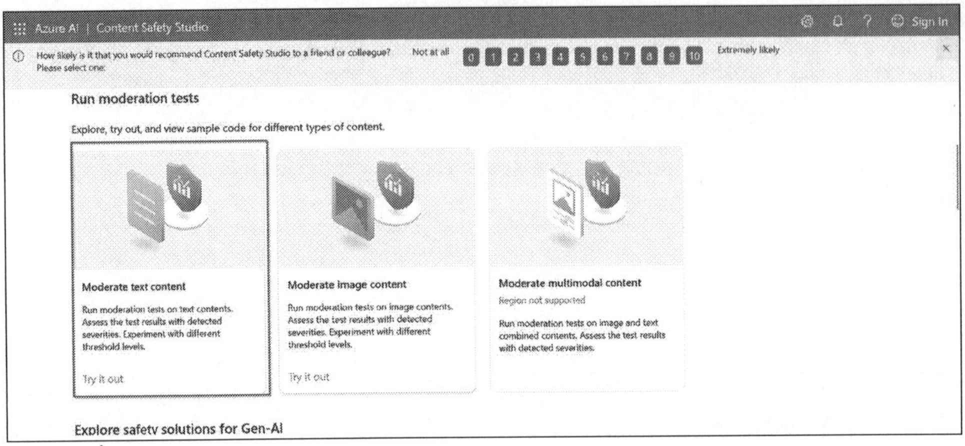

Figure 8.38: *Ways in which we can use azure content safety*

Purpose

Azure AI Content Safety has an end goal to assist software developers, corporations, and companies in sifting through and eliminating potentially harmful or inappropriate content. The uses of such a system are extensive, and it's primarily designed to be integrated with a variety of platforms and industries. It shows promise for use in various areas such as online marketplaces, gaming companies, social messaging platforms, large media enterprises, and educational solutions for K-12.

The service could be a valuable tool, and here's how:

- **Online marketplaces**

  These platforms often host a vast amount of user-generated content, including product catalogues, descriptions, and reviews. Azure AI Content Safety can aid in content moderation, ensuring the material posted on the platform adheres to the required safety and decency guidelines, thereby preserving its reputation.

- **Gaming companies**

  Multitudes of user-generated content, including chat rooms and game artefacts, can be moderated using Azure AI Content Safety. It ensures a safe and clean online gaming community by moderating and eliminating unacceptable material.

- **Social messaging platforms**

  With millions of images and text shared by users every day, the need for sophisticated content moderation is essential. Azure AI Content Safety can help regulate content, ensuring users don't post inappropriate or offensive material.

- **Enterprise media companies**

  Large companies that have huge amounts of content also need centralized moderation. With Azure AI Content Safety, it becomes possible to uniformly moderate the content and maintain the established standards.

- **K-12 education solution providers**

  Education solutions, such as online learning or resource platforms, have a responsibility to provide a safe environment for students and educators. Here, Azure AI Content Safety can play a significant role in filtering out material that is not suitable for the K-12 demographic.

In summary, Azure AI Content Safety offers a multipurpose solution that is adaptable to numerous industries requiring content moderation, thereby ensuring a safe, respectful online environment.

Application in Current Technological Landscape

Azure AI Content Safety, with its ability to analyze text and image content, effectively addresses the rising need for content moderation services in the current digital landscape. The **`'Analyze Text API'`** and **`'Analyze Image API'`** scan for harmful content, including sexual content, violence, hate, and self-harm. New features, such as **`'Jailbreak Risk Detection,'`** assess the risk of a jailbreak attack on a Large Language Model. **`'Protected Material Text Detection'`** pre-emptively scans AI-generated text for known content, thereby promoting safe AI interactions across varied interfaces.

To sum up, Azure's efforts towards Responsible AI contribute to a safer and more ethical digital landscape, reinforcing trust in AI solutions and its applications.

Conclusion

The transformation brought about by Generative AI and Large Language Models cannot be overstated. Their diverse benefits and applications, ranging from content creation to decision making, have revolutionized the field of artificial intelligence. Cloud computing platforms like Azure play a pivotal role in harnessing these advancements, making it easier for users to access and utilize them. Azure's integration with OpenAI, its innovative PromptFlow system for creating LLM-based applications, and its multimodal AI services in the form of Azure Speech and Vision, robustly cater to this fast-growing space. Particularly noteworthy is Azure's commitment to responsible and unbiased AI models, reinforcing the importance of ethics and safety in AI. Indeed, as Generative AI and Large Language Models continue to evolve, platforms like Azure will be crucial in shaping a future where AI can benefit humanity in a sustainable and responsible manner.

In the next chapter, we will delve into the concept of Responsible AI, exploring its importance, scope and application. We will understand the principles of designing and deploying ethical AI systems that are fair, trustworthy and accountable. We will also examine how to manage potential risks and pitfalls associated with AI while ensuring that it respects and safeguards human rights. This chapter will not only help understand AI's potential impact on society but also tackles the critical issue of ensuring its responsible use for the benefit of all.

Exercise

- What is the significance of Generative AI and Large Language Models in the contemporary digital context?
- Can you discuss a few potential applications of Generative AI and Large Language Models?
- How does Azure's OpenAI platform contribute to the advancement of Generative AI?
- What role does Azure's Model Catalog play in Generative AI?
- Elaborate on Azure's PromptFlow and its utility in creating Large LLM-based applications.
- What are the advantages of using Azure's PromptFlow in LLM applications?
- How do Azure Speech and Azure Vision impact the development and implementation of AI models?
- Can you provide a detailed implementation of an AI model using Azure Vision?
- Why is it crucial to create Ethical and Unbiased AI Models?
- How does Azure approach Responsible AI and how does this approach contribute to the creation of ethical and unbiased AI models?
- Does Azure's OpenAI platform provide capabilities to develop Generative AI models?
- Does Azure's Model Catalog have a direct relationship with Generative AI?
- Does Azure's PromptFlow facilitate the creation of LLM applications?
- Are Azure Speech and Azure Vision essential components of AI models?
- Does Azure have protocols to ensure AI content safety and ethical AI model development?

Multiple Choice Questions

1. What does Generative AI primarily focus on?
   a. Data analysis
   b. Predictive models
   c. Generating data
   d. Image classification
2. How does Azure utilize OpenAI?
   a. Image processing
   b. Text generation and understanding
   c. Predicting weather
   d. Financial analysis
3. What is the function of Azure's Model Catalog?
   a. Predictive analytics
   b. Classification of images
   c. Storing and deploying AI models
   d. Cyber Security
4. What is the main advantage of Azure's PromptFlow in LLM applications?
   a. Faster processing
   b. Generating human-like text
   c. Image classification
   d. Sound recognition
5. How is Azure's Speech used in AI models?
   a. Recognizing human voice
   b. Translating languages
   c. Text to speech conversion
   d. All of the above
6. What is the role of Azure's Vision in AI models?
   a. Recognition and processing of images
   b. Converting speech to text
   c. Analyzing social media activity
   d. Creating chatbots

7. Why is it important to create ethical and unbiased AI models?
    a. To increase efficiency
    b. To ensure fairness and prevent discrimination
    c. To improve accuracy
    d. To optimize storage space
8. What is Azure's approach to Responsible AI?
    a. Discourage the development of AI
    b. Prioritize fairness, inclusiveness, reliability and privacy
    c. Focus solely on efficiency and accuracy
    d. Encourage the use of AI in all aspects of life
9. What is the purpose of Azure AI Content Safety?
    a. Identify and mitigate harmful content in AI models
    b. Protect against cyber attacks
    c. Provide storage solutions
    d. Analyze social media content
10. What is a potential application of Generative AI and Large Language Models?
    a. Generating human-like responses
    b. Managing database systems
    c. Performing cardiac surgeries
    d. Designing buildings

Answers

1. c
2. b
3. c
4. b
5. d
6. a
7. b
8. b
9. a
10. a

CHAPTER 9
Responsible AI and Ethics

Introduction

In this chapter, *Responsible AI and Ethics*, we will delve deeply into the ethical considerations of Artificial Intelligence (AI) and data science. The chapter begins by introducing the importance of AI ethics and how it serves as the bedrock for responsible AI. We will then discuss the principles and best practices associated with responsible AI and move on to examine the ethical dilemmas that often surface in data science projects, discussing how these dilemmas can impact project outcomes and offering strategies for navigating them ethically.

As we delve further into the chapter, we will focus on the fundamentals of fairness, transparency, and interpretability in machine learning models, along with the need to ensure these models abide by these principles. We will also examine ways to mitigate biases and discrimination in AI models, thereby improving the model's reliability and trustworthiness. Privacy concerns and security risks associated with AI solutions are another key topic of discussion. Finally, we will explore how Azure, one of the leading cloud services providers, supports the development and deployment of responsible AI. This includes its tools and strategies for promoting fairness, transparency in AI, and mitigating bias and discrimination.

Structure

Let's delve into the topics we are going to explore:

- The Crucial Role of AI Ethics
- Understanding Responsible AI
- Responsible AI Principles and Practices
- Ethical Considerations in Data Science Projects
- Fairness, Transparency, and Interpretability of Machine Learning Models

- Mitigating Bias and Discrimination in AI Models
- Privacy and Security Concerns in AI Solutions
- Implementing Responsible AI with Azure

The Crucial Role of AI Ethics

Artificial Intelligence (AI) has permeated all aspects of modern life, becoming an indispensable part of business, healthcare, education, manufacturing, and more. As AI continues to permeate society, ethical considerations have come to the forefront. This section explores the central role that ethics play in AI, delving into why ethical considerations are crucial and outlining the potential consequences of unethical AI practices.

Understanding the Importance of Ethics in Artificial Intelligence

AI, given its potential impacts on human decisions and behavior, draws various ethical considerations. The technology's scope can affect individuals, communities, and society as a whole in unprecedented ways. Hence, ethical considerations are not just optional add-ons but necessary elements in AI's evolution.

Ethics in AI deal with a vast array of concerns, including fairness, accountability, transparency, privacy, safety, and human values. Fairness involves designing AI systems that do not discriminate against specific groups of people. Transparency and interpretability pertain to how these systems arrive at their outcomes, whereas privacy has to do with respecting user data, and safety involves ensuring these systems cause no harm.

AI systems must also stay within the bounds of human values, respecting human autonomy and dignity. Hence, AI ethics involve an amalgamation of perspectives from numerous disciplines, such as philosophy, law, sociology, psychology, and politics.

Consequences of Unethical AI

The consequences of neglecting ethical considerations in AI are substantial and could manifest in various ways. Firstly, if unchecked, AI systems can lead to unfair outcomes or discrimination, reinforcing existing societal biases. These biases in algorithms could predominantly affect marginalized groups, leading to societal harm.

Secondly, the misuse of data raises privacy concerns, with unethical AI practices leading to data theft and misuse causing severe harm to individuals and businesses.

Third and most importantly, the absence of transparency and interpretability can also result in unintended consequences, where humans don't understand what AI systems are doing or how they are doing it. Without clear mechanisms to hold these systems accountable, this could lead to public mistrust and resistance towards AI.

Therefore, a firm foundation in AI ethics is more than just a theoretical ideal – it is a practical necessity to avert significant consequences and ensure public trust in AI advancements.

Understanding Responsible AI

Artificial Intelligence (AI) has become a widely used technology, driving innovation across diverse sectors. It holds immense potential, but with great power comes an even greater responsibility. As AI continues to shape society's future, it becomes imperative to understand and implement Responsible AI. Here, we explore the concept of Responsible AI, its overarching significance, and related principles.

Definition and Overview of Responsible AI

Responsible AI refers to the practice of developing and utilizing AI in a manner that is ethical, transparent, and accountable. It's the idea of using AI systems and tools in a way that respects human rights and values, ensures fairness and non-discrimination, and safeguards autonomy and privacy.

AI drives complex algorithms that are capable of learning and making decisions "*independently*." However, these often rely heavily on the training data used to build them. They may inadvertently reflect and perpetuate biases embedded in this data, leading to discriminatory or unfair outcomes. As such, Responsible AI is rooted in the idea that anyone developing, using, or impacted by AI should be able to understand and inspect these systems' behavior.

Responsible AI emphasizes the significant responsibility of those who deploy AI systems to ensure that these systems function ethically, fairly, and transparently. The ultimate aim is to promote trust among all stakeholders while minimizing any potential negative impacts or misuse.

Importance of Responsible AI

With AI becoming increasingly pervasive in our lives, understanding the significance of Responsible AI becomes all the more important. As AI touches every aspect of our lives - from the way we work, travel, shop, and even socialize - it is important that it is designed, developed, and deployed in an ethically responsible manner.

Firstly, Responsible AI protects individuals and society from harmful biases that can perpetuate inequality and discrimination. Secondly, it instills public trust in AI systems by ensuring transparency and accountability. As we become more reliant on AI-powered devices and services, the trust ensures that we can use these technologies without fear of unfair treatment or privacy intrusion.

Thirdly, it safeguards privacy and data security. AI applications often depend on large swathes of data - sometimes private and sensitive. Responsible AI mandates due protection be given to this data, guarding against unlawful or unethical use.

Lastly, Responsible AI promotes innovation while minimizing risks. The ethical use of AI often sparks creativity, leading to developments that can drive social good and sustainable development. It ensures that systems are robust, secured, and well-maintained, mitigating risks of misuse or malfunction.

In conclusion, Responsible AI sits at the intersection of technology and ethics, requiring continuous dialogue, research, and regulatory effort. As data scientists, it's crucial to incorporate these principles in our work, contributing to shaping a future where AI serves humanity ethically and responsibly.

Responsible AI Principles and Practices

Artificial Intelligence, in its capacity to transform society, has also amplified the need for ethical principles and practices. The focus of these principles is to ensure AI technology respects our rights, values, and sensitivities. These principles drive its application and safeguard against any potential harm or misuse.

Introduction to Responsible AI Principles

Responsible AI Principles are the set of values and guidelines that should guide the development and use of AI technologies. They are widely agreed upon and recognized as the standard requirements for ethical AI. Although these principles may differ depending on the organization or institution, some key principles remain common among them:

- **Fairness**

  AI systems should not favor one group over another and should be free from any bias. They should respect diversity and uphold equality.

- **Privacy**

  AI systems must respect and protect people's privacy and personal data.

- **Transparency**

  There should be clarity about how AI systems make decisions and function. It is important that their workings are explainable and understandable.

- **Accountability**

  Those who design and deploy AI should be held accountable for the impact it has on those it interacts with.

- **Safety and Security**

  AI systems should be reliable, secure, and safe to use. They should be robust against manipulation or malicious use.

- **Human-Centric**

  AI should always augment human abilities and never undermine human agency.

Implementation of Responsible AI Practices

Turning these principles into reality requires proactive effort from everyone involved in the AI lifecycle. Developing responsible practices might include the following steps:

1. **Design**

   During the design phase, considerations for responsible AI should be incorporated into the technology's blueprint.

2. **Training**

   AI systems must be trained on diverse and representative datasets to eliminate biases.

3. **Testing**

   Rigorous auditing and testing for biases, fairness, and transparency must be conducted before the system is launched.

4. **Review**

   Frequently review and update AI systems to ensure they maintain ethical standards over time.

5. **Guidelines**

   Establish internal guidelines and compliance checks to ensure ethical AI systems.

6. **Education**

   Equip developers, users, and decision-makers with knowledge about responsible AI - its principles, benefits, and methods of implementation.

Moreover, data scientists and organizations should strive to collaborate with external regulators and lawmakers to strengthen the implementation of these principles and make AI ethics a legal requirement.

In conclusion, the advancement of AI must align with the principles of Responsible AI. It is our collective responsibility as a society, and particularly as data scientists, to work together to implement these principles and practices, promoting a more ethical use of AI.

Ethical Considerations in Data Science Projects

As a field that fundamentally influences today's digital solutions, data science is at the core of our technological advancements. However, the awesome power of data science comes with the equally critical need for ethical considerations. All data science projects should be pursuing the betterment of individuals and society as a whole.

Importance of Ethics in Data Science

In data science, ethics takes center stage due to a number of reasons. Firstly, data science often deals with personal and sensitive information. Ensuring the privacy and security of this data is a moral obligation. Secondly, misuse or mishandling of data can result in substantial harm or damage, emphasizing the ethical importance. Lastly, the potential of implicit biases in algorithms and datasets puts fairness and transparency at stake, hence, demanding ethical guidelines.

Beyond mitigating harm, ethical considerations in data science can help enhance trust among stakeholders, promote responsible innovation, and contribute to reputation management. It provides a foundation for building and deploying successful, beneficial, and respected AI systems.

Ethical Considerations and Their Practical Applications

When it comes to ethical considerations in data science projects, it's essential to implement practical measures for each phase of the project.

1. **Data Collection**

   Ensure all data collection is legal, consent granted, and privacy maintained. Data anonymization methods can be used to respect the privacy of individuals.

2. **Data Storage and Handling**

   Implement secure data storage and processing methods. Access to the data should be limited to authorized personnel only.

3. **Consenting and Choice**

   Users should be clearly informed about how and why their data will be used and be able to opt out whenever they want.

4. **Bias and Fairness**

   Audit datasets for biases and ensure your algorithms aren't discriminating between user groups. Corrective measures should be applied to neutralize bias.

5. **Transparency and Explainability**

   It should be clearly stated what data is being used and for what purpose. AI models should be interpretable and debuggable.

6. **Accountability**

   Be willing to take responsibility for any outcomes that might result from the use of the data or AI models.

In conclusion, ethical considerations are key to responsible data science and AI. They ensure the well-being of society and can prevent serious harm or adverse consequences. By keeping these considerations at the heart of data science projects, we can leverage data for progress, while respecting human rights, values, and freedom.

Fairness, Transparency, and Interpretability of Machine Learning Models

Machine learning models have the potential to transform various sectors and industries. However, the realization of this potential is contingent on these models aligning with principles of fairness, transparency, and interpretability.

Defining Fairness, Transparency, and Interpretability

Fairness in machine learning implies that the algorithms make unbiased decisions and do not discriminate against any particular group. The essence is to ensure equivalent outcomes for individuals who are equivalent in relevant respects.

Transparency reflects the openness about the workings of the AI system. It refers to a clear understanding of how the machine learning models operate, the steps they execute, and the decisions they make.

Interpretability describes the extent to which a machine learning model's behavior can be comprehended and predicted. It is about being able to explain how the model went from its raw input data to its final decision.

Importance of These Principles in Machine Learning

These three principles are crucial in addressing various ethical concerns in AI and achieving Responsible AI:

Fairness is essential to prevent any discriminatory behavior that the algorithm might inadvertently learn from its training data. It assures that the decisions made will be unbiased and equitable, having a positive societal impact.

Transparency is equally important in establishing trust among consumers. As we involve AI more in our lives and businesses, transparency assures that we understand these technologies, their capabilities, and limitations.

Interpretability is vital for accountability. It allows us to understand and explain why and how the model made a particular decision, enabling us to better analyze, debug, and improve the model.

Practices to Enhance These Principles in ML Models

Ensuring fairness, transparency, and interpretability within machine learning models involves diligent practice and strategy.

To promote fairness, it is important to examine training data for biases and balance it accordingly. We must carefully choose performance metrics that adequately represent all classes in the data. Regular audits for fairness should also be conducted.

Interpretability can be improved by using simpler models where possible, as they tend to be more interpretable. Techniques like **LIME** (Local Interpretable Model-agnostic Explanations) and **SHAP** (SHapley Additive exPlanations) provide explanations for individual predictions made by complex models, enhancing interpretability.

In conclusion, the principles of fairness, transparency, and interpretability are paramount for the ethical application of machine learning. By incorporating these principles, we can ensure that our AI systems are robust, ethical, and truly beneficial for society.

Mitigating Bias and Discrimination in AI Models

As AI continues to permeate our lives on personal, social, and professional levels, the need to ensure these systems are unbiased and non-discriminatory is increasingly vital. This necessitates a comprehensive understanding of bias and discrimination in AI and strategies to mitigate them.

Understanding Bias and Discrimination in AI

Bias in AI usually stems from the training data used to develop models. If the data includes discriminatory inclinations or is not representative of all groups, the model is likely to make unfair or biased predictions or decisions. Discrimination in AI can be direct or indirect, causing harm or disadvantage to certain individuals or groups based on their characteristics, such as race, gender, age, and more.

Such biases and discrimination can lead to unfair outcomes, breach of trust, harm to individuals, or legal implications for businesses. Therefore, understanding and addressing these issues is of paramount importance.

Techniques for Mitigating Bias and Discrimination

Several techniques can be employed to mitigate bias and discrimination in AI.

The first step is to ensure your data is representative of the diverse population you serve. Conducting a thorough data audit to identify and rectify biases in data is crucial.

Next, ensure diversity among AI developers to minimize inherent bias that may be unintentionally introduced during model development.

Algorithmic fairness techniques can also be employed to correct bias in AI models. These techniques can help ensure that similar individuals are treated similarly by the AI system.

Explainable AI techniques can increase transparency and allow for easier identification and correction of bias. Regular audits of AI models can also ensure that any biases that do emerge are promptly identified and corrected.

Case Studies: Impact of Mitigation Strategies

There are numerous instances where bias mitigation strategies have led to a more equitable AI ecosystem.

For instance, a major tech company found gender bias in the AI algorithm used for screening resumes. The algorithm was favoring male candidates as it was trained on a dataset primarily composed of male resumes. Once identified, the company retained its model on a more gender-balanced dataset, leading to fairer candidate screenings.

In another case, a healthcare AI system used to predict healthcare needs was found to be racially biased. The model was giving White people preferential treatment over sicker Black patients. The error was identified, and the model recalibrated to consider other factors beyond those that had introduced the initial racial bias, showing how ongoing monitoring and testing can lead to more equitable AI systems.

In conclusion, bias and discrimination in AI are multifaceted issues that require ongoing attention and refinement. Constant vigilance, corrective measures, and a commitment to diversity and fairness are quintessential for upholding the principles of Responsible AI.

Privacy and Security Concerns in AI Solutions

Given the amount of user data AI solutions consume and generate, privacy and security have emerged as top priorities. Protecting user data is not merely a legal obligation, but essential for building trust and providing users with control over their information.

Importance of Privacy and Security in AI

Privacy and security form the backbone of ethical AI solutions. When users interact with an AI solution, they often share personal or sensitive data. Ensuring privacy means keeping this data confidential and giving users choice and control over their information, which instills trust.

On the other hand, security in AI ensures that this data, along with the AI systems themselves, are protected against breaches, misuse, or cyberattacks. As AI systems are becoming increasingly complex, so are the potential threats, making security a crucial aspect.

Impact of Security Breaches on AI Solutions

Security breaches can have severe implications for AI solutions. Unauthorized access to AI systems and data could potentially allow for the exploitation of user data, subversion of the AI's behavior, or even malicious use of the AI system.

A breach not only exposes user data but can also have significant reputational damage, leading to a loss of trust among users and stakeholders. Furthermore, it can result in immense financial costs due to penalties, lawsuits, and loss of business.

Strategies to Ensure Privacy and Security in AI Solutions

Several strategies can be employed to ensure privacy and security in AI solutions.

Data minimization, which is collecting only the necessary data, and anonymization techniques can help protect user privacy. It's also important to provide clear user consent mechanisms and transparent data policies.

For security, it's crucial to implement strong encryption for data storage and transmission. Regular vulnerability assessments can help identify and remedy any potential weaknesses in the system.

Incorporating '*Privacy by Design*' and '*Security by Design*' principles can ensure that these aspects are not an afterthought but are embedded from the very beginning in the development process.

Effective identity and access management policies can prevent unauthorized access. Moreover, having incident response plans in place can help manage any breaches quickly and efficiently.

In conclusion, privacy and security are paramount in any AI solution. It's not enough to build AI systems that are powerful and effective – they must also be trustworthy and safe, ensuring that users can interact confidently without fear of privacy invasion or potential harm.

Implementing Responsible AI with Azure

AI and machine learning have the potential to revolutionize nearly every aspect of our lives. However, like any transformative technology, they must be used responsibly. Microsoft has always been a frontrunner in bringing ethics to the technology world, and Azure, Microsoft's cloud platform, is a key player in implementing Responsible AI.

Overview of Azure's Role in Responsible AI

Azure provides a wide range of tools and capabilities that data scientists can leverage to implement Responsible AI practices. Azure's commitment to Responsible AI is built on Microsoft's principles of fairness, reliability and safety, privacy and security, inclusiveness, transparency, and accountability.

Azure's AI services are designed to assist businesses in developing responsible AI solutions by providing features aimed at achieving machine learning interpretability, transparency, fairness, privacy, and security. Moreover, the Azure platform is designed to be user-friendly and draughts guidelines for designing and implementing AI systems ethically and responsibly.

Azure also offers an array of compliance offerings designed to help organizations comply with national, regional, and industry-specific requirements governing the collection and use of data.

Using Azure Machine Learning for Ethical AI Practices

Azure Machine Learning service empowers data scientists to design, deploy, and manage machine learning models responsibly. It incorporates numerous features and tools to support Responsible AI:

- **InterpretML**: This open-source package offers interpretability of machine learning models. It provides insights into your model's behavior, unlocking its black-box nature.
- **Fairlearn**: This tool helps assess and improve the fairness of your machine learning models, thus avoiding harmful discrimination.
- **Differentially Private Data Analysis**: Azure machine learning allows you to apply differentially private noise to your data during analysis, providing a balance between data utility and privacy.
- **Security**: Azure Machine Learning makes data protection its utmost priority, allowing you to encrypt data at rest and while in transit. Azure's robust identity and access management features also provide control over who can access your data and machine learning models.
- **Azure AI Content Safety:** Azure AI Content Safety serves as a valuable tool to identify and filter out insidious content generated by users or AI in diverse applications and services. This critical functionality encapsulates text and image APIs, which help pinpoint potentially detrimental materials. Furthermore, Azure AI Content Safety includes an engaging Content Safety Studio, where one can peruse, dissect, and experiment with sample codes aiming to detect harmful content across various modalities.

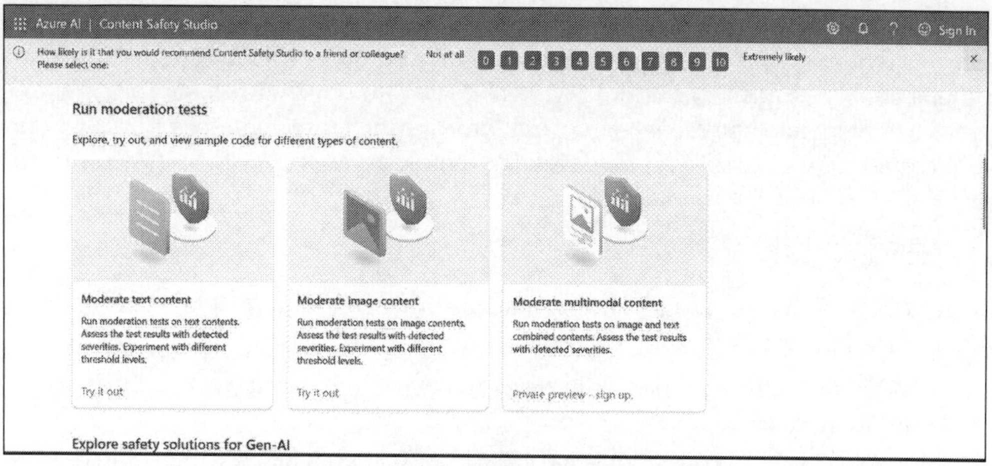

Figure 9.1: *Azure AI Content Safety Studio*

Moreover, Azure provides robust documentation with best practices. It also offers education on Responsible AI principles and ethical implications of AI, encouraging data scientists to think critically about the AI systems they are building.

By utilizing these features, data scientists can ensure the AI systems they develop and deploy adhere to established principles of Responsible AI. This enhances user trust and promotes the development of AI systems that are beneficial and fair to all.

Conclusion

Throughout this chapter, we explored the critical realm of Responsible AI and Ethics, understanding its implications in the world permeated by AI and machine learning. We delved into several aspects, including the principles of Responsible AI, the importance of ethics in data science, and factors such as fairness, transparency, and interpretability in AI models. Moreover, we probed into mitigating biases and discrimination in AI systems, addressing privacy and security concerns.

As the power of AI continues to amplify, understanding these principles and committing to ethical and responsible AI is more important than ever for data scientists. We are entrusted with more than just data; we are entrusted with people's lives and society's well-being. Ethics and responsibility in AI ensure that as we continue to push the boundaries of what AI can achieve, we also respect and uphold human values, rights, fairness, and trust. By incorporating these principles, we can ensure that AI serves all of humanity, fostering a future where AI and humans progress hand in hand.

In the upcoming chapter, we will be delving deep into the world of big data analytics with Azure. The focus will be on understanding the immense potentiality and utility of Microsoft's cloud computing platform - Azure - for managing and analyzing large datasets. We will be exploring various Azure tools and services that allow businesses to make insightful and data-driven decisions.

The next chapter promises to demonstrate how big data analytics with Azure can transform the way your organization functions by creating opportunities for innovation and reshaping business operations. We will delve into how Azure's Big Data Analytics services help in managing, analyzing, and interpreting large volumes of data to gain a competitive edge in today's rapidly evolving tech ecosystem.

Questions

- How can bias in AI algorithms inadvertently perpetuate social and economic discrimination? Provide examples.
- What measures can be put in place to ensure the privacy and security of data in AI operations?
- Discuss the potential pitfalls of neglecting ethical considerations in data science projects.
- How is the balance between model simplicity and interpretability important in the development of machine learning algorithms?
- How can regular auditing and testing aid in achieving fairness in AI and machine learning models?
- Is it important to include a diverse group of individuals in the development of AI systems?
- Can AI systems inherently hold bias?
- Is it possible for an AI system to be 100% transparent in its decision-making process?
- Would differentially private data analysis techniques always protect user data?
- Is '*Privacy by Design*' a necessary feature in AI development?

Multiple Choice Questions

1. What is Responsible AI?
    a. Using AI for useful purposes
    b. Implementing AI without glitches
    c. Developing and utilizing AI ethically, transparently, and with accountability
    d. Making AI tasks easier
2. Why is bias in AI a problem?
    a. Increases processing time
    b. Disrupts data flow

   c. Can result in unfair outcomes
   d. Enhances model efficiency
3. How can you ensure fairness in AI solutions?
   a. Use large datasets
   b. Use the latest algorithms
   c. Audit datasets for biases and balance them accordingly
   d. Increase execution speed
4. Which one of these is NOT related to interpretability in AI?
   a. The ability to understand how machine learning models operate
   b. Black-box nature of algorithms
   c. The color scheme used in the AI module
   d. Being able to predict a model's behavior
5. Which of the following cases reflect the impact of a security breach in an AI solution?
   a. Faster processing speed in the AI model
   b. Loss of trust among users and stakeholders
   c. Enhanced accuracy of AI predictions
   d. Increase in the number of AI users
6. Which tool within the Azure Machine Learning service is used to enhance the fairness of your models?
   a. PowerBI
   b. Fairlearn
   c. Databricks
   d. SQL Server
7. Which AI principle ensures that AI systems respect privacy and protect personal data?
   a. Accountability
   b. Safety and security
   c. Privacy
   d. Human-centric

8. What is a key technique for mitigating bias and discrimination in AI?
    a. Using bigger datasets
    b. Training with more neural networks
    c. Employing a diverse team of developers
    d. Utilizing more powerful hardware
9. Which responsible AI principle values amplifying human abilities while not undermining human agency?
    a. Accountability
    b. Safety and security
    c. Human-centric
    d. Privacy
10. In terms of Responsible AI, what principle does interpretation relate to the most?
    a. Accountability
    b. Transparency
    c. Privacy
    d. Fairness
11. Which Azure tool offers machine learning interpretability?
    a. Fairlearn
    b. Differentially private data analysis
    c. Identity and access management
    d. InterpretML
12. What type of bias did a major tech company find in the AI algorithm used for screening resumes?
    a. Ethnicity bias
    b. Age bias
    c. Gender bias
    d. Education bias
13. What is the first step in ensuring fairness in AI models?
    a. Ensuring data is representative of the diverse population
    b. Implementing strong encryption for data storage and transmission

c. Maintenance of thorough documentation about the model's development process

d. Applying differentially private noise to your data during analysis

14. Which tool is NOT used for enhancing interpretability in ML models?

    a. Differentially private data analysis

    b. LIME

    c. SHAP

    d. InterpretML

15. Which Azure feature is least related to ethical considerations in AI practice?

    a. Fairlearn

    b. InterpretML

    c. Azure Kubernetes Services

    d. Differentially private data analysis

Answers

1. c
2. c
3. c
4. c
5. b
6. b
7. c
8. c
9. c
10. b
11. d
12. c
13. a
14. a
15. c

CHAPTER 10
Big Data Analytics with Azure

Introduction

In this chapter, we will delve into the intricate world of big data and its analytical methods, with a keen focus on the capabilities of Azure. We begin with an introduction to the overarching concepts of big data analytics and its processing, familiarizing you with the foundational knowledge you need to navigate this space.

Following on, we will explore the Azure Databricks—an essential tool for scalable data processing. You will learn its core features and benefits and understand how to deploy and use it effectively. The discussion will then expand to the implementation of Apache Spark jobs on Azure, providing you a detailed guide on their execution.

But our exploration doesn't stop there. The chapter will also shed light on Azure HDInsight—a potent tool in the arsenal for big data solutions. Subsequently, we transition into real-time data processing using Azure Stream Analytics, arming you with the skill to tap into real-time insights from your data.

Wrapping up the chapter, we will discuss several real-world applications and case studies, helping you to draw from their best practices and successful strategies. Overall, this chapter aims to demystify Azure's role in big data analytics and processing and show you how to harness its full potential in real-world scenarios.

Structure

We will cover the following topics in this chapter:

- Introduction to Big Data Analytics and Processing
- Using Azure Databricks for Scalable Data Processing
- Implementing Apache Spark Jobs on Azure
- Leveraging Azure HDInsight for Big Data Solutions
- Real-Time Data Processing with Azure Stream Analytics
- Real-world Applications of Big Data Analytics Using Azure

Introduction to Big Data Analytics and Processing

In today's rapidly modernizing world where business and technology intersect with incredible dynamism, data stands as an unshakable pillar underpinning the crux of strategic decision-making processes. Partaking in the journey of exploration encompassed in this chapter will lead us down an enlightening path, helping us traverse the comprehensive panorama of big data analytics and processing. As we begin our expedition, we will bespeak the vital connection between data and innovation, illuminating how data, when interpreted and utilized efficiently, wields the power to drive forward the gears of progress.

Defining Big Data: Understanding its Scope and Importance

Azure provides various services such as analytics, computing, databases, mobile services, networking, and storage. One of the key features of Azure is its ability to handle big data - '*big data*' not just being a trendy tech term, but a revolution that is significantly altering the way we understand the business world. This perfectly aligns with Azure's offering of a clear, convenient, and cost-effective cloud-based environment for handling big data analysis.

Big data in Azure can encompass vast volumes of data sets within its infrastructure. These data sets could be of such prodigious size that it is beyond the ability of typical database software tools to capture, store, manage, and analyze. Azure gives big data the ability to be managed and processed flexibly and with speed. Leveraging Azure's scalable resources, it breaks up big data problems into smaller, more manageable parts that can be processed in parallel, thus doing its part to handle the **'Volume'** aspect of the 3Vs of Big Data.

Velocity, the second V in the 3Vs of Big Data, refers to the speed at which data accumulates. The rapid generation of data poses its own set of challenges, particularly in terms of storage and processing. Azure Big Data solutions come into play here offering real-time data processing capabilities using services like Azure Stream Analytics. Azure provides quick resource allocation which allows this massive influx of data to be processed and analyzed swiftly, accommodating the rapid accumulation of data and fulfilling the velocity element.

Variety, the third V, indicates the different types of data that can come in. The data handled by organizations come in various formats - structured, semi-structured, and unstructured. Azure caters to this variety by providing a broad list of services that can process and analyze data of any kind, be it from videos, social media posts, customer transaction data, machine logs or anything else.

The importance of big data analyzed through Azure is immense. It holds the potential to recognize observable patterns, identifiable trends, and associated relationships. Whether it's the health sector or consumer-oriented marketing, big data insights prove crucial to these industries. It's under this umbrella that Azure's formidable analytics capabilities have the power to deliver actionable and high-value insights for businesses. The reach and influence of big data is vast, and Azure is a strong apparatus standing at the helm, ready to decipher these mammoth data sets into relevant, valuable information for businesses.

Overview of Big Data Analytics: Techniques and Tools

When it comes to Big Data analytics, a multitude of tools are currently being employed to get the job done. Here is a list of such tools, including Azure-specific ones:

- **Azure HDInsight**

  This is an Azure product that deploys and provisions Apache Hadoop clusters in the cloud, providing a software framework designed for processing and analyzing large datasets across many computers.

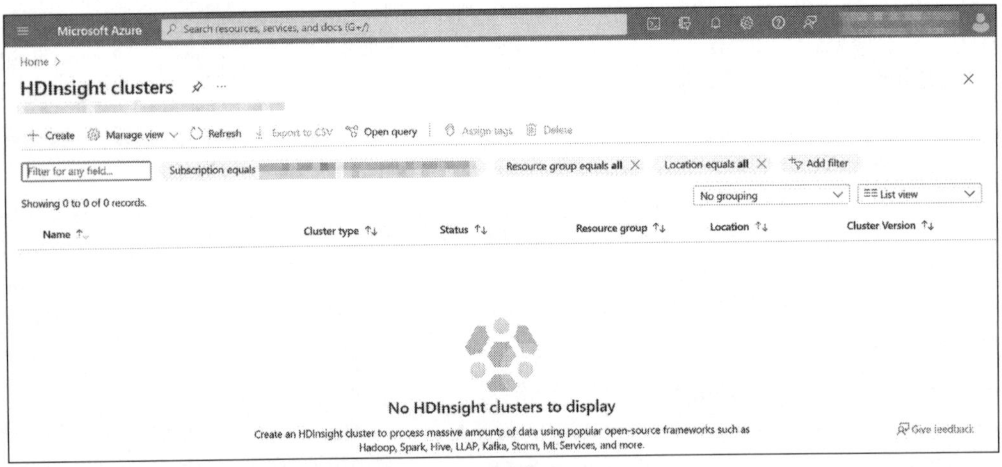

Figure 10.1: *Azure HDInsight dashboard*

- **Azure Data Lake Analytics**

  This is an on-demand analytics job service that simplifies big data. Instead of deploying, configuring, and tuning hardware, you write queries to transform your data and extract valuable insights using U-SQL, R, Python, and .NET.

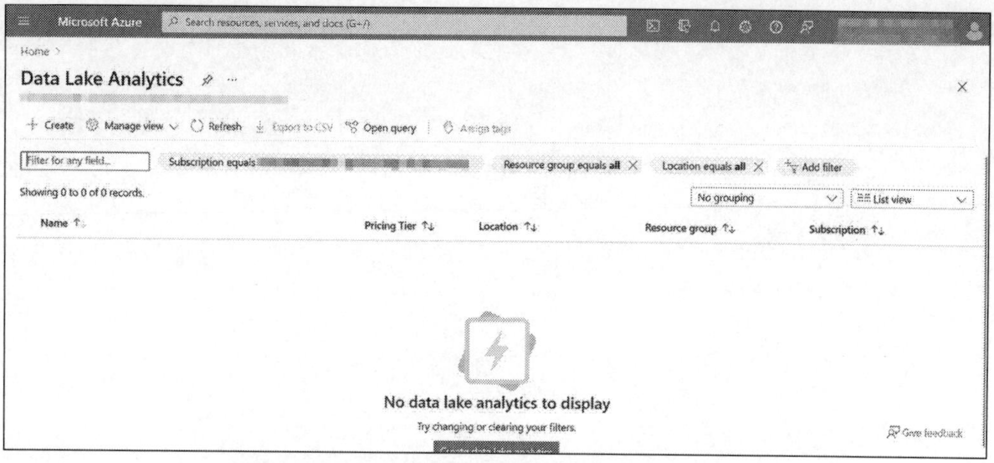

Figure 10.2: *Azure Data Analytics dashboard*

- **Azure Synapse Analytics (formerly SQL Data Warehouse)**

  This is Microsoft's enterprise analytics service that allows businesses to analyze massive amounts of data using on-demand or provisioned resources.

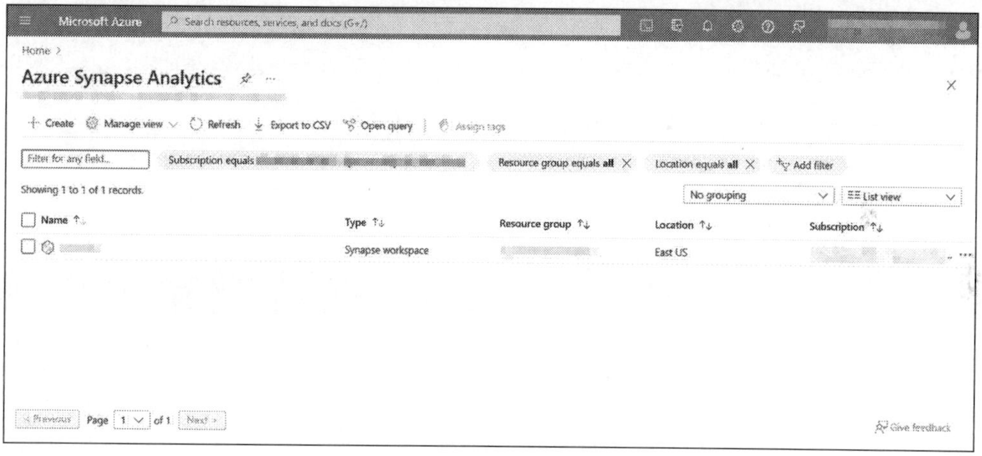

Figure 10.3: *Azure Synapse dashboard*

- **Azure Machine Learning**

  This tool provides cloud-based machine learning algorithms, enabling predictive analytics and anomaly detection.

- **Azure Stream Analytics**

  A real-time analytics and complex event-processing engine that is designed to analyze and visualize streaming data in real time.

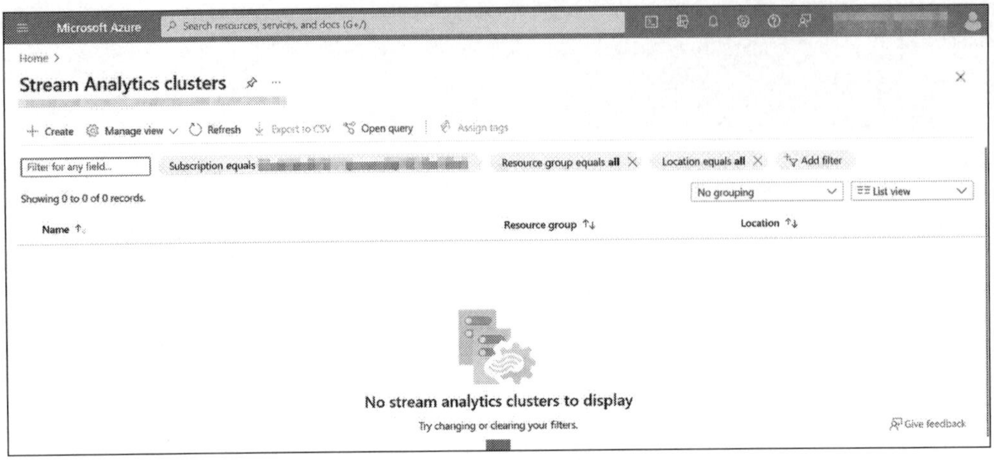

Figure 10.4: *Azure Stream Analytics dashboard*

- **Spark on Azure Databricks**

  A fast, easy, and collaborative Apache Spark based analytics platform that significantly simplifies the process of building big data analytics and AI solutions.

Figure 10.5: *Azure Databricks dashboard*

- **Hadoop**

  An open-source software framework capable of storing vast amounts of data and running applications on clusters of commodity hardware.

- **MongoDB**

  A NoSQL database, helps businesses transform their industries by harnessing the power of data. It is used for storing unstructured data that can be changed in real time.

- **Tableau**

  A business intelligence and data visualization tool that helps you generate visual insights of your data. It can connect with Azure data sources for real-time analytics.

- **Apache Flink**

  This tool is used for processing unbounded and bounded data sets and deploying large-scale data-driven applications. It can be used with Azure to analyze data in near real-time.

Each tool comes with its unique features that help with various aspects of big data analytics, from data storage and processing to visualization and machine learning. Depending on the organization's needs and the nature of the data, these tools are employed to derive actionable insights from the massive amounts of data. The choice between these tools would depend on factors such as the size of the data, the speed at which analysis needs to be done, the complexity of analytics, and the specific requirements of a given project.

Big Data Processing: Steps and Challenges

Big data processing encompasses various stages, each with its distinct utility and pertinence.

- **Data Ingestion**: The initial step involves bringing in the data from various sources. It can be in the form of live data feeds (streaming) or batch processing of accumulated data.
- **Data Storage**: Once the data is ingested, it needs to be stored somewhere. Depending upon the size and structure of the data, it could be stored in databases (SQL or NoSQL), data warehouses, or in data lakes.
- **Data Processing**: After it's stored, data has to be processed. Data processing could be batch processing, stream processing, or real-time processing. Technologies like Hadoop utilize batch processing while tools like Apache Flink and Azure Stream Analytics are used for real-time processing.
- **Data Cleaning**: It refers to preparing the data for analysis by handling missing values, removing outliers, and handling errors. This step is vital to improve the accuracy of further analysis.
- **Data Transformation**: Data from multiple sources often come in numerous formats. These disparate data sets need to be transformed and consolidated into a unified format for easier analysis.
- **Data Analysis**: This is the stage where statistical models and algorithms are run on the data to uncover patterns and insights. These models could range from predictive analytics to machine learning algorithms.

- **Data Visualization**: Lastly, these findings need to be communicated in an easily understandable way, and visualization tools like Tableau help in presenting the data in the form of charts and graphs.

However, big data processing does present a set of challenges, including:

- **Privacy and Security**: As data volumes increase, so do concerns around data privacy and security.
- **Integration and Validation**: Dealing with different data types and handling their successful integration can be challenging.
- **Infrastructure and Storage**: The infrastructural demands for Big Data processing can be immense, making storage a significant challenge.
- **Skills Gap**: There exists a dearth of data scientists and professionals skilled in big data technologies.

Despite these challenges, they can be managed through effective strategies such as keeping up-to-date with regulatory policies, using effective data management software and platforms, investing in scalable storage solutions, and building a team with the appropriate skills. Leveraging the offerings of cloud computing platforms like Azure, businesses can overcome many of these challenges while fully realizing the potential of big data.

Using Azure Databricks for Scalable Data Processing

As we progress further in our exploration of big data analytics, the significance of tools tailor-made for handling vast data repositories comes to the fore. Azure Databricks is one such powerful tool that stands out in the crowd. In this segment, we shall delve into Azure Databricks and its use for scalable data processing.

Introduction to Azure Databricks: Benefits and Features

Azure Databricks is an Apache Spark-based analytics platform optimized for the Microsoft Azure cloud services platform, providing a seamless and simplified platform for big data analytics and machine learning. Designed in collaboration with the founders of Apache Spark, Azure Databricks brings together the best of the Apache Spark framework and Azure's cloud capabilities.

Key Features of Azure Databricks:

- **Fast, Easy, and Collaborative Apache Spark-based Analytics**: Azure Databricks provides a fast, easy, and collaborative environment for data scientists, data engineers, and business analysts.

- **Interactive Workspace:** It provides an interactive workspace where you can create visualizations, use machine learning libraries, and write, run, and debug code.
- **Native Azure Integration**: Being integrated with Azure can make it easy to set up and manage connections to other Azure services, including Power BI, SQL Data Warehouse, and Cosmos DB.
- **Support For Multiple Languages**: It allows multiple programming languages, including Scala, Python, SQL, and R, thus catering to diverse developer requirements.
- **Automated Machine Learning**: Azure Databricks provides automated machine learning capabilities for streamlined and efficient model training and evaluation.

Benefits of Azure Databricks:

- **Performance**: Azure Databricks runs up to 50x faster than standard Apache Spark by leveraging state-of-the-art techniques and cutting-edge engineering solutions.
- **Productivity**: It can increase productivity with an interactive workspace and collaborative features for both data engineers and data scientists, with support for SQL queries, streaming, and machine learning.
- **Seamless Integration**: Azure Databricks offers out-of-the-box integration with various Azure services providing a streamlined workflow and better security.
- **Scalability and Flexibility**: It provides a serverless, cloud-based environment that scales with the needs of your business. You can set up a new Spark environment within minutes, and data engineers and data scientists can work on the same projects with their preferred languages.
- **Security**: Azure Databricks provides enterprise-level security with features like Azure Active Directory integration, role-based controls, and compliance standards.
- **Cost-effective**: Azure Databricks offers a cost-effective solution with the flexibility to choose between on-demand pricing or reserved instances. Being able to scale up and down on demand helps optimize costs while encountering varying loads.
- **Unified Analytics**: With Azure Databricks, organizations can perform streaming, machine learning, and graph processing all within a single solution, without having to worry about infrastructure management. This leads to faster-time-to-market and more efficient operations.

Through these features and benefits, Azure Databricks has carved a niche for itself in big data processing and analytics and continues to be a trusted platform for data professionals worldwide.

Setting Up Azure Databricks: A Step-by-Step Guide

Deploying Azure Databricks involves a sequence of steps to ensure it is correctly implemented. Here are the step-by-step instructions:

1. **Microsoft Azure Account**: The first requirement is to have a Microsoft Azure account and a subscription plan. If you do not have one, you can create an account and choose a suitable subscription.
2. **Create a Databricks Workspace**: In the Azure portal, go to the left-hand menu and click **`'Create a Resource.'`** In the **`'New'`** window that appears, search for **`'Databricks.'`** Select **`'Azure Databricks'`** and click the **`'Create'`** button.

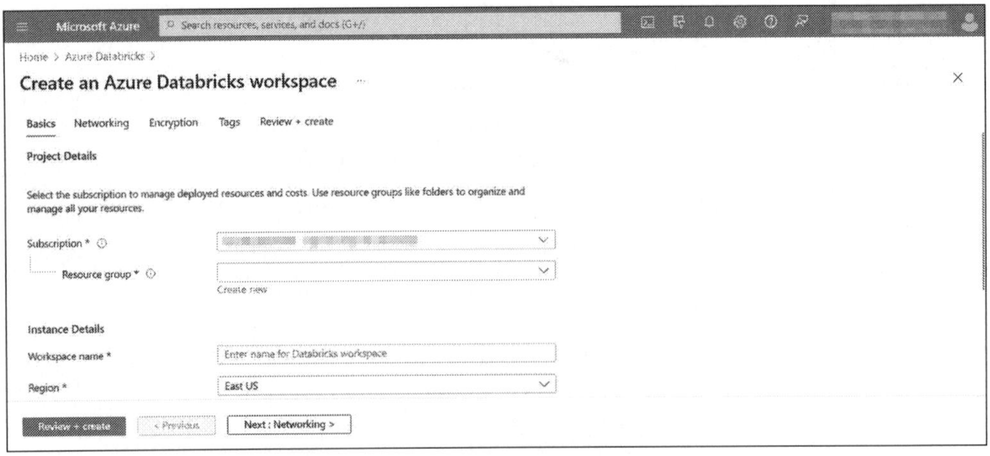

***Figure 10.6**: Creating Azure Databricks workspace*

3. **Configure the Workspace**: A **`'New Databricks workspace'`** page will open. You will need to fill in the required details like **`Subscription`**, **`Resource Group`**, **`Workspace name`**, **`Location`**, **`Pricing Tier`**, and so on.
4. **Review and Create**: After verifying all the details filled in the previous step, click **`'Review + Create'`** and then **`'Create'`** to initiate the deployment. The deployment could take several minutes.
5. **Launch Workspace**: Once the deployment is complete, navigate to the resource group where you created your Databricks workspace, and click the **`'Launch Workspace'`** button. This will open the **`Databricks workspace`** in a new tab.

6. **Create a Databricks Cluster**: Now that your workspace is set up, you can create a Databricks cluster. Go to the `'Clusters'` tab and click `'Create Cluster'`. Additionally, you can choose your specific configurations for the cluster (`number of workers`, `Databricks runtime version`, and more.)
7. **Use Databricks Notebook**: After the cluster is ready, you can use Databricks notebook functionality to write and execute your Apache Spark code. Click `'New Notebook'`, give it a name, select the language of your choice and attach it to the cluster you created.
8. **Collaborate and Execute Code**: Now, the setup is complete, and you can start writing and running code. Azure Databricks has a collaborative, interactive workspace, allowing multiple users to work together in real-time.

Always remember to terminate clusters when they are not being used, as Azure Databricks bills by the minute for the active usage of clusters. Also, regularly monitor and analyze your Databricks units (DBUs) consumption, ensuring you are optimally using Azure Databricks.

Finally, effective security practices for Azure Databricks include integrating it with Azure Active Directory and setting up role-based access controls to ensure that only authorized users can access and perform operations in your Databricks workspace. Also, periodically review who has access to what data and functionalities to ensure compliance and least privilege access.

Using Azure Databricks for Data Processing: Best Practices

Using Azure Databricks for data processing can yield significant efficiency and performance benefits when executed with best practices in mind:

- **Use Right-Sized Clusters**: Make sure you use the right number and size of nodes for each cluster. Azure Databricks can scale up and down but having the right configuration can ensure you are not overpaying for resources.
- **Turn Off Idle Clusters**: Azure Databricks allows the turning off of clusters when not in use. Set up auto termination settings for your clusters to reduce costs.
- **Optimize Data Formats**: It is recommended to use efficient data formats such as Parquet and Avro. These data formats can significantly speed up data processing tasks.
- **Partition Large Datasets**: When working with large datasets, utilize partitioning strategies. This can significantly boost the performance of data processes by reducing the volume of data that needs to be read.

- **Leverage Cluster Pinning**: For critical notebook workflows that require swift interactive responses, leverage cluster pinning. Pinning a notebook to a cluster can help bypass latencies that occur due to re-attaching notebooks or cluster idling.
- **Utilize Transformations**: Use transformations such as Filter and Select as early as possible in your pipeline to minimize the amount of data being processed in later stages.
- **Leverage Delta Lake**: Delta Lake is a storage layer that brings ACID transactions to Apache Spark and big data workloads. It enhances data reliability and simplifies the architecture.
- **Monitor Performance**: Use Azure Databricks built-in monitoring tools to keep a tab on the performance of your analytics jobs.
- **Security**: Implement role-based access control (RBAC) to ensure that only authorized users can access and perform operations.
- **Data Cleaning**: Ensure all data preprocessing, like eliminating duplicates, handling missing values and outliers, is conducted effectively within Databricks notebooks before further processing and analysis.

Implementing these best practices while using Azure Databricks can significantly enhance your data processing tasks and provide fast, efficient and cost-effective results, unlocking the full potential of this powerful toolkit.

Implementing Apache Spark Jobs on Azure

Apache Spark is a powerful, open-source processing engine built around speed, ease of use, and complex analytics. When combined with the might of Azure, it allows businesses to truly harness the power of their data through multi-fold data processing and analytical tasks. This section dives into the implementation of Apache Spark on the Azure platform.

Understanding Apache Spark: Its Role in Big Data Processing

Apache Spark is an open-source, distributed computing system renowned for its high-speed processing, ease of use, and sophisticated analytics. Basically, Apache Spark is designed for fast computation, making it ideal for processing a massive volume of data, thereby meeting the challenges presented by big data.

The features of Apache Spark are as follows:

- **Speed**: Apache Spark is fast. It can process large volumes of data at an amazing speed, processing tasks up to 100 times faster in memory and 10 times faster on disk than Hadoop.
- **Ease of Use:** Spark provides simple APIs for Python, Java, Scala, and R, and also supports SQL queries. It also provides a command line interface and a user-friendly web-based user interface.
- **Flexibility**: Apache Spark is compatible with various data sources, such as Hadoop Distributed File System (HDFS), Apache Cassandra, Apache HBase, and Amazon S3.
- **Powerful Analytics**: Spark not only supports `'Map'` and `'Reduce'`, but also supports SQL queries, streaming data, machine learning, and graph algorithms, among others.
- **Fault Tolerance**: Apache Spark is known for its fault-tolerant capability, thanks to the use of the RDD (Resilient Distributed Dataset) data structure.

Role of Apache Spark in Big Data Processing

Apache Spark plays a pivotal role in big data processing for its speed, ease of use, and comprehensive analytics. It is designed to handle batch processing, real-time data processing, data streaming, machine learning, and interactive queries in one system.

- **Data Processing**: Apache Spark allows for the processing of large datasets across a distributed network quickly and easily.
- **Real-time analytics**: Spark's lightning-fast analytics can process live data streams in real-time, making it perfect for creating real-time analytical dashboards or detecting anomalies instantly.
- **Machine Learning:** Spark's MLlib toolkit makes it possible to perform machine learning on large datasets. It includes several popular machine learning and statistical algorithms, making it a solid choice for data scientists.

By getting a firm understanding of Apache Spark, you can effectively employ it in your big data solutions, leveraging its speed and efficiency for data-processing tasks of all kinds, and thus unlocking its full potential.

Apache Spark and Azure: A Powerful Duo

Azure Databricks, as a powerful cloud-based big data processing solution, seamlessly integrates Apache Spark, a lightning-fast unified analytics engine for big data and machine learning. This integration unlocks a suite of benefits, making Azure Databricks and Apache Spark a truly powerful duo in handling and processing large swaths of data.

Here's how Azure and Apache Spark come together:

- **Enhanced Performance**: Apache Spark's in-memory processing capabilities, combined with Azure's optimized cloud infrastructure, yields enhanced speed and performance. Azure Databricks helps achieve up to 50x improved performance over on-premises Spark due to various enhancements.
- **Scalability**: The Spark on Azure Databricks architecture allows users to scale up and down according to their computational needs. This elasticity ensures optimal resource utilization and cost savings.
- **Ease of Use:** Azure Databricks offers a fully managed Spark service with one-click setup, streamlined workflows, and an interactive workspace for collaboration among data scientists, data engineers, and business analysts.
- **Integrated Workspace**: Azure Databricks includes a collaborative notebook environment that enables data scientists and engineers to work together efficiently. You can write in Python, Scala, SQL, and R, all languages supported by Apache Spark.
- **Real-time Analytics:** Azure Databricks integrates well with Spark Streaming to handle real-time data processing tasks. It helps transform and analyze live data streams and integrate them with machine learning models.
- **Security**: Azure Databricks provides robust security, including enterprise-grade Azure security, Azure Active Directory integration, and role-based access control to notebooks, clusters, jobs, and more. All the data processed using Apache Spark on Azure Databricks is secured through Azure's network encryption and access control features.
- **Integrations**: Azure Databricks easily connects with several Azure services, such as Azure Synapse Analytics, Power BI, Azure Machine Learning, Cosmos DB, Event Hubs, and more. This wide range of integrations provides users with a comprehensive data platform that can serve many different needs and applications.
- **Batch and Stream Processing**: Apache Spark on Azure Databricks can process both batch data and real-time data streams, providing flexibility depending on the use-case requirements.

By integrating Apache Spark with Azure, businesses can leverage the best of both worlds and build a robust and scalable big data pipeline that is perfect for their needs. With the ability to scale up processing power when needed and pare it back when it's not, the Spark and Azure combo is a cost-effective and powerful solution for big data processing.

Running Apache Spark Jobs on Azure: A Comprehensive Guide

Running Apache Spark jobs on Azure typically involves Azure Databricks, a cloud-based platform powered by Apache Spark. Here's a detailed guide:

1. **Create an Azure Databricks Workspace**: As mentioned earlier, create your workspace. In the Azure Portal, click `'Create a resource'`, search for `'Azure Databricks'`, and fill in the necessary details on the create blade.
2. **Create a Cluster**: Within the Databricks workspace, navigate to the `'Clusters'` section and create a new cluster. Select the runtime version, type of virtual machines, and enter the number of workers you need.
3. **Create a Notebook**: In the `Workspace` section, create a new Notebook. You can choose among several languages including Python, Scala, SQL, or R for your Spark job. Provide your notebook with a name and link it to the cluster that you have just created.
4. **Write Code**: You can start writing your Apache Spark code within this notebook now. You can read data from various Azure data sources, process this data using Spark transformations and actions, and write the processed data back to an Azure data source.
5. **Run the Notebook**: After writing your Spark job, click `'Run All'` to execute the notebook, which runs your Spark job on the cluster.
6. **Debug**: If your Spark job runs into issues, utilize the built-in debug features. If the data volume is large, consider adding more worker nodes to your cluster.
7. **Schedule Jobs**: On Azure Databricks, you can schedule jobs. Go to the `'Jobs'` tab, create a new job, select your notebook, the cluster, and configure your schedule.
8. **Monitor Performance**: Make use of the integrated monitoring features to keep track of the Spark job's performance.

Azure Databricks makes it simple to run Apache Spark jobs, providing an integrated workspace where you can code, schedule, and monitor your Spark jobs under one roof. By encapsulating the complexities of Apache Spark behind a user-friendly interface, Azure Databricks makes it easier for data scientists and data engineers to focus on what matters most - gleaning insights from the data.

Leveraging Azure HDInsight for Big Data Solutions

Further enhancing our discussion on Azure's capabilities is another noteworthy service - Azure HDInsight. It's a cloud distribution of Apache Hadoop components, designed to process large amounts of data. This section of our chapter will explore Azure HDInsight and how it fits into the big data solutions framework.

Introduction to Azure HDInsight: Capabilities and Functions

Azure HDInsight is a cloud-based, open-source analytics service provided by Microsoft. It enables organizations to analyze vast amounts of data and extract valuable insights, assisting in making informed business decisions. HDInsight is a fully managed cloud service that makes processing large amounts of data easy, cost-effective, and fast.

Here are some of the key capabilities and functions of Azure HDInsight:

- **Multi-Functional Analytical Platform**: HDInsight provides a set of high-performance analytical engines, including Apache Hadoop for batch processing, Apache Kafka for real-time messaging, Apache Hive for data warehousing, and Apache HBase for NoSQL data. This versatility lets companies tackle a variety of data processing tasks with one tool.
- **Scalability and Flexibility**: You can quickly scale clusters up or down in HDInsight, giving you the flexibility to meet workload requirements without paying for resources you don't need.
- **Productivity**: HDInsight integrates with familiar tools such as Excel, Power BI, and Visual Studio, allowing your team to work in an environment that they are comfortable with.
- **Data Security and Compliance**: Data stored in HDInsight is encrypted at rest and in transit, and the service includes capabilities to ensure regulatory compliance.
- **Big Data Integration**: Azure HDInsight can be integrated with big data technologies like Hadoop, Spark, Hive, LLAP, Kafka, Storm, HBase, and R Server, allowing for advanced analytics and machine learning capabilities.
- **Real-time Analytics**: HDInsight offers the ability to analyze data in real-time through Spark and Kafka, enabling organizations to gather insights instantly.
- **Cost-Effective**: With HDInsight, you can benefit from the power of on-demand clusters, paying only for what you use. This, combined with the ability to pause clusters, means you can minimize costs while still having the resources you need when you need them.

HDInsight makes it simpler to implement big data analytics in the cloud, using the tools and languages that data scientists and engineers are already familiar with. It's designed to handle any amount of data, scaling from terabytes to petabytes on demand, letting you focus on your data, not on your infrastructure.

Integrating Azure HDInsight with Big Data Analytics: Mastering the Process

Azure HDInsight is a fully managed, full-spectrum, open-source analytics service provided by Microsoft for enterprises. It facilitates the processing of big data and is designed to handle high volumes of data across a wide variety of types and sources. It provides popular open-source frameworks such as Hadoop, Spark, Hive, LLAP, Kafka, Storm, R, and more.

Here are the steps to integrate Azure HDInsight with Big Data Analytics:

1. **Create an HDInsight cluster**: Via the Azure portal, create an HDInsight cluster. Choose the type of cluster suited to your workload - Apache Spark for machine learning, Apache Hadoop for batch processing, or Apache Kafka for real-time processing.

2. **Data Storage**: HDInsight stores data in Azure Blob Storage or Azure Data Lake Storage. During the creation of the HDInsight cluster, you'll choose a default data source. Make sure the data to be analyzed is in the chosen data source.

3. **Ingest Data**: After setting up the cluster and storage, the next step is to ingest data. Data can be ingested using several Azure services, including Azure Data Factory or Azure IoT hub.

4. **Perform Analysis**: Once the data is in place, you can start analyzing. You can use Apache Hive for data summarization, query, and analysis of large datasets; Apache Spark for machine learning jobs; or use MapReduce for batch processing tasks.

5. **Visualize Data**: After performing the desired analysis, you can visualize the results using various tools such as Power BI, Excel, or Zeppelin notebooks.

6. **Delete the Cluster**: After you've finished analyzing and extracted valuable insights from your data, you can delete the cluster as HDInsight clusters are billed per minute.

Remember, when integrating HDInsight with your big data strategy, regular monitoring and management of resources and a strong governance policy is a must. Azure provides tools like Azure Log Analytics and Azure Monitor to track performance and send alerts for any operational issues, so use these tools to your advantage.

By integrating Azure HDInsight effectively into your big data analytics, you can take advantage of a scalable, robust, and versatile platform, simplifying complex data processing tasks and, thus, deriving valuable insights more efficiently.

Best Practices for Using Azure HDInsight in Big Data Solutions

Azure HDInsight is a fully managed, full-spectrum, open-source analytics service from Microsoft Azure for enterprises to utilize the capabilities of Apache Hadoop, Spark, and other open-source frameworks to analyze, visualize, and gather insights from the vast amounts of data.

The following are some of the best practices to consider when working with Azure HDInsight, helping you avoid common pitfalls and harness the power of HDInsight efficiently:

- **Right-Size Clusters**: Select the right types and the right number of nodes suitable for your workload. Keep in mind different node types perform differently and come at varying costs.
- **Use Managed Disks**: Managed disks provide better reliability for HDInsight and are resilient to failures. They automatically distribute data across different storage scales to limit the impact of hardware failures.
- **Utilize Autoscale**: Azure HDInsight provides an Autoscale feature which, when enabled, will scale the number of worker nodes in your cluster up or down based on the load. This can help you to handle varying workloads more efficiently.
- **Data Security**: Enable Azure Active Directory (Azure AD) integration to authenticate users who access your HDInsight clusters and use Apache Ranger together with Azure AD for role-based access control.
- **Encrypt Sensitive Data**: Always enable encryption-at-rest and encryption-in-transit for any sensitive data to mitigate the impact of security breaches.
- **Backup and Disaster Recovery**: Configure regular backups for critical data and use Azure's Geo-Replication feature for disaster recovery.
- **Monitoring and Diagnostics**: Use Azure Monitor and Azure Log Analytics to monitor usage and performance in real-time, helping to identify any issues quickly.
- **Cost Management**: Be sure to delete clusters when they are no longer needed. Since HDInsight clusters can be easily created and deleted, it's a best practice to remove clusters when you're finished with them to save cost.
- **Use Effective Data Formats**: When using Apache Hive, it's recommended to use either the ORC or Parquet format. Both of these formats are compressed columnar formats, and Hive can read, write, and process these formats extremely quickly compared to row-based formats.

- **Decoupling Storage and Computation**: Store your data in Azure Blob Storage or Azure Data Lake Storage which provides low-cost, highly reliable cloud storage, leaving HDInsight responsible only for computation.

By incorporating these best practices, organizations can make the most out of Azure HDInsight, ensuring the effective and efficient handling of their big data solutions.

Real-Time Data Processing with Azure Stream Analytics

In today's rapidly changing digital landscape, the demand for real-time data analytics is skyrocketing. Azure Stream Analytics, a powerful real-time analytics tool, caters to this need perfectly. In this section of the chapter, we will explore this Azure service and its use in real-time data processing scenarios.

Understanding Azure Stream Analytics: Features and Benefits

Azure Stream Analytics is a real-time analytics and complex event-processing engine that is designed to analyze and visualize streaming data in real-time. It is a fully managed, extremely scalable, and secure service that enables users to process and analyze large volumes of data streaming from devices, web sites, applications, and more.

The key Features of Azure Stream Analytics are as follows:

- **Real-time Event Processing**: It allows you to process millions of data streams simultaneously in real time, leveraging its high-speed data processing capabilities.
- **SQL Language Support**: It allows you to write queries and perform operations on real-time data using a SQL-like language, enabling immediate insights from data streams.
- **Time-Windowing Operations**: With Stream analytics, you can perform time-windowing operations such as sliding, tumbling, and hopping on data streams to extract trends over set periods.
- **Event Time Ordering**: Preserve the order of events exactly as they occurred while handling the out-of-order and late-arriving data.
- **Integration with other Azure Services**: It seamlessly integrates with other Azure services such as the Azure IoT Hub, Azure Event Hubs for real-time data ingestion, Azure Machine Learning, and Power BI for visualization.

The benefits of Azure Stream Analytics are:

- **Ease of Use**: A key advantage of Azure Stream Analytics is its ease of use. It enables writing queries using SQL language, which is familiar to many developers and data analysts.
- **Scalability**: It offers on-demand scalability, providing quick and easy scalability when required.
- **Cost-Effective**: It is a fully managed service that doesn't require significant hardware or personnel expenditure, reducing the total cost of ownership.
- **Reliable**: It delivers fault-detection, auto recovery from failures, and guarantees at least-once data delivery to provide a reliable service.
- **Security**: Data is always encrypted, whether at rest or in transit. Moreover, it is integrated with Azure Active Directory to ensure Enterprise-grade security.

Azure Stream Analytics is a perfect solution for businesses that need real-time insights from their data to make prompt decisions. It is a versatile tool that can be leveraged for scenarios ranging from IoT device telemetry to real-time analytics on e-commerce data, and many more.

Setting Up Azure Stream Analytics: Practical Steps

Setting up Azure Stream Analytics requires a methodical approach to ensure its optimal deployment. Here's a step-by-step guide on setting it up:

1. **Create a Stream Analytics Job**

   Firstly, you need to create a Stream Analytics job. In the Azure portal, navigate to **`'Create a Resource'`** and select **`'Stream Analytics job'`**. Fill in the **`subscription`**, **`resource group`**, **`job name`**, and other details then click **`'Create'`**.

2. **Define Input**

   Next step is to define the input to the Stream Analytics job. This is the data source that you would like to analyze. Click **`'Inputs'`** under job topology and then **`'+Add stream input'`**. There are several options you can select from like **`Event Hub`**, **`IoT Hub`**, or **`Blob storage`**, as per your requirement.

3. **Define Output**

   You then have to define the output. Click **`'Outputs'`** under job topology and then **`'Add'`**. This is where the output of your job will be written. There are several options you can choose like **`SQL Database`**, **`Blob storage`**, **`Event Hub`**, and so on.

4. **Write Query**

   The next step is to define the transformation you want to apply. In the `'Overview'` section, click `'Query'`. Here you can write SQL-like data transformation queries to select data from your input alias and write it to your output alias.

5. **Start Job**

   Once your job is configured, start the job. You can choose to start it immediately or schedule for a specific time.

6. **Monitor Performance**

   Finally, monitor the performance of your Stream Analytics job and check the output. The monitoring dashboard provides useful metrics such as `SU% Utilization`, `Input/Output Events`, and `Data Conversion Errors`, and more.

Remember to stop the job when you are not using it to prevent unnecessary costs. Understanding and implementing these steps can help you harness the capabilities of Azure Stream Analytics effectively.

Implementing Real-Time Data Processing with Azure Stream Analytics

Implementing real-time data processing with Azure Stream Analytics involves a sequence of steps that include setting up your streaming input, creating the Stream Analytics job, and configuring your output. Here's a step-by-step outline:

1. **Setup Azure Stream Analytics**: You'll need an Azure subscription. If you do not have one, you can create a free Azure account.

2. **Creating the Input Source**: The first step would be to set up the source of your streaming data. Data can be streamed from various sources including `Event Hubs`, `IoT Hub`, and `Blob Storage`.

3. **Setup Stream Analytics Job**: Once you have your streaming input setup, navigate to the Azure portal and create a new Stream Analytics Job. Fill in the necessary details such as `Job name`, `Resource group`, `Location`, `Streaming units`, and `Hosting environment`.

4. **Adding Input to the Job**: The next step would be to add an input to your job. Navigate to your job's details page, click `'Inputs'` under the `'Job Topology'` tab, and `'Add streaming input'`. From here on, follow the prompts to connect your previously defined input source.

5. **Define Query**: Use the SQL-like query language to define transformations and real-time analytics on your data stream. You can define the exact data you're interested in, perform aggregations, and filter data right from the incoming stream.

6. **Setting up the Output**: Similar to the Input setup, add an output to your job. Azure Stream Analytics can output to a variety of sinks like SQL Database, Cosmos DB, Blob Storage, Event Hub, Data Lake Storage, and Power BI.

7. **Starting the Job**: After all inputs, queries and outputs are set, start the job. You have the option to process data in real-time or process existing data.

8. **Monitor the Job**: After your job starts, make sure to monitor the job to ensure it's running as expected. Azure provides built-in monitoring metrics like Input/Output Events, Data Conversion Errors, Runtime Errors which are useful to gain insights about the running job.

Remember, implementing real-time data processing with Azure Stream Analytics is not a one-time activity. You'll need to monitor and potentially adjust your job to ensure it continues to meet your evolving business needs and handles the changes in incoming data. Ensuring your queries are written efficiently, and the appropriate streaming units are selected according to the volume and complexity of your data, will help reduce cost and improve performance.

Conclusion

In this chapter, we covered a wide range of topics related to using Azure for data science. We started by defining big data and discussing its scope and importance in today's data-driven world. We then provided an overview of big data analytics techniques and tools, highlighting their significance in extracting valuable insights from large datasets. Additionally, we explored the steps and challenges involved in big data processing, emphasizing the need for efficient and scalable solutions.

Moving forward, we focused on Azure Databricks and its advantages for scalable data processing. We explained the benefits and features of Azure Databricks, providing a step-by-step guide for its setup. Moreover, we discussed best practices for utilizing Azure Databricks for data processing, ensuring optimized performance and resource management. Next, we delved into Apache Spark and its role in big data processing, particularly on the Azure platform. We highlighted the synergy between Apache Spark and Azure, emphasizing their combined power in handling large-scale data processing tasks. Furthermore, we provided a comprehensive guide on running Apache Spark jobs on Azure, equipping data scientists with the knowledge to leverage this powerful combination effectively.

Our exploration then led us to Azure HDInsight, a cloud-based service for big data solutions. We introduced Azure HDInsight by highlighting its capabilities and functions, demonstrating its potential in handling complex analytical tasks. Furthermore, we discussed the process of integrating Azure HDInsight with big data analytics, offering insights into effectively harnessing its capabilities. We concluded this section by presenting best practices for utilizing Azure HDInsight in big data solutions, ensuring robust and efficient processing. Real-time data processing with Azure Stream Analytics was another crucial topic covered in this chapter. We discussed the features and benefits of Azure Stream Analytics, highlighting its ability to process streaming data in real-time. Additionally, we provided practical steps for setting up Azure Stream Analytics, enabling data scientists to implement real-time data processing solutions.

Lastly, we explored real-world applications of big data analytics using Azure. We analyzed case studies of successful big data implementations, showcasing how Azure has been instrumental in solving complex data challenges across industries. Additionally, we discussed future trends in Azure-based big data analytics, paving the way for cutting-edge advancements in the field. By the end of the chapter, we emphasized the significance of Azure in achieving success in big data analytics, enabling data scientists to extract valuable insights and drive meaningful outcomes.

Looking ahead, the next chapter will delve into real-world applications of data science using Azure. We will explore various industry-specific use cases and demonstrate how Azure can be effectively employed to address the specific challenges and opportunities faced by data scientists. Join us as we embark on an exciting journey into the practical applications of Azure in the realm of data science.

Questions

- Discuss the specific advantages and disadvantages of using Azure Databricks for scalable data processing.
- Elaborate on how Azure Databricks and Apache Spark collectively contribute to big data processing.
- Explain the integration process of Azure HDInsight with big data analytics, providing a detailed step-by-step guide.
- How does real-time data processing with Azure Stream Analytics cater to specific industry use-cases? Provide examples.
- Discuss the likely future trends in Azure-based big data analytics, and how these trends might impact businesses in various sectors.
- Is Azure Databricks capable of handling the processing of big data in real-time?
- Does Azure HDInsight support the integration with open-source platforms like Apache Hadoop and Spark?
- Can Azure Stream Analytics be used to analyze both real-time data and historical data?

- Are there any limitations to the kind of data that can be processed using Azure-based big data analytics tools?
- Has Azure proven instrumental in successful big data implementations in real-world scenarios?

Multiple Choice Questions

1. What type of data does Azure Databricks process?
   a. Structured
   b. Unstructured
   c. Semi-structured
   d. All of the above
2. What is one of the main benefits of implementing Apache Spark Jobs on Azure?
   a. Decreased data accessibility
   b. Managed clusters and scalability
   c. Limited programming flexibility
   d. Higher cost efficiency
3. Which feature of Azure HDInsight allows for the processing of large datasets?
   a. Real-time processing
   b. Memory-optimized processing
   c. Disk-based processing
   d. None of the above
4. Azure Stream Analytics primarily caters to:
   a. Real-time data processing
   b. Historical data analysis
   c. Both of the above
   d. Neither of the above
5. What is one of the future trends in Azure-based big data analytics?
   a. Reduced usage of cloud-based services
   b. Decreased reliance on real-time data

   c. Increase in machine learning applications

   d. Limiting data types for processing

6. In the context of Big Data Analytics, what does Azure Databricks primarily offer?

   a. A platform for data ingestion

   b. An environment for executing notebook-based workflows

   c. A secure data warehouse solution

   d. A machine learning framework

7. Which of the following is NOT an advantage of using Apache Spark on Azure?

   a. High cost of operation

   b. End-to-end data processing capabilities

   c. Skip the cluster management complexity

   d. Easy integration with other Azure services

8. Azure HDInsight is best described as:

   a. A fully managed, full-spectrum, open-source analytics service

   b. A real-time data processing tool

   c. An AI model training service

   d. A cloud storage service

9. Azure Stream Analytics is used to handle:

   a. Large-scale batch data

   b. Real-time streaming data

   c. Small data sets

   d. Non-streaming data

10. Future trends in Azure-Based Big Data Analytics include:

    a. Decreasing importance of data privacy

    b. Growing trend of on-premise data storage

    c. Increased adoption of IoT data analysis

    d. Decreased use of cloud-based services

11. Azure Databricks is optimized for performance with which cloud data platform?
    a. Google Cloud
    b. Amazon Web Services
    c. Alibaba Cloud
    d. Azure Data Lake Storage
12. Apache Spark Jobs on Azure can best be optimized with the use of:
    a. Azure Databricks
    b. Azure Functions
    c. Azure HDInsight
    d. Azure Batch
13. Azure HDInsight is based on which open source framework?
    a. Hadoop
    b. Spark
    c. Both Hadoop and Spark
    d. Neither Hadoop nor Spark
14. Azure Stream Analytics can be integrated with which real-time data ingestion service?
    a. Azure Data Explorer
    b. Azure Event Hubs
    c. Azure Cognitive Services
    d. Azure Batch
15. One key benefit of Azure-based Big Data Analytics is:
    a. Multi-language support
    b. Data size restrictions
    c. No real-time analytics support
    d. Limited integration with other Azure services

Answers

1. d
2. b
3. b
4. a
5. c
6. b
7. a
8. a
9. b
10. c
11. d
12. a
13. c
14. b
15. a

Chapter 11
Real-World Applications and Case Studies

Introduction

In this final chapter, we are set to explore practical applications of data science on Azure. You will be introduced to exemplary projects across various industries such as finance, healthcare, and e-commerce, providing a deeper understanding of data science implementation in the real world.

We will dive into critical case studies, highlighting how business problems were addressed using data science solutions on Azure. We will also share valuable lessons learned from implementing these projects.

Additionally, we will present you with a host of best practices for successful data science implementation on Azure and address some common queries in our Q&A section.

This chapter aims to bridge the gap between theory and application, equipping you with practical knowledge and insights about data science on Azure. Let's get started!

Structure

The topics covered in this chapter are as follows:

- Overview of Real-World Data Science Applications on Azure
- Real-World Examples of Successful Data Science Projects on Azure
- Case Studies: Data Science Applications in Various Industries
- Identifying Business Problems and Formulating Data Science Solutions
- Lessons Learned from Implementing Data Science Projects
- Best Practices for Delivering Value Through Data Science on Azure

Overview of Real-World Data Science Applications on Azure

The advent of the twenty-first century has seen a dramatic shift in the inclination of businesses; from traditional methods and tactics to a more data-driven approach. Harnessing and leveraging data has come to play a pivotal role, emerging as the vanguard of innovation and growth in various business sectors. Notably, this progress marks a significant rise in the functionalities of Data Science. This domain has become the marrow of structural decision making and strategic planning for businesses, enabling them to transform raw data into actionable insights. In this dawning era of Data Science, Microsoft's Azure platform stands out as a shimmering beacon. Azure, earmarked as one of the most transformative platforms, offers an impressive range of cutting-edge machine learning and Artificial Intelligence (AI) tools. It empowers data scientists and data analysts with the essential metrics and abilities to explore, process, and visualize complex data coherently and efficiently. It's a comprehensive cloud platform that carries a wide assortment of tools, ranging from simple data analyses to complex machine learning model designs, thereby simplifying the application of data science tasks and making them more manageable.

Azure, over the years, has rapidly metamorphosed into a substantial hub or rather, a fruitful soil from where robust and innovative data science applications can sprout, bloom, and grow beyond the boundaries of their sectors. Regardless of the industry - whether it's finance, healthcare, e-commerce, or any other field - Azure has proven its mettle in bringing the theoretical concepts and principles of data science to life, translating them into valuable, practical, and impactful industry applications.

In particular, Azure's application in finance has been revolutionary. By leveraging AI and machine learning capabilities, Azure facilitates in-depth analyses of financial markets, predicting market trends and behaviors, thereby prompting better investment decision-making. In the healthcare sector, Azure deploys machine learning techniques for predictive analysis, enhancing patient care, optimizing medical procedures, and promoting health data management. In the e-commerce realm, Azure helps businesses drive customer engagement, optimizing shopping experiences and predicting buying habits, thereby elevating sales and revenue.

Azure's cloud-based infrastructure is another feather in its cap. It ensures scalability, flexibility, robustness, and security for diverse applications, accommodating infinitely growing data volumes, complex computations, and extensive data traffic smoothly. This robust cloud-based framework not only provides affordable storage solutions but also ensures uninterrupted access to data, scalable computing power, real-time analytics, and effective disaster recovery methods. This flexibility allows businesses to choose the services that suit their particular needs and scale up or down as required. Azure has proved itself as a reliable and versatile platform in the realm of Data Science applications. Its robust nature, coupled with a multitude of tools, makes it a preferred choice for businesses of all scales and sectors. Microsoft Azure, with its focus on enhancing data analysis and processing methods, continues to be instrumental in driving the transformative power of data and setting milestones in the ever-evolving realms of Data Science and AI.

Explanation of Data Science Projects: Success Stories

To better understand how these data science projects translate to real-world applications, let's journey through a few success stories.

Our first story springs from the financial sector. Many financial institutions globally have successfully leveraged data science on Azure to build powerful credit risk models. By utilizing Azure's advanced machine learning tools, these organizations could analyze vast amounts of customers' financial history and transaction data, forming predictive models that could forecast potential defaults. Consequently, these models empowered them to make more intelligent credit offerings, reduce their risk exposure, and increase their profitability.

Our next anecdote comes from the healthcare industry. In a world where early detection can drastically improve patient outcomes, a leading healthcare provider utilized Azure to systematically analyze and predict patient health trends. Through Azure's machine learning services, they managed to collect and analyze medical data on a large scale, discern patterns, predict diseases, and formulate potential treatment paths. This approach resulted in enhanced patient care, predictive healthcare delivery, and significantly improved health outcomes.

These success stories exemplify the true power and potential of data science on Azure, and how it is redefining the modus operandi of a vast array of industries. As we delve deeper into more such case studies and examples, you will witness the sheer scale and diversity in applications of data science using Azure across the globe.

Real-World Examples of Successful Data Science Projects on Azure

As we delve deeper into the vibrant world of data science on Azure, it is pertinent to underscore its practical applications across diverse industries. Throughout this section, we will navigate the course of three successful data science projects implemented on Azure that have effectively addressed critical business problems. Each project will break down the problem, the applied Azure tools, and the final observations, offering a granular understanding of how Azure harnesses data science capabilities for real-world applications.

Let's pave the way into these projects, indulging in the details of how they were able to provide innovative solutions, change the operational landscape, and unlock unprecedented value for businesses.

Project A: Predictive Maintenance for the Manufacturing Industry

Introduction and Background

The manufacturing industry, an integral pillar of the global economy, has long been grappling with the unpredictability and high costs associated with machine failures and consequent downtime. Traditionally, manufacturing organizations have adhered to a reactive approach of equipment maintenance, wherein the faults and failures are addressed after they occur. Such unanticipated equipment breakdowns can lead to significant production losses, resultant delays, customer dissatisfaction, and cost overruns. Herein the concept of predictive maintenance comes into play, a methodology that is rapidly transforming how the industry operates.

Predictive Maintenance Concept

Predictive maintenance has brought about a strategic shift in the manufacturing industry – from a reactive approach to a proactive one. It focuses on foreseeing and preventing equipment faults before they culminate into complete machine failures that can abruptly halt the entire production line. For this purpose, a pioneering predictive maintenance application was developed leveraging Microsoft Azure's Machine Learning Studio, a cloud-based, drag-and-drop tool that eliminates the necessity of coding, making machine learning more accessible and manageable.

Project Execution

The core concept of the project revolved around predicting potential failures and taking preventive actions to avoid costly production interruptions. The execution of this project required capturing, processing, and analyzing colossal volumes of real-time and historical sensor data from production machinery. The captured data features incorporated machine parameters such as temperature, usage time, vibration patterns, error logs, and more, painting a comprehensive picture of each machine's operative state.

Post data capture, the preprocessing stage involved sifting and cleaning this raw sensor data, dealing with missing values, outliers, and insignificant variables. This clean, processed data was then ingested into Azure's Machine Learning algorithms meticulously designed to recognize intricate data patterns and correlations that would mark possible machine malfunctions.

The data science team, armed with domain knowledge, frequently contrasted machine learning-generated patterns against real-time machine performance data, enabling them to predict potential machine failures. Realizing that making such a system work in a real life setting required more than just robust algorithms, the team also paid significant attention to establishing a synergistic collaboration between data scientists and manufacturing engineers. This ensured that the machine learning outputs could be seamlessly incorporated into the existing maintenance framework, fostering a practical and workable approach.

Project Outcome

The successful implementation of the predictive maintenance model completely revolutionized the manufacturing industry's approach to equipment maintenance and failure prevention. The principal benefit of the system was its ability to signal potential machinery failures well ahead of time. This provided the manufacturing and maintenance teams with sufficient lead time for timely interventions, dramatically curtailing instances of unanticipated, crippling machine breakdowns.

In terms of tangible outcomes, the industry experienced a marked increase in overall operational efficiency and productivity. The frequency of unplanned machine downtimes dropped significantly, allowing for a smoother, more reliable production process. These improvements not only translated into substantial cost savings in the form of reduced waste and maintenance expenses but also brought about an upsurge in production levels, consequently boosting the revenue streams and positively impacting the bottom line.

Key Learnings

The project prominently underscored the transformative potential of predictive analytics in operationally intensive sectors such as manufacturing. Moreover, it reiterated the prowess and adaptability of Azure's Machine Learning tools when it came down to processing high-dimensional datasets and generating reliable, timely predictive outputs leading to meaningful actions on the ground.

In hindsight, the project reaffirmed two vital realities of successful data science projects. Firstly, the invaluable role of context-specific, quality data collection and preprocessing in developing meaningful machine learning models. Secondly, the indispensable need for proactive, cross-functional collaborations, in this case, between data scientists and manufacturing engineers, ensuring the workable implementation and application of data science outputs in a real-world industrial setting.

Overall, the project emerged as a resounding testimony of how Azure's data science capabilities could influence actionable insights in a real-world environment, fostering enhanced operational efficiency while also lighting the path for future technological advancements in the manufacturing landscape.

Project B: Customer Segmentation in E-commerce

Introduction and Background

The e-commerce industry's meteoric rise is equally credited to explosive technological advancements and evolving consumer behavior. Today, the e-commerce landscape is a sprawling, dynamic arena – buzzing with myriad opportunities and stiff competition. Amidst such intense market dynamism, customer segmentation serves as a linchpin for effective marketing strategy and customer relationship building. Recognizing this business imperative, a far-reaching customer segmentation project was enacted within a prominent e-commerce entity. This project effectively harnessed Microsoft Azure's Databricks platform and machine learning capabilities to breathe life into a new level of personalized marketing.

Customer Segmentation Concept

At its fundamental level, customer segmentation is a method of subdividing the customer base into definable, accessible, and actionable segments according to shared demographics, psychographics, lifestyle, purchase patterns, and preferences. The primary goal is to better understand customer behavior, thus allowing for more nuanced and efficient marketing strategies that transcend the confines of broad and generalized targeting. This transition to a more focused target strategy forms the core of personalized marketing, which boasts of higher efficacy and conversion rates.

Project Execution

In the execution of this project, Azure played a crucial role, providing robust computational capacities courtesy of its Databricks platform. Azure Databricks, an Apache Spark-based analytics platform, boasts of enhanced distributed computing power, making it better equipped to handle and process vast, diversified customer data sets at scale.

The data feed was a treasure trove of detailed customer records providing insights into past purchases, browsing and search patterns, product ratings, customer reviews, and engagements on the online platform. Aptly collected and collated, this data served as a critical input for the customer segmentation model.

Carving out meaningful clusters from this high-dimensional dataset required the use of unsupervised machine learning algorithms. Unsupervised learning, by nature, seeks out hidden structures in unlabeled data, making it the right choice for customer segmentation. Specifically, K-means clustering – an algorithm that identifies '*k*' number of centroids and then allocates every data point to the nearest cluster – was employed.

Project Outcome

The fruits of this project's exertions were gratifying. The successful segmentation facilitated the formation of distinct customer clusters, each reflecting a group of customers with similar buying behavior, tastes, and preferences. Now, armed with a profound understanding of these variants of customer clusters, the marketing teams could tailor their communication strategies precisely and effectively.

The customer segments offered a much-needed structure and direction to the marketing campaigns. The segmentation-driven personalized marketing led to enhanced customer engagement, satisfaction, and retention, as customers felt valued and catered to through individualized offers and communications.

Furthermore, the rich insights gleaned from customer clustering resulted in more powerful, '*customer-appealing*' product offerings and innovations. This led to higher customer conversions and up-selling instances, bolstering sales and revenues. An added advantage was the project's fluidity, allowing the e-commerce entity to continually refine and recalibrate customer segments and strategies based on real-time data and evolving shopping patterns.

Key Learnings

The project's triumph vividly exemplified the potential of data science in crafting customer-centric strategies and user experiences. It illustrated how Azure's robust capabilities could handle complex, large-scale datasets and leverage machine learning algorithms to facilitate profitable business solutions such as market segmentation.

The implications of this success story extend far beyond this particular e-commerce entity. It serves as a valid testimony to the transformative power of data-driven decision-making and machine learning in creating potent marketing strategies. With its ability to pivot marketing efforts from one-size-fits-all to a more personalized and effective approach, it underscores the important role technology and data science will play in the future of business growth and customer relationships.

Project C: Fraud Detection in Financial Services

Introduction and Background

The rapid ascent of e-commerce not only stems from technological advancements but also an evolving landscape of financial transactions and consumer behavior. Alongside its countless opportunities, the e-commerce market also faces substantial challenges, especially in the realm of security and fraud detection. The burgeoning issue of financial fraud in e-commerce necessitates robust deterrents and solutions. To address this, a state-of-the-art fraud detection initiative was implemented using

Microsoft Azure's sophisticated computing capabilities through the Azure Databricks platform.

Customer Segmentation Concept

Fraud detection in financial services involves identifying unusual or suspicious transactions that could be indicative of fraudulent activities. The process employs various data-driven techniques to analyze transaction patterns, flag inconsistencies, and prevent fraudulent losses. The objective is not only to detect and respond to fraud effectively but also to predict and prevent it, thereby protecting both the retailer and the customer.

Project Execution:

Azure's role was paramount in this project, providing the computational horsepower through its Databricks platform. Azure Databricks, built on Apache Spark, is renowned for its superior distributed computing prowess, making it an ideal choice for processing large volumes of transaction data efficiently and effectively.

Data for this project consisted of vast arrays of transaction records, including timestamps, transaction amounts, user IDs, merchant details, and more. This vast dataset formed the backbone of our fraud detection model, powered by sophisticated machine learning algorithms and real-time processing.

Anomaly detection techniques, employing supervised machine learning models like Random Forest, Logistic Regression, and Neural Networks, were integral to identifying fraudulent transactions. These models were trained on historical fraud data, allowing them to learn and identify patterns and anomalies indicative of fraud in new transactions.

Project Outcome:

The results of the fraud detection initiative were highly impactful. By implementing a real-time fraud detection system, the e-commerce entity succeeded in drastically reducing the occurrence of fraudulent transactions. This proactive approach not only saved potential revenue losses but also reinforced customer trust and confidence in the security of their transactions.

In addition, the capability to adapt and learn from new fraudulent patterns enabled the system to stay ahead of fraudsters, who continually evolve their techniques to bypass traditional detection systems. This dynamic adaptation led to continually improving fraud detection rates and reducing false positives, thereby enhancing overall customer experience.

Key Learnings:

This project showcased the immense potential of leveraging big data and machine learning in fraud detection. Using Azure's robust capabilities, the project demonstrated how handling complex, large-scale datasets and employing advanced analytics can lead to significant business solutions in fraud prevention.

The success of this initiative underscores the transformative power of data-driven decision-making and machine learning in developing robust security measures for the e-commerce environment. This approach not only helps in tailoring specific anti-fraud measures but also sets a benchmark for the industry in maintaining the integrity of digital transactions.

The project not only addresses the immediate needs of fraud prevention but also provides a scalable model that can adapt to emerging fraud tactics, ensuring long-term security and trust in the financial transactions landscape.

Case Studies: Data Science Applications in Various Industries

Data science has proved pivotal across numerous industries, offering solutions ranging from predicting stock market trends to customizing medical treatments and optimizing logistics. Let's delve further into specific case studies demonstrating how data science, particularly when implemented on Azure, has contributed significantly to business problem-solving in the finance, healthcare, and e-commerce sectors.

Finance

Case Study 1: Optimizing Trading Strategies

- **Problem Identification**: In the competitive world of financial services, firms are constantly seeking to optimize trading strategies to maximize profits and reduce risks. However, this task can be extremely challenging, given the high volatility and complexity of financial markets.
- **Solution via Data Science**: With Azure's machine learning capabilities, one hedge fund firm used a multitude of data, including market, alternative, and proprietary data, to devise new, more efficient trading strategies. Using Azure, they built and trained trading models that factored in external variables often overlooked by traditional models. These AI models identified patterns and predicted future price changes more accurately, thus enabling more profitable trades and paving the path for more dynamic risk management.

Case Study 2: Improving Loan Approval Processes

- **Problem Identification**: Many banks face a conundrum involving intricate loan approval processes and reducing potential credit risks while improving customer service for loan applicants.

- **Solution via Data Science**: A prominent bank used Azure to overhaul its burdensome loan approval process. They built predictive models that used extensive consumer data and sophisticated algorithms to quickly and accurately assess creditworthiness. This resulted in quicker loan approvals, reduced default rates, and improved customer satisfaction.

Healthcare

Case Study 1: Personalized Medical Treatments

- **Problem Identification**: The "*one-size-fits-all*" approach often falls short in healthcare. Personalized treatments can significantly enhance clinical efficiency and patient experience.
- **Solution via Data Science**: A healthcare institution used Azure to process and analyze massive genomic sequencing data paired with health records. It allowed them to develop personalized treatment plans based on underlying genetic conditions and medical histories. This approach proved to be highly transformative, improving patient care and health outcomes.

Case Study 2: Enhancing Drug Discovery

- **Problem Identification**: Traditional drug discovery processes are often time-consuming and costly, which can cause significant delays in addressing pressing health issues.
- **Solution via Data Science**: A pharmaceutical company implemented Azure to accelerate its drug discovery process. They analyzed vast amounts of biomedical data, identifying promising drug candidates in a fraction of the original time. Azure's machine learning capability managed to automate large parts of the process, significantly speeding up the drug discovery phase and reducing costs.

E-Commerce

Case Study 1: Supply Chain Optimization

- **Problem Identification**: In the fast-paced e-commerce industry, efficient supply chain management is crucial. Businesses are always on the lookout for ways to optimize the supply chain to reduce costs and improve customer satisfaction.
- **Solution via Data Science**: A major online retailer implemented data science on Azure to optimize its supply chain. They built predictive models on Azure to forecast product demand accurately and manage inventory effectively.

Case Study 2: Product Recommendation Engine

- **Problem Identification**: To enhance sales and customer experiences, e-commerce portals require effective product recommendation systems. However, developing personalized and responsive recommendation systems can be challenging.
- **Solution via Data Science**: Leveraging Azure's machine learning tools, an e-commerce company created a responsive product recommendation system. It analyzed user behavior, purchase history, and integrated real-time shopping data to provide customers with relevant and personalized product suggestions, significantly increasing conversion rates and customer satisfaction.

Identifying Business Problems and Formulating Data Science Solutions

Data science is an enabler that empowers businesses to find optimum solutions to complex problems, but the key is identifying the correct problem and translating it into a data science problem. Here, we propose methods to define business problems clearly and, subsequently, develop respective data science solutions.

Understanding Business Problems: Tips and Techniques

The first step towards effectively harnessing the power of data science is understanding and defining the business problem at hand.

1. **Engage with Stakeholders**: Involve key stakeholders to obtain a thorough understanding of the business problem. Engage with them individually, if need be, to determine the root causes and impacts.
2. **Define Goals and Metrics**: Clearly articulate what needs to be achieved. Outline goals for the project and identify key performance metrics to measure success.
3. **Understand the Data Landscape**: Familiarize yourself with the available data sources. This includes understanding what data is collected, how, and where it's stored.
4. **Feasibility Analysis**: It's crucial to examine the feasibility of the problem being solved through data science methods. Not all business problems can or should be solved by data science – some might benefit more from fundamental process changes.

Creating Suitable Data Science Solutions: A Step-by-Step Guide

With the business problem clearly defined, the next step is to create a data science solution on frameworks like Azure. Here, we offer a systematic approach.

1. **Problem Translation**: Translate the business problem into a data science problem. If your business problem is about improving customer retention, your data science problem could be predicting customer churn.
2. **Data Acquirement and Cleaning**: Gather the necessary data required to solve the query. The data needs to be cleaned and formatted correctly, making it suitable for analysis.
3. **Exploratory Data Analysis**: Uncover patterns, spot anomalies, or check assumptions with the help of summary statistics and graphical representations.
4. **Model Selection and Training**: Choose the most suitable predictive or prescriptive model that can help achieve business goals. Train this model on your dataset.
5. **Evaluation and Tuning**: Evaluate your model using pre-selected performance metrics and fine-tune its parameters to achieve the best results.
6. **Implementation**: Once the model is performing satisfactorily, it's time for deployment. Plug the model into your business processes or systems.
7. **Monitor and Update**: Data-driven models need to be monitored and updated periodically to ensure they continue to perform optimally as new data comes in.

Remember, the goal is not to create the most sophisticated model; instead, it is to find the model that best addresses the business problem and can be implemented effectively. Azure assists in this by providing a scouring suite of data science tools and services that can be adapted to a wide array of problems, data types, and domains.

Lessons Learned from Implementing Data Science Projects

Implementing data science projects involves not only the application of complex technical knowledge but also the management of numerous challenges recognized through past experiences. Continuous learning and adapting from these experiences shape the success of future data science projects. This section presents key lessons learned from implementing data science projects on Azure.

Challenges and How to Overcome Them

Implementing data science projects often comes with distinct challenges:

1. **Data Collection and Cleaning**: Often, the biggest hurdle isn't building the model itself but preparing the data that the model will use. Overcoming this challenge requires investing time in data cleaning and utilizing tools and resources.
2. **Missing or Incomplete Data**: It's quite common to encounter missing data or data not collected properly. To manage this, data imputation techniques or model training methods that handle missing data could be employed.
3. **Skill Gap**: Data science projects often require varied skills, including programming, statistical analysis, and machine learning. Building a well-rounded team is essential. Azure provides numerous resources and user-friendly interfaces that make it accessible to people even with a basic understanding of data science.
4. **Scalability**: Testing models on a small dataset is different from deploying it to handle a large, real-world dataset. Ensuring proper infrastructure and support, such as Azure's scalable ML solutions, is essential.
5. **Data Privacy**: When dealing with customer data, it's crucial to keep privacy in mind. Always use data anonymization techniques for sensitive data.

Key Takeaways from Past Projects

1. **Define Clear Objectives**: Ensure the data science project has well-defined objectives aligning with the business's overall goals.
2. **Understand the Data**: Devote time to understanding the data thoroughly before jumping into model building. What data is available? Is more needed? How does it need to be manipulated or altered?
3. **Choose the Right Tool**: Not every tool or language is suitable for all problems. Choose the one best fitting the problem scope, data, and team skills. Azure offers a range of tools, making it flexible for different tasks.
4. **Model Simplicity**: A simpler model that works is always better than a complex one. Prototype quickly and improve iteratively.
5. **Regular Monitoring**: A model can drift over time, delivering less accurate results. Regular monitoring after deployment can help you identify this and update the model, if necessary.

Approaching data science projects without acknowledging these key lessons can lead to significant obstacles in the project flow. Keeping a learner's approach is perhaps the best practice a data scientist may adopt. Wisdom gathered from the past can serve as the guiding beacon for future projects.

Best Practices for Delivering Value through Data Science on Azure

Implementing data science in the business environment must be carried out thoughtfully to effectively tap into its vast potential. It's one thing to execute a successful data science project; it's another to generate continuous business value out of it. Here, we discuss some key practices for delivering sustained business value through data science on Azure.

- **Adopt a business-centered approach**: Start with a compelling business problem and then apply data science, not the other way around. Ensure that data science projects align with the overall business strategy.
- **Assemble a diverse team**: Effective data science implementation calls for a team with a mix of skill sets, such as business understanding, data wrangling, modeling, project management, and more.
- **Lay a strong data foundation:** Before embarking on analysis or modeling, ensure you have clean and well-structured data ready for use.
- **Iterate and improve**: The first solution won't often be the best one. Continually test, refine, and improve your models to achieve better results. Azure ML allows you to manage and track various versions of your models for comparison.
- **Translate technical results into business language**: Stakeholders will be interested in how your results affect business parameters. Thus, it's essential to translate technical results into business terms.
- **Make results actionable**: Always strive for results that can be directly acted upon to improve business.

Conclusion

In this chapter, we explored real-world applications of data science on Azure and investigated some successful cases that demonstrate the remarkable potential of Azure for data science applications. We delved into a variety of projects spanning multiple industries, including finance, healthcare, and e-commerce, analyzing each case in terms of problem identification and their data science-mediated solutions. Furthermore, the chapter sheds light on the key aspect of understanding business problems and devising fitting data science strategies to provide solutions. This involved arming readers with practical tips and techniques for comprehending business issues and mapping out data science solutions.

An in-depth discussion on common challenges faced during the implementation of data science projects and how to tackle these obstacles served as a pivotal part of this chapter. We also extracted key learnings from these past projects to better equip data scientists for future ventures. Finally, the chapter compiled essential best practices and expert responses to frequently voiced concerns for successful data science implementation. Overall, the chapter not only aims to educate on the vast applications of data science on Azure but also provides a blueprint for successfully executing future data science projects.

We understand that preparing for Azure certification exams can be a daunting task, but remember, the journey of a thousand miles begins with a small step. We are confident that the knowledge acquired from this chapter and the entire book will serve as an invaluable resource in your preparation. As you endeavor to master Azure for data science, keep in mind the real-world applications, best practices, and common challenges elaborated here. Use them not only to ace your certification exams but also to solve actual business problems with data science on Azure. All the best in your certification journey and may success crown your efforts. Happy learning!

As we near the next chapter, which is the last in our series, we will take a moment to rewind and review all the key learnings we have discussed throughout. The concluding chapter will serve as a comprehensive recap of our journey, synthesizing the vital insights and strategies that have been highlighted, ensuring that they are well-understood and can be effectively applied in future endeavors.

Q&A: Frequently Raised Concerns and Expert Responses

1. **Question**: How can we ensure data privacy and security while implementing data science projects on Azure?

   Answer: Azure provides many built-in security measures like encryption, access controls, and compliance certifications. It's imperative to leverage these and follow the principle of least privilege.

2. **Question**: What is the best way to handle missing or incomplete data in Azure?

   Answer: Azure ML offers various methods to handle missing data, such as removal, imputation, or using algorithms robust to missing values. The best method depends on the data nature and missingness mechanism.

3. **Question**: How can we ensure a smooth transition from older data analytics methods to Azure's data science capabilities?

   Answer: A phased approach can be adopted, beginning with pilot projects, learning, and gradually increasing the scale. Azure's compatibility with various languages and tools also eases the transition.

4. **Question**: What if the developed models fail to perform in the real world as they do in test scenarios?

   Answer: Real-world data can often behave differently. Quick iteration and regular model monitoring for accuracy losses can help here. Azure provides model management and monitoring services that make this process easier.

CHAPTER 12
Conclusion and Next Steps

Introduction

This chapter aims to summarize the key concepts discussed throughout the book and encourage readers to continue exploring and learning about data science and its application in Azure. The ultimate goal is to inspire readers to deepen their knowledge and enhance the skills they have acquired throughout their journey.

The advent of data science has opened numerous opportunities in multiple sectors. Azure, as a leading cloud computing service, provides an extensive array of tools that facilitate data storage, analysis, and insights generation. The book begins by introducing these two crucial domains and shows how they intersect to provide powerful solutions that drive industries forward.

Throughout the book, we delved deep into the concepts of data ingestion, storage, transformation, machine learning, and AI, specifically in the Azure platform. We also discussed the importance of ethical AI and explored big data analytics in Azure. Real-world case studies were presented to elucidate the practical applications of these concepts, and elaborate Q&A challenges were designed to help you achieve your data science certifications.

Each chapter offered a unique perspective and critical knowledge of various aspects of data science within Azure. It is hoped that the chapters have provided immense value, understanding, and application of data science on the Azure platform.

Now, as we come to the concluding chapter of this enlightening journey, let's take a moment to reflect on the path we have traversed and see where to go next.

Structure

This chapter will contain the following:

- Recap of Key Concepts Covered in the Book
- Reflection on the Journey from Designing to Implementing Data Science Solutions
- Encouraging Readers to Explore Advanced Topics and Continue Learning
- Next Steps for Further Enhancing Data Science Skills on Azure

Recap of Key Concepts

Let us revisit and review the key concepts covered in the book.

Review of Data Science and Azure

In the first chapter, the fundamental concepts of data science and Azure were introduced. Understanding the intersection of data science and Azure provided the foundation from which further comprehension of the synergy between complex data analysis techniques and cloud technologies would be built.

Reflection on Setting Up Your Azure Environment

Next, readers were guided on the process of configuring an optimal Azure environment. Tips were offered to select the right services and resources, understand the Azure portal navigation, and configure key security measures to ensure a safe and efficient platform for data science projects.

Recap on Data Ingestion and Storage in Azure

Diving into the technical aspects, the third chapter covered data ingestion and storage – two fundamental stages in any data science pipeline. We explored Azure Data Factory for data integration services and Azure storage solutions such as Azure Blob Storage, Azure Data Lake, and more.

Summary of Data Transformation and Cleaning

Chapter 4, *Data Transformation and Cleaning*, stressed the importance of data quality for effective data science. It covered a range of Azure tools and services, such as Azure

Data Catalog for data governance and Azure Data Lake Analytics for cleaning and transforming raw data into insights-ready data.

Review of Machine Learning

Chapter 5, Introduction to Machine Learning, provided an overview of machine learning as a universally pivotal component of data science. Basic ML concepts were defined and an introduction to Azure's ML services and capabilities was provided.

Reflection on Azure Machine Learning Studio

In *Chapter 6, Azure Machine Learning Studio*, we delved into detail about Azure Machine Learning Studio, offering an overview of its drag-and-drop feature for building, testing, and deploying ML models. We explored the use of Azure ML Studio in machine learning experimentation and deployment.

Summary of Model Deployment and Monitoring

Chapter 7, Model Deployment and Monitoring, dealt with the practical aspects of deploying, managing, and monitoring machine learning models in Azure. Essential security and governance practices were discussed, alongside exploring the Azure Model Registry and other useful tools.

Recap on Embracing AI Revolution with Azure

In *Chapter 8, Embracing AI Revolution with Azure*, we introduced AI services available in Azure and how businesses can utilize them to gain strategic advantages. We particularly focused on Cognitive Services, Azure Bot Services, and Azure Databricks.

Reflection on Responsible AI and Ethics

In *Chapter 9, Responsible AI and Ethics*, we discussed essential principles of ethical AI, stressing responsible AI development, fairness, privacy, transparency, and AI's societal impacts. It aimed to address the growing importance of ethical considerations in AI deployment.

Summary of Big Data Analytics with Azure

In *Chapter 10, Big Data Analytics with Azure*, we explored how Azure caters to Big Data needs with services such as Azure Synapse Analytics, HDInsight, and Databricks. It focused on how these services can be leveraged to analyze large datasets and extract valuable insights.

Review of Real-World Applications and Case Studies

In the final chapter, *Real-World Applications and Case Studies*, before this recap, readers were introduced to real-world applications of Azure in data science with detailed case studies. Additionally, certification-oriented Q&A challenges were presented to further prepare readers for their professional advancement in the field of data science.

Reflection on the Journey from Designing to Implementing Data Science Solutions

Since the early chapters, this book emphasized the application of the data science problem-solving process. Embarking on this journey, you understood the significance of asking the right questions, acquiring and preparing the necessary data, selecting and applying appropriate machine learning algorithms, and evaluating, refining, and ultimately deploying models to solve real-world problems. These processes were further explored through various Azure services, reflecting the flexibility and power of cloud platforms in implementing data science solutions.

Importance of Designing to Implementing Data Science Solutions

As the book evolved, developing a systematic design approach to tackling and implementing data science solutions became a central theme. You discovered how Azure's comprehensive set of tools and services assists in designing seamless data pipelines from start to finish. You learned about integration, storage, cleaning, transformation, and analytics tools that all work together to form a cohesive environment for designing and executing data science tasks.

Reflection on Learned Skills and Techniques

As you journeyed from understanding basic concepts in data science and Azure to learning about data cleaning, transformation, machine learning, AI, and Big Data Analytics with Azure, you have essentially developed essential skills and techniques in data science. Reflecting on the journey, you will realize the development of your abilities in cloud computing, programming, statistical analysis, machine learning, artificial intelligence, data management, data governance, and ethical considerations in AI. This journey might have been challenging, but it is undoubtedly rewarding as you are now equipped with the comprehensive knowledge and technical skills to excel in any data science role or project.

Progressing Further: Diving Deeper into Azure and Data Science

Venturing on this journey, you have built a strong foundation in Azure and data science. However, learning in such dynamic and transformative fields is never-ending. Hence, it is necessary to delve deeper and explore the advanced aspects that can enhance your skills and broaden your horizons further.

Emphasizing Continuous Learning in Data Science

The essence of Data Science lies in its dynamic nature and the constant evolution it undergoes. Likewise, Azure continues to update its features and capabilities. Adapting to these changes and staying updated is pivotal to achieving success in this field. So, cultivating a habit of continuous learning is a prerequisite.

A Glimpse into Advanced Azure Topics

Moving beyond the foundational concepts, there is an entire landscape of advanced topics in Azure waiting to be explored. These include areas like Azure's IoT services, real-time analytics with Azure Stream Analytics, and even venturing into quantum computing with Azure Quantum. If you find machine learning particularly interesting, delve deeper into the nuances of deep learning and explore reinforcement learning possibilities with Azure Machine Learning Service.

Inspiring More Engagement with Real-World Applications

The key to mastering data science lies not just within understanding its theoretical aspects, but more importantly in practical implementation. Nothing beats the satisfaction and understanding gathered from applying your knowledge to real-world applications. Be it healthcare, finance, marketing, or even e-commerce, Data Science and Azure are becoming indispensable tools for transforming industries. Thus, for those aspiring to create an impact, it's a must to venture beyond the books and immerse yourself in the practical application of the acquired knowledge.

Future Directions: Amplifying Your Data Science Expertise in Azure

As we officially draw this journey to a close, remember that your exploration and learning in data science and Azure are only beginning. Let us venture into future steps to enhance your skills while shedding light on the importance of continuous learning in the evolving world of data science and Azure.

Strategies for Skill Augmentation in Data Science

As with any field, the more you practice, the more proficient you become. It is advisable to keep strengthening the foundational skills you have gained throughout this guide in real-world scenarios by solving problems and implementing solutions using Azure tools and services. Utilize online resources such as Azure's official documentation, hands-on tutorials, and think tanks to keep honing your data science skills.

Resources for Continued Learning

Consider exploring educational resources such as Microsoft Learn, online courses on data science and Azure from platforms like Coursera and Udemy, and interactive coding platforms like Kaggle and Codecademy. Keeping a tab on the Azure Blog also helps you stay informed about updates and new features.

Future Trends and Technologies to Look Out

As the saying goes, foresight is 20/20. Always keep an eye out for emerging trends in data science and Azure, from the potential of quantum computing and edge computing, and the growing popularity of serverless computing, to shifts in AI and machine learning paradigms. Exploring these trends will help ensure you and your skills progress with the tides, rather than being swept away by them.

Certifications to Validate Your Skills

For those looking to establish their credentials formally, Azure offers a variety of certifications for different roles and levels of expertise – from Azure Data Scientist Associate to Azure AI Engineer Associate. These globally recognized certifications can further improve your career trajectory and endorse you as a certified professional in the field.

As a data scientist focused on Microsoft Azure, you can follow a specific path to validate your skills and knowledge. Here is a potential roadmap:

Fundamentals Certification

- **Microsoft Certified: Azure AI Fundamentals (AI-900):** This certification covers core AI concepts such as machine learning, computer vision, natural language processing, and conversational AI. This is a good starting point if you are new to AI or Azure.
- **Microsoft Certified: Azure Data Fundamentals (DP-900):** This certification covers the basics of core data concepts and how they are implemented, including the use of relational and non-relational data.

Associate Certifications

- **Microsoft Certified: Azure Data Scientist Associate (DP-100):** This certification validates your knowledge of implementing and running machine learning workloads on Azure. This includes tasks such as setting up an Azure Machine Learning workspace, running experiments and training models, optimizing and managing models, and deploying and maintaining models.

Specialty Certifications

- **Microsoft Certified: Azure AI Engineer Specialty:** This certification is for candidates with subject matter expertise in designing and implementing AI apps and agents that use Microsoft Azure Cognitive Services, Azure Bot Service, Azure Cognitive Search, and data storage in Azure. While this is not strictly a data science certification, it can be beneficial if your role involves implementing AI solutions in addition to performing data science tasks.

  Remember, the roadmap might vary depending on your current skills, experience, and career goals. You can choose to start at the associate level if you already have some foundational knowledge of Azure and data science.

Conclusion: Reflecting, Engaging, and Envisioning the Future in Data Science with Azure

As we approach the end of this enlightening journey, we pave the way for independent exploration, continual growth, and practical engagement in the versatile field of data science and Azure.

Reflection on the Learning Journey

From understanding the intricacies of data science to deploying machine learning models using Azure – this book has been a trove of knowledge. Grasp the importance of the learnings from this guide and adopt a lifelong learning approach to stay updated in this ever-evolving space.

Encouraging Engagement in Data Science Endeavors

With the world of data science and Azure now open to you, it's time to engage with practical projects and challenges that integrate and reinforce what you have learned. Do not be intimidated by challenges, but welcome them as milestones in your data science journey.

Envisioning the Future – Data Science and Azure

To conclude, let us look into the future. With the knowledge you have gained, recognize your ability to harness the power of data science and Azure and bring significant changes in various fields. Surging ahead, keep in mind the limitless potential of these combined domains and how they can be leveraged to redefine the world as we know it.

Index

A

ADLS Gen2
about 62
advantages, features 62, 63
concepts 62
real-world, applications 63
AKS (Azure Kubernetes Service) 185
AKS, setting up
application, deploying 186
cluster, connecting 185
cluster, creating 185
troubleshoot, monitoring 186
AMLS (Azure Machine Learning Studio) 27
about 127
capabilities 132
data, importing 140-142
data, scaling 150, 151
experiments, preventing 137, 138
interface, navigating 128-131
resources, organizing 138, 139
roles, utilizing 131, 132
setting up 132-137
structures 127
AMLS, benefits
computer 34
data, labeling 34
link, service 34
monitoring 34
AMLS Code Elaborated, steps
data, encoding 149
data, inspecting 145
data, loading 143-145
data, transforming 148
data types, converting 148
duplicates, handling 146
miss value, handling 145, 146
outliers, handling 147, 148
AMLS, functionalities
components 33
data 32
endpoint 34
environment 33
jobs 33
model 33
pipelines 33
AMLS, sections
Assets 28
Authoring 28
Manage 29
AMLS, tools
AutoML 31
designer 30
notebooks 30
Prompt flow 32
Apache Spark 264
Apache Spark, benefits
easy, use 266
integrating 266
performance, enhancing 266
real-time, analytics 266
scalability 266
security 266
stream, processing 266
workspace, integrating 266

Apache Spark, features
easy, use 265
fault tolerance 265
flexibility 265
speed 265
SQL Queries 265
Apache Spark, roles
data, processing 265
Machine Learning 265
real-time, analytics 265
Artificial Intelligence (AI)
about 228
aspects 238
Azure Approach, utilizing 229
breaches, impacting 246
consequences 238, 239
ethics, importance 238
importance 228, 229
privacy, importance 246
strategies, utilizing 247
Azure Advisor 14, 15
Azure AI 10
Azure AI, capabilities 10, 11
Azure AI, principles
Application, ability 233
content, safety 229
purpose 232, 233
resources, steps 230, 231
Azure Application 188
Azure Application, key steps
diagnostics, logs 189
insights, setup 189
ML Algorithms, analyzing 189
performance, utilizing 189
Azure Architecture, key components
data storage, analyzing 6
environment, managing 6
tasks, computing 6
Azure Cloud Platform 39
Azure Container Instances (ACI) 186
Azure Databricks
about 9, 83
best practices 263, 264
deploying, instructions 262, 263
Azure Databricks, benefits
cost, effectiveness 261
performance 261
productivity 261
scalability, flexibility 261
seamless, integrating 261
security 261
unified, analyzing 261
Azure Databricks, key features
languages, supporting 261
ML, automating 261
Native Azure, integrating 261
spark-based, analyzing 260
workspace, interacting 261
Azure Data Factory (ADF)
about 79
aspects 80
benefits 80
features 79
Azure Data Factory, guiding steps
control flow, configuring 81
data pipeline, running 81
factory, creating 80
monitoring 81
pipeline activities, optimizing 81
pipeline, creating 81
troubleshoot, debugging 81
Azure Data Ingestion, techniques
Azure Data Factory (ADF) 59-61
Azure Stream Analytics 61, 62
Data Ingestion Pipeline 62
Azure Data Lake Storage 9, 10
Azure Data Science, project enhancing 282-288

Azure Data Storage, options
ADLS Gen2 51-54
Azure Blob Storage 56-58
Azure SQL Database 54-56
Azure Environment
about 22
importance 22
setting up 297
Azure Environment, setting up
account, establishing 22, 23
subscription, selecting 23
Azure, features
Azure Boards 43
Azure DevOps 43
Azure Notebooks 43
Azure Pipelines 43
Azure HDInsight
about 268
best practices 270, 271
Big Data, analyzing 269
Azure HDInsight, capabilities
cost-effective 268
data, integrating 268
data security, compliance 268
multi-functional, platforms 268
productivity 268
real-time, analytics 268
scalability, flexibility 268
Azure Machine Learning (AML)
about 8
best practices 173
cost, managing 175, 176
version control 173, 174
Azure Machine Learning, practices
AI Content, safety 248
fairlearn 248
interpretML 248
private data, analyzing 248
security 248
Azure Machine Learning SDK
about 152
data, constructing 154-158
models, training 158, 159
structures 152
Azure Machine Learning SDK, components
experiment 153
model 154
run 153
workspace 152
Azure Machine Learning, security aspects
access control, managing 174
compliance, regulatory 175
encryption, isolating 175
threats, protecting 175
Azure Machine Learning Service 183, 184
Azure ML
about 24
features, benefits 27
workspace, setting up 26
Azure Monitor 187
Azure Monitor, key steps
activating 187
alerts, creating 188
log, analyzing 188
metrics, setting up 188
Azure Notebooks
about 37
AutoML, collaborating 38
Data Science, executing 38
structure, utilizing 37
Azure OpenAI
about 204, 205
function, usages 209
Generative AI, utilizing 209
Microsoft Azure, harnessing 209-213
Model Catalog 208
resources, utilizing steps 206-208
Azure Pricing 12
Azure Resource Manager (ARM) 14
Azure Resource Manager, functionalities
Azure Portal, navigating 16
resources, exploring 17
service, managing 17

Azure Resources manager, tools
Azure Advisor 14, 15
Azure Role-Based Access Control (RBAC) 14
Azure Role-Based Access Control (RBAC) 14
Azure's Data Security
cloud storage, importance 66
data, encrypting 64, 65
user, authenticating 65, 66
Azure, services
big data, operations 25
small project, start-ups 25
Azure's Speech services 225
Azure Stream Analytics
about 271
benefits 272
best practices 272, 273
key features 271
real-time data, implementing 273, 274
Azure Synapse Analytics 10
Azure Vision Services
about 226
AI Models, roles 228
AI Models, utilizing 227
Azure Speech 226
Azure Vision 227
content, implementing 228
practical, implementing 227

B

Big Data Analytics 255, 256
Big Data Analytics, challenges
integration, validating 260
privacy, security 260
skill gap 260
storage, infrastructures 260
Big Data Analytics, stages
data, analyzing 259
data, cleaning 259
data ingestion 259
data, processing 259
data, storage 259
data, transforming 259
data, visualizing 260
Big Data Analytics, tools
Apache Flink 259
Azure Databricks 258
Azure Data Lake, analyzing 256
Azure HDInsight 256
Azure Machine Learning 257
Azure Stream Analytics 257
Azure Synapse Analytics 257
Hadoop 258
MangoDB 258
Tableau 259

C

CI/CD 189, 190
CI/CD ML, implementing 190, 191
Classification Algorithms, types
decision tree 102
logistic, regression 102
naive bayes, classifying 103
random forest 102
SVM 102
Classification Metrics, concepts
accuracy 111
F1 Score 111
precision 111
Recall 111
ROC, curve 111
specificity 111
Classification Metrics, terms
False Negatives (FN) 110
False Positives (FP) 110
True Negatives (TN) 110
True Positives (TP) 110
Compute Resources
about 36
autoscalling 36
capability 35
data, monitoring 37
importance 35
need, optimizing 36
role, utilizing 35
Cross-Validation 166

D

Data Cleaning,
techniques 78
Data Governance
about 67
Azure Policy 68
compliance, policies 67, 68
principles, utilizing 67
roles, analyzing 67
Data Governance, tools
Azure Policy 69
blueprints 69
cost, managing 70, 71
monitor 70
security center 70
Data Ingestion 50, 51
Data Preprocessing 77, 78
Data Science
about 2
best practices 293
business problems,
utilizing 290
concepts 3, 297
design, implementing 299
ethics, importance 242
future, directories 301, 302
importance 2
process, utilizing 3, 4
roles, analyzing 5
structures 2
tools, utilizing 4, 5
Data Science, aspects
application, inspiring 300
data, emphasizing 300
IoT Services, utilizing 300
Data Science, Azure services
Azure ML 24
cognitive 25
Databricks 24
HDInsight 25
synapse, analyzing 25
Data Science Azure, utilizing
account, creating 13
service, permissions
managing 13
subscription, buying 13
Data Science, industries
E-Commerce 289, 290
Finance 288
healthcare 289
Data Science, phase
accountability 243
content, consenting 243
data, collecting 242
data storage, handling 242
fairness, bias 243
transparency 243
Data Science, project
analyzing 282
Data Science Project,
challenges
data, cleaning 292
data, missing 292
data, privacy 292
scalability 292
skill gap 292
Data Science Project,
key point
data, utilizing 292
model, simplicity 292
monitoring 292
objective, clearing 292
tools, choosing 292
Data Transformation 77
Data Transformation Pipeline
about 91
Azure Features, using 92
Orchestration, role 91, 92
Data Wrangling
about 82
benefits 83
data, enriching 83
goals, utilizing 83
structure, analyzing 82

F

Feature Engineering 107
Feature Engineering,
process steps
attribute, selecting 108
variable, creating 107, 108
variable, transforming 107

G

Generative AI
about 199, 200
concepts 200, 201
importance, benefits 201, 202
principles 201
Generative AI Application, technologies
art, designing 203
language service, translating 203
media, entertaining 203
potential, future 203
service, communicating 203
technologies, editing 203
Git 39

H

Hyperparameter Tuning
about 160
challenges 160
process, optimizing 160
SDK, comprehensing 161, 162
strategies, implementing 162, 163
techniques, utilizing 160

L

Large Language Models (LLMs) 199

M

Machine Learning
best, practices 244
Bias, using 113, 114
Ethics, revolving 119
fairness, interpretability 243
principles, importance 244
Machine Learning, algorithms
Classification 101
Clustering 105
Regression 103
Machine Learning Bias, types
algorithmic 116
exclusion 115
Measurement 115
outlier 116
Prejudice 115
sample 114
selection 116
Machine Learning, clustering
Affinity Propagation 106
DBSCAN 106
Hierarchical 105
K-Means 105
Mean-Shift 106
spectral 106
Machine Learning Fairness, techniques
algorithm, modifying 118
Bias-Awareness, training 118
data, preprocessing 118
evaluation, metrics 118
feature, selecting 118
post, processing 118
stratified, sampling 118
Machine Learning, fundamental
Reinforcement Learning 100, 101
Supervised Learning 98
Unsupervised Learning 98, 99
Machine Learning Metrics, types
Classification Metrics 110
Regression Metrics 112
Machine Learning Models 170, 171
Machine Learning Models Retraining, strategies
automated 172
Champion-Challenger, framework 172
model, updating 173
Model Version Control 173
validation 172

Machine Learning Stream, steps
- environment, setting up 168
- model deploy, preparing 167
- real-time prediction, creating 169

Machine Learning Tasks, types
- Classification Task 164, 165
- Clustering Task 165
- Ranking Task 165
- Regression Task 164

Microsoft Azure
- about 5
- Azure Architecture 6
- benefits 6
- data science, utilizing 7
- structure, utilizing 6

Microsoft Azure, models
- Enterprise Agreement 12
- Pay-As-You-Go 12

Model Deployment 182, 183
Model Monitoring 182, 183
Model Version Control 192

P

Principal Component Analysis (PCA) 109
Programming 3
PromptFlow
- about 214
- advantages 215
- enterprise, readiness 215
- key steps 216-221
- LLMs Application, analyzing 215
- nodes, optimizing 221-224
- structure, agility 215

R

Recursive Feature Elimination (RFE) 109
Regression Algorithms, types
- Bayesian Linear 105
- Elastic Net 104
- LASSO 104
- linear 103
- logistic 104
- poisson 104
- polynomial 104
- ridge 104

Regression Metrics, concepts
- Mean Absolute Error (MAE) 112
- Mean Squared Error (MSE) 112
- Root Mean Squared Error (RMSE) 113
- R-squared 113

Responsible AI
- about 239
- ethical, considering 298
- importance 239, 240

Responsible AI, practices
- design 241
- education 241
- guidelines 241
- review 241
- testing 241
- training 241

Responsible AI, principles
- accountability 241
- fairness 240
- human-centric 241
- privacy 240
- safety, security 241
- transparency 240

Rollback 192
Rollback, key steps
- automating 193
- implementing 193
- model, versioning 192
- performance, tracking 193
- version, archiving 193

S

Structured Data 89
Structured Data, challenges
inflexibility 87
time, cost 87
Structured Data, techniques
ML, algorithms 89
SQL Queries 89
statistical, analyzing 89

U

Univariate Selection 108
Unstructured Data
about 89
challenges 88
techniques 90

V

Version Control
about 39
Git, integrating steps 40-42
importance 40

Made in United States
Orlando, FL
04 November 2026

90209893R00186